Driving Green Consumerism Through Strategic Sustainability Marketing

Farzana Quoquab
Universiti Teknologi Malaysia, Malaysia

Ramayah Thurasamy
Universiti Sains Malaysia, Malaysia

Jihad Mohammad
Universiti Teknologi Malaysia, Malaysia

A volume in the Practice, Progress, and Proficiency in Sustainability (PPPS) Book Series

IGI Global
DISSEMINATOR OF KNOWLEDGE

Published in the United States of America by
IGI Global
Business Science Reference (an imprint of IGI Global)
701 E. Chocolate Avenue
Hershey PA, USA 17033
Tel: 717-533-8845
Fax: 717-533-8661
E-mail: cust@igi-global.com
Web site: http://www.igi-global.com

Library of Congress Cataloging-in-Publication Data

Names: Quoquab, Farzana, 1978- editor. | Thurasamy, Ramayah, 1964- editor. | Mohammad, Jihad, 1970- editor.
Title: Driving green consumerism through strategic sustainability marketing / Farzana Quoquab, Ramayah Thurasamy, and Jihad Mohammad, editors.
Description: Hershey, PA : Business Science Reference, [2018]
Identifiers: LCCN 2017012411| ISBN 9781522529125 (hardcover) | ISBN 9781522529132 (ebook)
Subjects: LCSH: Green marketing. | Consumer behavior--Environmental aspects. | Environmentalism. | Consumption (Economics)--Environmental aspects.
Classification: LCC HF5413 .D75 2018 | DDC 658.8/02--dc23 LC record available at https://lccn.loc.gov/2017012411

This book is published in the IGI Global book series Practice, Progress, and Proficiency in Sustainability (PPPS) (ISSN: 2330-3271; eISSN: 2330-328X)

British Cataloguing in Publication Data
A Cataloguing in Publication record for this book is available from the British Library.

For electronic access to this publication, please contact: eresources@igi-global.com.

Practice, Progress, and Proficiency in Sustainability (PPPS) Book Series

Ayman Batisha
International Sustainability Institute, Egypt

ISSN:2330-3271
EISSN:2330-328X

Mission

In a world where traditional business practices are reconsidered and economic activity is performed in a global context, new areas of economic developments are recognized as the key enablers of wealth and income production. This knowledge of information technologies provides infrastructures, systems, and services towards sustainable development.

The **Practices, Progress, and Proficiency in Sustainability (PPPS) Book Series** focuses on the local and global challenges, business opportunities, and societal needs surrounding international collaboration and sustainable development of technology. This series brings together academics, researchers, entrepreneurs, policy makers and government officers aiming to contribute to the progress and proficiency in sustainability.

Coverage

- Global Business
- E-Development
- Innovation networks
- Socio-Economic
- Intellectual Capital
- Green Technology
- ICT and knowledge for development
- Knowledge clusters
- Technological learning
- Sustainable development

IGI Global is currently accepting manuscripts for publication within this series. To submit a proposal for a volume in this series, please contact our Acquisition Editors at Acquisitions@igi-global.com or visit: http://www.igi-global.com/publish/.

The Practice, Progress, and Proficiency in Sustainability (PPPS) Book Series (ISSN 2330-3271) is published by IGI Global, 701 E. Chocolate Avenue, Hershey, PA 17033-1240, USA, www.igi-global.com. This series is composed of titles available for purchase individually; each title is edited to be contextually exclusive from any other title within the series. For pricing and ordering information please visit http://www.igi-global.com/book-series/practice-progress-proficiency-sustainability/73810. Postmaster: Send all address changes to above address.

Titles in this Series

For a list of additional titles in this series, please visit: www.igi-global.com/book-series

Sustainable Local Energy Planning and Decision Making Emerging Research and Opportunities
Vangelis Marinakis (National Technical University of Athens, Greece)
Information Science Reference • © 2017 • 171pp • H/C (ISBN: 9781522522867) • US $140.00 (our price)

Sustainable Potato Production and the Impact of Climate Change
Sunil Londhe (International Centre for Research in Agroforestry (ICRAF), India)
Information Science Reference • © 2017 • 323pp • H/C (ISBN: 9781522517153) • US $180.00 (our price)

Handbook of Research on Green Economic Development Initiatives and Strategies
M. Mustafa Erdoğdu (Marmara University, Turkey) Thankom Arun (University of Essex, UK) and Imran Habib Ahmad (Global Green Growth Institute, South Korea)
Business Science Reference • © 2016 • 747pp • H/C (ISBN: 9781522504405) • US $335.00 (our price)

Impact of Water Pollution on Human Health and Environmental Sustainability
A. Elaine McKeown (Independent Researcher, USA) and George Bugyi (Pennsylvania State University, USA)
Information Science Reference • © 2016 • 422pp • H/C (ISBN: 9781466695597) • US $220.00 (our price)

Impact of Meat Consumption on Health and Environmental Sustainability
Talia Raphaely (Curtin University, Australia) and Dora Marinova (Curtin University, Australia)
Information Science Reference • © 2016 • 410pp • H/C (ISBN: 9781466695535) • US $210.00 (our price)

Handbook of Research on Sustainable Development and Economics
Ken D. Thomas (Auburn University, USA)
Business Science Reference • © 2015 • 479pp • H/C (ISBN: 9781466684331) • US $325.00 (our price)

Handbook of Research on Pedagogical Innovations for Sustainable Development
Ken D. Thomas (Auburn University, USA) and Helen E. Muga (University of Mount Union, USA)
Information Science Reference • © 2014 • 800pp • H/C (ISBN: 9781466658561) • US $345.00 (our price)

Sustainability Science for Social, Economic, and Environmental Development
Nilanjan Ghosh (Multi Commodity Exchange of India Limited, India) and Anandajit Goswami (The Energy and Resources Institute, India)
Information Science Reference • © 2014 • 324pp • H/C (ISBN: 9781466649958) • US $195.00 (our price)

IGI Global
DISSEMINATOR OF KNOWLEDGE

701 East Chocolate Avenue, Hershey, PA 17033, USA
Tel: 717-533-8845 x100 • Fax: 717-533-8661
E-Mail: cust@igi-global.com • www.igi-global.com

Editorial Advisory Board

Table of Contents

Detailed Table of Contents

Foreword

Driving Green Consumerism Through Strategic Sustainable Marketing is written to increase awareness of environmental issues among consumers, marketing managers, students, policy makers and researchers. Green consumerism is a form of consumption that is compatible with the safeguard of the environment for the present and for the next generations. A consumer whose purchasing behavior is persuaded by environmental concerns is known as a green consumer. Examining how consumers' pattern of consumption can safeguard the environment for current and future generation is fascinating and interesting topic. Therefore, it is very reasonable to take steps to prevent the negative future environmental outcomes from occurring. This involves modifying the ways we live, consume, and make marketing decision. I believe that considering the impact of consumer decision in term of their consumption pattern is a step in the right direction.

This book is crucial for the readers in many aspects: First, it enhances their knowledge about the influence of green awareness on human behavior in several ways, e.g., reducing consumption, changing wasteful or harmful consumption patterns and raising preference for environmentally friendly products. Second, it explains how consumer green attitude and behaviour can have positive effect on sustainability of environment. In reality, there has been a change in consumer attitudes and behavior towards the green consumption and people are actively trying to reduce their impact on the environment. This involves developing positive attitude and behavior towards forming a consumption pattern that harms the environment as little as possible, or even benefits the environment. This consumption is characterized by purchase and use of products with lower environmental impacts, such as biodegradable products, recycled or reduced packaging, and low energy usage. Third, this book demonstrated the different green marketing strategies that involve focusing on Reduce, Reuse, and Recycle (3Rs) that can help green consumption. These green marketing strategies can be examined according to four components of marketing mix such as product, price, distribution and promotion. Last but not least, this book addresses the sustainability phenomenon which has become an important issue. Sustainability is the business strategy that drives the long-term corporate growth and profitability by mandating the inclusion of environmental and social issues in the business model and implies the responsibility of the business to execute its operations in such a way as to have the minimum impact on its environment.

The obligation to protect the environment and the people health from the effects caused by industrial pollutants has developed this new idea of consumption. The first green brands began to appear during 1980s. During the next decades, green products had showed a steady growth. Again, in the early 2000, evidence suggests that a growing number of consumers' interest around the world became more environmentally responsible in terms of their personal habits and lifestyles, and has been continuing to grow.

The ultimate goal of this book is to enhance consumers', practitioners', and academicians' awareness and knowledge about their responsibility or co-responsibility for tackling environmental problems through adoption of environmentally friendly behaviors, such as the use of organic products, clean and renewable energy and the research of goods produced by companies with zero impact. In turn, this situation is expected to have positive impact on marketers of consumer products and organizations since they have to respond to this green challenge. Moreover, this will also affect policy makers and researchers who seek to influence consumers' behavioral change in order to address environmental issues.

Abu Bakar Abdul Hamid
Universiti Putra Malaysia, Malaysia

Preface

This book, *Driving Green Consumerism Through Strategic Sustainability Marketing*, is meant to provide a broad research perspective on latest trend of consumerism, its effect and implications from developing country perspective. Providing a forum for the exchange of research ideas and practices, this book is a reference convergence point for academicians, professionals, managers, and researchers in the consumer behavior and sustainability marketing field, including the development practitioners.

WHY WE ARE WRITING THIS BOOK

Environmental concern is now in forefront in the recent world. This is due to the fact that the environmental pollution became a major challenge which is caused by several human activities such as over consumption of natural resources, expansion of industries, water and air pollution and the like. Daily human consumption that is drawing on natural resources poses a serious threat to the sustainability of the natural environment. Therefore, individuals are required to adopt changes in behavior to prevent further deterioration of the environment. Lot of research attention has been paid to the green chemistry, green consumer behavior and green supply-chain. However, discussion on environmental significant behaviour and sustainable consumption are comparatively new which certainly requires further investigation in different context and different cultural setting.

Certainly, the traditional consumption activities no longer follow a linear path. It is now shaped by global changes and baked by different kinds of wants and demands which deserve researchers' attention to discuss more to understand its micro as well as macro level impacts. Indeed, the organizations have also started to think differently by considering the environmental welfare. In this instance, green organization and pro-environmental behavior at work emerged. Being the internal customers, the changes in behavioral aspect of the front-line employees also calls for research attention.

On the whole, the strategic approach of marketers as well as policy makers need to be changed based on the recent changes in the global economy. There are numerous studies that are conducted in the developed country perspective, whereas, little attention has been paid to the developing country aspect which this book attempts to address. This book will enhance readers' understanding of the latest trend in consumerism in regard to the environmental aspects. Additionally, the book attempts to clarify issues related to recent changes in consumer behavior particularly in developing country perspective.

THE TARGET AUDIENCES OF THIS BOOK

The target audiences for this book include policy makers, academicians, researchers, advanced-level students, libraries and information centers, and government officials. All these parties will find this book useful in furthering their research exposure to pertinent topics in sustainability marketing and assisting in furthering their own research efforts in this field.

HOW THIS BOOK IS ORGANIZED

This book is organized in four sections and 13 chapters. The book encompasses both theoretical aspects as well as practical aspects of green marketing related issues. A brief summary of each section and chapter are provided below.

Section 1: Building Awareness About Green Consumerism

Chapter 1, "Awareness of Environmental Issues Among Consumers in the Malaysian Hotel Industry" by Yusnita Yusof, Yahaya Ibrahim, and Zainudin Awang of Universiti Sultan Zainal Abidin from Malaysia, investigates the effect of environmental management practices towards customer satisfaction and customer loyalty in the Malaysian hotel industry. The authors found that, customers usually look for maximum facilities provided by the hotel and its employees, compared to green practices applied within the hotel. And thus, the green practices of the hotels are not so popular among Malaysian consumers.

Chapter 2, "Consumers Consciousness Towards Environmental Aesthetics in Using Nutricosmetics Products" by Ruzanna Shahrin and Rossilah Jamil of Universiti Teknologi Malaysia from Malaysia, discusses notion of environmental aesthetics in the context of Malaysian nutricosmetics industry. More particularly, this chapter addresses four research questions: (1) How does green marketing contribute to consumer consciousness towards environmental aesthetics? (2) How do nutricosmetic products offer aesthetic values to the consumers? (3) How consumers perceive environmental aesthetics in purchasing nutricosmetic products? (4) How environmental aesthetics is interconnected with the environment? In this way, this chapter highlights consumers' awareness about health, quality of life and wellbeing while using nutricosmetics products.

Chapter 3, "A Review on Green Trust and Environmental Quality Awareness Affect Towards Environmental Attitude" by Trianna Rosli and Fauziah Sh. Ahmad of Universiti Teknologi Malaysia from Malaysia, develops a conceptual framework pertaining to the environmental quality awareness. Although environmental awareness is gaining more ground among consumers, it is still not clear how this influence their cognitive thinking and action. This chapter focuses on the issues related to green trust and environmental quality awareness and provides understanding about how these could stimulate environmental attitude.

Section 2: Understanding Green Attitude and Behavior

Chapter 4, "Understanding Green Attitudes" by Aysen Coskun of Akeniz University from Turkey, discusses about green attitudes. This chapter provides a comprehensive and coherent framework on green attitudes. It is also discussed that new research methods on attitude measurement may provide new understanding. The implications for marketers and policy makers are outlined, and recommendations for future research are made.

Chapter 5, "Green Attitudes and Thinking in the New Green Market: Using Mathematical Modeling to Satisfy Green Customers' Needs" by Florea Nicoleta Valentina of Valahia University of Targoviste from Romania, proposes analysis of few different approaches regarding the implementation of green marketing policies and the situation of green marketing in the world and the green customers behaviours in choosing a green product (using Markov chains), in the context of Romania.

Chapter 6, "Driving Green Marketing in a Developing Country: Reducing the Attitude-Behaviour Gap" by Shweta Pandey and Deepak Chawla of International Management Institute from India, provides examines the social-normalisation process and its impact on adoption of green practices in India based upon an empirical study. Using various techniques (Heat maps, factor analysis and regression) this chapter indicates that while greater number of customers shows positive attitudes green activities, it does not result in the same being perceived as part of the normal routine, thereby leading to an attitude-behavior gap.

Chapter 7, "Pro-Social Behavior and Philanthropy in Conflict and Post-Conflict Contexts" by Shaza Aldairani and Rosmini Omar of Universiti Teknologi Malaysia from Malaysia, highlights the pro-social behavior during conflict as well as post-conflict context and addresses three research inquiries: (1) Do individuals and corporate perform pro-social behaviour in conflict context? (2) If so, how do they perform such behavior? (3) How does literature approach specifically consumer pro-social behavior in conflict and post-conflict locations?

Section 3: Green Marketing Strategies

Chapter 8, "Green Marketing Strategies and Marketing Performance: The Case of Turkey" by Serkan Kılıç and Erkan Özdemir of Uludağ University from Turkey, examines the effects of green product, green pricing, green marketing channel and green marketing communication strategies on the marketing performance. The results of this study are particularly important in terms of shaping the marketing mix strategies of businesses that focuses on marketing of green products.

Chapter 9, "Green Brand Personality: Its Relevance to the Green Marketing Practices" by Anitha Acharya and Manish Gupta of IFHE University from India, discusses about the green brand, its characteristics, and its implications. This chapter would help readers understand the need for studying green brand personality and appreciate its importance in the current market scenario.

Chapter 10, "Marketing Strategies for Trendy Animal Products: Sustainability as a Core" by Alfredo Escribano who is an independent researcher and consultant from Spain, reviews consumers' behaviour towards meat and dairy products claiming different attributes related to sustainability. This chapter reviews, synthesize and discusses the existing knowledge on the topic with an integrative-interdisciplinary approach. Finally, marketing strategy recommendations are provided.

Section 4: Sustainability Paradox

Chapter 11, " Sustainable Development Values: What Do We Know From Developing Country Perspective?" by Farzana Quoquab, Fong Teng, and Jihad Mohammad of Universiti Teknologi Malaysia and Ramayah Thurasamy of Universiti Sains Malaysia from Malaysia, furthered the understanding about sustainable development values by discussing the knowledge gap from developing country perspective. By utilizing qualitative method this study found that there is a difference of sustainability values between developed and developing countries. More specifically, the findings suggest for considering two additional values and group together certain values based on their priority.

Chapter 12, "Sustainable Software Lifecycle for Green Consumerism" by Shah Muhammad Nazmus Saquib of Technical University of Munich from Germany, discusses about the accountable digital consumers who care to keep the earth green through their purchases and simultaneously those who design and administrate these digital products, that includes senior and mid-level professionals from industries and from government authorities. This chapter suggests that cell phones outfitted with sustainability software could profit to associate consumers' choices with their environmental and biodiversity impacts.

Chapter 13, "A Conceptual Model of Green HRM Adoption Towards Sustainability in Hospitality Industry" by Yusmani Mohd Yusoff of Universiti Sains Malaysia and Mehran Nejati of Edith Cowan University from Australia, provides a better understanding on the predictors of green human resource management which can result in improved environmental and financial performance across hospitality industry. The proposed model has been constructed from the perspective of external pressure (i.e., normative) and internal pressure (manager's environmental concerns) by using the Institutional Theory and Resource Based View Theory. The chapter examines the antecedents of sustainability in hospitality industry in terms of improved financial and environmental performance. It therefore expands the level of understanding on mechanisms which leads to corporation sustainability.

Farzana Quoquab
Universiti Teknologi Malaysia, Malaysia

Ramayah Thurasamy
Universiti Sains Malaysia, Malaysia

Jihad Mohammad
Universiti Teknologi Malaysia, Malaysia

Acknowledgment

First and foremost, all praises be to the Creator Almighty, the most merciful the most benevolent for His guidance and blessings for giving us the inspiration and opportunity to embark on this project and to make this dream a reality.

We would especially like to thank all chapter contributors who have diligently addressed reviewers' feedback and amended the chapters several times. Special thank goes to the reviewers who have taken their time off from their busy schedule to review the chapters and to provide their feedback to enhance the quality of the write up.

We are highly indebted to the pioneer researchers in the field, whose published work enhanced our understanding about the issue and made us more thoughtful. Ultimately it made us to think further and to initiate this book.

It has been a great pleasure to work with entire IGI Global team. Thank you very much for your continuous support and cooperation.

The special appreciation goes to our family members for their unconditional love, support and encouragement which became our true inspiration to devote ourselves to the completion of this book.

Farzana Quoquab
Universiti Teknologi Malaysia, Malaysia

Ramayah Thurasamy
Universiti Sains Malaysia, Malaysia

Jihad Mohammad
Universiti Teknologi Malaysia, Malaysia

Section 1

Building Awareness About Green Consumerism

Chapter 1
Awareness of Environmental Issues Among Consumers in the Malaysian Hotel Industry

Yusnita Yusof
Universiti Sultan Zainal Abidin, Malaysia

Yahaya Ibrahim
Universiti Sultan Zainal Abidin, Malaysia

Zainudin Awang
Universiti Sultan Zainal Abidin, Malaysia

ABSTRACT

Global issues such as climate change, global warming and pollution have become some of the most critical issues happening around the world for quite some time. Previous research has found that the environmental issues are closely linked with human activities. Generally, the hotel industry is closely related to the environment, particularly through daily operations that can lead to these environmental issues. Beginning a few decades ago, there was an increase in environmental awareness in the hospitality industry. In this light, green hotels seem to be becoming a growing niche in the competitive lodging industry and the number of customers who are interested in staying at green hotels has also increased. Due to the lack of studies that explore the green efforts that influence customer satisfaction and customer loyalty, this study was therefore conducted to investigate the effect of environmental management practices towards customer satisfaction and customer loyalty in the Malaysian hotel industry.

INTRODUCTION

In the recent decades, environmental issues become one of the most critical issues in the world. The most significant issues are global warming and pollution. Global warming, that is causing climate change across the world, gives a direct impact on the environment (NASA, 2015a). Since the 1970s, the global temperature has been increasing due to human activities (NASA, 2015; American Association for the

DOI: 10.4018/978-1-5225-2912-5.ch001

Advancement of Science, 2007). In the 20th century, the average global temperature expansion was approximately 1 degree Fahrenheit (NASA, 2015a). Although the number is seen as only a slight change, it makes a huge impact on the environment. For instance, glaciers becoming smaller, ice on the rivers or lakes dispersing more quickly, trees flowering early, sea levels rising more quickly and heat waves becoming more intense. However, environmental issues have plagued Malaysia for some time which is began with water pollution from tin mining operation, followed by air pollution from industrial and waste disposal and continues with climate change, global warming and also deforestation (Central Intelligence Agency, 2015; Mohamad, Tengku Arifin, Samsuri, & Mior Badrul Munir, 2014). The effects of climate change differ among regions, and depends on the environmental systems in use to alleviate the changes (NASA, 2015a). Recently, the haze that hit Malaysia due to forest fires in Indonesia was a big environmental problem (Central Intelligence Agency, 2015). All industries related to the environment will be affected if these environmental issues are not addressed. Tourism industry is directly related to the environment. Since hotels are part of the service industry that is people-oriented (Al-Shourah, 2007), this means that the hospitality industry is interrelated between humans and the environment. However, an increase in tourist arrivals is seen to have an effect on the environment (Hassan & Nezakati, 2014; Siti-Nabiha et al., 2011).

Since tourism industry play a negative role in climate change, reduce poverty, capacity building, cultural and natural conservation, in 2009, the Special Working Group on ASEAN Tourism Integration created ASEAN Tourism Strategic Plan (ATSP) for 2011-2015 in Phnom Penh. This plan is aimed to draft policies, programs and projects of the ASEAN National Tourism Organizations (ASEAN NTOs). There are three strategic directions in the ASEAN Tourism Strategic Plan including, development of experiential regional products and creative marketing and investment strategies; strategically increase the quality of services and human resource in the region; and enhance and accelerate travel facilitation and ASEAN connectivity. Additionally, in the plan also created six ASEAN Tourism Standards which are led by Thailand, namely Green Hotel, Food and Beverage Services, Public Restroom, Home Stay, Ecotourism and Tourism Heritage as showed in Figure 1.

ASEAN Green Hotel Standards was presented to identify the hotels that meet the standards which have been agreed upon by the ASEAN National Tourism Organization. Ministry of Tourism and Sports of Thailand (2013) summarized the best practices for use by hotel management in the ASEAN Tourism Standards Book 2011-2015. The Ministry of Tourism and Culture of Malaysia (MOTAC) has adapted these standards to be applied in the context of Malaysia, as shown in Table 1. Hotels will receive the ASEAN Green Hotel Award if they meet the standards, and they were nominated from each ASEAN member country (Ministry of Tourism and Sports of Thailand, 2013). There were 10 hotels in Malaysia awarded as a green hotel in 2014 and the list of hotels is as illustrated in Figure 2.

Excessive pollution has led to the establishment of acts related to environmental conservation, starting in 1955 (Kirk, 1995). Malaysia also has a few relevant plans and policies to decrease environmental problems such as the Five-Year Malaysia Plan, the National Tourism Policy and the National Ecotourism Plan. The 10th Malaysia Plan concentrated on solving global warming, environmental conservation and sustainability, while the 11th Malaysia Plan (2016-2020) focused on four areas including intensify the elasticity to climate change and natural disasters, enabling the environment for green development, adopting the concept of sustainable consumption and production, and conservation of natural resources for present and future generations (Economic Planning Unit, 2015).

Figure 1.

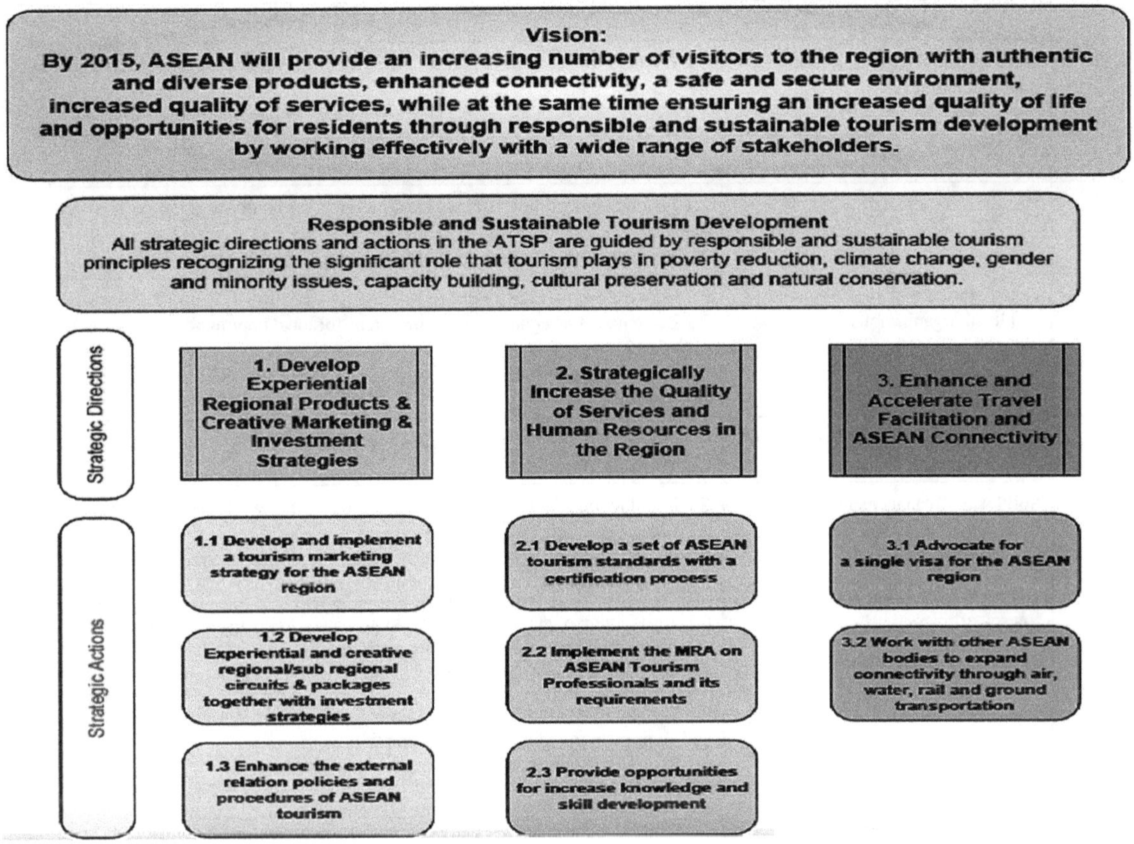

Figure 2.

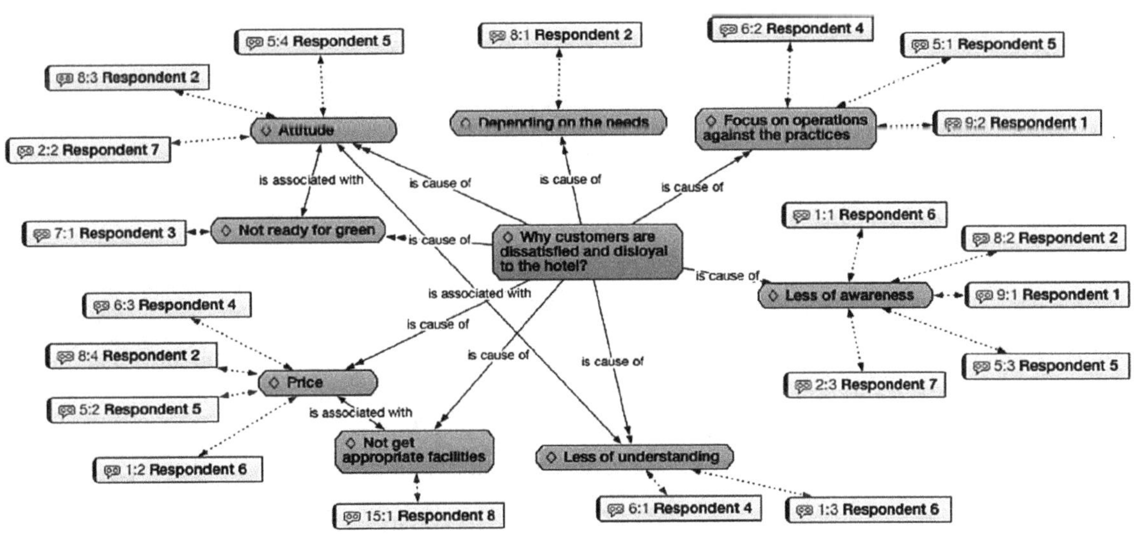

Table 1. ASEAN green hotel standards

	Major Criteria	Requirements: Hotels
1	Environmental policy and actions for hotel operation	1.1 Promotion of environmental activities in order to encourage the involvement of hotel staff, clients 1.2 Existence of plan for raising staff to be aware of environment; i.e. training. 1.3 Existence of environmental management plan for hotel operation. 1.4 Existence of monitoring program for environmental management of hotels.
2	Use of Green products	2.1 Encouragement for the use of local products for hotel operation i.e. food and handicrafts. 2.2 Encouragement for the use of environmentally friendly products.
3	Collaboration with the community and local organizations	3.1 Existence of plans/activities to help improve quality of life of the community. 3.2 Existence of awareness raising programs for local community on environmental protection. 3.3 Creation of activities in promoting culture and traditional performance and local ways of life.
4	Human resource development	4.1 Provision of training programs for operation and management staff on environmental management.
5	Solid waste management	5.1 Introduction of waste management techniques e.g. wastes reduction, reuse, recycling, waste separation and composting. 5.2 Encouragement of the involvement of hotel staff in waste reduction, reuse, recycling, waste separation and composting program.
6	Energy efficiency	6.1 Introduction of energy saving techniques and / or energy-saving technology and equipment for hotel to reduce energy consumption. 6.2 Installation of meters/equipment to monitor energy consumption.
7	Water efficiency	7.1 Introduction of water saving techniques and / or use of water-saving technology and equipment to reduce water consumption. 7.2 Regular maintenance for water saving equipment.
8	Air quality management (indoor and outdoor)	8.1 Designation of smoking and non-smoking area. 8.2 Regular monitoring and maintenance for equipment and hotel facilities to ensure the air quality i.e. air conditioning.
9	Noise pollution control	9.1 Existence of noise control program from hotel operation.
10	Wastewater treatment and management	10.1 The use of mechanisms to prevent water contamination and reduce wastewater generation. 10.2 Promotion of the use of recyclable/grey water in operation; i.e. watering trees. 10.3 Encouragement for an appropriate use of wastewater treatment.
11	Toxic and chemical substance disposal management	11.1 Provision of clear signs for toxic substance. 11.2 Appropriate hazardous waste disposal management. 11.3 Regular inspection, cleaning and maintenance for storage in order to avoid leakage of gas or toxic chemical substance.

Source: Ministry of Tourism and Sports of Thailand (2013)

According to Mohamed (2008), inappropriate development and management of tourism that does not comply with the law can destroy habitats and natural resources. To overcome this problem, an organized development approach should be taken to ensure natural resources are preserved, such as sustainable tourism development. Sustainable tourism is believed one of the effort that can contribute to environment protection and also be able to provide employment opportunities for the local community (Siti-Nabiha et al., 2011; Mohamed, 2008; Kasim & Scarlat, 2007). Natural tourism, green tourism, eco-tourism and rural tourism are listed as sustainability concepts of tourism (Faulkner, Mascardo, & Laws, 2000) which may transform mass tourism to become more ecological.

Community awareness towards environmental issues has started more than half a century ago (Cohen, 2014; Mattera & Moreno-melgarejo, 2012; Eggeling, 2010; Islam, 2008). Historically, in the 1970s, business organizations in many developing countries had little awareness towards the environment and carried out their activities and development without any sense of responsibility towards environmental preservation. Around the 1980s, a number of environmental calamities that occurred, such as the chemical contamination in Bhopal and the Exxon Valdez oil spill in Alaska, caused the world to pay more attention to the importance of environmental conservation (Kasim, 2009). However, a growing interest in research on tourism development and environmental quality started in 1990s (Erdogan & Tosun, 2009; Kirkpatrick, 1990) with the development of special interest tourism such as green tourism (Kirkpatrick, 1990). This was due to economic instability factors (Claver-Cortes, Molina-Azorin, Pereira-Moliner, & Lopez-Gamero, 2007) and global climate change (Kasim, 2004). Green tourism has a different focus and meaning, however, in general term, it is related to environmentally friendly tourism (Furqan, Mat Som, & Hussin, 2010). Additionally, green tourism is related to a product or service when it is beneficial to the manufacturer and consumer without damaging the environment (Millar & Baloglu, 2008).

The involvement of business organizations towards environmental awareness begins with the concept of eco-efficiency. According to DeSimone and Popoff (1997), the concept of eco-efficiency that is emphasized in Western countries has four elements, namely the formation of value with the environment; promotion of externalities reduction such as waste products, pollution and excessive resource consumption; the relationship between environmental excellence with business excellence; and identification of pollution control that covers all business networks such as suppliers and intermediaries. This concept gives advantages to the industry such as cost reduction, pollution and resource consumption, improvement on the quality of products and services that meet customer needs while improving environmental quality, increase in market share and business opportunities as well as enhanced image of the product (DeSimonc & Popoff, 1997).

The Rio Earth Summit, with the theme of environment and sustainable development focused on developing a global framework for addressing environmental deterioration. The conference produced several documents such as the Convention on Biological Diversity; The Framework Convention on Climate Change; Principles of Forest Management; The Rio Declaration on Environment and Development; and Agenda 21. The main document that came out of the conference was Agenda 21. The main goal of Agenda 21 was to ensure maximum output of sustainable development, improve quality of life, eliminate poverty, and improve waste management. According to this conference, hotels can minimize environmental impact by implementing the use of ecological equipment such as solar panels, low flow showerheads, and recycling bins. At the same time, this will attract more tourists to stay on. From observation made on environmental issues, the hotel management now understands that sustainability and economic growth depends on the type of environment policy put in place. In this case, a clean environment is now seen as a fundamental component of quality service and it is important for the development of the tourism and hospitality industry.

Thus, this paper was prepared to investigates to what extent and the impact of environmental management practices to the customer satisfaction and customer loyalty in Malaysian non-green hotel. The rational of non-green hotel selected is because the possibility this types of the hotel still apply environmental management practices in their hotel even though they are not awarded as a Green Hotel by ASEAN Tourism National Organization.

ISSUES AND PROBLEMS

Since the hotel industry gives a huge effect on the environment, especially through their daily operations, thus this industry is important to be explored. According to Bohdanowicz (2005) the hotel industry contributed 75% to the environment impacts through improper water, energy and waste disposal management. Thus, this research chose the hotel industry in Malaysia as the subject to examined. According to Lita, Surya, Ma'ruf and Syahrul (2014), attention to environmental issues and business practices is more popular in developed countries compared to developing countries, particularly in the aspect of community awareness and government policies and regulation. This statement is supported by the research by Kang, Stein, Heo and Lee (2012) which found that the world's leading hotels have made initiatives to invest in becoming environmentally friendly since a few years ago. However, hotels in Malaysia focused more on facilities and services rather than environmental policy and practices (Abdul Samad, Abdul Rahman & Ibrahim, 2008).

Due to the increasing environmental awareness among the management of the hospitality industry, the green hotel seems to be a growing niche in the competitive lodging industry and the number of customers who are interested to stay in green hotels has also increased (Mohd Noor & Kumar, 2014; Chikita, 2012; Kasanava, 2008; Claver-Cortes, Molina-Azorin, Pereira-Moliner, & Lopez-Gamero, 2007; Manaktola & Jauhari, 2007). According to Benson (2013) and Cometa (2012), the demand for hotels which implement green practices will lead to competitive advantage. Thus, many hotels have purposely implemented this innovative approach to increase consumer's perception towards environmental friendliness, accommodate green consumer's needs and actively participate in eco-friendly activities which can decrease negative impacts on the environment (Ham & Han, 2013). However, Mohamad et al. (2014) and Chong and Verma (2013) argue that the demand for green hotels is still unclear. Meanwhile, on the flipside, the research conducted by The J. Power and Associates on hotel guest satisfaction found that 75% of hotel guests would be willing to take part in environment friendly hotel (Bruns-smith, Choy, Chong, & Verma, 2015; Butler, 2008).

Green initiative or environmental initiative is among the programs that were adopted in many parts of the tourism sector (Siti-Nabiha et al., 2011). According to Chan (2013), green initiative is a marketing strategy that can attract customers. This is supported by Mohd Noor and Kumar (2014) and Kang et al. (2012) who indicate that environmental initiatives includes environmental friendly activities or practices that influence a customer's intention (Tang, 2015) to choose a green hotel, customer satisfaction (Gao & Mattila, 2014), customer loyalty (Scott, Ipkin, & Wong, 2015) and return intentions (Berezan, Raab, Yoo, & Love, 2013). However, Lita et al. (2014) and Chong and Verma (2013) consider the green initiative as a challenge to the hotelier to meet customer expectations. As green initiatives are moving forward at a fast pace, examining consumer attitudes and behaviors towards environmental management practices in the hospitality industry has received more attention from researchers. In this study, environmental management practices are among the green initiatives, as based on Tang (2015), Berezan et al. (2014), Singh, Cranage and Lee (2014) and Kang et al. (2012), it is linked to eco-friendly programs such as recycling programs, water saving devices and green landscaping. Additionally, it is believed that green initiatives through green image, energy and resource management will give benefit to the hotel industry (Park, 2009).

Environmental Management Practices refer to ongoing processes adopted by the management of which the activities and programs of the hotel are monitored to minimize negative environmental impact (Al-Shourah, 2007). Previous studies have indicated that the three core sustainable tourism practices are energy management, waste management and water conservation (Styles et al., 2013; Zhao, 2011; Chan, Wong, & Lo, 2009; Park, 2009; Mensah, 2006; Bohdanowicz, 2005; Sloan, Legrand, & Chen, 2004). However, Wolff (2008) stated other practices, such as eco-cuisine, energy efficient lighting, installing hinge activated lighting, using electronics such an e-mail and check in using the internet rather than using paper, were also important to be considered. Additionally, some hotels started implementing the green practices in their housekeeping department, food and beverage products and services, laundry, rooms and other facilities (Kasimu, Zaiton, & Hassan, 2012). Siti-Nabiha, Abdul Wahid, & Kamalul Ariffin (2010) proposed five drivers for adopting environmental management practices in the hospitality includes regulation or government policies, demand from customers, level of competition, green awareness at the organizational level and organization's attitude towards change. However, Md Salleh et al. (2010) found that the challenges in the hospitality industry are the customer's awareness. This finding supported the research by Doherty (2013) and Abdul Wahid, Abustan, Khalid and Amran (2008) that indicated the lack of awareness towards the green practices in the hotel industry.

Most hotels are faced with the challenge of fulfill customer's expectations to ensure repeat patronage, which is the bedrock of any business (Caruana, Money, & Berthon, 2000). Although several factors have been reported as relevant for gaining customer loyalty, customer satisfaction is highly recognized for its fundamental role (Jamal & Naser, 2002). According to Nurul Syaqirah and Putra Faizurrahman (2014) the success of the tourism industry, especially in the hotel sector, depends on customer satisfaction. Moreover, an emotional link to customer loyalty is one of the key strengths of any green product (Hartmann & Ibáñez, 2006).

To ensure customer satisfaction is achieved, it is important to recognize and anticipate customer needs (Dominici & Guzzo, 2010). This statement is agreed by Ranjbarian, Dabestani, Khajeh and Noktehdan (2011), who state that customer satisfaction is related to the needs and expectations of the customers towards factors such as previous personal experience, the products or services the company has promised and the price of the goods or service. Customers are satisfied if they have positive feelings, resulting from having received products and services that was beyond what was expected, and also the purchase decision and the needs associated with the purchase (Wiele, Boselie, & Hesselink, 2002; Akbar & Parvez, 2009). Loyalty is a result of customer satisfaction with the quality of services received at a hotel. A loyal customer not only engages in repeated patronage, but also delivers information to others, thus enabling the possibility of increasing hotel revenues (Poku, Zakari, & Soali, 2013). Since the cost of attracting new customers is higher than the cost of retaining the existing ones, in order to be successful, managers must concentrate on retaining existing customers by implementing effective policies for customer satisfaction and loyalty (Dominici & Guzzo, 2010).

Han, et al. (2010) described green behavioral intention as a possibility of an individual to visit a green hotel, optimistic towards the green initiative and be willing to pay for the premium service and product offered. Furthermore, there have been many research that explored and investigated customer satisfaction and customer loyalty from many various fields, but none of the research focussed on green and environmental issues (Asgharian, et al. 2012). This is supported by Meta analysis studies related to the hotel industry that have been conducted by Berezan, Millar, and Raab (2014) and Dolnicar and Otter (2003). Reading through the analysis, the researcher has identified the attributes that have always been and still are given less emphasis in studies related to the hotel industry such as service, room, price, food and beverage, location, security, image, green efforts and marketing. The most popular attribute being studied in this sector was service quality while the least popular being marketing. Interestingly, the studies related to green efforts has been increasing each year. This shows that the community's awareness towards environmental preservation has increased and is expected to increase even more with time, thus increasing the number of relevant studies. From this meta analysis, Berezan, Millar and Raab (2014) concluded that the green efforts related to hotel's environmental record and environmentally friendly practices in the hotel. Due to the lack of studies that explore the green efforts that influence customer satisfaction and customer loyalty, this study was therefore managed to explore the effect of environmental management practices which can be considered as new indicator among hotel practitioner in Malaysia on customer satisfaction and loyalty in the Malaysian hotel industry.

METHODOLOGY

This research involve mixed method approach, initial by quantitative approach followed by qualitative. This study involved hotel customer where the sampling frame for the study cannot be determined as there is no complete list of hotel guests available. The sampling frame was developed based on the Confidence Interval Method (Burns and Bush, 2014) and the sampling size formula by Krejcie and Morgan (1970). Using the formula, the proposed number of respondents for quantitative approach is 281. For quantitative research, this study involves three sections (A, B, and C) of the self-administered questionnaire. Section A was consisted of statements related to the environmental management practices, while Section B of the questionnaire includes statements to measure customer satisfaction and the last section was designed to measure customer loyalty towards the hotel. All section in this questionnaire using 10-point numerical scale. Meanwhile, for qualitative approach, the in-depth interview with three selected expert and five of respondents in focus group discussion done to elaborate result of the regression analysis. To simplify the results, researcher used Atlas.ti software to model the feedback from respondents.

RESULTS AND DISCUSSIONS

Based on Table 2, from the total of 281 respondents, this study consisted of 45.9% males and 54.1% females. The respondents were aged between 21-30 years (the majority, 48.8%), between 31-40 years (24.9%), between 41-50 years (13.2%), and the rest were aged 50 years and above. The results of this study found that the intention of the respondents for staying at a hotel included for filling up their spare time (33%), for business purposes (17.8%), for educational purposes (10.7%), and the rest were for miscellaneous reasons such as visiting friends, religious activities, and sporting events (39.4%).

Level of Environmental Management Practices

Table 3 shows the mean value of environmental management practices in Malaysian non-green hotels. The values shown are from the perception of a customer towards the environmental management practices applied or used in the hotel they stayed at. The item which states "this hotel offers an option to reuse towels for guests staying more than one night" indicates the highest mean value (6.80) compared to other items. This means that most hotels nowadays try to apply this practice. Meanwhile, the item "this hotel purchases organically grown food" shows the lowest mean value (5.82). The respondents agreed with this statement; however, sometimes they did not know whether or not the hotel uses organic products in the food provided, unless the hotel specifically mentions the fact. Based on Table 3, all the item of

Table 2. Demographic profile

Profile	Frequency (N=281)	Percentage (%)
Gender		
Male	129	45.9
Female	152	54.1
Age		
< 20 Years Old	27	9.6
21-30	137	48.8
31-40	70	24.9
41-50	37	13.2
51-60	10	3.6
Reason		
Relaxation	90	32.0
Visit relatives and friends	24	8.5
Business	50	17.8
Education	30	10.7
Culture	4	1.4
Fun	17	6.0
Sports	5	1.8
Health	3	1.1
Religious purposes	2	.7
Others	56	19.9

Table 3. Level of environmental management practices

Item	Mean	Std. Deviation
Environmental activities (EMP1)	6.44	2.080
Energy efficient lighting (EMP2)	6.34	2.029
Programmable thermostats (EMP3)	6.57	2.231
Refillable amenity dispensers (EMP4)	6.46	2.387
Recycling program (EMP5)	6.09	2.296
Air filtration (EMP6)	6.44	2.214
Designation of smoking and non-smoking area (EMP7)	6.84	2.353
Regular maintenance of equipment (EMP8)	6.68	2.008
Reuse of towels (EMP9)	6.80	2.197
Water saving technology (EMP10)	6.20	2.196
Organically food (EMP11)	5.82	2.297
Noise control (EMP12)	6.31	2.250
Soundproofing system (EMP13)	6.39	2.209
Sound-proof rooms (EMP14)	6.35	2.133
Toxic substances signage (EMP15)	6.30	2.198
Awareness programs (EMP16)	6.36	2.243

environmental management practices variable were in good value because the mean values for all items of environmental management practices are 5.8 and above. Since this study used a 10-point scale, the results revealed that all the items in this study were at a good level (5.8 and above) when the mean value was between 5.51 to 7.75 (Rist & Allen, 2011).

The Influences of Environmental Management Practices on Customer Satisfaction

To determine the dimensions of environmental management practices and customer satisfaction that most influence customer satisfaction, *stepwise* regression analysis was carried out. The dimension of environmental management practices was come out from Exploratory Factor Analysis (EFA). There are four dimension of environmental management practices this variable, namely Environmental Management Practice Component 1, Environmental Management Practice Component 2, Environmental Management Practice Component 3 and Environmental Management Practice Component 4. All these dimension of environmental management practices cannot be renamed as specific name because of the items contained in that dimension are jumbled. The list of items with their dimension were summarized in Table 4.

Based on Table 5, it is found that three variables that are Environmental Management Practice Component 4, Environmental Management Practice Component 1 and Environmental Management Practice Component 3 are entered into the regression model. Table 3 shows that Environmental Management Practice Component 4 influences customer satisfaction as much as 55.7 percent. The combination of Environmental Management Practice Component 4 and Environmental Management Practice Component 1 adds on 3.9 percent towards customer satisfaction. This means that the combination of Environmental

Table 4. Items of environmental management practices

Component	Item	Statement
Component 1	11	This hotel uses water saving technology.
	16	This hotel purchases organically grown food.
	17	This hotel has a noise control program.
	18	This hotel has soundproofing system in guest rooms.
	19	This hotel has soundproof rooms.
	20	This hotel provides clear warning signs for toxic substances.
	21	This hotel organizes awareness programs for environmental protection.
Component 2	1	This hotel promotes environmental activities for the guest.
	2	This hotel uses energy efficient lighting fixtures.
	5	This hotel has a refillable amenity dispenser for bathrooms.
	6	This hotel has an active recycling program for guests and employees.
Component 3	4	This hotel uses programmable thermostats to control temperature in guest rooms.
	7	This hotel has an air filtration system in place for guestrooms.
	10	This hotel offers an option to reuse towels for guests staying more than one night.
Component 4	8	This hotel has designated smoking and non-smoking areas.
	9	This hotel carries out maintenance for all equipment regularly.

Table 5. Regression model summary

Model	R	R^2	R^2 Change	Std. Error of the Estimate
1	.746[a]	.557	.555	1.15096
2	.772[b]	.596	.593	1.10072
3	.780[c]	.608	.604	1.08664

a. Predictor: (Constant), Environmental Management Practice Component 4
b. Predictor: (Constant), Environmental Management Practice Component 4, Environmental Management Practice Component 1,
c. Predictor: (Constant), Environmental Management Practice Component 4, Environmental Management Practice Component 1, Environmental Management Practice Component 3

Management Practice Component 4 and Environmental Management Practice Component 1 contributes 59.6 percent towards customer satisfaction. Meanwhile, the combination of Environmental Management Practice Component 4, Environmental Management Practice Component 1 and Environmental Management Practice Component 3 adds another1.2 percent making the overall contribution of all three variables to 60.8 percent towards customer satisfaction.

Results of the regression analysis show that Environmental Management Practice Component 4 [F (1, 279) = 350.735, p<0.05] contributes 55.7 percent of variance (R^2= .557) towards Customer Satisfaction. This shows that Environmental Management Practice Component 4 (β= 0.746, p<0.05) is the main predictor that influences Customer Satisfaction. The combination of Environmental Management Practice Component 4 and Environmental Management Practice Component 1 (β=0.553, p< 0.05) adds on 3.9 percent more influence on Customer Satisfaction. Meanwhile, the combination of Environmental Management Practice Component 4, Environmental Management Practice Component 1 and Environmental Management Practice Component 3 (β=0.402, p< 0.05) adds on 1.2 percent towards Customer Satisfaction. The results of this study also show that Environmental Management Practice Component 2 does not contribute towards Customer Satisfaction.

Dependent Variable: Customer Satisfaction

Based on the regression analysis in Table 5, Table 6, and Table 7, this shows that customer satisfaction was influenced by several items of environmental management practices applied in the hotel. However, items in Component 2 did not contribute to their satisfaction. Therefore this study will expose the factor of customer dissatisfaction on the environmental management practices applied in the hotel through in-depth interview and focus group discussion.

Figure 2 shows the eight factors causing customer to be dissatisfied with and disloyal to the hotel they are staying at. These include customer's attitude, price, customer not ready for green, inadequate facilities, customer less of understanding about green, lack of awareness, focus on operations instead of practices, and depending on the customer needs. Nevertheless, lack of awareness of green practices is most frequently cited among respondents. This shows less of awareness is a key factor of customer dissatisfaction. This factor indicates customers insensitive to environmental issues that occur. In addition, the price factor is also an important matter evaluated by customers when they want to stay at a hotel. Since the hotel that adopts environmental management practices usually imposes a relatively higher price, customers are less satisfied and loyal to the hotel if the charges are not comparable with the services provided. Customer attitude also plays a significant role in ensuring the successfulness of

Table 6. Analysis of variance for the influence of environmental management practices and customer satisfaction towards customer loyalty

Model		Sum of Squares	dk	Mean Square	F	Sig.
1	Regression	464.626	1	464.626	350.735	.000[b]
	Residual	369.597	279	1.325		
	Total	834.223	280			
2	Regression	497.404	2	248.702	205.271	.000[c]
	Residual	336.818	278	1.212		
	Total	834.223	280			
3	Regression	507.146	3	169.049	143.167	.000[d]
	Residual	327.077	277	1.181		
	Total	834.223	280			

Dependent Variable: Customer Satisfaction
Predictor: (Constant), Environmental Management Practice Component 4
Predictor: (Constant), Environmental Management Practice Component 4, Environmental Management Practice Component 1
Predictor: (Constant), Environmental Management Practice Component 4, Environmental Management Practice Component 1, Environmental Management Practice Component 3

Table 7. Analysis of coefficients environmental management practice and customer satisfaction towards customer satisfaction

Model		Unstandardized Coefficients	Standardized Coefficients	t	Sig.
		B	Beta		
1	(Constant)	2.594		10.637	.000
	Environmental Management Practice Component 4	.648	.746	18.728	.000
2	(Constant)	2.227		9.144	.000
	Environmental Management Practice Component 4	.463	.533	9.533	.000
	Environmental Management Practice Component 1	.259	.291	5.201	.000
3	(Constant)	2.054		8.288	.000
	Environmental Management Practice Component 4	.350	.403	5.650	.000
	Environmental Management Practice Component 1	.186	.209	3.358	.001
	Environmental Management Practice Component 3	.211	.226	2.872	.004

green practices adopted. There may be customers that act inappropriately by letting the electricity and air conditioner running while they are out of the room. This can be attributed to their lack of knowledge on green practices and/or the fact that they are less willing to go green. Customers have different needs when staying in hotels. Therefore, the customer is looking at the operation of hotels and facilities provided compared to green practices applied within the hotel. Even so, this can be overcome if the hotel management informs the customer earlier, i.e when they check in. This can help them understand and encourage support for the concept or practices of going green in the occupied hotel.

As a result of the face-to-face interviews, and also the focus group discussion with eight respondents, Figure 3 reveals 12 necessities of customers when staying in the hotel, of which these, at the same time, can increase the level of satisfaction and loyalty for the hotel. Among the needs of customers are comfort, cleanliness, safety, quality, friendly staff, price, good environment, appropriate facilities, website appearance, efficient action on customer feedback, information of green practices and parking space. Cleanliness is a top priority when staying at the hotel. This was proven when four of the eight respondents cited room cleanliness as their top priority when staying in hotels. Apart from cleanliness, comfort was also a priority if they wanted to book a hotel room.

Normally, customers will assess and review the comments or feedback from other customers who have previously stayed in the hotel, through the hotels own web site or through sites that offer promotional prices for the rooms such as Booking.com, Agoda.com, and Trivago.com. This shows that the hotel's website should have an attractive appearance and is user-friendly, which are important in ensuring customers get the detailed information they need to make the right choice. In addition, customers require appropriate facilities and quality services that are comparable to the prices they are required to pay for. Facilities provided should also be in usable and good condition, and managed properly. For example, gym equipment and the swimming pool available should be managed properly to satisfy new customers. High-speed Internet connection is also becoming a priority for customers.

Additionally, the external environment is also considered when choosing a hotel. For those who prefer hotel rooms with windows, they need an attractive environment. However, safety factors inside and outside the hotel have also become a priority to customers. This means that every hotel should provide sufficient parking space and security for customers even if the location of the hotel is located in a crowded area so that customers feel secure when parking their vehicles. Customers will also expect

Figure 3.

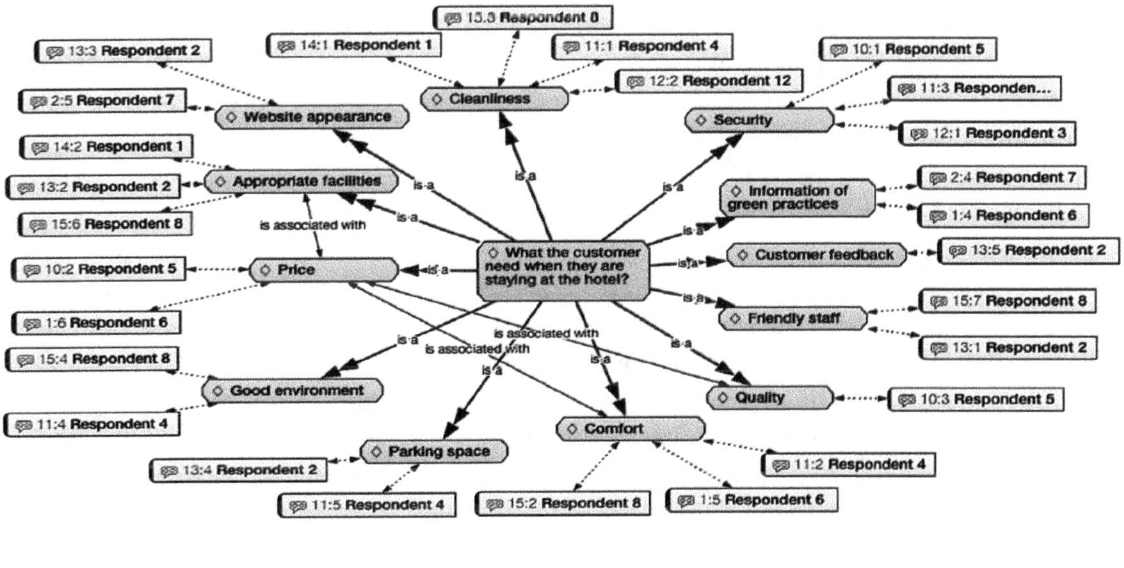

to get good service from hotel staff, especially employees who they are in direct contact with, such as when making a reservation and during checking in and out.

If a hotel has adopted green practices, they should provide information for the customer so that the customers in turn will understand the needs of the hotel and are more likely to act as required. The hotel employees must also understand and adopt the green practices. If there is feedback from the customer, the hotel must investigate and take action for improvement. If all this can be done and provided by the hotel, it is possible the customers would come back for another stay at the hotel, at the same time spreading good impressions about the hotel. This will increase the number of customers and be profitable for the hotel. As a conclusion it can be seen that environmental management practices are not as high a priority for customers when they choose to stay at the hotel compared to other factors. They are more concerned on the quality of products and services provided.

SOLUTIONS AND RECOMMENDATIONS

Until now, there have been no specific environment laws and regulations on the service industry in Malaysia especially in the accommodation sector. Therefore, the government plays a role in drafting and establishing laws and special regulations on the management of hotels that can help promote sustainable development. At the same time, the regulations can encourage hotel management to commit to environmental preservation. Many awareness programs and training should be given to the employees in the hotel industry as a way to increase knowledge. Programs related to environmental awareness can be conducted in collaboration with other organizations such as the Ministry of Natural Resources and Environment; the Ministry of Education; the Ministry of Energy, Water and Communication; the Ministry of Science, Technology and Innovation; and the Malaysian Hotel Association and NGOs that are directly and indirectly related to hotels in Malaysia. The programs and campaigns related to the environment at university or community level could be intensified and expanded to national level. Among the programs implemented are "My Beautiful Malaysia by Universiti Teknologi Malaysia", "Youth Environmental Expo by Universiti Putra Malaysia", "Program cintai Alam Sekitar, Go Green Help Clean by Universiti Kebangsaan Malaysia", "Kempen Jom Jimat Tenaga by Open Universiti Malaysia", "Pertandingan Debat Alam Sekitar by University Malaya", "Majlis Sambutan Hari Bumi by Universiti Teknikal Malaysia", and "Kempen Kitar Semula by Universiti Pendidikan Sultan Idris". In addition, in primary and secondary schools, environmental protection modules should be included in the teaching syllabus. One of its advantages is to give exposure to the students about the importance of the environment to individuals, the local community and society as a whole.

Mass media and social media play an important role in disseminating news and facts. Nowadays, social media has become a prime source for obtaining information. Therefore, the government should cooperate with the media, especially television and radio, to inform the general public about the significance of shielding the environment and create awareness about the problems that currently occur all over the world. Besides that, campaigns can also make use of advertising through billboard or signboard displays on the road. This way, the information can reach consumers faster.

In order to increase public awareness on protecting the environment, participation in celebrations such as the "World Environment Day" at international level is vital, increasing attention and action from both government and private agencies. The celebrations started in 1974 and have expanded to become a global platform, widely celebrated in more than 100 countries and hosted by countries selected according to specific themes.

Hotel managements also have their own roles to play in increasing the level of environmental awareness among customers. Customers usually do not understand or realize the importance of environmental stewardship. Thus, one of the efforts that can be made is by placing informational brochures in the guest rooms or in the lobby. This brochure should be made from recycled material or environmentally friendly material. Although eco-booklets are quite difficult to produce and it is difficult to determine whether these brochures are effective in attracting customers, the comprehensive information provided in them will give customers a better understanding and influence their behavior towards the environment such as the need to minimize the use of water and energy and the impact of their behaviors on the environment. The information can be illustrated using attention-grabbing images and graphics that can encourage customers to read and understand. In addition, posters placed around the hotel that contain information about environmental care can also attract consumers.

Customers can be educated through labeling or signage. Hotels should place environmental signage such as for saving water, switching off lights when not in use, switching off all electrical appliances when leaving a room, reusing towels and so on, so that customers can understand the concept of environmental protection. Additionally, feedback forms should be provided to get response from customers regarding the eco-friendly products and services offered by the hotel, to enable the hotel to rectify problems related to environmental protection.

Additionally, hotels that have its own websites should make modifications towards becoming environmental friendly. The websites can be placed with elements of environmental stewardship. In this way, easy to understand information can be provided to customers who are looking to book or make reservations. E-brochure is one of the initiatives that can be applied using the hotel's website. This action not only reduces the cost of hardcopy brochures, but it is one of the practices (going paperless) that can be implemented to support environmental preservation. Any reservations through the Internet and customers checking in can be done paperless, with customers only needing to provide proof of booking through a reference number.

Each customer who stays at the hotel has different needs and desires. Therefore, the hotel management should review what the appropriate customers needs are to ensure that customers are satisfied when staying at the hotel. To gain support from customers, they need to be informed about green practices on the property. Hotel employees such as the receptionist or front desk officers who deal directly with customers should inform the customers about the green practices being practiced and applied in the hotel, thus helping customers understand and encourage them to act accordingly.

CONCLUSION

Although the term 'green' is not new for people around the world, it seems not well-known among hoteliers and customers in Malaysia. This green approach in the hotel industry was introduced a long time ago after environmental awareness increased. Now, greening the hotel is one of the initiatives to change the way a hotel operates and attract both practitioners and visitors. Thus it is important for hotel management to identify and understand the importance of environmental management practices applied in the hotel. Generally, customer were not satisfied or loyal based on the environmental management practices due to having less awareness about green practices, less information about green practices, and having more concerns on facilities and price of accommodations rather than environmental issues. Thus, to increase awareness among customers on the environmental issues, there are several approaches that hotel management can apply. Among these include disseminating information through brochures, a comprehensive website and environmental signage. The government also must play a role in helping hotels apply environmental management practices in their hotel. This is due to the high cost required at the initial phase of adopting environmental management practices in the hotel. However, the practices should be well maintained by the hotel management to save costs and to be able to attract pro-environmental customers. These outcomes are important to the government and institutions that have an authority to improve the laws and regulations related to environmental protection. Hotels or accommodation providers can intensify environmental campaigns across the country to provide information to the society regarding environmental issues and create awareness. The results from this study will help hotel managements to improve their environmental management practices, as the environmental awareness among consumers and employees is important to increase satisfaction towards a hotel.

Interestingly, this study creates a theoretical contribution by expanding the Theory of Planned Behavior (TPB) by Ajzen (1991). Based on previous research, this research is further improved by integrating environmental management practices as a green initiative which is novelty factor that may give impact to the intention and behavior among hotel customers. Even though there are many theories that are used to predict human behavior and are widely used to explain individual's decision-making process (Han, 2015), however, TPB was chosen because this theory encompasses both volitional and non-volitional sides (control belief-perceived behavioral control) (Han, 2015; Ajzen, 1991). This theory indicates that behavior can be deliberated according to the three constructs, such as behavioral attitude, subjective norms and perceived behavioral control. Behavioral attitude is the belief about the possible effect, whether it is negative or positive, from the behavior. Subjective norms refer to the beliefs about expectation from other external factors, while perceived behavioral control is a belief about the factors which exist that may simplify or interfere with the behavior performance and how the person feels in handling these factors. The combination of these three constructs is a predictor to the behavioral intention, which then leads to an actual behavior. According to Ajzen (1991), common behavior intention will affect actual behavior positively, unless the person has other constraints such as financial and time problems that would obstruct them from accomplishing the behavior. The Theory of Planned Behavior seems suitable for this research because this study investigates the behavior of customers related to satisfaction and loyalty. In this research, customer satisfaction acts as the behavioral intention while loyalty reacts as the behavior. Since environmental management practices are the external factors that affect the behavior among customers, these two constructs were considered as behavioral attitude and subjective norms. According to Ajzen (1991), an individual will accept and purchase green products and practices when their pro-environmental behavior (environmental awareness) is in line with their interests (normative).

FUTURE RESEARCH DIRECTIONS

This study covered only three variables: environmental management practices, customer satisfaction and customer loyalty. However, there are many other determinants that can be used in further research to identify the correlation between environmental management practices and customer behavior. Besides that, this research only involved hotel customers as respondents. To obtain more comprehensive and holistic results, future research could involve other respondents such as hotel management, hotel employees, policy makers, stakeholders and communities. The findings from various representatives will help hotel managements improve their hotel based on the recommendations given.

REFERENCES

Abdul Samad, M. H., Abdul Rahman, A., & Ibrahim, F. (2008). Green Performance Ratings for Malaysian Buildings With Particular Reference to Hotels. *International Conference on Environment Research and Technology (ICERT 08).*

Abdul Wahid, N., Abustan, I., Khalid, S.-N., & Amran, A. (2008). Green indicators in hospitality industry: Identification of common attributes applied by hotels in American and Latin American continents. *Proceedings of National Symposium on Tourism Research*, 79–90.

Ajzen, I. (1991). The Theory of Planned Behavior. *Organizational Behavior and Human Decision Processes, 50*, 179–211. doi:10.1016/0749-5978(91)90020-T

Akbar, M. M., & Parvez, N. (2009). Impact of service quality, trust, and customer satisfaction on customers loyalty. *ABAC Journal, 29*(1), 24–38.

Al-Shourah, A. A. (2007). *The Relationship Between Environmental Management Practices (Emp) And Hotel Performance : Emp Drivers And The Moderating Role Of Perceived Benefits.* Academic Press.

American Association for the Advancement of Science. (2007). *AAAS Board Statement on Climate Change.* Retrieved August 15, 2015, from http://www.aaas.org/sites/default/files/migrate/uploads/aaas_climate_statement.pdf

Asgharian, R., Salehi, M., Saleki, Z. S., Hojabri, R., & Nikkheslat, M. (2012). Green product quality, green customer satisfaction, and green customer loyalty. *International Journal of Research in Management & Technology, 2*(5), 499–503.

Berezan, O., Millar, M., & Raab, C. (2014). Sustainable hotel practices and guest satisfaction levels. *International Journal of Hospitality & Tourism Administration, 15*(1), 1–18. doi:10.1080/15256480.2014.872884

Berezan, O., Raab, C., Yoo, M., & Love, C. (2013). Sustainable hotel practices and nationality: The impact on guest satisfaction and guest intention to return. *International Journal of Hospitality Management, 34*(1), 227–233. doi:10.1016/j.ijhm.2013.03.010

Bohdanowicz, P. (2005). European hoteliers environmental attitudes: Greening the Business. *The Cornell Hotel and Restaurant Administration Quarterly, 46*(2), 188–204. doi:10.1177/0010880404273891

Caruana, A., Money, A. H., & Berthon, P. R. (2000). Service quality and satisfaction - the moderating role of value. *European Journal of Marketing, 34*(11/12), 1338–1352. doi:10.1108/03090560010764432

Central Intelligence Agency. (2015). *The World Factbook- Environmental- Current issues.* Retrieved August 24, 2015, from https://www.cia.gov/library/publications/the-world-factbook/fields/2032.html

Chan, E. S. W. (2013). Managing green marketing: Hong Kong hotel managers perspective. *International Journal of Hospitality Management, 34*(1), 442–461. doi:10.1016/j.ijhm.2012.12.007

Chan, W., Wong, K., & Lo, J. (2009). Hong Kong hotels sewage: Environmental cost and saving technique. *Journal of Hospitality & Tourism Research (Washington, D.C.), 33*(2), 329–346. doi:10.1177/1096348009338525

Chong, H. G., & Verma, R. (2013). Hotel sustainability : Financial analysis shines a cautious green light. *Cornell Hospitality Report, 13*(10), 1–15.

Claver-Cortes, E., Molina-Azorin, J. F., Pereira-Moliner, J., & Lopez-Gamero, M. D. (2007). Environmental strategies and their impact on hotel performance. *Environmental Strategies and Their Impact on Hotel Performance., 15*(6), 663–679.

Cohen, S. (2014). *The Growing Level of Environmental Awareness.* Retrieved December 11, 2015, from http://www.huffingtonpost.com/steven-cohen/the-growing-level-of-envi_b_6390054.html

DeSimone, L. D., & Popoff, F. (1997). *Eco-efficiency: The Business Link to Sustainable Development.* London: The MIT Press.

Doherty, L. (2013). *Environmental sustainability practices in the hospitality industry of orange county.* California Polytechnic State University.

Dolnicar, S., & Otter, T. (2003). Which hotel attributes matter? A review of previous and a framework for future research. In *Proceedings of the 9th Annual Conference of the Asia Pacific Tourism Association (APTA).* University of Technology Sydney. http://doi.org/http://ro.uow.edu.au/commpapers/268

Dominici, G., & Guzzo, R. (2010). Customer satisfaction in the hotel industry : A case study from Sicily. *International Journal of Marketing Studies, 2*(2), 3–12. doi:10.5539/ijms.v2n2p3

Economic Planning Unit. (2015). *Eleventh Malaysia Plan 2016-2020. Rancangan Malaysia Kesebelas (Eleventh Malaysia Plan): 2016-2020.* Kuala Lumpur: Percetakan Nasional Malaysia Berhad. Retrieved from http://rmk11.epu.gov.my/book/eng/Elevent-Malaysia-Plan/RMKe-11 Book.pdf

Eggeling, J. (2010). *Sustainable Tourism Practices in the Hospitality Sector : A Case Study of Scandic.* Mid Sweden University Östersund.

Engel, J. F., Blackwell, R. D., & Miniard, P. W. (1990). *Customer Behavior* (6th ed.). Hinsdale: Chicago Dryden Press.

Erdogan, N., & Tosun, C. (2009). Environmental performance of tourism accommodations in the protected areas: Case of Goreme Historical National Park. *International Journal of Hospitality Management, 28*(3), 406–414. doi:10.1016/j.ijhm.2009.01.005

Faulkner, B., Mascardo, G., & Laws, E. (2000). *Tourism in the 21st century: Lessons from experience.* London: Continuum.

Furqan, A., Mat Som, A. P., & Hussin, R. (2010). Promoting green tourism for future sustainability. *Theoretical and Empirical Researches in Urban Management*, *8*(17), 64–74.

Gao, Y., & Mattila, A. S. (2014). Improving consumer satisfaction in green hotels: The roles of perceived warmth, perceived competence, and CSR motive. *International Journal of Hospitality Management*, *42*, 20–31. doi:10.1016/j.ijhm.2014.06.003

Han, H. (2015). Travelers pro-environmental behavior in a green lodging context: Converging value-belief-norm theory and the theory of planned behavior. *Tourism Management*, *47*, 164–177. doi:10.1016/j.tourman.2014.09.014

Han, H., Hsu, L.-T., & Sheu, C. (2010). Application of the Theory of Planned Behavior to green hotel choice: Testing the effect of environmental friendly activities. *Tourism Management*, *31*(3), 325–334. doi:10.1016/j.tourman.2009.03.013

Hartmann, P., & Ibáñez, V. A. (2006). Green value added. *Marketing Intelligence & Planning*, *24*(7), 673–680. doi:10.1108/02634500610711842

Hassan, H., & Nezakati, H. (2014). Green Tourism Practices in Malaysia. In Selected Issues in Hospitality and Tourism (pp. 24–36). Serdang, Selangor: Universiti Putra Malaysia Press.

Islam, N. (2008). Public Awareness About Environmental Issues: Perspective Bangladesh. *Asian Affairs*, *30*(2), 30–56.

Jamal, A., & Naser, K. (2002). Customer satisfaction and retail banking: An assessment of some of the key antecedents of customer satisfaction in retail banking. *International Journal of Bank Marketing*, *20*(4), 146–160. doi:10.1108/02652320210432936

Kang, K. H., Stein, L., Heo, C. Y., & Lee, S. (2012). Consumers willingness to pay for green initiatives of the hotel industry. *International Journal of Hospitality Management*, *31*(2), 564–572. doi:10.1016/j.ijhm.2011.08.001

Kasim, A. (2004). Socio-environmentally responsible hotel business: Do tourists to Penang Island, Malaysia care? *Journal of Hospitality & Leisure Marketing*, *11*(4), 5–28. doi:10.1300/J150v11n04_02

Kasim, A. (2009). Managerial attitudes towards environmental management among small and medium hotels in Kuala Lumpur. *Journal of Sustainable Tourism*, *17*(6), 709–725. doi:10.1080/09669580902928468

Kasim, A., & Scarlat, C. (2007). Business Environmental Responsibility in the Hospitality Industry. *Management*, *2*(1), 5–23.

Kasimu, A. B., Zaiton, S., & Hassan, H. (2012). Hotels involvement in sustainable tourism practices in Klang Valley, Malaysia. *International Journal of Economics and Management*, *6*(1), 21–34.

Kirk, D. (1995). Environmental management in hotels. *International Journal of Contemporary Hospitality Management*, *7*(6), 3–8. doi:10.1108/09596119510095325

Kirkpatrick, D. (1990). *Environmentalism: The new crusade*. Retrieved February 21, 2015, from http://archive.fortune.com/magazines/fortune/fortune_archive/1990/02/12/73069/ index.htm

Lita, R. P., Surya, S., Maruf, M., & Syahrul, L. (2014). Green attitude and behavior of local tourists towards hotels and restaurants in West Sumatra, Indonesia. *Procedia Environmental Sciences*, *20*, 261–270. doi:10.1016/j.proenv.2014.03.033

Mattera, M., & Moreno-melgarejo, A. (2012). Strategic Implications of Corporate Social Responsibility in Hotel Industry : A Comparative Research Between NH Hotels and Meliá Hotels International. *Higher Learning Research Communications*, *2*(4), 37–53. doi:10.18870/hlrc.v2i4.85

Md Salleh, N. Z., Abdul Hamid, A. B., Hashim, N. H., & Omain, S. Z. (2010). *Issues and challenges in Malaysian hotel operations. In 3rd Asia-Euro Tourism, Hospitality and Gastronomy*. Subang: Taylor's College.

Mensah, I. (2006). Environmental management practices among hotels in the Greater Accra Region. *Journal Hospitality Management*, *25*(3), 414–431. doi:10.1016/j.ijhm.2005.02.003

Millar, M., & Baloglu, S. (2008). Hotel guests' preferences for green hotel attributes. *Proceedings of the European Council for Hotel, Restaurant, and Institutional Education Conference*.

Ministry of Tourism and Sports of Thailand. (2013). *ASEAN Tourism Standards*. Bangkok: ASEAN Tourism Standards.

Mohamad, Z. Z., Tengku Arifin, T. R., Samsuri, A. S., & Mior Badrul Munir, M. F. (2014). Intention to visit green hotel in Malaysia : The impact of personal traits and marketing strategy. *International Journal of Business and Social Science*, *5*(7), 167–173.

Mohamed, B. (2008). *Pelancongan lestari*. Kuala Lumpur: Dewan Bahasa dan Pustaka.

Mohd Noor, N. A., & Kumar, D. (2014). Eco friendly "Activities" vs Eco friendly "Attitude": Travelers intention to choose green hotels in Malaysia. *World Applied Sciences Journal*, *30*(4), 506–513. doi:10.5829/idosi.wasj.2014.30.04.14062

NASA. (2015a). *Climate change: How do we know?*. Retrieved August 15, 2015, from http://climate.nasa.gov/evidence/

NASA. (2015b). *Scientific consensus: Earth's climate is warming*. Retrieved August 15, 2015, from http://climate.nasa.gov/scientific-consensus/

Nurul Syaqirah, Z., & Putra Faizurrahman, Z. (2014). Managing customer retention of hotel industry in Malaysia. *Procedia: Social and Behavioral Sciences*, *130*, 379–389. doi:10.1016/j.sbspro.2014.04.045

Oliver, R. L. (1999). Whence consumer loyalty?. *Journal of Marketing*, *63*(Special Issue), 33–44. doi:10.2307/1252099

Park, J. (2009). *The Relationship Between Top Managers' Environmental Attitudes and Environmental Management in Hotel Companies*. Virginia Polytechnic Institute and State University.

Poku, K., Zakari, M., & Soali, A. (2013). Impact of service quality on customer loyalty in the hotel industry: An empirical study from Ghana. *International Review of Management and Business Research*, *2*(2), 600–609.

Ranjbarian, B., Dabestani, R., Khajeh, E., & Noktehdan, I. (2011). An investigation of influencing factors customers' loyalty in a four star hotel in Iran. *International Journal of Business and Social Science*, *2*(21), 243–246.

Rist, S., & Allen, D. (2011). *Tales from the Field: Evaluating a University Residential Living- Learning Community*. Retrieved March 31, 2016, from http://www.performancexpress.org/2011/07/tales-from-the-field-evaluating-a-university-residential-living-learning-community/

Scott, M., Ipkin, R., & Wong, A. (2015). Green marketing programs as strategic initiatives in hospitality. *Journal of Services Marketing*, *29*(2).

Singh, N., Cranage, D., & Lee, S. (2014). Green strategies for hotels: Estimation of recycling benefits. *International Journal of Hospitality Management*, *43*, 13–22. doi:10.1016/j.ijhm.2014.07.006

Siti-Nabiha, A. K., Abdul Wahid, N., & Kamalul Ariffin, N. S. (2010). The drivers and the outcomes of environmental management practices in the hotel industry : A proposed framework. *TEAM Journal of Hospitality and Tourism*, *7*(1), 13–26.

Siti-Nabiha, A. K., George, R. A., Abdul Wahid, N., Amran, A., Abustan, I., & Mahadi, R. (2011). A field survey of environmental initiatives at selected resorts in Malaysia. *World Applied Sciences Journal*, *12*, 56–63.

Sloan, P., Legrand, W., & Chen, J. S. (2004). Factors influencing German hoteliers attitudes toward environmental management. *Advances in Hospitality and Leisure*, *1*, 179–188. doi:10.1016/S1745-3542(04)01011-2

Styles, D., Schönberger, H., & Martos, J. L. G. (2013). *Best Environmental Management Practice in the Tourism Sector*. European Union; doi:10.2788/33972

Tang, M. (2015). Evaluating green hotels in Taiwan from the consumer's perspective. *International Journal of Management Research and Business Strategy*, *4*(1), 1–15.

Van Der Wiele, T., Boselie, P., & Hesselink, M. (2002). Empirical evidence for the relationship between customer satisfaction and business performance. *Managing Service Quality*, *12*(3), 184–193. doi:10.1108/09604520210429259

Wolff, C. (2008). Second Nature. *Lodging Hospitality*, *64*(2), 24–26.

Zhao, C. (2011). *An Analysis of Hotels' Green Activities and Its Influence on Hotels' Projected Image Using a Mixed Methodology*. Purdue University.

KEY TERMS AND DEFINITIONS

Customer Loyalty: Customer loyalty refers to psychological character and emotional attachment with the product and service provided by an organization that leads to a repurchase, delivering of information to other persons and being price insensitive (Oliver, 1999).

Customer Satisfaction: Customer satisfaction refers to the feelings resulting from the expectations and what customers get when they are staying at the hotels (Engel, Blackwell, & Miniard, 1990). Customers will respond positively if the products and services meet or exceed their requirements. However, if their needs are not achieved, they will respond to the contrary. In this study, customer satisfaction is the feeling reflected by the environmental management practices applied in the hotel.

Environmental Management Practices: Environmental Management Practices are activities and programs used by the hotel to reduce negative impacts on the environment.

Non-Green Hotel: Non-green hotel refers to the hotel that has been registered with the Ministry of Tourism and Culture, Malaysia, but not recognized as a green hotel by the ASEAN Tourism National Organization. However, this type of hotel has the probability of adopting green practices and image even if it is not awarded as a green hotel.

Chapter 2
Consumers Consciousness Towards Environmental Aesthetics in Using Nutricosmetics Products

Ruzanna Shahrin
Universiti Teknologi Malaysia, Malaysia

Rossilah Binti Jamil
Universiti Teknologi Malaysia, Malaysia

ABSTRACT

The present paper attempts to shed some light on consumers' consciousness on environmental aesthetics in using nutricosmetics products. More particularly, this paper seeks to answer the following questions: (1) How does green marketing contribute to consumer consciousness towards environmental aesthetics? (2) How do nutricosmetic products present its aesthetic values towards its consumers? (3) How do consumers perceive environmental aesthetics in purchasing nutricosmetic products? (4) How are environmental aesthetics interconnected with the environment? In answering these research questions, relevant literature is reviewed, analysed, compared and synthesized as a way to gather the required information. The present paper contributes to the understanding of environmental aesthetics in the context of nutricosmetics industry.

INTRODUCTION

There is a recent trend in cosmetics industry which is cosmetic hybrids or nutricosmetics. Cosmetic hybrids are results of innovative scientific research and development on beauty products (Van den Bulte and Joshi, 2007) which breeds a range of health and beauty products particularly Nutricosmetics (Ancarani and Gisco, 2014). Green formulations and environmental-friendly features are the focus of the current nutricosmetics industry. Even though the shift to 'green' is likely to incur extra costs to both consumers

DOI: 10.4018/978-1-5225-2912-5.ch002

and businesses, yet it is worthwhile in the long run. In this aspect, the notion of environmental aesthetics plays a vital role in shaping consumers' preference towards purchasing nutricosmetics products. The core idea of environmental aesthetics is to create values between people and the environment. It also contributes in preserving the planet if green consumption is adopted in practice. Environmental aesthetics helps to support connectivity among people with their healthy environment and widens choices to practice green lifestyle.

Kim and Damhorst (1998) stated that consumers' desire to choose eco-friendly products for healthier living has given birth to the opportunities for businesses to gain profits using green/eco-friendly platforms. As such, the eco-friendly products are regarded as a novel selling point for businesses to embark on a completely new line of products and services (Lau, Chiu and Yau, 2014). Within this trend, effective green marketing emerges and forms a foundation in understanding the role of 'environmental aesthetics'. Environmental aesthetics refer to the interaction between an individual and the environment, related to beauty (Mandoki, 2016). Human environment interaction includes physical environment and its associated objects, as well as the psychological and physiological processes that are involved in human perception and cognition.

Due to the increasing awareness among consumers about environment and quality life, significant studies have focused on topics pertaining to green marketing. However, little has been known about consumers' awareness about environmental aesthetics, particularly in the context of nutricosmetics product usage. Considering this, the present paper aims to fill this gap in the existing literature. More clearly, this study seeks to answer the following research questions:

- How does green marketing contribute to consumer consciousness towards environmental aesthetics?
- How nutricosmetic products offer aesthetic values to the consumers?
- How consumers perceive environmental aesthetics in purchasing nutricosmetic products?
- How environmental aesthetics is interconnected with the environment?

The rest of the paper is organized into the following structure. *First*, how the information was gathered is briefly mentioned. *Second*, how green marketing contributes to consumer consciousness towards environmental aesthetics is discussed. *Third*, the paper discusses the aesthetic values that nutricosmetic products use to attract its customers. *Lastly*, consumers' perception towards environmental aesthetics in purchasing nutricosmetic products is highlighted followed by an overall concluding remark.

GATHERING INFORMATION

This study utilized content analysis approach to review relevant literature in the field. Literatures of environmental aesthetics were reviewed, compared and synthesized using key words 'environmental aesthetics', 'green cosmetics', 'nutricosmetics', 'environmental consciousness', and 'consumer behaviors' to further understand the terms. Several databases were utilized to search and download relevant journal articles such as Elsevier, Science Direct, Emerald and Taylor & Francis. Furthermore, Google scholar was used to search conference papers. To gain a different angle to the subject, industrial reports for example Euromonitor, websites of selected government and non-government institutions, and the World

Health Organization (WHO) were also reviewed. The collected information was carefully scrutinized for its credibility and novelty. The articles were reviewed in order to answer the research questions that are mentioned in the introduction section.

HOW DOES GREEN MARKETING CONTRIBUTE TO CONSUMER CONSCIOUSNESS TOWARDS ENVIRONMENTAL AESTHETICS?

Environmental issues have been highlighted in many areas of life. Delafrooz, Taleghani and Nouri (2014) mentioned the influence of green marketing tools such as the eco-label, green claims and environmental advertisement were used to have significant effects on consumer consciousness and purchasing behaviour.

Green marketing supports environmental agenda by spreading the benefits of going green through the production and consumption of green products. Meeting demands for green consumption is the departure point of green marketing. Green consumption helps consumer to be aware about the impacts of environmental deterioration on their lives (Akenji, 2014). Green operation is the foundation for the enterprise to implement the green marketing (Wilson and Schwarzman, 2016). According to Husted et al (2014) consumer willingness to pay for green products is an indication of environmental consciousness. Hence companies must take the opportunity to get into the green marketing bandwagon. Three aspects must be considered in order to implement green marketing strategy, i.e. profit, cost and responsibility (Zhu, Li, Geng and Qi, 2013). According to Öberseder, Schlegelmilch and Murphy (2013), the emphasis for sustainable business practices by corporations around the world is a result of increased consumer awareness towards environmental protection and social welfare.

A study by Baker, Davis and Weaver (2013) highlights that green marketing has a strong role in influencing consumers' intentions to purchase environmentally-friendly products. Stahl (2012) suggested that customers' actions have progressed through the years with the spirited environmental changes and this change is reflected in their shopping i.e. checking if the packaged items are in a recyclable material (e.g. CFC-free hair products, deodorants, biodegradable paint, etc.) The marketers also respond to the behavioural change of consumers by developing the right eco-friendly quality of the product/brand and customers satisfaction. Lamb and Peretiatkos, (2013) supported the idea of environmental friendly packaging by stating that packaging and its labelling are some important way to assert the consumers about the visibility about the eco-friendly product/brand. It happens similar to cosmetic industry, which cosmetic hybrids, especially nutricosmetics aimed to assert such trend to build consumer confidence on product/brand (Raj et al, 2012).The prime definition of a brand is "distinctive name, term and symbol (such as a logo, trademark, or package design) anticipated to recognize the goods or services of either one seller or a group of sellers, and to differentiate those goods or services from those of competitors" (Aaker and Equity, 1991, p. 7). Care for the environment is always a positive approach and business practice as it has many beneficial factors such as employee motivation, more committed consumers (brand loyalty) which in turns generate increase profitability (Forte & Lamont, 1998). As such, cosmetic hybrid e.g. Nutricosmetic made to have these environmental qualities to offer consumer better green choices. Pujari (2006) asserts that consumers value performance, reliability, and designs much more than a product's ecological soundness. Indeed, to overcome their image problem, green products must often outperform over traditional counterparts.

HOW DO NUTRICOSMETIC PRODUCTS OFFER ITS AESTHETIC VALUES TO THE CONSUMERS?

Increased consciousness towards quality of life, environment and health results more people to look for eco-friendly products. Eco-friendly products mean much more than just saving the environment and protecting the planet. Also, it ensures general well-being and sustainability of the human species (Haws, Winterich, and Reczek, 2013). Cosmetic hybrids are thought to be more beneficial as they maintain consumers health and protect them from the use of unsafe chemicals (Foster, 2012). Most standard-quality products nowadays contain harmful substances which may potentially lead to serious health problems (Folashade, Omoregie and Ochogu, 2012). Dureja et al (2005) state cosmetic hybrids like nutricosmetics product was invented to minimize the use of any potential toxins or harmful chemicals in their production. Thus, many nutricosmetics products are made from plant-based, organic ingredients that are safe for human and environments (Neves, 2014).

It is important to understand the core of nutricosmetic products' manufacturers' strategy to present its aesthetic values towards its consumers. Corporations are increasingly recognizing the benefits of green marketing, although many companies are doing it for their own benefit and not for social responsibility reasons (Wolch et al, 2014). Additionally, many nutricosmetics companies use 'greenwashing' approach. The term *greenwashing* refers to the act of misleading consumers by using any symbol or color (e.g., green color in the package) that generally represents the concept of 'green', without really adopting the green concept. The primary objective of greenwashing is to provide consumers with the feeling that the organization is taking the necessary steps responsibly manage its ecological trail. However, in reality, the company may be doing nothing that is environmentally effort and societies are constrained by environmental limits (Esty and Winston, 2009). The part where the nutricosmetics do is always looking greener than other does. Ottman et al (2006) pointed out most of the products in this industry selling the "brand" and its outrageous claims which known without scientific evidences and means to deceive consumer with their green/eco-friendly features.

Nutricosmetics market produced drinks, liquid, powder and pill, and even by-injection and dripping methods is increasing on demand as the solution for skin enhancing (e.g. whitening) and problem like aging, wrinkles, anti-oxidant, blemishes, or pigmentation (Kapoor, 2005). Growing consumer awareness for natural products and despicable claims for the effectiveness and green/eco-friendly practices for such products are the major factors driving the demand for nutricosmetic products. People are becoming more concerned about healthier lifestyle and are looking for products that beyond the normal causes (Heasman and Mellentin, 2001). Natural ingredients such as fruit extracts, green tea, Shea Butter, coconut oil, camu-camu, herbs like turmeric and ginger are commonly used in nutricosmetics products. Such ingredients reside with natural values and people believe for its effectiveness through traditional medicine. Scientifically proved that ingredients of nutricosmetics products such as bark, coconut oil, root and stem among others have shown positive effects in the beautification of skin, and improving health (Mukherjee, Maity, Nema, and Sarkar, 2011). Therefore, Taylor et al (2014) identifies the nutricosmetics market has experienced diversified trends across different region such as North America, Europe, and Asia Pacific.

The product image/design also considering as part of aesthetics concerns of products. Green or eco-friendly industry marked as the area to educate the consumer about the features, benefits, and product efficacy towards consumer and environment (Kim et al., 2016). Yet, getting that message across via packaging alone is a challenge to attain consumer trust on products. The utmost issue, which nutricosmetics confront, is the formulations. Hunt et al (2016) found that the various claims perceived natural, organic and non-chemical based ingredients made the products are greener and healthier to consumers. As explained by Sagalowicz and Leser (2010) the benefits are beyond what consumer would obtain from just eating normal foods or applying surface cosmetic products. So what exactly goes into nutricosmetics products? The ingredients and the designs came to show the eco-friendliness and natural in the formulations. They often used many types of ingredients with generally known as a good food for example as vitamin E, C, broccoli, alfafa, goji berries and spirulina, Turmeric, and etc. (Khan and Abourashed, 2011). The key is in the product's ingredients, and manifestly green on its appearances with green claims and labels. However, there is a gap between the "green claim" and "the effectiveness of the product based on the claims"

Through green marketing, the perception of environmental aesthetics is revealed through various aesthetic elements in products and its benefits towards consumers and environments. The aesthetic sense that inherited from successful green marketing drew toward conditions that made for survival and reproductive success for products. Aesthetic interests are widely spread, from landscapes and environments, to non-human animals, and to the product appearance and behaviour of fellow humans (Davies and Aperson, 2015). Consumer experience led to the robust environmental changes and this change is reflected in lifestyle (e.g. shopping and checking if the product is made from natural ingredients and packaged items are in a recyclable material). D'Souza, Taghian, Lamb, and Peretiatkos (2006) supported the idea of environmental aesthetic by stating that designing, packaging and its labelling is one important way to assert the consumers about the visibility of eco-friendly product/brand. Hence, green marketing plays important role for positive understanding of environmental aesthetics.

HOW CONSUMERS PERCEIVE ENVIRONMENTAL AESTHETICS IN PURCHASING NUTRICOSMETIC PRODUCTS?

Being environmentally friendly involves several engagements including purchasing green products. The significant of environmental aesthetics on consumers' perception of green marketing may provide insight into the expanding aesthetics offered with ecological integrity as well as product personal appearance. Environmental aesthetic inspired by nature's beauty to make them environment beautiful (Shapshay, 2013). Pleasing own personal appearances is an important because individual personal aesthetic reflects the appearance of the earth. Denison and Ren (2001) claim green products selling point combines natural/green ingredients incorporates self-esteem into its promotions for its products, reconciling traditional trends with natural beauty ideals and environmental ethic for powerful message of green marketing.

Thus, the marketing of environmentally friendly products involves series sense of aesthetics, one that invokes connections between health and beauty. The connections between self and community, ethics and aesthetics, and humans and nature synthesize aesthetic values to motivate environmental awareness. Green marketing strategies merge consciences and aesthetics so that people attracted by such products. Therefore, it grows to understand and value the insight of environment benefits behind the products on consumer and environs. The connection between natural/green ingredients and performance encourage consumers to make the connection between the ethics of production and the aesthetics of products. It fosters an understanding of the relationship between consumer choices and environmental beauty. This environmental aesthetic promotes an ethic that is guided by holistic nature. The ethical principles of green marketing are based on perspective of humans as part of a complicated and intrinsically valuable ecosystem. Essa, Dekker and Groot (2015) assert that the environmental messages improved ethical individuality where being green is not just cool, but people are hip to the need for action to protect the environment. Thus, it is necessary to consider the green movements upon the actions as consumers. The cosmetic hybrids turn in green marketing creates concepts of aesthetic, as being healthy is the real beauty.

The environmental effects of green consumerism are contested and it needs to increase in consumer green behaviours. However, Todd (2004) argue that the green consumerism does not address the root cause of environmental problems because it does not encourage a decline in consumption, and in fact encourages corporate greenwashing that misleads consumers about "environmental" business practices. Being healthy is more important. Sometimes in order to get beautiful people use harmful chemicals on their hair and skin. However often people forget that these products definitely improve their looks but harmful on health. One of the biggest challenges in defining "green", whether it be consumers, products or ads, is that "green," like the planet itself, encompasses everything; air, water, biological life, chemicals, and energy. What is a question the challenge of knowing which questions to ask help to understand green market opportunities? "Green" is a simple, easy to remember term, but it may not be so useful in communicating with consumers who likely have their own interpretations of "green" expressed throughout their day-to-day lives. To those willing to take a shot at rebuilding interest and credibility in all things "green", remember some important things first most consumers want to do the right thing. They want clean air and clean water, healthful food to eat, litter-free and beaches to play in, and energy to run their lives. Whether it be keeping their bathroom clean, saving for retirement, driving the speed limit or eating healthfully, all consumers tend to overstate virtuous behaviours to pollsters. Thus, just like for all products, most consumers will only pay a premium when products demonstrate genuine added value (Luck and Ginanti, 2013).

Although it might take a little doing, most consumers have the ability to understand the building blocks of "green", e.g., "recycled", "recyclable" and "biodegradable". Happily, businesses have the wherewithal to address consumers' needs and their motivations. For green marketing, using eco-labels or green certification systems are part of strategies (Delmas, 2014). Questions such as which label is better, which product is safer for the environment and what does a label even mean are common questions that well-intended green shoppers may find themselves asking when trying to make an environmentally responsible purchase. Brecard (2014) claims confusion can arise from labels that certify too much or too little information. Some eco-labels focus on a single product attribute (e.g., recycled content), which keeps things simple but can inadvertently mislead consumers into thinking the product is green overall. That is greenwashing attributes if it does mislead consumer. Some products, such as electrical appliances, foods, household cleaning items have a number of labels and certifications, while others, such as mattresses, shoes or cookware, have none. Bose, Vira and Garcia (2016) argue another common reason for confusion is the inconsistency in the levels of accuracy applied to some eco-labelling. The labelling issues made such green products better but may also cause consumer to be fooled by claims that are not true and exaggerate. Understanding the eco-labels and know its roles benefits consumers as some labels have different interpretation that require independent, third-party verifications while others allow self-certification (Bonsi, Hammett and Smith, 2008).

The eco-label and customer purchase behaviours need to be addressed as the increased awareness on eco-labels (Testa et al., 2015). They have a strong ability to promote green product consumption among other potential green consumers. However, government take serious monitoring on the credibility and reliability of green claims and eco-labels. Government should endeavour to educate citizens about the meaning and availability of the new eco-labels and existing environmental certification for consumer awareness. Moreover, the question on environmental aesthetics and consumer purchase behaviours. Environmental aesthetics is the personal experience of consumer towards specific products, which influence purchasing behaviours, and this opportunity helpful to increase familiarity with environmental products today. Chen and Chang (2013) stated the factors contributing to the failure of applying green marketing to enhance purchase behaviour is due to the low credibility of green claims among consumers and price competitions. Chen and Chang (2013) claimed not all consumers are strongly influenced by green marketing. Thus, there is a need to identify and concentrate promotion of goods or products on green market targets that are environmentally concerned.

HOW ARE ENVIRONMENTAL AESTHETICS INTERCONNECTED WITH THE ENVIRONMENT?

Being physically and mentally healthy is rather important point instead of only focusing on beauty. The sense that environmental aesthetics brings upon the rest of environment includes the protection, utility, and communication among all unit of ecosystem. All these functions are important to be analysed when creating a new product in the market. It is necessary to bypass negative perceptions and the price offered must be reasonable or the product can be unappealing to consumers. Therefore, consumer will not be able to change and spend their money to purchase it. There is always probability the products could be recognised only from the packaging without identifying the brand. Nutricosmetics products usually focus to use organic, natural ingredients and greatly appeals to consumers (Larsen and Tambo, 2014). Enlightening consumer on the green practices and innovative technologies in product packaging plays as a strong positioning factor for products. It is important because products' primary and secondary packaging always needed to support logistics and prolong self-life. Consumers vote for products with their wallets, and consumer alertness for superficial sustainability claims are more important than ever. There are clearly solutions for difficult-to-recycle waste streams when companies provide the resources necessary to make them possible, and consumers have the influence to reward them instead of the many brands, retailers and companies that are jumping on the sustainability trend for profit. There quite many scientific understanding to bear on one's environmental aesthetic appreciation provided in different area.

There are number of questions for further investigation that hope to be taken on environmental aesthetics. It has clearly emerged studying of environmental aesthetics contribute immensely to environmental awareness and inspire companies in participation of environmental projects. Also, being aware of the aesthetic benefits of the totality of the environment (both natural and built environments) promotes a sense of community by providing a convenient and attractive public place in which people can meet and share ideas as well as common goals (Gulsrud, Gooding and van den Bosch, 2013). This confirms Kaplan (2000) assumption that this can foster community spirit when environmental aesthetics is embedded in products and service to enhance the environment. Environmental aesthetic and can be discovered when one is exposed to experiences. This insight of aesthetic of the environment enlarges the frontiers of the world of to aim at environmental protection. Indeed, green marketing strengthen the environmental aesthetics that have the potential to cultivate consumer environmental behaviours.

CONCLUSION AND FUTURE RESEARCH DIRECTIONS

This paper points that environmental aesthetics may simultaneously evoke positive responses of green consumers and promote a growing number of environmentally-equipped nutricosmetic products. A large number of nutricosmetic products offer natural ingredients as well as various health benefits. The wide consumption of cosmetic hybrids, such as nutricosmetic raises a question: how can environmental aesthetic be achieved through both environmental packaging and use of natural ingredients to influence consumer purchase behaviours? A combination of environmental packaging and health benefits of green products stimuli requires a higher level of elaboration because of the complexity of aesthetic stimuli. Further, environmental packaging may have ambience, design, and social factors in which all create a dynamic, multi-sensory stimuli (Marzano, 2003). Thus, the effects of broader sources of environmental aesthetic stimuli on consumers' cognitive, affective, and behavioural responses can be extremely intricate. Certainly, this will provide challenging opportunities for future research.

Depletion of non-renewable resources accompanied by non-disposal pollutants has led to an increase in consumer and corporate awareness towards green marketing. There is limited research that has sufficiently examined the impact of green marketing on consumers from emerging economies like India, Bangladesh, and Southeast Asia (McMichael, 2016). Related studies on green consumerism have been mostly conducted in well-developed countries. It is quite clear that there is a large research gap in identifying and conceptualizing the impacts of consumer awareness. Care for the environment is always a positive approach and surprisingly, less has been focused to explicitly address the principles for green marketing to further understand environmental aesthetic .

This paper contributes to academic literatures on environmental aesthetics, green marketing, green consumerism, and future marketers in different areas of specialization. This paper suggests that green marketing gives the plain idea of cosmetic hybrids. Environmental aesthetics consists of the designs, formulations and experiences of consumers on green products. Environmental aesthetics plays an important role in moving consumers' evaluations of green purchase and leading marketers to improve their products to achieve green image and reputations. Thus for marketers, environmental aesthetic should be given more prominence in implying green marketing. For academics, appreciation of innovation in the cosmetic hybrids industry may contribute in understanding consumers' cognitive, affective, and conative responses and their motivational orientations. It helps in pushing for a step further for future research to discover new contributions for industrial and educational advancement.

The discussion on the consumers' consciousness towards environmental aesthetics in using nutricosmetics products has highlighted the area where future efforts need to be directed. Environmental factors which are inconsistently associated with consumptions and lifestyle warrant greater research. Further research should seek the importance mixture of behaviours and beliefs about consumer green consumption. The awareness and desire to make informed ethical options lead to suggest that there are probably numbers of people who can be considered as 'conscious consumers'. Environmental aesthetics is an important factor in a decision to accept green products.

Much of the existing research on this topic has been undertaken in the Western and developed countries. More work is required to investigate whether environmental aesthetics is present in different settings, such as Europe or Asia, countries where the nature of built environments, and the ways in which they are used are quite different. In addition, existing studies have often examined the influence of the environmental aesthetics in relation to architecture, geographical areas, often in cities or metropolitan areas. Clear positive perception of natural, organic ingredients and certification standard have a huge impact on conscious consumer choices.

Thus, nutricosmetics products involve a sense of aesthetics, one that invokes connections between health and beauty. This is defined by a set of values that reflects the eco-experience of a product. Green marketing strategies merge ethics and aesthetics so that people are appealed by the aesthetics of natural personal care products then grow to understand and believe the ethics of environment behind the products. The relation between natural ingredients and performance encourages consumers to make the connection between the ethics of production and the aesthetics of the beauty products. Thus, it fosters an understanding of the relationship between consumer preferences and environmental aesthetics. This transparency opens us up towards the possibility of increased connection; making the connections more visible, and emphasizes harmony between humans and nature. Eco-brand is considered as a new topic in cosmetic research hence needs more investigation. Information and articles on this topic are scarce, thus require further research.

Consumer consciousness on the environmental aesthetic promotes the acceptance of ethical and moral beliefs that are guided by holistic beauty (Mandoki, 2016). Environmental message delivered to an ethical consumer where being green is not just cool, but it is a healthy trend to protect the environment. This article provides suggestions in an effort to enlighten the perspective of environmental aesthetics in cosmetic hybrids. Consumer movement towards sustainable lifestyles and green consumptions will be a gradual process (Vergragt, Akenji and Dewick, 2014). Therefore it provides important information on the current market situations of the cosmetic hybrids industry. Research on consumer purchasing and expenditure behaviours on cosmetics is always needed due to the dynamism in the tastes and preferences of consumers.

Green consumption and consumer consciousness are useful for organizations and governments to better develop and encourage environmental knowledge to foster healthy and green environment among consumers. In addition, extra attention needs to be focused to examine the factors of perceived consumers' environmental in different contexts. Additionally, studies investigating social norms can inform future research to understand the impact of personal norms in consumers consciousness towards environmental aesthetics in green products. Future studies should also focus on consumer attitudes and perceptions to contribute to the understanding of environmental aesthetics. It includes understanding on the green label, green packaging and green values or green service on a specific type of green product in the market. Finally, future research should consider embedding the perceptions on environmental aesthetics towards green buying commitment.

REFERENCES

Aaker, D. A., & Equity, M. B. (1991). Capitalizing on the Value of a Brand Name. New York: Academic Press.

Akenji, L. (2014). Consumer scapegoatism and limits to green consumerism. *Journal of Cleaner Production, 63*, 13–23. doi:10.1016/j.jclepro.2013.05.022

Ancarani, F., & Gisco, A. (2014). *Wellness Marketing: New strategies for new trends*. EGEA spa.

Baines, T., Brown, S., Benedettini, O., & Ball, P. (2012). Examining green production and its role within the competitive strategy of manufacturers. *Journal of Industrial Engineering and Management, 5*(1), 53. doi:10.3926/jiem.405

Baker, M. A., Davis, E. A., & Weaver, P. A. (2013). Eco-friendly attitudes, barriers to participation, and differences in behavior at green hotels. *Cornell Hospitality Quarterly*.

Bonsi, R., Hammett, A. L., & Smith, B. (2008). Eco–labels and International Trade: Problems and Solutions. *Journal of World Trade, 42*(3), 407–432.

Bose, A., Vira, B., & Garcia, C. (2016). Does environmental certification in coffee promote business as usual? A case study from the Western Ghats, India. *Ambio, 45*(8), 946–955. doi:10.1007/s13280-016-0796-3 PMID:27329139

Brécard, D. (2014). Consumer confusion over the profusion of eco-labels: Lessons from a double differentiation model. *Resource and Energy Economics, 37*, 64–84. doi:10.1016/j.reseneeco.2013.10.002

Bullot, N. J., & Reber, R. (2013). The artful mind meets art history: Toward a psycho-historical framework for the science of art appreciation. *Behavioral and Brain Sciences, 36*(02), 123–137. doi:10.1017/S0140525X12000489 PMID:23507091

Carlson, A. (2010). Contemporary environmental aesthetics and the requirements of environmentalism. *Environmental Values, 19*(3), 289–314. doi:10.3197/096327110X519844

Chen, Y. S., & Chang, C. H. (2013). Greenwash and green trust: The mediation effects of green consumer confusion and green perceived risk. *Journal of Business Ethics, 114*(3), 489–500. doi:10.1007/s10551-012-1360-0

Cherian, J., & Jacob, J. (2012). Green marketing: A study of consumers attitude towards environment friendly products. *Asian Social Science, 8*(12), 117. doi:10.5539/ass.v8n12p117

D'Souza, C., Taghian, M., Lamb, P., & Peretiatkos, R. (2006). Green products and corporate strategy: an empirical investigation. *Society and Business Review, 1*(2), 144-157.

Davies, S., & Alperson, P. (2015). *The philosophy of art*. John Wiley & Sons.

Delafrooz, N., Taleghani, M., & Nouri, B. (2014). Effect of green marketing on consumer purchase behavior. *QScience Connect*, 5.

Delmas, M. A., & Grant, L. E. (2014). Eco-labeling strategies and price-premium: The wine industry puzzle. *Business & Society, 53*(1), 6–44. doi:10.1177/0007650310362254

Denison, E., & Ren, G. Y. (2001). *Packaging prototypes 3: Thinking green* (Vol. 3). Rotovision.

Dureja, H., Kaushik, D., Gupta, M., Kumar, V., & Lather, V. (2005). Cosmeceuticals: An emerging concept. *Indian Journal of Pharmacology, 37*(3), 155. doi:10.4103/0253-7613.16211

Essa, S. A. G., Dekker, H., & Groot, T. (2015). Improving outsourcing negotiations. *Amsterdam in Science, Business and Society, 2015*(2), 28-29.

Esty, D., & Winston, A. (2009). *Green to gold: How smart companies use environmental strategy to innovate, create value, and build competitive advantage*. John Wiley & Sons.

Folashade, O., Omoregie, H., & Ochogu, P. (2012). Standardization of herbal medicines-A review. *International Journal of Biodiversity and Conservation*, *4*(3), 101–112.

Forte, M., & Lamont, B. T. (1998). The bottom line effects of greening. *The Academy of Management Executive*, *12*(1), 89–90.

Foster, S. (2012). *Tyler's honest herbal: a sensible guide to the use of herbs and related remedies*. Routledge.

Fritz, A. J. (2013). A Critique of the Relationship between Scientific Cognitivism and Positive Aesthetics. American Society for Aesthetics Graduate E-Journal, 5(2).

Gulsrud, N. M., Gooding, S., & van den Bosch, C. C. K. (2013). Green space branding in Denmark in an era of neoliberal governance. *Urban Forestry & Urban Greening*, *12*(3), 330–337. doi:10.1016/j.ufug.2013.03.001

Hansson, S. O. (2014). Agricultural Biotechnology for Health and the Environment. In Biotechnology and Biodiversity (pp. 67-76). Springer International Publishing. doi:10.1007/978-3-319-09381-9_5

Hasler, C. M. (2000). The changing face of functional foods. *Journal of the American College of Nutrition, 19*(sup5), 499S-506S.

Haws, K., Winterich, K. P., & Reczek, R. W. (2013). Seeing the world through GREEN-tinted glasses: Green consumption values and responses to environmentally friendly products. *Journal of Consumer Psychology*.

Heasman, M., & Mellentin, J. (2001). *The functional foods revolution: healthy people, healthy profits?* Routledge.

Hummel, R. P. (2016). Arendt, Kant and the beauty of politics: a phenomenological view. In *Political Phenomenology* (pp. 93–120). Springer International Publishing. doi:10.1007/978-3-319-27775-2_7

Hunt, L., Rosin, C., Campell, H., & Fairweather, J. (2015). Organic Farmers: Contributing to the Resilience of the Food System?. In Re-Thinking Organic Food and Farming in a Changing World (pp. 187-211). Springer Netherlands.

Husted, B. W., Russo, M. V., Meza, C. E. B., & Tilleman, S. G. (2014). An exploratory study of environmental attitudes and the willingness to pay for environmental certification in Mexico. *Journal of Business Research*, *67*(5), 891–899. doi:10.1016/j.jbusres.2013.07.008

Kaplan, S. (2000). New ways to promote proenvironmental behavior: Human nature and environmentally responsible behavior. *The Journal of Social Issues*, *56*(3), 491–508. doi:10.1111/0022-4537.00180

Kapoor, V. P. (2005). Herbal cosmetics for skin and hair care. *Nat Prod Radiance*, *4*(4), 306–314.

Khan, I. A., & Abourashed, E. A. (2011). *Leung's encyclopedia of common natural ingredients: used in food, drugs and cosmetics*. John Wiley & Sons.

Kibert, C. J. (2016). *Sustainable construction: Green building design and delivery*. John Wiley & Sons.

Kim, H. S., & Damhorst, M. L. (1998). Environmental concern and apparel consumption. *Clothing & Textiles Research Journal, 16*(3), 126–133. doi:10.1177/0887302X9801600303

Kim, S. Y., Kim, S. Y., Yoon, J., Yoon, J., Choi, I., & Choi, I. (2016). What matters to promote consumers intention to patronize sustainable business-and-industry (B&I) food services?. *British Food Journal, 118*(11), 2710–2731. doi:10.1108/BFJ-02-2016-0050

Larsen, R. H., & Tambo, T. (2014). Managing cosmetics technologies in dynamic environments. In *Proceedings of the 4th Nordic Retail and Wholesale Conference*. Nordic Retail and Wholesale Association.

Lau, W. K., Chiu, S. M., & Yau, Y. (2014). Economising subsidies for green housing features: A stated preference approach. *Urbani Izziv, 25*(2).

Leder, H., & Nadal, M. (2014). Ten years of a model of aesthetic appreciation and aesthetic judgments: The aesthetic episode–developments and challenges in empirical aesthetics. *British Journal of Psychology, 105*(4), 443–464. doi:10.1111/bjop.12084 PMID:25280118

Ligade, V., Sreedhar, D., Manthan, J., & Udupa, N. (2009). Cosmeceuticals: Are they truly worth the cost? *Indian Journal of Dermatology, Venereology and Leprology, 75*(1), 8. doi:10.4103/0378-6323.45213 PMID:19172024

Luck, E., & Ginanti, A. (2013). Online environmental citizenship: Blogs, green marketing and consumer sentiment in the 21st Century. *Electronic Green Journal, 1*(35), 1–26.

Mandoki, K. (2016). *Everyday aesthetics: Prosaics, the play of culture and social identities*. Routledge.

Marzano, S. (2003). *The new everyday: Views on ambient intelligence*. 010 Publishers.

McMichael, P. (2016). *Development and social change: A global perspective*. Sage Publications.

Mendleson, N., & Polonsky, M. J. (1995). Using strategic alliances to develop credible green marketing. *Journal of Consumer Marketing, 12*(2), 4–18. doi:10.1108/07363769510084867

Mukherjee, P. K., Maity, N., Nema, N. K., & Sarkar, B. K. (2011). Bioactive compounds from natural resources against skin aging. *Phytomedicine, 19*(1), 64–73. doi:10.1016/j.phymed.2011.10.003 PMID:22115797

Neves, M. F. (2014). *The future of food business: the facts, the impacts and the acts*. World Scientific. doi:10.1142/8567

Öberseder, M., Schlegelmilch, B. B., & Murphy, P. E. (2013). CSR practices and consumer perceptions. *Journal of Business Research, 66*(10), 1839–1851. doi:10.1016/j.jbusres.2013.02.005

Ottman, J. A., Stafford, E. R., & Hartman, C. L. (2006). Avoiding green marketing myopia: Ways to improve consumer appeal for environmentally preferable products. *Environment: Science and Policy for Sustainable Development, 48*(5), 22–36.

Pujari, D. (2006). Eco-innovation and new product development: Understanding the influences on market performance. *Technovation*, *26*(1), 76–85. doi:10.1016/j.technovation.2004.07.006

Raj, S., Jose, S., Sumod, U. S., & Sabitha, M. (2012). Nanotechnology in cosmetics: Opportunities and challenges. *Journal of Pharmacy and Bioallied Sciences*, *4*(3), 186. doi:10.4103/0975-7406.99016 PMID:22923959

Richey, R. G. Jr, Musgrove, C. F., Gillison, S. T., & Gabler, C. B. (2014). The effects of environmental focus and program timing on green marketing performance and the moderating role of resource commitment. *Industrial Marketing Management*, *43*(7), 1246–1257. doi:10.1016/j.indmarman.2014.06.014

Sagalowicz, L., & Leser, M. E. (2010). Delivery systems for liquid food products. *Current Opinion in Colloid & Interface Science*, *15*(1), 61–72. doi:10.1016/j.cocis.2009.12.003

Shapshay, S. (2013). Contemporary environmental aesthetics and the neglect of the sublime. *The British Journal of Aesthetics*, *53*(2), 181–198. doi:10.1093/aesthj/ays067

Stahl, F., Heitmann, M., Lehmann, D. R., & Neslin, S. A. (2012). The impact of brand equity on customer acquisition, retention, and profit margin. *Journal of Marketing*, *76*(4), 44–63. doi:10.1509/jm.10.0522

Sutton, R. K. (2014). *Aesthetics for green roofs and green walls*. Academic Press.

Taylor, M. L., Coates, T. L., Anyansi-Archibong, C., & Tanaka, N. (2014). The Twenty-First's Second Decade-Whither the Beauty Industry?. *Business Case Journal, 21*(1).

Testa, F., Iraldo, F., Vaccari, A., & Ferrari, E. (2015). Why Eco-labels can be Effective Marketing Tools: Evidence from a Study on Italian Consumers. *Business Strategy and the Environment*, *24*(4), 252–265. doi:10.1002/bse.1821

Todd, A. M. (2004). The aesthetic turn in green marketing: Environmental consumer ethics of natural personal care products. *Ethics and the Environment*, *9*(2), 86–102. doi:10.2979/ETE.2004.9.2.86

Van den Bulte, C., & Joshi, Y. V. (2007). New product diffusion with influentials and imitators. *Marketing Science*, *26*(3), 400–421. doi:10.1287/mksc.1060.0224

Vergragt, P., Akenji, L., & Dewick, P. (2014). Sustainable production, consumption, and livelihoods: Global and regional research perspectives. *Journal of Cleaner Production*, *63*, 1–12. doi:10.1016/j.jclepro.2013.09.028

Wilson, M. P., & Schwarzman, M. R. (2016). Toward a new US chemicals policy: rebuilding the foundation to advance new science, green chemistry, and environmental health. *Industrial Chemistry: New Applications, Processes and Systems*, 176.

Wolch, J. R., Byrne, J., & Newell, J. P. (2014). Urban green space, public health, and environmental justice: The challenge of making cities just green enough. *Landscape and Urban Planning*, *125*, 234–244. doi:10.1016/j.landurbplan.2014.01.017

Zhu, Q., Li, Y., Geng, Y., & Qi, Y. (2013). Green food consumption intention, behaviors and influencing factors among Chinese consumers. *Food Quality and Preference*, *28*(1), 279–286. doi:10.1016/j.foodqual.2012.10.005

KEY TERMS AND DEFINITIONS

Consumer Consciousness: A social movement based around increased awareness of the impact of purchasing decisions on the environment and the consumer's health and life in general.

Cosmetic Hybrids: Expanding new technology (encapsulation, double chamber packaging, applicators) and formula transformations which are intended to enhance beauty through ingredients providing additional health related function or benefit.

Eco-Friendly: It is a philosophy that refers to the environmentally friendliness of a product, service or policy. More clearly, it promises to reduce or minimize harm upon ecosystems or the environment.

Environmental Aesthetics: The interaction and appreciation of natural environments between an individual and the environment, in relation to beauty.

Green Marketing: The process of offering products and/or services based on their environmental benefits.

Greenwashing: Greenwashing is the practice of making an unsubstantiated or misleading claim about the environmental benefits of a product, service, technology or company practice.

Nutricosmetics: The concept of beauty through a healthy body by consuming food or drink which intended to be anti-ageing to support the function and the structure of the skin and enhance the appearance.

Chapter 3
A Review on Green Trust and Environmental Quality Awareness Affect Towards Environmental Attitude

Trianna Rosli
University Technology of Malaysia, Malaysia

Fauziah Sh. Ahmad
University Technology of Malaysia, Malaysia

ABSTRACT

There are literally thousands of the global warming and pollution issues affecting the living resources, habitats and residents of an ecosystem. The question is, do the issues affects consumers' environmental attitude? Although environmental awareness is gaining more ground among consumers, it is still not clear how this influence their cognitive thinking and consequently their action. The findings on this issue are still equivocal. There are also arguments that most consumers expect others to solve environmental issues which seems to be more of future concerns while they seek immediate gratification or short term personal satisfaction. To date, marketers are still struggling to convince consumers towards eco-products. Furthermore, green halo effect and greenwashing continues distorting buyers and caused them to be more skeptical. This chapter intends to consolidate the literature on green trust factors and environmental quality awareness and assess how these could stimulate environmental attitude.

INTRODUCTION

During the past decades, researchers from multidisciplinary areas relating to environmental studies recognized the importance knowledge and practices that can lead to more responsible ecological decisions and sustenance of environment. While advance nations have been more action oriented towards green and reported to take more initiatives to control and manage environmental issues (Otman, 2011), the developing nations including Malaysia are building up their stronger perceptions on the importance

DOI: 10.4018/978-1-5225-2912-5.ch003

to go green. Slowly it builds concerted effort to provide solutions to protect, develop and sustain the environment. The government as well as other responsible parties have been increasingly educating and undertaking the responsibility to enhance the nation's capacity in dealing with the environment issues. The consumption issues of natural resources such as water, energy as well as the protection of natural habitats and endangered species are making it more important for all individuals to practice green in their daily life. However, the national effort may not necessarily translated into a better green perceptions of customers.

However, in a different perspective, it is believed that conscious customers are socially performing daily decision making to minimize the impact of environmental burden and some voluntarily join the green movements to highlight the importance of being green. They even called themselves as 'green people' or more fashionably known as 'pro-environmentalist' (Ottman, 2011). Often, these environmentalist are not leaving the responsibility of environmental issues entirely on the government and businesses (Thøgersen, Jørgensen, & Sandager, 2012).

The environmental movement has extended into organization's practice that determines environmental performance. This includes higher environment standards to innovate and stimulate technology performance that affects companies' efficiency (Peng & Lin, 2009). The implementation of environmental regulations and development of environmental technology (improvement) are one of the critical factors in the organizations towards environmental performance. However, many firms are not capable of undertaking the green marketing strategies and integrating the green concept within all aspects of marketing routine (Ottman, 2011). The implementation of environment performance in the organization has proven such environment oriented practice can support customers to become greener practical within the company. It may not reflects individual's practice-related activities such as practicing product recycling at home or using the green product in the daily routine (Grimmer & Bingham, 2013).

Generally, people who are aware of the environmental problems tend to possess the environmental attitude, and it will translate into supporting or encouraging environment movements. Several research findings support that individuals who possess the environmental awareness have the tendency to perform the environmental behavior (Boztepe, 2012). Unfortunately, the past results seemed to be inconsistent. No matter how severe is the environmental degradation issues and people are expected to monitor lifestyles ethically, yet, there is an indication of poor green practice. People may take the environment for granted, as well as to some, leave for the others to solve the issue (Carrington, Neville, & Whitwell, 2010) because bio-gradable or green products may often cost more money and efforts (Markkula and Moisander, 2011). Customers are likely to seek personal gain (self-fulfillment) and satisfaction rather than a future outcome (Oliver, 2014). Furthermore, the reality in Malaysia shows the presence of a green idea in individual perspective but it is still limited (Goh & Wahid, 2014; Mei, Ling, & Piew, 2012; Ramli, 2009; Sinnappan et, 2011).

Based on Boztepe (2012), people behavior has a complex spectrum of habit, personality, and lifestyle. Hence, the attitude problem is rooted in customers' deep confusion on the green idea. Therefore, marketers are still struggling to change people behavior to be greener as well as to convince them on green consumption. Furthermore, it is difficult to overstate the effectiveness of the green initiatives and marketing strategy due to many possible constraints to make people going green.

The famous green constraints are known as green halo effect and greenwashing that are distorting the reality of green products. These restrictions are escalating the misconception and skeptical towards eco-label, claims, and advertising. Time to time, it has become a serious challenge for marketers to create a solid marketing strategy that will 'move' people towards being green.

Past literature has been discussed about people awareness and trust. However, the results still remain inconclusive to influence environmental attitude. Many initiatives by government bodies present the eco-labelling and advertisement, yet, how much people trust the green claims to actually persuading them to practice green in their daily activities? Although Malaysia has Environmental Performance Index to monitor how significant the performance of country's environment, but what are the perceptions of customers towards our environmental quality or development? How well the customers aware of the environmental issues and to what extend they will go about it? It is thus crucial to consolidate the literature on green trust and environmental quality awareness to bridge environmental attitude gap. Furthermore, an adaptation of the Theory of Reason Action; Three Paradigm Model as well as Trust-Based Situation Awareness Model would explain the potential relationship of the proposed constructs.

GREEN TRUST

Trust has numerous background from diverse disciplines including sociology, psychology, and economics. In psychology, trust "compromises the intention to accept the vulnerability based on positive expectations of the intentions or behavior of another" (Rousseau, Sitkin, Burt, & Camerer, 1998, p. 395).Two criteria in the definition, the first criteria relates to 'positive expectancy' from another individual. It explains the individual's belief towards another person will act in a manner that is responsible and integrity. The second criteria is related to 'accepting the vulnerability' where people will accept it with an open heart (willingly accept) of whatever outcomes.

Early researchers discussed the trust antecedent in the Commitment-Trust Theory where it is conceptualizing trust "as an existing when one party has confidence in an exchange partner's reliability and integrity" (Morgan and Hunt, 1994, p. 5). The definition is similar to another early study that claimed: "trust is defined as a willingness to rely on an exchange partner in whom one has confidence" (Moorman, Deshpande, and Zaltman, 1993, p. 82). Furthermore, it is suggested that positive trust could influence the relationship between partners. For instance, when a customer has high competence trust towards a service provider, it is presumed that the customer holds a high-performance expectation of the provider in the subsequence relationship exchange (Singh & Sirdeshmukh, 2000).

The popular example of green constraints are called a greenwashing and green halo. These terms are considered as marketing strategy or tactics to make customers feel safe in a placebo way.. The modern western 'greenwash' term started in the early 1970s when Earth Day began on April 22, 1970; the US government encouraged companies to advertise themselves as being friendly to the environment. During that green period, western public utilities spent 300 million dollars to portray themselves as a green company. A New York writer, Jay Westervelt who created the first term of greenwashing in 1986, wrote about environmental issues essay concerning hotel industry's practice of placing placards in each room promoting reuse of towels to 'save the environment.' Westervelt (1986) said, in most cases, no significant effort had contributed to reducing energy wastage, and companies claimed that they were green but demonstrated nonexistence cost reduction due to this practice. Therefore, the greenwash term used to describe the practice of businesses over claiming the environmental products or practice that cannot be validated. Hence, the false claims are broad misleading marketing tactics by dishonest companies which often result in suspicion about green claims (Parguel, Benoît-Moreau, & Larceneux, 2011; Self, Self, & Bell-Haynes, 2010).

Green products are associated with the direct impact on the environment in every phase of the product's life-cycle, and this also serves vague promises that guaranteed by the profit-making companies. The exaggeration of the environmental value of their products will rise the suspicions which make customers distrust and hesitate to buy. Thus, such greenwash claims can damage and lead to confusion, skeptical as well as uncertainty towards the green products (Obermiller, Spangenberg, & MacLachlan, 2005; Tahir Albayrak et, 2011, Pomering and Johnson, 2009). As a result, it will potentially destroy the green market in the future (Kalafatis, Pollard, East, & Tsogas, 1999; Peattie, 1999; Polonsky & Rosenberger, 2001).

Another example of marketing strategy is called the Green Halo tactic; it is a cognitive bias that most companies influence their customers' feelings and thought about the characters of the products. For example, organization claim is to saving the world by driving a Prius, selling the organic beauty products and safe product made by bio-ingredients. This halo effects seems to give false feelings or thoughts of consumers that they are doing good for the society. Edward Thorndike who is a psychologist that named Halo Effect term which refers to a person who being perceived as having a halo when he or she influenced by products claims or branding. The University of Toronto shows that when people spend money on eco-friendly products, believe they earned 'moral credit' for saving the world.

Turnbull (2000) define the green consumer confusion as a 'customer failure' to develop a correct interpretation of green product's preference during their purchase decision process (Turnbull, Leek, & Ying, 2000). Therefore, the confusion and mistrust arise when companies fail to develop a real situation or give a misleading interpretation of a various aspect of their products during information decision making (Peattie, 1999; Turnbull et al., 2000). As a result, consumer's misunderstanding creates a confusion of the green market when the products are too similar, complex, ambiguous or too much of information of the products (Y.-S. Chen, 2007, 2009; Y.-S. Chen & Chang, 2012b; Mitchell & Papavassiliou, 1999; Turnbull et al., 2000). Hence, this will raise people suspicions and undermine their trust and eventually, this will stop them to purchase or consume green products again. (Singh & Sirdeshmukh, 2000). Even worse, they will tell their friends and influence them not to try or buy green products.

Therefore, an interesting extension study by Chen (2009) has developed antecedent in sustainability research, and coined the Green Trust term. This precursor serves customer's 'willingly to depends' on green products characteristic, attributes as well as advertising. Trust defines the trustworthy or an act of willingness to rely on products, service or brand based on beliefs or expectation resulting in its credibility, benevolence, and ability to its environmental performance (Schurr & Ozanne, 1985).

Adapt by Chen (2010); there are four items proposed as below:

1. Green product's environmental reputation is reliable.
2. Green product's performance is dependable.
3. Green product have assurance towards environment protection.
4. Green product's environmental claims are trustworthy.

ENVIRONMENTAL QUALITY AWARENESS

According to Han, Hsu, Lee, & Sheu (2011), environmental awareness is a positive attitude towards eco-friendly activities and encourages people to engage more frequently in ecological behaviors in their everyday life. Chen (2010) defines an individual with environmentally awareness has the environmentally concerned attitude that can be described as the perception of self and the extent to which a person identifies him/herself to be an essential part of the environmental setting. Past result shows that the environmental quality issues have brought up the idea of being more exposed to efficiency and favorable attitude (Simmons & Widmar, 1990).

For many years, environmental awareness has received significant attention and extensive coverage of studies among academicians and practitioners (Bran, Radulescu, & Ioan, 2011; Grimmer & Bingham, 2013; Peng & Lin, 2009). According to philosophy science study, self-awareness is an effort "to describe consciousness in clear terms that develop awareness of the qualia drawn up by other networks" (Ferrari & Sternberg, 1998, p. 6). A person with environmental awareness practices energy saving, recycling, and efficiently consuming bio-gradable products; they are the individuals who acknowledge the importance of environment protection (Ottman, 2011).

There were extensive coverage studies on environmental awareness (Bran, Radulescu, & Ioan, 2011; Grimmer & Bingham, 2013; Peng & Lin, 2009). The environmental awareness can be associated with business success by communicating various products' ecology credibility and impact towards social and environment. Although, the early models were based on the linear progression of environmental awareness that hypothesized to influence pro-environmental behavior, yet, it was claimed that environmental awareness does not promote sustainable lifestyle efficiently (Hobson, 2001).

Unfortunately, in the case of Malaysia, there is discrepancy between individual's stated and actual behaviour. The commitment does not necessarily translated into pro-environmental behavior (Mat Said, Ahmadun, Hj. Paim, & Masud, 2003). Behavioral researchers argues that individual hardly change their behavior when their lifestyle is rooted deep in a social context (Jackson, 2005). Another study supported that awareness about a green product does not affect the purchasing green product decision (Suki, 2013). Hence, the question is, why environmental awareness is still not enough to influence environmental attitude?

In 2009, the introduction of Environmental Performance Index had become a favorite indicator which numerically marking the environmental performance of states policies and provides a ranking of the whole countries. Even so, EPI cannot provide feedback on the level of customers' sensitivity (Carrington et al., 2010). To date, there is no inclusive evidence on the study of environmental quality awareness (EQA) in Malaysia.

Environmental Quality Awareness defines as an acknowledgment the quality of environmental towards Human Health, Ecosystem Vitality and Socioeconomic Sustainability of the country (Trianna R, 2017). EQA investigates customers' awareness towards environmental quality and seeing to what extent the customers will receive a response in their lifestyle regarding human health, ecosystem vitality and socioeconomic sustainability of the country (Trianna R, 2017). It postulates to support the attitude/behavior gap issues, as well as structuring the solutions for the current ecological concerns in Malaysia. By considering this, the researcher proposed the environmental awareness quality could contribute towards the sustainability area of knowledge (Trianna, 2017). EQA will deliver four question items:

1. I am aware environmental burden can affect my health and ecosystem vitality.
2. I know that air and water quality may affect my health and ecosystem vitality.
3. I believe that water sanitation system is important to maintain a good health.
4. I am aware that open fire, transportation, and industrial hazardous waste can affect my health and ecosystem vitality.

ENVIRONMENTAL ATTITUDE

Historically, people are worried about their health because the fear of losing the ability to sustain healthy life environment and they felt the environment has diluted by many unethical actions (J. Ottman, 2011). In social psychology research, the customer's attitudes have been continuously used to predict energy conservation and ecologically informed purchase which specifically focused on the relationship between environment attitudes as well as environmentally related behavior (Ajzen, 1991; Ajzen & Sexton, 1999).

Environment attitude refers to the individual's value judgment and it taps the person's cognitive assessment to participate in environmental-supportive behavior (Lee, 2008; Sinnappan et, 2011) in instances such as to ride public transport, recycling, or to get environmental products. However, supported by Carrington's study shown that most of the people expect others to solve on the environment issues (Carrington, Neville, & Whitwell, 2010). Furthermore, the deceiving cases about organizations that are trying to compete by claiming things that untrue. Therefore, it has been formed as customers' constraint to rely on and depends on green product's claims.

Many green attitudes constraints that evolved with people trust and awareness have restricted to influence them to behave environmentally. People are driven by the curiosity and added precaution to protect their health, and some of them are skeptical with the reputations of product manufacturers towards social and environment responsibility (Ottman, 2011).

Adding to this, customers are overwhelming with complex information on green products (Moisander, 2007). The increasing skeptical and confusion towards green claims would negatively influence green consumption (Y.-S. Chen, 2009; Y.-S. Chen & Chang, 2012a, 2012b, 2013; Walsh & Mitchell, 2010) as well as outperform the ability to act in a green way.

Hence, it is best to study the environmental quality awareness influence towards environmental attitude. The researcher will access Environmental Attitude antecedent as to gain the understanding about individual's belief. The proposed variable items are adapted from Sinnapan et al. (2011);

1. It is essential to promote green living in Malaysia.
2. I strongly agree Malaysia needs more environmental protection.
3. It is important to raise environmental awareness among Malaysia people.

THEORIES AND MODEL

As proposed by Theory of Reasoned Action (TRA), 'evaluation of outcome' constitutes the attitude of a person which lead to the behavior, by this mean, people must be observant to the consequence (Azjen, 2011). TRA theory suggests 'beliefs' are the novels that play the first role in human behavior (Figure 1). In another word, these beliefs guide the human behavior by three kinds of considerations, the first belief is about the consequences of the behavior, which is called behavioral beliefs. Then, a normative belief that defines as beliefs about the normative expectations of others. Followed by control beliefs, which constitutes the beliefs about factors that may facilitate that performance of the behavior (Ajzen, 2002). The theory delivers in-depth information on three salient beliefs are behavioral beliefs, normative beliefs and as well as control beliefs. These three salient beliefs that people who hold onto which considered principal determinants of individual's intention and action (Ajzen & Sexton, 1999).

Figure 1. The theory of planned behavior. Organizational behavior and human decision processes.
Source: Ajzen (1975)

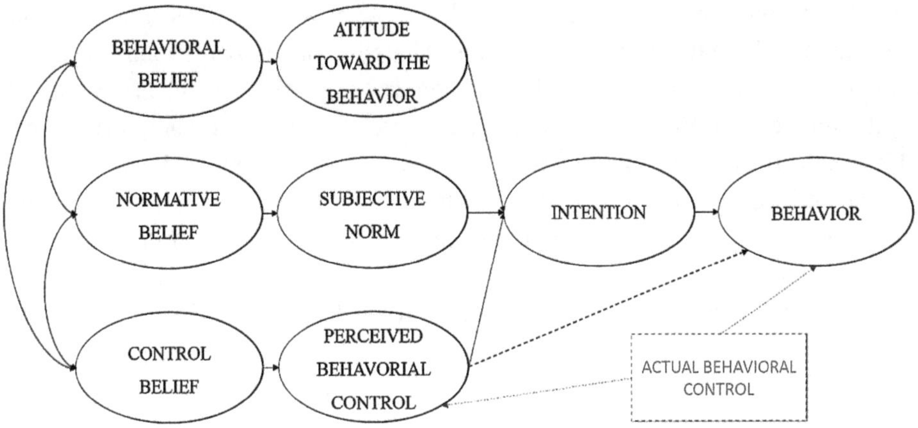

According to this underpinning theory from Icek Ajzen, behavioral beliefs is predicted to influence attitudes towards the behavior, normative beliefs constitute the underlying determinants of subjective norm, and lastly, control beliefs provides the foundation perceptions of behavior control.

Meanwhile, Sterling's of Three Paradigm model (2009) also explains that the individual must have the ethical sensibility or consciousness through perception (seeing) and followed by the conception (understanding). Stephen Sterling (2009) suggested a critical understanding of pattern and the consequence will help a person to connect towards the subject. In the study of ecology learning, people need to have 'cognitive domain' (aware and understanding) and 'affective domain' (seeing, emotion, assumption, values), then people will have 'intentional domain' (doing or practical) in order to respond towards environmental issues. Correspond to futures expert Paul Raskin argues that "the shape of the global future rests with the reflexivity of human consciousness – the capacity to think critically about why we believe what we do – and then to think and act differently" (Raskin, 2008, p. 469). The Three paradigm model suggests that the people awareness is critical to shaping the people values and attitude.

Moreover, the addition of Environmental Performance Index (EPI) literature has shown that contents raw data (index) is insufficient which it does not play the part of taking account of customers' awareness or standpoint, nor it examines how well green practice as they exposed to the environmental performance (Alex de Shernin et, 2013). Hence, the theories and model support the relationship between green trust and environmental quality awareness towards the environmental attitude that will discuss further.

PROPOSED MODEL

In this chapter, the researcher proposed the Theory of Situation Awareness (SA) as a foundation for the model relationship. SA theory is a significant contributor to the "Quality of decision-making in complex, dynamically changing environments" (Aydoğan, Sharpanskykh, & Lo, 2014,p. 22). SA refers to knowing what is happening around oneself and generally, this theory is adapted in intelligent software agent and aviation organizations. The operational of SA model has been vigorously debated about two main streams of the traditional information-processing approach of psychology versus ecological psychology.

Based on Endsley (1995), the concept of situation awareness refers to the level of knowledge that an individual has of a situation and an operator's dynamic understanding of 'what is going on.'

A decision-making process developed by considering from what sources should be taken into the information fusion of making that particular decision. Therefore, an individual must be in somewhere to 'depend' on the information sources. Alas, the decision-making process may vary because the persons influenced by the source of information given and the degree of (un)certainty of information provided by this source. Hence, the person must determine to what extent of communicated or observed information contributes to the activation level to correspond or to decide (Aydoğan, Sharpanskykh, & Lo, 2014). Moreover, one of the major factors influencing both misuse and disuse is trust in automation (Parasuraman, Sheridan, & Wickens, 2008).

Therefore, this chapter adapted the model concept by R. Aydo˘gan et al. (2015) study which extended the SA theory in the study of an aircraft. This study integrated the interpersonal trust in the framework which previously SA Theory does not take it in the model range. The study suggested that the more person trusts the information source, the more it affects that person to make an assessment of the situation. Thereby, the ability examines of what kind information source should be taken into account and how well person aware of the situation is important in decision making.

The model noted that the choices or alternative would depend not only on the content of information but also on the trustworthiness of the information source is important to put into the consideration (Aydoğan et al., 2014). Thus, R. Aydo˘gan et al. (2015) proposed integrated model between SA which activated by communicated or observed information and the trust towards information sources affect decision maker's assessment of the situation.

R. Aydo˘gan et al. (2015) performed Endsley and Hoogendoorn's computational model of SA which manage to introduced agent-based situational awareness model incorporating trust to enable humanlike decision-making tools in the computational area. The finding proved that significant impact of trustworthiness of information sources had an effect on airline operation controller's situation awareness and implication on its decision-making.

Therefore, this chapter adapted Trust Based-Situation Awareness model by R. Aydo˘gan et al. (2015) that has extended the knowledge area by integrated the trust antecedent and stimulate in an airline's operation control domain case. This chapter aims to investigate the relationship between green trust and environmental quality awareness towards environmental attitude using the Trust Based-Situational Awareness model. Figure 2 shows a study by R. Aydo˘gan et al. (2015). Both are hypothesized that the independent variables are affecting the dependent variable (outcome).

Figure 3 showed the example of prior study and proposed green trust and environmental quality awareness towards environmental attitude. The first construct of green Trust discusses on the willingness of the people to depend on the marketing information sources, for instance, advertisements, eco-label, and claims. The second novel discusses the environmental quality awareness which explains about people's awareness is towards environmental quality to fit the environmental discipline study. Therefore, this chapter suggests that based on this adapted model, the integration of green trust and environmental quality awareness potentially affects environmental attitude. Therefore, it is postulated that when people trust towards information source and there is sufficient awareness towards environmental quality, it will lead them to have the environmental attitude.

Figure 2. Airline operation control decision-making in complex sociotechnical systems
Source: Aydoğan, Sharpanskykh, and Lo (2014)

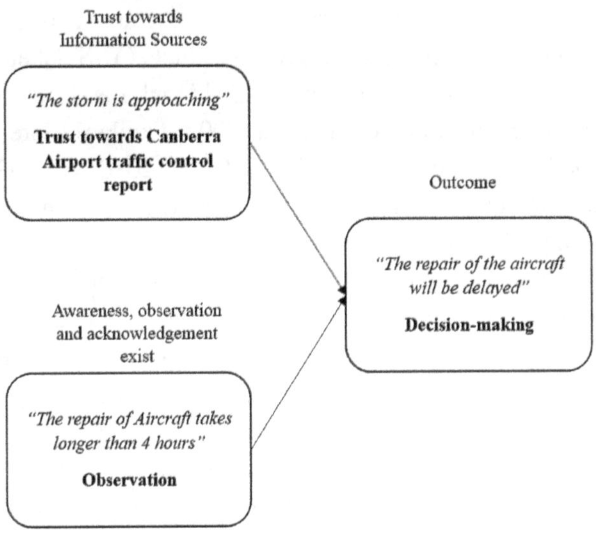

Figure 3. Green trust: environmental quality awareness towards environmental attitude

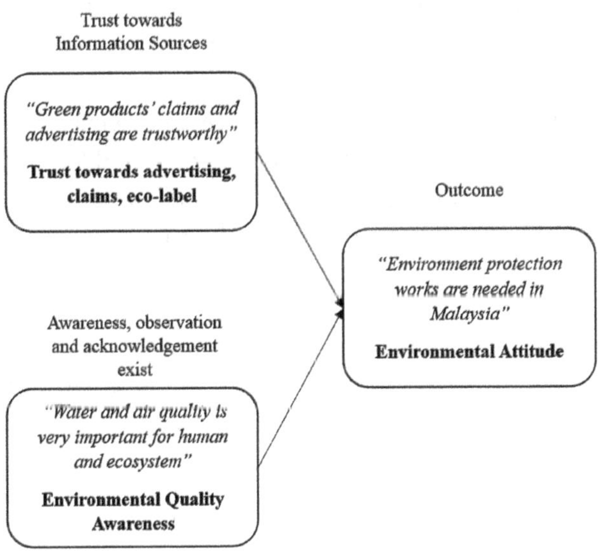

CONCLUSION

Overall, the chapter explains the opportunity to strengthen the relationship between green trust and environmental awareness towards environmental attitude for future research. Furthermore, a discussion of Trust Based-Situational Awareness model has extended the EQA framework that proposed by Tri-anna R (2017). Hence, the future research could test the Planned Behavior theory to provide a necessity bridge between green trust, environmental quality awareness and environmental attitude relationship in the framework.

As supported by Chen et al., (2009, 2010, 2013) behavioral study, people must trust the green claims, eco-label, characteristics and attributes to make them purchase green products. Hence, no matter how well perspective or attitude towards environmental, if the people are skeptical or confuse about green products, they will not be interested in purchasing green products (Y.-S. Chen, 2009, 2013; Y.-S. Chen & Chang, 2013; Walsh & Mitchell, 2010). Chen et al. (2013) who is developed green trust novel has tested in Taiwan and environmental awareness (Zsóka, 2005; Dunlap, Liere, Mertig, & Jones, 2000; Kollmuss & Agyeman, 2002; Connolly & Shaw, 2006; Chen, 2010; Han, Hsu, Lee, & Sheu, 2011; Boztepe, 2012) has tested in many Western countries, hence, the study should not be generalized and presented as a whole customer's behavior.

The differences of background and multi-culture of Malaysian people contributed different findings as compare to Western countries. The interaction between behavior, organizational factor and personal factors described in triadic reciprocal determinism (Bandura, 1986) which has multicultural society dominated by Malay, Chinese and Indian. Thus, the personality behavior possibly will influence by culture as Schein stated that "one can view personality and character as the accumulation of cultural learning that an individual has experienced in the family, the peer group, the school, the community and the occupation. In this sense, culture is within us as people and yet constantly evolving as we join and create new groups that eventually creates new cultures" (Shein, 2004, p. 8). In addition, environmental quality awareness (EQA) provides another spectrum of scale has contributed towards the sustainability area of knowledge. This chapter proposed environmental quality awareness variable that is assumed the person will make more initiatives to control and manage environmental issues. Hence, the research hypothesizes that if individuals are aware of environmental quality; it will translate it to their environmental attitude by supporting as well as encouraging environment movements.

Dunlap (2000), suggested that to understand any specific environmentally significant behavior requires empirical analysis and the roles of environmentalist tendencies are different from behavior, the actor and the context. Furthermore, "environmental intent and environmental impact are two separate things, theories explaining environmentalism are necessarily insufficient for understanding how to change environmentally significant behaviors" (Dunlap, Liere, Mertig, & Jones, 2000, p. 9). As a conclusion, Green Trust and Environmental Quality Awareness are hypothesized to affect an environmental attitude that further study, especially in developing country like Malaysia. Therefore, by assessing proposed model will extend the understanding of people trust to influence environmental attitude and to what extent of awareness towards environment quality that could influence them to gain environmental attitude as well as change social and lifestyle.

REFERENCES

Ajzen, I. (1991). The theory of planned behavior. *Organizational Behavior and Human Decision Processes*, *50*(2), 179–211. doi:10.1016/0749-5978(91)90020-T

Ajzen, I., & Sexton, J. (1999). Depth of processing, belief congruence, and attitude-behavior correspondence. *Dual-process theories in social psychology*, 117-138.

Aydoğan, R., Sharpanskykh, A., & Lo, J. (2014). *A Trust-Based Situation Awareness Model.* Paper presented at the European Conference on Multi-Agent Systems.

Chen, Y.-S. (2007). The Driver of Green Innovation and Green Image – Green Core Competence. *Journal of Business Ethics*, *81*(3), 531–543. doi:10.1007/s10551-007-9522-1

Chen, Y.-S. (2009). The Drivers of Green Brand Equity: Green Brand Image, Green Satisfaction, and Green Trust. *Journal of Business Ethics*, *93*(2), 307–319. doi:10.1007/s10551-009-0223-9

Chen, Y. S. (2013). Towards green loyalty: Driving from green perceived value, green satisfaction, and green trust. *Sustainable Development*, *21*(5), 294–308. doi:10.1002/sd.500

Chen, Y.-S., & Chang, C.-H. (2012a). Enhance green purchase intentions: The roles of green perceived value, green perceived risk, and green trust. *Management Decision*, *50*(3), 502–520. doi:10.1108/00251741211216250

Chen, Y.-S., & Chang, C.-H. (2012b). Greenwash and Green Trust: The Mediation Effects of Green Consumer Confusion and Green Perceived Risk. *Journal of Business Ethics*, *114*(3), 489–500. doi:10.1007/s10551-012-1360-0

Chen, Y.-S., & Chang, C.-H. (2013). Towards green trust: The influences of green perceived quality, green perceived risk, and green satisfaction. *Management Decision*, *51*(1), 63–82. doi:10.1108/00251741311291319

Dunlap, R., Liere, K., Mertig, A., & Jones, R. E. (2000). Measuring endorsement of the new ecological paradigm: A revised NEP scale. *The Journal of Social Issues*, *56*(3), 425–442. doi:10.1111/0022-4537.00176

Ferrari, M. D., & Sternberg, R. J. (1998). *Self-awareness: Its nature and development.* Guilford press.

Goh, Y.-N., & Wahid, N. A. (2014). A Review on Green Purchase Behaviour Trend of Malaysian Consumers. *Asian Social Science*, *11*(2), 103. doi:10.5539/ass.v11n2p103

Grimmer, M., & Bingham, T. (2013). Company environmental performance and consumer purchase intentions. *Journal of Business Research*, *66*(10), 1945–1953. doi:10.1016/j.jbusres.2013.02.017

Hobson, K. (2001). Sustainable lifestyles: rethinking barriers and behaviour change. *Exploring sustainable consumption: Environmental policy and the social sciences*, 191-209.

Jackson, T. (2005). *Motivating sustainable consumption: a review of evidence on consumer behaviour and behavioural change: a report to the Sustainable Development Research Network.* Centre for Environmental Strategy, University of Surrey.

Kalafatis, S. P., Pollard, M., East, R., & Tsogas, M. H. (1999). Green marketing and Ajzens theory of planned behaviour: A cross-market examination. *Journal of Consumer Marketing*, *16*(5), 441–460. doi:10.1108/07363769910289550

Lee, K. (2008). Opportunities for green marketing: Young consumers. *Marketing Intelligence & Planning*, *26*(6), 573–586. doi:10.1108/02634500810902839

Lee, K. (2009). Gender differences in Hong Kong adolescent consumers green purchasing behavior. *Journal of Consumer Marketing*, *26*(2), 87–96. doi:10.1108/07363760910940456

Mat Said, A., & Ahmadun, F. l.-R., Hj. Paim, L., & Masud, J. (2003). Environmental concerns, knowledge and practices gap among Malaysian teachers. *International Journal of Sustainability in Higher Education*, *4*(4), 305–313. doi:10.1108/14676370310497534

Mei, O. J., Ling, K. C., & Piew, T. H. (2012). The antecedents of green purchase intention among Malaysian consumers. *Asian Social Science*, *8*(13), 246. doi:10.5539/ass.v8n13p246

Mitchell, V.-W., & Papavassiliou, V. (1999). Marketing causes and implications of consumer confusion. *Journal of Product and Brand Management*, *8*(4), 319–342. doi:10.1108/10610429910284300

Obermiller, C., Spangenberg, E., & MacLachlan, D. L. (2005). Ad skepticism: The consequences of disbelief. *Journal of Advertising*, *34*(3), 7–17. doi:10.1080/00913367.2005.10639199

Ottman, J. (2011). *The new rules of green marketing: Strategies, tools, and inspiration for sustainable branding*. Berrett-Koehler Publishers.

Ottman. (2011). *The New Rules of Green Marketing*. Academic Press.

Parasuraman, R., Sheridan, T. B., & Wickens, C. D. (2008). Situation awareness, mental workload, and trust in automation: Viable, empirically supported cognitive engineering constructs. *Journal of Cognitive Engineering and Decision Making*, *2*(2), 140–160. doi:10.1518/155534308X284417

Parguel, B., Benoît-Moreau, F., & Larceneux, F. (2011). How sustainability ratings might deter greenwashing: A closer look at ethical corporate communication. *Journal of Business Ethics*, *102*(1), 15–28. doi:10.1007/s10551-011-0901-2

Peattie, K. (1999). Trappings versus substance in the greening of marketing planning. *Journal of Strategic Marketing*, *7*(2), 131–148. doi:10.1080/096525499346486

Polonsky, M. J., & Rosenberger, P. J. III. (2001). Reevaluating green marketing: A strategic approach. *Business Horizons*, *44*(5), 21–30. doi:10.1016/S0007-6813(01)80057-4

Ramli, N. (2009). *Awareness of Eco-label in Malaysia's Green Marketing Initiative*. Academic Press.

Rousseau, D. M., Sitkin, S. B., Burt, R. S., & Camerer, C. (1998). Not so different after all: A cross-discipline view of trust. *Academy of Management Review*, *23*(3), 393–404. doi:10.5465/AMR.1998.926617

Schurr, P. H., & Ozanne, J. L. (1985). Influences on exchange processes: Buyers preconceptions of a sellers trustworthiness and bargaining toughness. *The Journal of Consumer Research*, *11*(4), 939–953. doi:10.1086/209028

Self, R. M., Self, D. R., & Bell-Haynes, J. (2010). Marketing tourism in the Galapagos Islands: ecotourism or greenwashing?. *International Business & Economics Research Journal (IBER)*, *9*(6).

Shove, E., & Warde, A. (2002). Inconspicuous consumption: the sociology of consumption, lifestyles and the environment. *Sociological theory and the environment: classical foundations, contemporary insights*, *230*, 51.

Singh, J., & Sirdeshmukh, D. (2000). Agency and trust mechanisms in consumer satisfaction and loyalty judgments. *Journal of the Academy of Marketing Science*, *28*(1), 150–167. doi:10.1177/0092070300281014

Sinnappan. (2011). *Antecedents of Green Purchasing Behavior among Malaysian Consumers*. Academic Press.

Tahir Albayrak. (2011). *The Influence of Skepticism on Green Purchase Behavior*. Academic Press.

Trianna Rosli (2016). *Measuring Environmental Performance Awareness: A Qualitative Approach*. SOSHUM.

Turnbull, P. W., Leek, S., & Ying, G. (2000). Customer confusion: The mobile phone market. *Journal of Marketing Management*, *16*(1-3), 143–163. doi:10.1362/026725700785100523

Walsh, G., & Mitchell, V.-W. (2010). The effect of consumer confusion proneness on word of mouth, trust, and customer satisfaction. *European Journal of Marketing*, *44*(6), 838–859. doi:10.1108/03090561011032739

KEY TERMS AND DEFINITIONS

Eco-Label: A certification that provides the understanding of ecological benefits to the customers in the long run.

Environmental Attitude: An expression of psychological tendency between favor and un-favor towards things, situations, and people.

Environmental Performance Index: Global metrics for the environment that rank the countries' environmental performance of the human health protection and the protection of ecosystems.

Environmental Quality Awareness: Explains customers' awareness towards environmental quality that consists of three sustainable pillars which are environmental health, ecosystem vitality, and socio-economic sustainability.

Green Consumerism: Defined as the customers' purchasing habits towards environmentally friendly products and services.

Green People: Also called pro-environmentalists, these are people who belong to environment-society. These people are supporters of green or environmental movements whether political or ethical movements.

Green Products: Environmentally safe products that are safe, energy efficient and often have low maintenance requirements.

Green Purchasing Behavior: Spending on products that are beneficial to the environment.

Green Self-Efficacy: People's degree of involvement, effort and how long they will persist in facing the obstacles as well as aversive experiences.

Green Trust: Defined as the willingness to depend on a product or service based on the belief or expectation resulting from its credibility, benevolence, and ability about environmental performance.

Section 2
Understanding Green Attitude and Behavior

Chapter 4
Understanding Green Attitudes

Aysen Coskun
Akdeniz University, Turkey

ABSTRACT

Many environmental researches are interested in attitudes. Particularly in consumer behavior studies, attitudes are frequently used to identify the determinants of behavior. This chapter provides a framework for green attitude, first by focusing on its components and formation. The attitude-behavior gap is also discussed by categorizing a number of variables that are found to affect this relationship in the environmental literature. Following sections provide well-established scales of green attitudes and how they are measured. Finally, insights for green attitude change are discussed, along with future research directions, which underline the importance of new methods for attitude measurement.

INTRODUCTION

To date, there has been considerable discussion about the results and origins of human behaviors that are detrimental to environmental sustainability. The ability of the earth to support human consumption is being questioned increasingly (Assadouirian, 2010; Kotler, 2011). Some researchers have suggested that if the entire population of the world were to consume at the same rate as the average Western consumer, more than two Earths' worth of resources would be required to support this demand (Global Footprint Network, http://www.footprintnetwork.org/). Policy makers and marketers have recognized the need for consumers to change the ways in which they meet their needs (Polonsky, 2011).

Environmental pressures have produced extensive research examining approaches to marketing more responsible (i.e. less harmful) consumption behaviors (Leonidou & Leonidou, 2011; McDonagh & Prothero, 2014). Attempting to understand green consumer behavior, many theoretical frameworks emphasize personal factors such as values, norms, beliefs and attitudes. In Ajzen's (1985) Theory of Planned Behavior, the most well-known theoretical model for explaining people's intentions and behaviors, attitudes are assumed to directly affect the intentions that turn into behavior; along with attitudes, intentions are also influenced by social pressures.

The relationship between attitude and behavior has been structured in several theoretical models. Fazio's (1990) MODE (motivation and opportunity as determinants of behavior) model proposes that attitudes

DOI: 10.4018/978-1-5225-2912-5.ch004

are linked to behavior either automatically (spontaneously), or deliberately (reasoned). The possession of strong motivation and opportunity is a guide to the probability of an individual's enacting a behavior.

As a social psychology and consumer behavior concept, attitudes are widely used in predictions of behavior. Additionally, for more than half a century, scientists have been interested in the major themes of attitudinal change. There is, currently, a growing body of literature recognizing the significance of green attitudes as a predictor of green consumer behavior. Therefore, it is important to understand what underlies green attitudes, since, if individuals hold positive attitudes towards the environment, they are more likely to engage in environmentally-friendly behavior (McIntyre & Milfont, 2016).

The possession of a positive attitude, however, neither necessarily nor automatically corresponds with the desirable behavioral outcome. Several situational and individual factors interfere in the behavior formation process. Since consumer behavior plays a major role in environmental outcomes, it is important to understand why consumers might fail to engage in environmentally-friendly behaviors. Individuals are expected to regulate their consumption (Connolly & Prothero, 2008), while companies are under pressure to meet the needs of multiple stakeholders: consumers, who are demanding environmental responsibility; shareholders seeking dividends; and governments imposing stricter environmental legislation to regulate their activities. From another quarter, environmental activism continues to raise awareness on local and global fronts, encouraging and enabling community action, and often compelling governments to intervene on the side of the environment.

The objective of this chapter is to examine the green attitude within a comprehensive analysis of attitude formation and change. After defining green attitude, three salient issues are then addressed: the imperfect relationship between green attitude and behavior; the measurement of green attitude; and how change towards a green attitude, as a precursor of green behavior, might proceed. The sections which elaborate these three issues also provide the sequential structure of the chapter. Prior to the conclusion, the implications for marketers and policy makers are outlined, and recommendations for future research are made.

Defining Green Attitude

Attitudes are based on the evaluative feelings of what is favorable or unfavorable, with regard to particular objects, things, actions, or abstract concepts (Wicker, 1969), as well as an individual's life experience (Newhouse, 1990). As a result, attitudes can be observed in people's beliefs, feelings, and behaviors (Eagly & Chaiken, 1993; Fishbein & Ajzen, 1975).

The research on green attitudes uses various, interchangeable terms such as environmental attitudes, ecological attitudes, environmentally-friendly attitudes, and environmentally sustainable attitudes, all of which conceptualize individuals' evaluative judgments about the environment. In this chapter, the terms "green" and "environmental" are used interchangeably, and green attitude is explained in two contexts: (1) attitudes towards the environment, and (2) attitudes towards pro-environmental behavior. Therefore, definitions will vary accordingly. For instance, Schultz et al. (2004) defines green attitudes as the collection of beliefs, affect, and intentions about environmental activities. Heyl et al. (2013) describes green attitudes as the predisposition to respond in a consistently favorable or unfavorable manner regarding environmental issues. On the other hand, McIntyre and Milfont (2016) defines environmental attitudes as the evaluation of natural and built environments and factors affecting their quality. To gain a fuller understanding of green attitude, its components and formation must first be clarified.

Attitude Components

Whereas a number of studies treat attitudes as a unidimensional construct (Dunlap & Van Liere, 1978), the tri-component attitude model distinguishes components as affective, cognitive and behavioral. These different perspectives may contribute to either general or particular aspects of evaluations concerning the environment.

Of these three attitudinal dimensions – affective, cognitive and behavioral (conation) – the *cognitive dimension* refers to the perceptual component, or evaluation of the attitudinal object. Fishbein and Ajzen (1975) argue that attitudes, as the sum of our expected values, are evidence of the cognitive component, where expectancy refers to the estimation of probability that the object has a given attitude (Fazio & Olson 2003). The *affective dimension* reflects emotions and feelings associated with preferences in relation to objects/things/people/actions. Existing research recognizes the critical role played by learning theories (classical conditioning, operant conditioning and exposure) in attitude formation. Since attitudes can be learned, and treated as responses to an object, they are highly predictive of positive outcomes. Negative feelings, on the contrary, decrease the chances of that future occurrence. Finally, the *behavioral (conation) dimension* refers merely to an intention, and shapes action towards the attitudinal object. The behavioral route explains how attitudes are formed without the holding of either beliefs or feelings about the attitude object, i.e. attitudes can be inferred from experiences. For instance, a consumer may be dissatisfied when an energy bill reveals that a recently bought "energy-efficient" appliance has used more electricity than the previous, regular appliance. As a result, the consumer would choose another brand for the next domestic appliance purchase and/or spread negative word-of-mouth feedback. The components of attitude and their definitions are summarized in Table 1, along with examples from within an environmental context.

All three dimensions can be observed in attitude formation, and each must correspond with the others. Otherwise, attitude-behavior inconsistency, which prevents the individual from enacting the behavior, results. For instance, an individual may be harshly critical of people who pollute the environment; at the same time, he doesn't want to pay a penalty because he has (inadvertently or otherwise) put his cart outside before the trash collection day and time (attitude-behavior inconsistency).

The tricomponent attitude model is useful for categorizing attitudinal responses, provides a road map for attitude formation and change, and helps to distinguish between the components of attitude. It is important to note however that while the correspondence of these three dimensions implies a balanced and stable attitude, it does not necessarily follow that the individual will perform the behavior. There are several factors that may prevent the individual from acting, which will be explained in detail in the following section.

Table 1. Attitude components

Components	Definition	Example
Cognitive	Based on cognitions of the attitude object as to its desirable or undesirable outcomes	Belief in making a difference to environmental outcomes through behavior
Affective	Based on emotional reactions to the attitude object	Feeling virtuous when engaging in environmental friendly behaviors
Behavioral	Based on the tendency to act in favor of the attitude object.	Choosing to buy a hybrid car

Source: Schiffman & Kanuk (2007)

The Imperfect Relationship Between Green Attitude and Behavior

There is no doubt that environmental problems are induced by human behavior. Many consumers are aware of the facts of environmental degradation, and also that the costs are immense and widespread. Yet, awareness does not necessarily translate into action.

The circumstances of such an attitude-behavior gap have, over the last 30 years, been discussed within social psychology and consumer behavior literature. While much research has been published on the attitude-behavior gap, no consensus has, to date, been reached about the relationship between green attitudes and pro-environmental behavior. Although several studies posit green attitudes as significant predictors of pro-environmental behavior (Hines et al., 1987), others (Gatersleben et al., 2002; Mainieri et al., 1997; Tan & Lau, 2011) indicate that pro-environmental behavior is not significantly related to green attitudes, or report low correlation between the two constructs.

Numerous studies have analyzed the variables which may explain this gap, and several studies have discussed variables as barriers in the attitude-behavior relationship (i.e., Gleim et al., 2013, Gifford, 2011). However, no definitive framework providing a generalized conception of these various factors has been produced. Therefore, this chapter attempts to integrate each factor, in detail, into two main categories according to their role to provide a basis for understanding the attitude-behavior gap: situational variables, such as social surroundings, the means of measurement, or availability (opportunity or constraint); and individual factors, such as beliefs, norms, and values.

1. **Situational Variables:** Situational variables, accepted as lying beyond the individual's control (Tanner et al., 2004), will vary according to the environment (Wicker, 1969). Such variables can be significant in attitude-behavior inconsistency, given their accepted characteristics which are delineated as follows:
    a. **Level of Specificity:** General (or broad) attitudes are insufficient predictors of specific behavior, and the measurement of attitudes should be equal to the level of specificity (Ajzen & Fishbein, 1980; Conner & Armitage, 1998; Kaiser et al., 2007). For instance, knowing that a person has a positive attitude towards the environment may not predict/infer specific behavioral actions such as recycling, buying environmentally friendly goods, or reducing household energy consumption.
    b. **Social Desirability Bias:** In environmental studies, people tend to present themselves publicly in favorable ways, which seems to affect their responses in self-reported measures (Liere & Dunlap, 1978). However, Milfont (2009) found no measurable social desirability bias effect in responses to environmental issues and further, reported only limited evidence of this effect having been tested, with the balance of research merely noting it as a potential limitation of self-report measures.
    c. **Presence of Others:** Individuals tend to justify their responses when they know they are being observed. Moreover, people with low-prejudice scores were found to also have low attitude-behavior gaps when their answers were kept private (Warner & Defleur, 1969).
    d. **Unexpected Incidental Changes:** Life events such as losing money or possessions, getting fired, illness, death, birth, natural disasters, and meeting new people may prompt behavior change and thereby decrease the predictability of the behavior (Wicker, 1971). For example, the advent of unemployment might affect a person's usual buying behavior (such as the regular purchase of organic food).

e. **Contextual Settings (Availability):** Availability refers to assumed situational obstacles that restrain the person from action. For instance, a consumer with a high level of environmental awareness may prefer to buy recycled toilet paper, but the most convenient local store doesn't offer it. Similarly, people who rent, rather than own the house they live in choose not to buy insulation because their tenure is uncertain.

f. **Product Characteristics:** Perception of quality, price, and performance considerations contribute to consumers' evaluations of green products (Osterhus, 1997; Wagner, 2003). For example, since green products are generally perceived to be more costly (Bhate & Lawler, 1997), price could be a powerful (de)motivator in green consumer decision making. Many consumers habitually select the lowest-priced product without regard to its environmental impact, while others will purchase the less harmful product regardless of price.

g. **Non-Monetary Costs:** Consumers tend to evaluate benefits over costs not only on a price basis, but also on the time and effort involved. Thus, the perception of higher price in addition to the time required to research and understand the benefits of the environmentally friendly product will tend to make the green choice less likely (Gleim et al., 2013).

2. **Individual Variables:** Individual variables, or the distinctive characteristics of individuals which determine their patterns of behaviour, include the following:

a. **Problems in Motivated Reasoning:** The motivation and ability to process available information affects consumers' elaboration of cognitive processing (Rucker & Petty, 2006), whereby the cognitive cost of sourcing additional information may impede buying behavior. For instance, a consumer's main motivation may be monetary if disposable batteries are chosen over the more expensive rechargeable product, but buying the cheaper alternative comes at the cost of ignoring that the green option saves money in the long run. The lack of motivation or ability to take a longer-term view also applies when non-green choices and behaviors, such as using plastic bags or littering, are perceived as acceptable (Atkinson & Kim, 2014), and persist despite the availability of alternatives, and public awareness/education campaigns.

b. **Lack of Locus of Control:** The extent to which an individual believes in their capacity or power to change the way things are (Hines et al., 1987) indicates their locus of control and, therefore, the degree to which consumers believe their actions matter. People without a strong, internal locus of control have no expectations of their behavior influencing outcomes.

c. **Lack of Awareness**: Environmental awareness is significantly associated with individual behavior (Lillemo, 2014). Consider, for example, that a person who habitually buys bottled water may not be aware of the negative impact of its disposal on the environment.

d. **Cognitive Dissonance:** A person may have a desire to act environmentally responsibly, but nonetheless fail to realize the desired behavior. For instance, Juvan and Dolnicar (2014) reported that a high level of awareness of the negative environmental consequences of tourism activities did not in fact lead to behavior change; instead, participants justified their behavior using a range of explanations.

e. **Normative Influences:** Social norms, traditions and customs have an effect on people's attitudes (Dawes, 1980). Being raised in a culture that values the environment would probably form positive attitudes towards its protection. By way of example, in the village of Piplantri in India, whenever a girl is born, 111 trees are planted to unite the people in collective causes (One Green Planet, http://www.onegreenplanet.org/environment/village-in-india-plants-plants-trees-every-time-a-little-girl-is-born/).

f. **Lack of Trust:** When individuals feel that businesses exploit the "environmentally friendly" concept, they tend to be skeptical of marketing claims that decreasing the impacts of production, packaging, and transportation is making a difference. They also perceive such environmental messages to be examples of "greenwashing", i.e., ambiguous or misleading (Kangun et al., 1991), and largely symbolic rather than substantive actions.
g. **Expertise**: A person who has direct experience of the context (e.g. recycling one's own waste), rather than only indirect experience (e.g. hearing/reading a public service announcement) would have a stronger attitude-behavior relationship.

To date, in endeavors to fully understand the underlying dimensions of behavior, researchers have also sought to bridge the attitude-action gap by suggesting interaction effects through the use of mediator[1] and moderator[2] variables. Table 2 presents several moderators that have a significant effect on the magnitude of the relationship between attitude and behavior. For instance, attitudes are stronger and more likely to predict the subsequent behavior if the individual perceives his effectiveness within context.

Table 2. Examples of intervening variables in attitude-behavior relationship

Variable	Author	Type of Variable	Significance of Relationship
Consumer demographics	Ling-yee (1997)	Moderator	Males earn higher incomes and tend to make more extensive green product information searches and purchases.
Effort required for behavior	Bagozzi et al. (1990)	Moderator	When the level of effort required for behavior is high, intentions fully mediate the effect of attitude on behavior.
Faith in others	Berger & Corbin (1992)	Moderator	When individuals have greater faith in others, the correlation between attitude and behavior is higher.
Involvement	Ling-yee (1997)	Moderator	When individuals are highly involved with a product, they are more likely to show verbal commitment to environmental protection.
Perception of effectiveness	Berger & Corbin (1992)	Moderator	When individuals perceive greater efficacy, the correlation between attitude and behavior is higher.
Time perspective	Rabinovich et al. (2010)	Moderator	When individuals have a long-term perspective, the attitude-behavior consistency increases.
Appreciative recreation activities	Tarrant & Green (1999)	Mediator	Appreciative recreation activities mediate the relationship between environmental attitudes and behavior.
Green purchase intention	Chan (2001)	Mediator	Intention mediates the relationship between attitudes and behavior.

Measuring and Scaling of Green Attitudes

Attitudes, being a type of cognition, cannot as such be measured directly; it is necessary, therefore to "go to the people" to understand what lies behind these cognitions. In this way, essential pathways to attitudinal change can be determined (Maloney & Ward, 1973).

Measurement Techniques

Researchers frequently use explicit (e.g., depth interviews, focus groups, surveys) and implicit (e.g., observation, experimental design) techniques to measure attitudes. Explicit measurement techniques are also considered to be self-report methods. They are easy to use, flexible (Kormos & Gifford, 2014), and useful for obtaining factual information about the individual's disposition towards the environment (e.g., Nigbur et al., 2010; Steel, 1996; Thøgersen, 2009; Wu, 2012). Self-reported attitudes are generally assessed through questionnaires using different types of attitude scales – single-item, multi-item and continuous rating. Singe-item scales (such as rank-order scales, constant-sum scales, and paired-comparison scales) deal with one item at a time. Multi-item scales (Likert-type scales, semantic-differential scales, Guttman scale, and Stapel scale) are most frequently used to measure a specific construct. Finally, continuous-rating scales represent a continuum between the two extremes along which participants select a point that indicates their response to a stimulus.

Implicit measurement techniques are meant to determine uncontrolled, unintentional and purely stimulus-driven outcomes (De Houwer et al., 2009) and of these, the most frequently used technique relies on response time measures (Wittenbrink & Schwarz, 2007). According to cognitive psychology, when individuals are exposed to a stimulus, they can easily recognize subsequent, related objects. Another important implicit measurement procedure involves the "implicit association test" (IAT) developed by Greenwald et al. (1998), which aims to measure participants' automatic (without forethought) associations in seven sequential steps. The logic of IAT relies on its access to the subconscious mind, and preferences derived using this method may help to circumvent social desirability bias (see Greenwald et al., 1998 for further reading).

Since each of these methods, as outlined, has its advantages as well as drawbacks, no single method, therefore, applies to attitude measurement. The researcher, then, requires insight into the nature of his research, and must choose the technique that best suits the research objective. For instance, Oppenheim (2000) suggests that where the aim of the research is to identify attitude patterns, or theoretical explanations, the Likert-type scale is the most relevant; for understanding the hierarchical structure of an attitude or how attitudes are changed, the Guttman scale is more appropriate.

Green Attitudes Scales

Research into attitude measurement has an extensive history in environmental psychology, which studies interrelationships of people and their surroundings and has produced a great number of analytical studies (Kaiser et al., 1999; Milfont & Duckitt, 2010). While numerous types of scales have been used to measure green attitudes, among the most frequently used are the *Ecology Scale* (Maloney & Ward, 1973), the *Inventory of Social Issues* (Steiner & Barnhart, 1972), the *Environmental Response Inven-*

tory (ERI) (McKechnie, 1977), the *Environmental Concern Scale* (Weigel & Weigel, 1978), the *New Environmental Paradigm* (NEP) *Scale* (Dunlap & Van Liere, 1978), and the *Environmental Attitudes Inventory* (Milfont & Duckitt, 2010).

- **Ecology Scale:** Developed by Maloney and Ward (1973), this scale originally consisted of 130 items under four subscales: verbal commitment (36 items), actual commitment (36 items), affect (34 items), and knowledge (24 items). Initially, verbal commitment, actual commitment and affect subscales were measured with dichotomous (yes/no) questions, while knowledge items were presented in a multiple-choice format. Items were selected from among 500 items to reflect varying degrees of each context. Three PhD psychologists then assessed each item for suitability and six items were excluded from the scale. In the following years, a shorter, 45-item version of the scale was developed, reducing verbal commitment, actual commitment and affect to ten items each, and the knowledge subscale to 15 items. Critics have questioned the ability of the Ecology Scale to provide adequate measurement, since aspects of current and emerging environmental issues are not accommodated (McIntyre & Milfont, 2016). This scale, therefore, needs to be interpreted with caution.
- **Inventory of Social Issues:** Steiner and Barnhart (1972) selected items from a pool of approximately 250, and obtained answers from university and high school student samples. In the pre-test, 100 items were excluded so that the final version of the scale consisted of seven factors covering a total of 60 items. Importantly, the Inventory of Social Issues does not solely apply to environmental concerns. In their study, the authors have integrated attitudes related to regard for human life, pessimism about the outcomes of man's scientific and technological interventions in nature, the need to cooperate with nature, the implications and consequences of an increasing population and the need for its control, taking personal responsibility for current societal problems, optimistic belief in the ability and desirability of science and technology to solve societal problems and to deal with environmental deficiencies, and the desire for individual freedom (Steiner & Barnhart, 1972).
- **The Environmental Response Inventory:** The earlier version of McKechnie's (1977) scale consisted of 218 items measuring the behavioral and experiential differences in the way people interact with the environment. In the final version of the Environmental Response Inventory, 184 items were grouped under the eight subscales of pastoralism, urbanism, environmental adaptation, stimulus seeking, environmental trust, antiquarianism, need for privacy, and mechanical orientation, measured using a 5-point Likert-type scale. One additional measure (communality) validated the accuracy and attentive test-taking attitudes of respondents. The scale encompassed multiple topics relevant to the environment, such as attitudes toward conservation (pastoralism) and the degree to which people believe in humans' ability to modify the environment to their advantage (environmental adaptation). Additionally, several subscales measured people's enjoyment of fast-growing urban settings (urbanism) and/or traditional and historical structures (antiquarianism). There is even a subscale measuring individuals' kinesthetic skills with technology (mechanical orientation). In sum, the salience of the Environmental Response Inventory lies in its wide-ranging diversity and the environmental specificity of its content.
- **Environmental Concern Scale:** Weigel and Weigel's (1978) 16-item scale (refined from 31 initial items), relates to conservation and pollution issues. The scale assesses individuals' prevailing beliefs and feelings about ecological problems, and their predisposition to act in eco-friendly ways

(Weigel & Weigel, 1978). The authors measured the attitudes of respondents with seven positively- and nine negatively-stated items on a 5-point Likert-type scale. The scale was successful in its ability to comprehensively assess individuals' tendencies relative to specific environmental topics, conservation and pollution, which specificity is, at the same time, also a limitation of this particular scale.

- **New Environmental Paradigm (NEP) Scale:** The original NEP scale, developed in 1978 by Dunlap and Van Liere, consisted of 12 items measured on a 4-point Likert-type scale. In environmental research literature, this attitudinal scale is one of the most frequently used to assess people's beliefs about their relationship with nature, according to eight pro-traits and four con-traits. Although the scale is a unidimensional measure, it features three distinct dimensions which seek to understand human interrelationships with the natural world – humankind's domination of nature, the limits to growth, and the balance of nature. As such, the scale is very general in character, being more concerned with ethical attitudes than with particular environmental problems. A shorter, six-item version of the scale was developed for the Continental Group for use in a United States national survey (Dunlap et al., 2000). In 2000, the authors revised the scale for gender-neutrality, and a better balance between pro-traits and con-traits in items pertaining to two main aspects. The revised NEP scale consists in 15 items with five dimensions: the reality of limits to growth; anti-anthropocentrism; the fragility of nature's balance; the rejection of exceptionalism; and the possibility of an eco-crisis (Dunlap et al., 2000). Numerous studies have consistently used and validated the NEP scale in various interest groups (known-group validity). Moreover, extant research recognizes its predictive validity by reporting significant relationships between this scale and various types of intentions and behaviors which confirm its criterion validity. Overall, the later NEP scale has maintained its currency owing to its capacity to identify and accommodate emerging environmental issues.
- **Environmental Attitudes Inventory:** Specifically developed to capture the multidimensionality of environmental attitudes, this scale's 120 items and 12 subscales assess individuals' perceptions and beliefs pertaining to the natural environment on a 7-point Likert-type scale. Milfont and Duckitt's (2010) scale also captures the hierarchical nature of environmental attitudes horizontally and vertically – the horizontal structure comprising first-order factors, and the vertical structure relating to second-order factors in psychometric terms. The subscales of the inventory encompass enjoyment of nature, support for interventionist conservation policies, environmental movement activism, conservation motivated by anthropocentric concerns, confidence in science and technology, environmental fragility, altering nature, personal conservation behavior, human dominance over nature, human utilization of nature, eco-centric concern, and support for population growth policies. Each of the unidimensional subscales includes ten items of high internal consistency. The scale has also been tested in a cross-cultural study involving New Zealand, Brazil, and South Africa. The authors reported their development of a shorter, 24-item version of the scale which takes into account the time constraints of several research situations (Milfont & Duckitt, 2007).

Green Attitude Change

Attitude change is a complex process, and is precursory to behavior change. Policy-makers and marketers should therefore consider attitude change as an essential strategy for meeting their objectives. For instance, marketers strive to keep their customers within the firm as competitors offer unique selling propositions. Damage to the environment and the consequences for social welfare will continue to be increasingly challenging issues for policy-makers. Also, the shift in the perceptual paradigm of the environment offers new opportunities. Through attitude change, an increase in empathy and motivation, or a perceptual change may be achieved. Consequently, it is essential to understand the characteristics of attitude in any context of attitudinal change, which are outlined as follows.

- **Explicit vs. Implicit Attitudes:** Research on environmental attitudes frequently evaluates explicit attitudes, easily measurable and self-reportable by typical survey items. Results, as previously noted, are however likely subject to social desirability bias. By contrast, the implicit attitudes of people may produce less biased results, since they are held to be automatic, rapid, spontaneous and uncontrolled reactions to a stimulus.
- **Symbolic vs. Non-Symbolic Attitudes:** People attribute several meanings to an attitude. If an individual's attitude is based on affect, rather than formed through a cognitive process of gaining information, it is assumed to be symbolic. Non-symbolic attitudes are, on the contrary, formed as a result of reasoning. Given how attitudes are formed, non-symbolic attitudes can be more easily modified than those that derive from feeling in cases of influential rationalization.
- **Strong vs. Weak Attitudes:** Strong attitudes are relatively more stable and less susceptible to environmental influences than less firmly held attitudes.
- **Positive vs. Negative Attitudes:** Negative attitudes are less subject to influence or change because negative attitudes tend to typify people who are not open to new experiences or information about the disliked object (Fazio & Olson, 2003).
- **Relative Importance:** The degree to which an individual thinks a particular attitude is important has several bases, namely (1) the link to other attitudes, beliefs, and values in memory, (2) the setting, and size of relevant knowledge in individual memory, and (3) the impact of society (Krosnick, 1988). Taking all of these affects into account, it is apparent that the importance accorded by an individual will determine an attitude's stability.

There are various specific strategies and theoretical models explaining the process of attitudinal change. In the next section, the process and the mechanisms of altering attitudes is explained in detail, along with theoretical models.

Processes of Attitude Change

Attitudinal change, manifesting in a concordant behavior change, may happen through three different processes (Kelman, 1958):

- **Compliance:** When the individual believes that changing a behavior will provide rewards or approval, satisfaction is the result of the social effect.
- **Identification:** When a person believes that adopting the induced behavior will enhance their self-identity in relation to others, satisfaction derives from conformity with others. Moreover, the behavioral content is irrelevant, since the main motivation is self-defining.
- **Internalization:** When one believes that the induced behavior aligns with one's values, satisfaction results from the content of the new behavior.

Compliance, identification and internalization are three concepts explaining how attitude change may come about. How each of the processes are distinguished should, then, be ascertained by looking at their respective precursors. Kelman (1958) proposes that (a) the relative importance of the anticipated affect, (b) the relative power of the influencing agent, and (c) the appreciable power of the induced response will determine the process of attitude change.

Mechanisms of Attitude Change

Bodenhausen and Gawronski (2013) classifies how attitude change works, in the following three contexts:

1. **Learning-Based:** It is assumed that learning new information plays a critical role in attitude change. Essentially, persuasive message-learning affects the degree of attitude change. The role of persuasion has been important in attitude change research, and was elaborated on three levels by Baum et al. (1981): the source of the communication, its transmission, and the audience or recipient of the message. In Baum et al.'s (1081) scheme, the source is a signal of credibility (or otherwise) and the persuasiveness of the message increases with its attributed authority or trust. The transmission of the message influences the persuasion process depending on the characteristics of the medium. The audience that receives the message is made up of individuals, who will each be persuaded to varying degrees.

The role of environmental education (the cognitive component) in attitude change has been studied extensively (Iozzi, 1989a). However, it is essential to address attitudes, as the affective component, rather than simply transmitting knowledge about environmental concerns (Iozzi, 1989b), since merely presenting information about ecological issues, no matter how convincing, will not in itself achieve greener thinking, or green attitudes.

2. **Behavior-Induced:** In some situations, it has been found that even when individuals have no particular perspective on an attitude object, it is still likely that they will be influenced as a result of engaging in the associated behavior (Olson & Stone, 2005). Cognitive dissonance theory provides an explanation of this phenomenon in its assumption that people are motivated to reduce experiential disparities in order to avoid discomfort and negative feelings (Festinger, 1957). In other words, as long as individuals can justify their own behaviors, their attitudes will remain unchanged. An alternative mechanism is proposed by self-perception theory, which posits that people infer their attitudes and beliefs from their observable behavior (Bem, 1967).
3. **Context-Induced:** Contextual cues, especially those occurring in specifically-themed presentations can trigger attitude change by activating knowledge stored in memory. Automatic biases will come into play more strongly when, for example, someone sees on the news that their favorite car manufacturer has been sued for polluting the environment; conversely, if the person learns from the news that the same company supports an environmental charity, a more positive attitude would result. In short, when a given context stimulates a positive set of associations, positive attitudes are more likely to be formed.

Theoretical Models of Attitude Change

- **Elaboration Likelihood Model (ELM):** In this simple but multi-faceted attitude change theory, Petty and Cacioppo (1986) described two paths to persuasion (the central route vs. the peripheral route), which diverge in the amount of thought and consideration given to the object of persuasion. This model integrates people's motivation and ability to process the persuasive message, and proposes that the likelihood of attitude change will tend to be high when an individual is motivated and able to process the communication. Conversely, at the low end of the process continuum, lack of motivation and ability tends to result in retention or regaining of the initial attitude, rather than change. ELM also emphasizes motivational factors such as personal relevance, need for cognition, and personal responsibility, and recognizes that a person's ability to process may be affected by prior knowledge, distractions, time pressures, and the number of message repetitions. According to this theory, attitudes will persist, or not, depending on the route of persuasion. Attitudes formed via the central route (high motivation and ability) tend to last over time. The peripheral route (low motivation and ability) of the persuasion process could, however, have practical value in prompting immediate changes of attitude (Rucker & Petty, 2006). ELM has been applied in various fields such as advertising (Grau & Folse, 2008), health communications (Petty & Briñol, 2006), and has also proved useful in environmental attitude change (Grimmer & Bingham, 2013; MacDonald et al., 2015; Wolsko et al., 2016).
- **Functional Approach:** Katz (1960) provides a psychological framework designed to understand the reasons for holding attitudes. Four major functions of attitude are identified as utilitarian, ego-defensive, value-expressive, and knowledge. Each function performs a different role and is differently motivated: the role of the utilitarian function satisfies needs, the ego-defensive function protects the self, the value-expressive function provides the satisfaction of individual expression, and the knowledge function helps individuals to understand their surroundings. Substantive research using the functional approach to attitudes has yielded insights into motives such as brand loyalty (Russell-Bennett et al., 2013), and volunteering (Houle et al., 2005). In environmental studies, Milfont and Duckitt (2010) extended this approach by specifying the distinctive environmental attitude functions of preservation (symbolic values) and utilization.
- **Self-Monitoring:** Assuming that an individual's identity is shaped, in part, by social interactions, the theory of self-monitoring proposes that people consciously strive to create favorable images particular to situational contexts (Snyder, 1979). People who engage in high-level self-monitoring do so for social acceptance, and are prone to adjusting their self-presentation to the dynamics of social situations.

It can be claimed that certain mechanisms assist in understanding the attitude change context. The application of theoretical models to attitude change has advanced the knowledge of how attitude change occurs, as well as the complexity of attitudes. ELM continues to dominate theoretical approaches to attitude change through the mechanism of message-induced persuasion. Finally, given the significant role of attitudes in research across multiple disciplines, attitudinal change will continue to command attention.

MANAGERIAL IMPLICATIONS

Understanding why and how green attitudes are essential for the enacting of behavior that reduces environmental harm is critical for all sections of society. In fiercely competitive markets, companies are motivated to satisfy consumers' needs more effectively than their competitors can. When attitudes are deconstructed, methods and techniques for their measurement assessed, and the individual and situational barriers to attitudinal change considered, the gap between consumers' attitudes and behavior can be more easily explained, and marketers able to develop specific strategies to influence their customers' attitudes.

In the public realm, policy makers can initiate behavior change programs with a clearer understanding of the barriers to attitudinal change, given that attitudes are highly significant predictors of behavior. Change at the societal level would involve various parties in society, including local communities and peer groups focusing on change at the individual level (Jackson, 2004).

Educating people in more sustainable consumption is also a means of raising environmental awareness, with the evidence suggesting that environmental awareness is associated with environmental benefits (Cowan & Kinley, 2014). It is also important to emphasize the type of environmental benefit accruing from green behavior, whether a social, environmental, economic or psychological benefit.

Finally, evidence suggests that "behavioral spillover", which proposes that behaviors do not occur in isolation but are linked serially to others, in progressive or reactionary ways, is an important determinant of whether consumers adopt green behavior (Lacasse, 2016). The empirical evidence for behavioral spillover has received mixed reviews in the literature. Positive behavioral spillover situations have been claimed to demonstrate that pro-attitudes and adoption of more complex behavior (Thøgersen & Noblet, 2012) can be achieved in simple sequential steps. In the environmental context, it has been shown that when people perform small, environmentally-friendly actions, they are more likely to then proceed to enact other pro-environmental behaviors in the future (Poortinga et al., 2013).

FUTURE RESEARCH DIRECTIONS

Understanding consumers' attitudes to predict their behavior has been an enduring focus of marketers. In a globalized world where technological advances continue apace, researchers would benefit from the utilization of new research methods.

Explicit measurement techniques, particularly surveys, remain the most popular method for investigating attitudes. Notwithstanding the significant results that have been obtained using explicit measurements, the overreliance on such methods has been questioned in the context of attitude research (McIntyre & Milfont, 2016). Future studies of attitude change might focus on innovative approaches, such as from neuroscience, which may potentially help to overcome the human tendency to give socially desirable answers. Neuromarketing is an emerging practice whose aim is to gain insight into the physiology of response behind thoughts, reasoning, attitudes and decision-making processes. Research may benefit from using the tools of this interdisciplinary field, such as functional magnetic resonance imaging (fMRI), positron emission tomography (PET), electroencephalography (EEG), magnetoencephalography

(MEG), transcranial magnetic stimulation (TMS), eye tracking, and measuring physiological responses and response times. These techniques allow researchers to keep continuous track of psychophysiological responses, and in combination, such techniques can lead to a highly validated quality of information (Bercea, 2013).

In sum, explicit attitude measurement relies heavily on individuals' reports that are subject to certain types of bias. Moreover, when the various individual and situational variables that affect attitudes, as this chapter has described, are taken into account the validity and reliability of the measurement may be reduced. Therefore, using hybrid measurement techniques would provide greater clarity about how attitude structures work. At the same time, knowledge on this subject will continue to be enriched by the integration of qualitative and quantitative methods.

CONCLUSION

This chapter focused on the concept of green attitudes, and attitudinal change as the precursor to behavior change, firstly by defining the components and describing the formation of attitudes. The imperfect correlation between attitude and subsequent behavior was identified, and variables – situational and individual – affecting the attitude-behavior gap were then categorized and discussed. An overview of frequently used measurement techniques and scales measuring green attitudes provided insight into how to conduct attitude research. To provide a framework for the subject, attitude change mechanisms, process, and theoretical models were explained. Finally, the implications of gaining a clearer picture of attitude formation and change for managers were outlined, and recommendations for future research highlighted innovations which could produce deeper insights into attitude measurement. In conclusion, the chapter has provided a comprehensive view of green attitudes from multiple perspectives.

REFERENCES

Ajzen, I. (1985). From intentions to actions: A theory of planned behavior. In J. Kuhl & J. Beckman (Eds.), *Action control: From cognition to behavior*. Heidelberg, Germany: Springer. doi:10.1007/978-3-642-69746-3_2

Ajzen, I., & Fishbein, M. (1980). *Understanding attitudes and predicting social behavior*. Englewood Cliffs, NJ: Prentice-Hall.

Assadourian, E. (2010). Transforming cultures: From consumerism to sustainability. *Journal of Macromarketing*, *30*(2), 186–191. doi:10.1177/0276146710361932

Atkinson, L., & Kim, Y. (2014, June). "I Drink It Anyway and I Know I Shouldn't": Understanding Green Consumers' Positive Evaluations of Norm-violating Non-green Products and Misleading Green Advertising. *Environmental Communication: A Journal of Nature and Culture*, 1–21. 10.1080/17524032.2014.932817

Bagozzi, R. P., Yi, Y., & Baumgartner, J. (1990). The level of effort required for behaviour as a moderator of the attitude-behaviour relation. *European Journal of Social Psychology, 20*(1), 45–59. doi:10.1002/ejsp.2420200105

Baron, R., & Kenny, D. (1986). The moderator-mediator variable distinction in social psychological research. *Journal of Personality and Social Psychology, 51*(6), 1173–1182. doi:10.1037/0022-3514.51.6.1173 PMID:3806354

Baum, A., Singer, J. E., & Baum, C. S. (1981). Stress and the Environment. *The Journal of Social Issues, 37*(1), 4–35. doi:10.1111/j.1540-4560.1981.tb01056.x

Bem, D. J. (1967). Self-Perception: An Alternative Interpretation of Cognitive Dissonance Phenomena. *Psychological Review, 74*(3), 183–200. doi:10.1037/h0024835 PMID:5342882

Bercea, M. D. (2013). *Quantitative versus qualitative in neuromarketing research.* Retrieved from https://mpra.ub.uni-muenchen.de/44134/

Berger, I. E., & Corbin, R. M. (1992). Perceived Consumer Effectiveness and Faith in Others as Moderators of Environmentally Responsible Behavior. *Journal of Public Policy & Marketing, 11*(2), 79–89.

Bhate, S., & Lawler, K. (1997). Environmentally friendly products: Factors that influence their adoption. *Technovation, 17*(8), 457–465. doi:10.1016/S0166-4972(97)00006-0

Bodenhausen, G. V., & Gawronski, B. (2013). Attitude Change. In D. Reisberg (Ed.), *The Oxford Handbook of Cognitive Psychology* (pp. 957–969). Oxford University Press.

Chan, R. Y. K. (2001). Determinants of Chinese Consumers Green Purchase Behavior. *Psychology and Marketing, 18*(4), 389–413. doi:10.1002/mar.1013

Conner, M., & Armitage, C. J. (1998). Extending the Theory of Planned Behavior: A Review and Avenues for Further Research. *Journal of Applied Social Psychology, 28*(15), 1429–1464. doi:10.1111/j.1559-1816.1998.tb01685.x

Connolly, J., & Prothero, A. (2008). Green consumption: Life-politics, risk and contradictions. *Journal of Consumer Culture, 8*(1), 117–145. doi:10.1177/1469540507086422

Cowan, K., & Kinley, T. (2014). Green spirit: Consumer empathies for green apparel. *International Journal of Consumer Studies, 38*(5), 493–499. doi:10.1111/ijcs.12125

Dawes, R. M. (1980). Social Dilemmas. *Annual Review of Psychology, 31*(1), 169–193. doi:10.1146/annurev.ps.31.020180.001125

De Houwer, J., Teige-Mocigemba, S., Spruyt, A., & Moors, A. (2009). Implicit measures: A normative analysis and review. *Psychological Bulletin, 135*(3), 347–368. doi:10.1037/a0014211 PMID:19379018

Dunlap, R. E., & Van Liere, K. D. (1978). The New Environmental Paradigm.. *The Journal of Environmental Education, 9*(4), 10–19. doi:10.1080/00958964.1978.10801875

Dunlap, R. E., Van Liere, K. D., Mertig, A. G., & Jones, R. E. (2000). Measuring Endorsement of the New Ecological Paradigm : A Revised NEP Scale. *The Journal of Social Issues*, *56*(3), 425–442. doi:10.1111/0022-4537.00176

Eagly, A. H., & Chaiken, S. (1993). *The psychology of attitudes*. Fort Worth, TX: Harcourt Brace Jovanovich.

Fazio, R. H. (1990). Multiple processes by which attitudes guide behaviour: The MODE model as an integrative framework. In M. P. Zanna (Ed.), *Advances in experimental psychology* (Vol. 23, pp. 75–109). San Diego, CA: Academic Press.

Fazio, R. H., & Olson, M. A. (2003). Implicit measures in social cog- nition research: Their meaning and use. *Annual Review of Psychology*, *54*(1), 297–327. doi:10.1146/annurev.psych.54.101601.145225 PMID:12172003

Festinger, L. (1957). *A theory of cognitive dissonance*. Evanston, IL: Row, Peterson.

Fishbein, M., & Ajzen, I. (1975). *Beliefs, attitude, intention and behavior*. Reading, MA: Addison-Wesley.

Gatersleben, B., Steg, L., & Vlek, C. (2002). Measurement and Determinants of Environmentally Significant Consumer Behavior. *Environment and Behavior*, *34*(3), 335–362. doi:10.1177/0013916502034003004

Gifford, R. (2011). The dragons of inaction: Pychological barriers that limit climate change mitigation and adaptation. *The American Psychologist*, *66*(4), 290–302. doi:10.1037/a0023566 PMID:21553954

Gleim, M. R., Smith, J. S., Andrews, D., & Cronin, J. J. Jr. (2013). Against the Green: A Multi-method Examination of the Barriers to Green Consumption. *Journal of Retailing*, *89*(1), 44–61. doi:10.1016/j.jretai.2012.10.001

Global Footprint Network. (n.d.). Retrieved from http://www.footprintnetwork.org/

Grau, S. L., & Folse, J. A. G. (2008). Cause-Related Marketing (CRM): The Influence of Donation Proximity and Message-Framing Cues on the Less-Involved Consumer. *Journal of Advertising*, *36*(4), 19–33. doi:10.2753/JOA0091-3367360402

Greenwald, A. G., McGhee, D. E., & Schwartz, J. L. (1998). Measuring individual differences in implicit cognition: The implicit association test. *Journal of Personality and Social Psychology*, *74*(6), 1464–1480. doi:10.1037/0022-3514.74.6.1464 PMID:9654756

Grimmer, M., & Bingham, T. (2013). Company environmental performance and consumer purchase intentions. *Journal of Business Research*, *66*(10), 1945–1953. doi:10.1016/j.jbusres.2013.02.017

Heyl, M., Díaz, E. M., & Cifuentes, L. (2013). Environmental attitudes and behaviors of college students: A case study conducted at a chilean university. *Revista Latinoamericana de Psicología*, *45*(3), 487. doi:10.14349/rlp.v45i3.1489

Hines, J. M., Hungerford, H. R., & Tomera, A. N. (1987). Analysis and Synthesis o f Research on Responsible Environmental Behavior: A Meta-Analysis. *The Journal of Environmental Education*, *18*(2), 1–8. doi:10.1080/00958964.1987.9943482

Houle, B. J., Sagarin, B. J., & Kaplan, M. F. (2005). A Functional Approach to Volunteerism: Do Volunteer Motives Predict Task Preference? *Basic and Applied Social Psychology*, *27*(4), 337–344. doi:10.1207/s15324834basp2704_6

Iozzi, L. A. (1989a). What research says to the educator. Part one: Environmental education and the affective domain. *The Journal of Environmental Education*, *20*(3), 3–9. doi:10.1080/00958964.1989.9942782

Iozzi, L. A. (1989b). What Research Says to the Educator Part Two: Environmental Education and the Affective Domain. *The Journal of Environmental Education*, *20*(4), 6–13. doi:10.1080/00958964.1989.9943033

Jackson, T. (2004). Consuming Paradise? - Unsustainable consumption in cultural and social-psychological context. *International Workshop on Driving Forces of and Barriers to Sustainable Consumption*, 402.

Juvan, E., & Dolnicar, S. (2014). The attitude–behaviour gap in sustainable tourism. *Annals of Tourism Research*, *48*, 76–95. doi:10.1016/j.annals.2014.05.012

Kaiser, F. G., Oerke, B., & Bogner, F. X. (2007). Behavior-based environmental attitude: Development of an instrument for adolescents. *Journal of Environmental Psychology*, *27*(3), 242–251. doi:10.1016/j.jenvp.2007.06.004

Kaiser, F. G., Wölfing, S., & Fuhrer, U. (1999). Environmental attitude and ecological behaviour. *Journal of Environmental Psychology*, *19*(1), 1–19. doi:10.1006/jevp.1998.0107

Kangun, N., Carlson, L., & Grove, S. J. (1991). Environmental advertising claims: A preliminary investigation. *Journal of Public Policy & Marketing*, *10*(2), 47–58.

Katz, D. (1960). The Functional Approach to the Study of Attitudes. *Public Opinion Quarterly*, *24*(2), 163–204. doi:10.1086/266945

Kelman, H. C. (1958). Compliance, identification and internalization: Three process of attitude change. *Conflict Resolution*, *2*(1), 51–60. doi:10.1177/002200275800200106

Kormos, C., & Gifford, R. (2014). The validity of self-report measures of proenvironmental behavior : A meta-analytic review. *Journal of Environmental Psychology*, *40*, 359–371. doi:10.1016/j.jenvp.2014.09.003

Kotler, P. (2011). Reinventing Marketing to Manage the Environmental Imperative. *Journal of Marketing*, *75*(July), 132–135. doi:10.1509/jmkg.75.4.132

Krosnick, J. A. (1988). Attitude importance and attitude change. *Journal of Experimental Social Psychology*, *24*(3), 240–255. doi:10.1016/0022-1031(88)90038-8

Lacasse, K. (2016). Dont be satisfied, identify! Strengthening positive spillover by connecting pro-environmental behaviors to an environmentalist label. *Journal of Environmental Psychology*, *48*, 149–158. doi:10.1016/j.jenvp.2016.09.006

Leonidou, C. N., & Leonidou, L. C. (2011). Research into environmental marketing/management: A bibliographic analysis. *European Journal of Marketing*, *45*(1/2), 68–103. doi:10.1108/03090561111095603

Lillemo, S. C. (2014). Measuring the effect of procrastination and environmental awareness on households energy-saving behaviours: An empirical approach. *Energy Policy*, *66*, 249–256. doi:10.1016/j.enpol.2013.10.077

Ling-yee, L. (1997). Effect of Collectivist Orientation and Ecological Attitude on Actual Environmental Commitment. *Journal of International Consumer Marketing*, *9*(4), 31–53. doi:10.1300/J046v09n04_03

MacDonald, E., Milfont, T., & Gavin, M. (2015). Applying the Elaboration Likelihood Model to increase recall of conservation messages and elaboration by zoo visitors. *Journal of Sustainable Tourism*, *9582*(November), 1–16. doi:10.1080/09669582.2015.1091464

Mainieri, T., Barnett, E. G., Valdero, T. R., Unipan, J. B., & Oskamp, S. (1997). Green Buying: The Influence of Environmental Concern on Consumer Behavior. *The Journal of Social Psychology*, *137*(2), 189–204. doi:10.1080/00224549709595430

Maloney, M. P., & Ward, M. P. (1973). Ecology: Lets Hear from the People An Objective Scale for the Measurement of Ecological Attitudes and Knowledge. *The American Psychologist*, *28*(July), 583–586. doi:10.1037/h0034936

McDonagh, P., & Prothero, A. (2014). Sustainability marketing research: Past, present and future. *Journal of Marketing Management*, *30*(11–12), 1186–1219. doi:10.1080/0267257X.2014.943263

McIntyre, A., & Milfont, T. L. (2016). Who Cares? Measuring Environmental Attitudes. In Research Methods for Environmental Psychology (pp. 93–114). John Wiley & Sons, Inc. doi:10.1002/9781119162124.ch6

McKechnie, G. E. (1977). The Environmental Response Inventory in Application. *Environment and Behavior*, *9*(2), 255–276. doi:10.1177/001391657792006

Milfont, T. L. (2009). The effects of social desirability on self-reported environmental attitudes and ecological behaviour. *The Environmentalist*, *29*(3), 263–269. doi:10.1007/s10669-008-9192-2

Milfont, T. L., & Duckitt, J. (2007). *A brief version of the environmental attitudes inventory*. Unpublished manuscript.

Milfont, T. L., & Duckitt, J. (2010). The environmental attitudes inventory: A valid and reliable measure to assess the structure of environmental attitudes. *Journal of Environmental Psychology*, *30*(1), 80–94. doi:10.1016/j.jenvp.2009.09.001

Milfont, T. L., Sibley, C. G., & Duckitt, J. (2009). Testing the Moderating Role of the Components of Norm Activation on the Relationship Between Values and Environmental Behavior. *Journal of Cross-Cultural Psychology*, *41*(1), 124–131. doi:10.1177/0022022109350506

Newhouse, N. (1990). Implications of Attitude and Behavior Research for Environmental Conservation. *The Journal of Environmental Education*, *22*(1), 26–32. doi:10.1080/00958964.1990.9943043

Nigbur, D., Lyons, E., & Uzzell, D. (2010). Attitudes, norms, identity and environmental behaviour: using an expanded theory of planned behaviour to predict participation in a kerbside recycling programme. *The British Journal of Social Psychology*, *49*(Pt 2), 259–84. http://doi.org/10.1348/014466609X449395

Olson, J. M., & Stone, J. (2005). The influence of behavior on attitudes. In D. Albarracín, B. T. Johnson, & M. P. Zanna (Eds.), *Handbook of attitudes and attitude change* (pp. 223–271). Mahwah, NJ: Erlbaum.

One Green Planet. (n.d.). Retrieved from http://www.onegreenplanet.org/environment/village-in-india-plants-plants-trees-every-time-a-little-girl-is-born/

Oppenheim, A. N. (2000). *Questionnaire design, interviewing and attitude measurement*. Bloomsbury Publishing.

Osterhus, T. L. (1997). Pro-social consumer influence strategies: When and how do they work?. *Journal of Marketing*, *61*(4), 16–29. doi:10.2307/1252084

Petty, R., & Cacioppo, J. (1986). The elaboration likelihood model of persuasion. *Advances in Experimental Social Psychology*, *19*, 123–205. doi:10.1016/S0065-2601(08)60214-2

Petty, R. E., & Briñol, P. (2006). Understanding Social Judgment: Multiple Systems and Processes. *Psychological Inquiry*, *17*(3), 217–223.

Polonsky, M. J. (2011). Transformative green marketing: Impediments and opportunities. *Journal of Business Research*, *64*(12), 1311–1319. doi:10.1016/j.jbusres.2011.01.016

Poortinga, W., Whitmarsh, L., & Suffolk, C. (2013). The introduction of a single-use carrier bag charge in Wales: Attitude change and behavioural spillover effects. *Journal of Environmental Psychology*, *36*, 240–247. doi:10.1016/j.jenvp.2013.09.001

Rabinovich, A., Morton, T., & Postmes, T. (2010). Time perspective and attitude-behaviour consistency in future-oriented behaviours. *The British Journal of Social Psychology*, *49*(1), 69–89. doi:10.1348/014466608X401875 PMID:19224678

Rucker, D. D., & Petty, R. E. (2006). Increasing the Effectiveness of Communications to Consumers: Recommendations Based on Elaboration Likelihood and Attitude Certainty Perspectives. *Journal of Public Policy & Marketing*, *25*(1), 39–52. doi:10.1509/jppm.25.1.39

Russell-Bennett, R., Härtel, C. E. J., & Worthington, S. (2013). Exploring a functional approach to attitudinal brand loyalty. *Australasian Marketing Journal*, *21*(1), 43–51. doi:10.1016/j.ausmj.2012.08.001

Schiffman, L. G., & Kanuk, L. L. (2007). *Consumer Behavior. Its Origins and Strategic Applications. Consumer Behavior* (9th ed.). Upper Saddle River, NJ: Pearson Education Inc.

Schultz, P. W., Shriver, C., Tabanico, J. J., & Khazian, A. M. (2004). Implicit connections with nature. *Journal of Environmental Psychology*, *24*(1), 31–42. doi:10.1016/S0272-4944(03)00022-7

Snyder, M. (1979). Self-monitoring processes. *Advances in Experimental Social Psychology*, *12*, 85–128. doi:10.1016/S0065-2601(08)60260-9

Steel, B. S. (1996). Thinking Globally and Acting Locally? Environmental Attitudes, Behaviour and Activism. *Journal of Environmental Management*, *47*(1), 27–36. doi:10.1006/jema.1996.0033

Steiner, R. L., & Barnhart, R. B. (1972). The development of an instrument to assess environmental attitudes utilizing factor analytic techniques. *Science Education*, *56*(3), 427–432. doi:10.1002/sce.3730560320

Tan, B., & Lau, T. (2011). Green Purchase Behavior: Examining the Influence of Green Environmental Attitude, Perceived Consumer Effectiveness and Specific Green Purchase Attitude. *Australian Journal of Basic and Applied Sciences*, *5*(8), 559–567.

Tanner, C., Kaiser, F. G., & Wofing Kast, S. (2004). Contextual Conditions of Ecological Consumerism: A Food-Purchasing Survey. *Environment and Behavior*, *36*(1), 94–111. doi:10.1177/0013916503251437

Tarrant, M. A., & Green, G. T. (1999). Outdoor recreation and the predictive validity of environmental attitudes. *Leisure Sciences*, *21*(1), 17–30. doi:10.1080/014904099273264

Thøgersen, J. (2009). The Motivational Roots of Norms for Environmentally Responsible Behavior. *Basic and Applied Social Psychology*, *31*(4), 348–362. doi:10.1080/01973530903317144

Thøgersen, J., Haugaard, P., & Olesen, A. (2010). Consumer responses to ecolabels. *European Journal of Marketing*, *44*(11), 1787–1810. doi:10.1108/03090561011079882

Thøgersen, J., & Noblet, C. (2012). Does green consumerism increase the acceptance of wind power? *Energy Policy*, *51*, 854–862. doi:10.1016/j.enpol.2012.09.044

Van Liere, K. D., & Dunlap, R. E. (1978). Moral Norms and Environmental Behavior: An Application of Schwartzs Norm-Activation Model to Yard Burning. *Journal of Applied Social Psychology*, *8*(2), 174–188. doi:10.1111/j.1559-1816.1978.tb00775.x

Wagner, S. A. (2003). *Understanding Green Consumer Behaviour: A Qualitative Cognitive Approach*. Academic Press.

Warner, L. G., & Defleur, M. L. (1969). Attitude as an Interactional Concept: Social Constraint and Social Distance as Intervening Variables Between Attitudes and Action. *American Sociological Review*, *34*(2), 153–169. doi:10.2307/2092174 PMID:5778086

Weigel, R., & Weigel, J. (1978). Environmental Concern: The Development of a Measure. *Environment and Behavior*, *10*(1), 3–15. doi:10.1177/0013916578101001

Wicker, A. W. (1969). Attitudes versus Actions: The Relationship of Verbal and Overt Behavioral Responses to Attitude Objects. *The Journal of Social Issues*, *25*(4), 41–78. doi:10.1111/j.1540-4560.1969.tb00619.x

Wicker, A. W. (1971). An Examination of The Other Variables Explanation of Attitude-Behavior Inconsistency. *Journal of Personality and Social Psychology*, *19*(1), 18–30. doi:10.1037/h0031090

Wittenbrink, B., & Schwarz, N. (2007). *Implicit Measures of Attitudes*. New York: Guilford.

Wolsko, C., Ariceaga, H., & Seiden, J. (2016). Red, White, and Blue Enough to be Green: Effects of Moral Framing on Climate Change Attitudes and Conservation Behaviors. *Journal of Experimental Social Psychology*. 10.1016/j.jesp.2016.02.005

Wu, L. (2012). Exploring the New Ecological Paradigm Scale for Gauging Childrens Environmental Attitudes in China. *The Journal of Environmental Education*, *43*(2), 107–120. doi:10.1080/00958964.2011.616554

KEY TERMS AND DEFINITIONS

Attitude: A disposition to act favorably or unfavorably with regard to particular objects/things/events/people.

Attitude-Behavior Gap: Failure of positive attitudes to translate into behavior.

Behavioral Spillover: The idea that adopting a behavior in one domain will spill over into other domains in a sequential process.

Green Attitude: A disposition to act favorably or unfavorably with regard to the environment.

Individual Variables: The distinctive characteristics of individuals which determine their patterns of behaviour.

Situational Variables: Dimensions that will vary by context.

ENDNOTES

1 A mediator is a variable that helps to explain or provide a causal link between independent and dependent variables (Baron & Kenny, 1986).

2 A moderator is a variable that affects the direction and/or strength of the relation between independent and dependent variables (Baron & Kenny, 1986).

Chapter 5
Green Attitudes and Thinking in The New Green Market:
Using Mathematical Modeling to Satisfy Green Customers' Needs

Nicoleta Valentina Florea
Valahia University of Targoviste, Romania

ABSTRACT

People are concerned by the implications of product consumption on their health, which is why they become followers of a healthy and sustainable lifestyle, using green products and becoming aware of a sustainable environment. To have a viable business and to respond to customers' needs, the organization must have an attractive product that offers utility, value, health, joy, and satisfaction to consumers. This chapter analyses a few approaches regarding the implementation of green marketing policies and the situation of green marketing in the world and in Romania. Green customers' behaviour in choosing a green product (using Markov chains), the impact this could have on the number of specialists and the surfaces used in ecological agriculture on green production (using a regression function) are also anaylsed, and the author developed some measures in order to improve companies' involvement in implementing green activities.

INTRODUCTION

The world is facing enormous challenges like never before. The Earth's systems are under constant pressure due to adverse impacts from human activity: using more energy, creating more waste, and produce more air pollutants (Iannuzzi, 2016, p. xiii). The world is constantly changing and is trying to have a sustainable behaviour and attitude. Global companies have embraced sustainability and are triggering companies to build eco-innovation into their product offerings. Governments have responded by putting pressure on product developers to consider tough new requirements such as removing materials of concern, designing more recyclables, and minimizing packages and facilitating product take-back. These global regulations started out in Europe and have exploded throughout the world, making it very complicating for business to keep up with the ever-changing requirements and be compliant.

DOI: 10.4018/978-1-5225-2912-5.ch005

Global companies must eco-innovate products for the market and its customers from the new green economy—who is favoured by politicians, businesses, and policy-makers (Gasparatos &Willis, 2015, p. 19)—and generate economic growth and protect the environment (Vasile & Nicolo, 2017, p. xiv), bringing changes first in the culture (Danaher, Biggs, & Mark, 2016). They must inform their customers about this thing, because a greener product is useless if no one knows it exists. Appropriate marketing of eco-improved products is a critical aspect of a sustainability program (Iannuzzi, 2016, p. xiv). Degradation of environment led to green economy (Ayuk, Oku, Asubonteng, & Nutakor, 2017, p. 1) and its role is to minimize or to eliminate the factors that affect the environment (Nhamo & Mjimba, 2017, p. 3). This analysis is relatively recent and focuses on the need of reaching the consumer with wide spectrum of environmentally friendly products. A window of opportunity has opened up for those firms willing to take the lead in establishing positions of advantage based on greenness (Sahay, Stough, Sohal, & Goyal, 2006, pp. 96-97). It is clear now that the demands will continue to grow, and firms must respond to this challenge to achieve performance.

Every activity supposes a high cost for every stakeholder; this cost consists of consumption of valuable, rare, and unique resources: human, financial, technological, and especially natural. This affects the stakeholder efficiency and also the environment: use of energy for electronics and houses, driving cars, wearing trend-driven fashion, enjoy a wide range of fresh and processes food (Ha, 2008, p. 9). Every product bought is an investment of resources, and its production can contribute to pollution, climate change, and the destruction of habitats. Ecological footprinting has become a popular way of measuring the environmental impact of a given person's way of life. The interest in environmental, organizational, and individual protection and safety is growing every day. Starting in 1960s, the attention grew for environmental issues (Telesiene & Gross, 2016, p. 1; Kahle & Gurel-Atay, 2015), and for green economy, starting with 2000s (Shmelev, 2016, p. 143), and this has created many changes: policies, regulations, rules, and many studies and research made for a greener lifestyle, greener innovations (Peiry, Ziegler, & Baumgartner, 2016, p. xv), and green marketing. Thus, many studies regarding green marketing policies, green consumers' attitudes, green products characteristics, and green thinking and behaviours have been done.

Green business has grown rapidly and it has important expectations from customers, employees, managers, organizations, politicians, and the world in general. Green is not just about protection of the environment; it is about protection and safety of humans and organizations. Before, in order to develop a sustainable strategy, time to convince management to obtain the benefits was needed, but now major companies are making sustainability a platform for growth and funding significant advertising campaigns. Today's climate encourages sustainability improvements and shows how these can help us in the marketplace. People have moved from looking at environmental issues as a risk management function to something that has enormous potential for innovation and growth. Greener products play a bigger role than ever before and should be a growing part of every company's business model (Iannuzzi, 2016, p. 3).

Concern for the environment first appeared in the 1970s, gained momentum for the next two decades, and in recent years, has exploded onto the world business scene (Iannuzzi, 2016, p. 4). Using a green behaviour, the benefits are for everyone: saving resources consumption (natural, human, money), (re) using of waste, and improving personal and professional life.

This chapter brings to the foreground the literature made in the green marketing field, the behaviours of individuals and organizations, the policies made, especially the measures taken by our specialists at the Romanian level compared to European level. The objective of this chapter is to analyse the green market on the Romanian level by simulating customers' behaviours using probabilities calculations and Markov chains. The model used consists of analysing the impact the number of specialists and the surfaces used could have on ecological agriculture and green production by using a simulation model and Excel program. Using these calculations, we proposed some measures in order to improve companies' involvement in developing green activities and improve behaviours with green consumers.

The chapter starts with the definition of the concept of green marketing, and then with a brief discussion about some new ideas: green strategy, objectives, management and employees, green marketing and its four green Ps, and green consumers. These aspects are important for any manager who wants to use the limited resources to obtain maximum performance; this means that by acting efficiently into a new green economy, they could obtain important benefits for their organizations, for their employees, for customers, for the environment, and for stakeholders by implementing a green perspective. This is a step in showing how profitable a green strategy can be for the people, organization, and for the environment.

Green behavior is broader than IT and more global than the Internet and is about developing innovative solutions to advance our society while enhancing our most valuable asset: Earth (Koester, 2016, p. xxv). The best and most successful entrepreneurs recognize an opportunity and create products, services, and businesses that fill that unmet need. As sustainability evolves and takes into account social considerations, a change is occurring in green marketing: to be sustainable the reduction of energy and the resource consumption is needed, and to be green means to change behaviours (Polonsky, 1999, p. 12).

Along the years, some changes have occurred in the managerial perspective, thus appeared the new green marketing perspective. In the opinion of Saxena (2005, p. 657) these changes that affect the green marketing are goals (customer satisfaction, organizational goals, ecosystem compatibility), decision-making (integrated thinking, boundary spinning, long-term orientation), philosophical basis (biocentric, ecosystem a physical limiting factor, eco-costs must be paid), ecological accountability/responsibility (product risk, global/international, full accounting of ecological costs, PSLC members are mutually accountable, joint public-private sectors are mutually accountable), general tools (use life cycle assessment and environmental audits to minimize the impact, the waste, focus on industrial processes, total quality environmental management, use of strategic alliances to accomplish sustainable goals). As the concern for the environment increased in the past three decades, organizations had in mind two goals (Cox, 2010, p. 335): link corporate goals and behavior to the values of environmental quality and avoid if possible any additional environmental regulations that will affect their business.

To define what green means is difficult (The John Marshal Review of Intellectual Property Law, 2010), thus, in this chapter we offer some ideas about what green marketing is:

- Is a term used to refer to a corporation's attempt to associate its products, services, or identity with environmental values and images (Cox, 2010, p. 335).
- Presents managers with the challenge to turn environmentalism into a source of differential advantage and growth (Sahay, Stough, Sohal, & Goyal, 2006, p. 97).
- Is a strategic process involving stakeholders in order to create meaningful long-term relationships with customers while maintaining, supporting, and changing the natural environment (Ferrell, 2008, p. xix).
- Is an ecological issue that concerns all corporates who are called to maintain the ecological balance through developing biodegradable products and reducing the consumption of natural resources (Saxena, 2005, p. 653).
- Is an initiative that has been started by the business professionals where the focus is on the conservation of natural resources (Tehrani & Sinha, 2011, p. 328).
- Seeks to inform and persuade consumers about environmentally friendly options (including product labeling and advertising) (Cook & Ryan, 2015, p. 350).

- Is friendly with the environment, developing a success marketing strategy (Johnson, 2011).
- Influences and models the consumers' attitudes and life styles (Grant, 2009).
- Is the marketing of products that are presumed to be environmentally safe (AMA).
- Incorporates a broad range of activities (product modification, changes to the production process, packaging changes, promotion changes) which happen in a manner that is less detrimental to the environment (Chandrasejar, 2010, p. 458).

Marinova, Annandale, and Philliomore (2008, p. 257) say that for any organization to have green marketing activities they must achieve some important tasks such as:

- **Targeting:** Developing a new business unit must design promotion targeting on specific segments of consumers.
- **Green Design:** Production process must be integrated environmental principles to remain competitive.
- **Green Positioning:** The firm must promote the product or the firm's environmental performance as being a core component.
- **Marketing Waste:** The firm seeks to improve efficiency and to reduce waste and to identify viable consumers of waste products.
- **Green Alliances:** Developing joint activities that have some environmental linkage: co-branding activities, more substantive programs, work together to deal with environmental issues.

In the opinion of Florea (2011, p. 283), to obtain success in implementing green marketing the organizations must:

- Increase investment in green branding (without spending money and time) and technology,
- Make green innovation,
- Produce green products,
- Procure green materials,
- Make green manufacturing, advertising, sales, distribution,
- Be implicated in green awareness, education, development, evaluation and monitoring of employees,
- Attract, retain, and maintain green employees and customers.

Many people associated green marketing with organic, biodegradable, carbon neutral, energy efficient, natural, environmentally friendly, low carbon technology, sustainable, and renewable energy used (Kaufmann, 2014, p. 134).

Kotler says that to understand green marketing one also must understand some approaches such as (Rajagopal & Castano, 2015, p. 73-74):

- **Product:** Product design should carefully consider the materials and designs used in order to reduce the amount of materials, waste, and the energy required to produce products.
- **Price:** Businesses can offer products that vary in their level of environmental friendliness and price to appeal to consumers with different environmental and price sensitivities.

- **Place:** Production and distribution facilities can be placed closer to the market. More local production and decentralized distribution can be implemented.
- **Promotion:** Businesses should consider shifting promotion from print to online. Labels and advertising should be more specific about ingredients, sourcing, and carbon footprint.

With rising awareness among the mass market consumers about green products and practices, organizations are changing their manufacturing process and marketing strategy. The purchases of the consumers directly affect the manufacture of products and the purchasing decisions of the organization. When the demand of green products increases in the consumer market, the organizations have to produce green products to stay competitive (Tehrani & Sinha, 2011, p. 334).

ISSUES, CONTROVERSIES, CONSEQUENCES

Green is no longer simply a market position, it is a feature (Management Assoc, Info Res, 2014, p. 91) and an important element for the success of every organization, but in this new environment, it must be also important for every leader, manager, supervisor, employee, customer, supplier, producer.

Green business is a complex aspect and analysed by different specialists in the field, and in this chapter, we analysed its importance and its role in the present market by describing some important issues: green strategy, green objectives, green management, green employees, green product, price, place and promotion, green consumers, and green organizations (behavious and attitudes). Understanding these features of the green market all the participants will have a new vision on these relationships, attitudes, behaviours, businesses, and environment – a green one.

Green Strategy

Now is the moment for managers to have a green strategy (Roettgers, 2011, p. 9) and to satisfy the green needs.

From the studies made on this issue are extracted and presented two visions:

- **First Vision:** The firms have developed green strategies based on the 4Rs (reduction, recycling, reusing, and retrieval), which must be reviewed with regard to design and selection of environmentally friendly packaging method (Kirgiz, 2016), and sustainable consumption consists of the 3Rs (reduce, reuse, recycle) view, providing an interesting contrast to traditional environmental views (Kaufmann, 2014, p. 134). Recycling has a positive impact on performance activity of organizations by reducing their costs (OECD, 2015, p. 163).
- **Second Vision:** Based on the benefits the organization could win, it develops a strategy seated on the "4S", going from the green product concept (Kirgiz, 2016):
    - **Satisfaction:** Satisfying the needs of consumers.
    - **Social Acceptability:** Acceptance as a product or a firm being friendly with the environment.
    - **Safety:** Not jeopardizing the health of individuals.
    - **Sensitivity:** Companies are realising their products according to the sensitivity of the environment and its pressures: economical, social, political, environmental.

More and more analyses and studies describe the importance of implementation of green strategies; thus, Ottman defines its seven winning strategies for green marketing (Ottman, 2011, p. 47):

- Understand environmental and social beliefs and values of consumers and other stakeholders and develop a long-term plan to align with them.
- Create new products/services that balance consumers' desires for quality, convenience and affordability with minimal impact on environment.
- Develop brands that offer practical benefits with empowering and engaging consumers in meaningful ways about the important issues that affect their lives.
- Establish credibility for your efforts by communicating your corporate commitment and striving for complete transparency.
- Be proactive to solve emerging environmental and social problems. Go beyond what is expected from stakeholders.
- Think holistically. Underscore community with users and with the broad array of corporate environmental and societal stakeholders.
- Don't quit. Promote responsible product use and disposal practices. Continuously strive for "zero" impact.

Sahay, Stough, Sohal, and Goyal (2006, p. 104) say that a strategy for green marketing must have four pillars:

- **Promoting Reconsumption:** The ability to use and reuse goods in whole or in part.
- **Redirecting Customer Needs:** Redirect them towards consumption and the current marketing tools toward such redirection.
- **Reorienting the Entire Marketing:** Everything from product and packaging may be reoriented, but also through assessing the impact of manufacturing, content, package, label, advertising, distribution, use, and disposal of its products on environment.
- **Reorganizing Business:** Restructure and redesign of many processes and systems within a corporation according to the green vision encouragement.

The central idea of achieving green advantage is consisting of the four Ps (Boston Consulting Group, in Tehrani & Sinha, 2011, p. 333):

- **Planning:** Embedding green targets and green resources into corporate strategy (Corporate Social Responsibility).
- **Process:** Reducing wastes in operations, encouraging others especially their suppliers, partners, partners and customers to operate in green way.
- **Promotion:** Communicating the message of company sustainability to its various stakeholders.
- **Products:** Determining offerings, packaging, and pricing, Innovating the consumers to live a green way, knowing which green benefits will really matter to the consumer.

Green Objectives

In the opinion of Cohen (2011, p. 400), the organization will successfully implement green strategies if they align green objectives to the vision of the organization.

Unhelkar (2016, p. 65) thinks that green objectives are the core objectives of a business undertaking green transformation and these may be:

- Ensuring a synergy between the core business objectives and the accompanying green objectives.
- Length of time for potential application: 3-5 years being ideal.
- Key drivers and dimensions that are impacting the organization.
- Identify the growth potential and means for the returns on green investment.
- Finding the niche where the competitive advantage for the organization lies.
- Identifying the areas for formal green IT audits.
- Development of green HR as a part of the strategy.
- Optimization and integration of supply chain systems.
- Attention to collaborative opportunities.
- Incorporation of government rules and regulations.

Green Management

Sustainability of an organization is given by the capabilities and the skills of the leadership to obtain resources used in order to obtain organizational efficiency. Accepting sustainability in a world where the resources are limited involve responsibility towards future generations. Social responsibility belongs to sustainability, due to resource depletion.

Successful leadership requires a more complex mix of skills than in the past. Managers will need to be able to recognise and understand trends and to navigate roadblocks effectively. They must be capable of developing efficient and innovative responses to key challenges and opportunities since the sustainability concept is relatively new (Polonsky, 1999, p. 9). To make decisions and balancing different domains, the managers are facing challenges such as environmental protection, satisfaction of new green demands of consumers, be socially responsible, and offer environmentally friendly products and services. Eco-efficiency is driven by the vision of making the challenge of sustainability a business opportunity.

Green Employees

Employees involved in the sustainable activities and adopting sustainable development principles will become sustainable human resources (Florea & Florea, 2009). Human factor is known as one of the key factors in obtaining international organization success (Holbeche, 2012). The practitioners recognize the importance of the role played by human resources in achieving the objectives of the organizations (Edstrom & Lorange, 1984).

According to the principle "healthy people in healthy organizations", human resources must play an important role in applicating the sustainable development activities. In the last decade, human resources management has played an important role in solving problems like recruitment and selection, performance evaluation, training, processes based on not-discriminating, ethics, equity, diversity, and sustainable development principles. The efficiency of a human resources system is given not only by human resources behavior, knowledge, and capabilities but by the strategic human resource management ethics and sustainable development. Ulrich (1997) says that human resources professionals must create politics and practices that make the employees more competitive (Burke & Cooper, 2005).

Green Product

Products today need to be green and brands need to be socially responsible (Management Assoc, Info Res, 2014, p. 91). To understand better the green product we offer a few definitions from specialists in the field.

Thus, green products:

- Are the products which don't pollute the world or deplete natural resources and are recyclable or preservable and do not threaten the human or animal health. No product has zero impact on the environment, thus any organization must minimize the use of energy, the waste, and the unnecessary use (Kirgiz, 2016).
- Refer to those products that incorporate the strategies in recycling or with recycled content, reduced packaging or using less toxic materials to reduce the impact on the natural environment (Chen & Chai, 2010, p. 29).
- Need special efforts to be noticed by consumers. Since consumers are unwilling to pay more for green products, they need to be persuaded by marketing communication strategies. Advertising is the most popular way to promote awareness of environmental products and create demand for them (Kaufmann, 2014, p. 134). The first environmental advertisements appeared in the late 1960s, and in 1980s green advertising started to become a popular marketing strategy, and 1990s represented the period of making false messages and give confusion among consumers.
- Are generally regarded as more expensive than other alternatives (Kaufmann, 2014, p. 137).

We also offer and present other features linked by product:

- **Green Packaging**: Packaging is costing, thus the producers, the consumers and the activists search for cost-efficiently (Kirgiz, 2016), environmentally friendly and sustainable packaging, focusing on functionality, cost-effectiveness, and support for long-term human and ecological health. Green packaging means that the containers are not affecting future generations (Mansvelt, 2010, pp. 329-330) and must not go to waste and reduce the use of underground resources, respect human needs in terms of pay, working conditions (Mansvelt, 2010, p. 330). Using biodegradable materials in place of plastic which take centuries to decompose, the decomposition takes few weeks.
- **Green Labels**: (Or eco-labels) help consumers differentiate between green and non-green choices by emphasizing various green attributes (rigor and credibility). Some of green labels are carefully regulated by the government entities or nonprofit groups (Cook & Ryan, 2015, p. 350).

Green Price

Green price takes into consideration the people, planet and profit in a way that takes care of the health of employees and communities and ensures efficient productivity (Patil & Bhakkad, 2014, p. 85). Value can be added by changing ways of thinking, behaviours, and attitudes.

Green price mix aims at delivering superior value and greater benefits to price ratio guided by the objectives of green marketing-oriented companies rather than factors determining sales. For example, high quality standards can be promoted for money can be promoted for low-priced green products (Management Assoc, Info Res, 2014, p. 2001). Green price is an area of concern (Chandrasekar, 2010, p. 462). Most of the products are being sold at a premium which makes it unattractive. Considering that it is not mandatory on the part of the people to buy the green products, the prices in the initial times are definitely higher. Economies of scale can provide a lower price. Green pricing take into consideration the people, planet and profit in a way that takes care of the health of employees and communities and ensures efficient productivity. Value can be added to it by changing its appearance, functionality through customization. Organic vegetables, products are priced at a premium and are now unaffordable to masses. Green products need to be offered through the government's support channel and create more awareness among people. The firm must move beyond simply discussing out of cost price to identify the price of utilizing the good green logistics must be designed to minimize the utilization of resources that will frequently include reverse logistic systems that move packaging and used products back to the firm (Marinova, Annandale, & Phillimore, 2008, p. 257).

Green Place

The distribution of goods generates noise and vibration, causes accidents, and contributes to global warming, being the reason it needs to be analysed in order to decrease its impact on environment (McKinnon, Browne, & Whiteing, 2015, p. 3). Economic theory tells us that higher priced products can and should result in lower levels of customer participation and renewable energy purchases (Wilson & Olson, 2004, p. 25).

Green logistics:

- Is about managing logistics to cut down on transportation emissions (Patil & Bhakkad, 2014, p. 85), thereby in effect aiming at reducing the carbon footprint (Chandrasekar, 2010, p. 462).
- Must be designed to minimize the utilization of resources that will frequently include reverse logistic systems that move packaging and used products back to the firm (Marinova, Annandale, & Phillimore, 2008, p. 257).
- Meaning green transportation and green warehousing consist of pollution prevention, emission control, reduce costs, and fast deliveries (Emmet & Sood, 2010, p. 132).
- Is about saving money and reduces the effects on environment, having economic and social implications (McKinnon, Browne, & Whiteing, 2015, p. 4).

Green logistic is a relatively young but rapidly evolving subject. Without green logistics, a green supply chain will have not ensure success (Emmet & Sood, 2010, p. 132). The supply chains changed, too; now, the green products are found into specialized stores or on the online sites of organizations (Ottman, 2011, p. 8).

Green Promotion

Green promotion involves configuring the tools of promotion, such as advertising, marketing materials in such a manner that will not affect environment (Patil & Bhakkad, 2014, p. 85). Green promotion mix effectively communicates the value in a company's green product offerings in forms of environmental information about green products, processes and practices, and their environmental significance (Management Assoc, Info Res, 2014, p. 2001). Green marketers link green products and green promotion to enable them making effective purchase decisions. Green promotion involves the tools, such as advertising, marketing materials, signage, white papers, web sites, videos and presentations by keeping people, planet, and profits in mind (Chandrasekar, 2010, p. 462). The firm must include information in its promotional activities that mention environmental benefits of products in addition to other activities green logistics must be designed to minimize the utilization of resources that will frequently include reverse logistic systems that move packaging and used products back to the firm (Marinova, Annandale, & Phillimore, 2008, p. 257).

Green advertising has risen since 1980s and is the inclusion of environment-friendly features and attributes as a persuasive selling point. Criticism on green advertising relies on superficial and unsubstantiated claims at best, misleading and deceptive claims at worst. To protect consumers from false green advertising, the official commissions changed theirs guides and advised marketers on making claims about green product attributes that are truthful and nondeceptive (Cook & Ryan, 2015, p. 351).

The awareness of green products is done through green advertising, blogs, and social networking sites. In green advertising, the green ads are created to influence the homemakers to buy and use environmentally friendly products in their day-to-day activities (Tehrani & Sinha, 2011, p. 328). Green awareness among consumers may occur by using blogs. Green blog is a website that hosts daily updates and posts from people around the world solely devoted to environmental actions and discuss only with green community.

The most successful green marketing campaigns must (Iannuzzi, 2016, p. xv):

- Have a credible greener product story,
- Meet customers' greener product demands,
- Appropriately communicate the products greener attributes.

Green Consumers

Green consumers are sincere in their intentions, with a growing commitment to greener lifestyles (Patil & Bhakkad, 2014, p. 85). They are the individuals who are careful to purchase products that are biodegradable, recyclable or otherwise safe for the environment. They are sometimes called "tree huggers" because of their concern for preserving natural resources. Consumers' attitudes towards green products is increasing (Kaufmann, 2014, p. 128). If producers want to attract the green consumers, then they must have to understand the stages of consumer behavior and try to engage the green consumer more with their green products. To create awareness organizations must develop simple messages according to AIDA principle (attention, create interest, desire and action itself), targeting the wanted consumers, use promotion and focus on positive impacts (Tehrani & Sinha, 2011, p. 323).

A green consumer is someone who make purchases on the basis of firms' roles in society, who is concerned about their everyday habits and the impact on the environment, who translate their environmental concern into actively purchasing green products commitment, who is aware of and interested in environmental issues, who usually makes organized petitions, boycotted manufacturers, and actively promotes the preservation of the planet, and who wants a higher quality and is willing to pay a higher price (Universal-Publishers, 2011, p. 46). With the commencement of the new millennium and consumers became center of interest, in 2000s consumers started questioning eating habits, fuel consumption, car usage, energy saving, and recycling methods (Kaufmannn, 2014, p. 129).

The evolution of green marketing made develop a green consumer typology (Kaufmann, 2014, pp. 129-130):

1. Made by Ogilvy and Mather:
    a. **Activists (16%):** Likely to buy green products and services,
    b. **Realists (34%):** Are worried about the environment but skeptical about the green bandwagon,
    c. **Complacents (28%):** See the solution as somebody else's problem,
    d. **Alienated (22%):** Are unware of green issues or see them as transient.
2. Made by US Roper Starch Worldwide:
    a. **True Blue Greens (11%):** Major green purchasers and recyclers,
    b. **Greenback Greens (5%):** Will buy or give green but won't make lifestyle changes,
    c. **Sprouts (33%):** Care but would only spend a little more to buy green,
    d. **Grousers (18%):** Environment is somebody else's problem,
    e. **Basic Browns (31%):** Essentially don't/won't care.

Green Organizations: Behaviours and Attitudes

The environment, the options, the needs, and the consumers' desires, leading implicitly to changing products, vision, mission, behaviours and organization strategies are changing. Thus, a continuous loop of product and organization development according to environment changing and consumers desires is created.

Changes in consumer behaviour (Megicks, Donnelly, & Harrison, 2009, p. 51; Florea, 2014, p. 114):

1. Demographic
    a. Access to sport, due to a rapid aging process of young people and children and exposition to the new technologies and media campaigns,
    b. Changing family relationships (a more reduce size of the houses).
2. Segment Structure
    a. Appearance of monoparental families,
    b. Large number of single persons,
    c. Raising number of working women (70%).
3. Social
    a. Raising the percentage of using the internet (the number of Internet users worldwide increased from 0.36 mil. in 2000 to 19.66 mil. in 2010, to 30.35 mil. in 2014 and to 36.11 mil. in 2016 [www.internetworldstats.com], the growth from 2000 to 2016 being of 900.4%).
    b. Raising the percent for online orders and home deliveries,
    c. Concern for prices raising,
    d. Raising the importance of relationship quality/price/value.

4. Ethical
   a. Equity in buying,
   b. Buyers with conscious,
   c. Cynicism,
   d. Raising degree of knowing and information,
   e. Implication, human and environment rights defence,
   f. Lifestyle,
   g. Knowing the risks of smoking and alcohol consumption,
   h. Adapting of a healthy lifestyle,
   i. Raising the level of green products consumption.
5. Cultural
   a. Minimizing sugar consumption,
   b. Decreasing the consumption of products with a great level of fat,
   c. Participating to sport activities and fitness.
6. Natural Marketing Institute survey (2009) offered some data in which show, that the green concept became a normal phenomenon for customers and organizations, implying (Ottman, 2011, p. 8):
   a. Recycling materials from plastic, glass and paper (65% of consumers),
   b. Affecting less of the environment,
   c. Consuming less of the resources,
   d. Throwing less of toxic substances in the environment,
   e. Using bicycles (31%), and common transportation (subway and by bus), reducing the consumption of fuel (17%),
   f. Making shopping and using recyclables bags (48%),
   g. Prcscrving energy by stopping the light sources (95%) and water (85%),
   h. Producing clothing articles using recyclables or natural fibres, eco-detergents, raising healthy animals, making bio dyings, biological pesticides (84% from organizations).

Many organizations made new products, which are at fashion (Ottman, 2011, p. 2):

- Cell-phones which use solar batteries,
- Cars who use eco-fuels,
- Food and juices who are natural in a great proportion,
- Clothes made form recyclable materials,
- Packaging for cosmetics which are made from recyclable paper,
- Phosphate-free detergents (Soundarapandian, 2007, p. 221),
- Cadmium-free batteries,
- Energy-efficient computers,
- Solar water heating (Koester, 2016, p. 48),
- Water purifying systems,
- Cool roofing installation,
- Green building,
- Green cement.

And many other organizations are implicated in developing new green products in order to satisfy green consumers:

- Toyota Prius had made the first car that has had a green platform from its inception (Iannuzzi, 2016, p. 6).
- Starbucks is well known for their fair and ethical sourcing of coffee and their sustainability program to the visible part of their product (their cup, who ensure that 100% of their cups are reusable or recyclable.
- Kimberly Clarck initiated an advertising campaign about their new, sustainable toilet paper, without the cardboard tube under the brand name "Scott Naturals".
- Toyota presented in 1997 the rechargeable electrical hybrid vehicle and it provides performance and fuel economy today (Kirgiz, 2016).
- Ecologist Dish Washer is one of the best examples of the environmentalist production approach in all products developed by Arcelik A.S.
- AEG Electrolux use a diminished quantity of water, and lowering energy.
- McDonalds is using paper packages in lieu of plastic packages.
- Cell phone producers announce when the battery is fully charged to unplug the charger.
- Olive oil producers like Paksoy are using glass bottles.
- The producers of glass bottles lightening their weight in order to reduce the consumption of natural resources.
- IKEA started charging consumers when they opted for plastic bags and encouraged people to shop using its "Big Blue Bag".
- WalMart unveiled its first recyclable cloth shipping bag (Chandrasekar, 2010, p. 462).

These actions lead to obtaining profit by healthy organizations, growing the level of health of the population, and developing a healthy environment.

Benefits Obtained by Stakeholders by Implementing Green Marketing

Green market is growing, evolving due to new legislation and rules realized for a green consumer, which bring development opportunities for organizations, growing opportunities for sales, increasing opportunities for market shares or in positioning on a new segment and in satisfying new consumers desires. All stakeholders will have to gain, and all will receive benefits.

Using green products conducted to benefits as benefits for organizations and their brand.

Companies all over the world are striving to reduce the impact of products and services on the climate and other environmental parameters. Marketers have taken the cue and are going green (Chandrasekar, 2010, p. 458).

Implementing green marketing, the organizations could obtain the following benefits:

- Increasing the operational costs (Johnson, 2011), including for recruitment and selection (Florea, 2013, p. 56), offering a healthy work environment (Stegaroiu & Florea, 2013, p. 12),
- Reducing the degree of the competition,
- Reducing the consumption of materials.

Companies like Coca Cola (has lightened the silhouette of bottles by reducing the consumption of glass and plastic), Este Lauder (found a new melting method for packaging), Nestle, Procter & Gamble (offers products which are not transported in cardboard boxes), and McDonalds (who is using recycling for packages) are contributing to the reduction of costs and for attracting the attention of customers (Kirgiz, 2016).

Organizations who apply green marketing are:

- Increasing the morale of the employees (Ottman, 2011, p. 2),
- Making a correct functioning of all activities,
- Establishing clear objectives, who may be achieved on long term,
- Encouraging green employees,
- Recruiting of talented green employees,
- Growing the motivation of employees,
- Growing the degree of innovation,
- Growing the level of employees' skills,
- Ensuring price positioning over market value (Kirgiz, 2016),
- Preventing information tangle,
- Protecting against competitive attacks,
- Raising productivity,
- Creating loyalty in the consumer.

Benefits for Consumers

Organizations and retailers came in front of green consumers with new tactics:

- Offer recyclable packaging (for example, McDonalds and Burger King have offered these packaging in order to reduce waste, Coca-Cola pumped syrup directly from tank instead of plastic saving money) (Patil & Bhakkad, 2014, p. 85),
- Offer reduced air pollution for consumers (for example Sheraton Hotels used furniture made of wood harvested from managed forests and all carpets, draperies, paint and wall paper were made free of toxic chemicals; they forbade smoking and use ventilation systems that ensures fresh air in all rooms),
- Retailers use tools to save environment (for example, Wal-Mart runs videos to educate consumers, open ecofriendly stores where rainwater is collected from parking lots, and use solar powered for road signs) (Chandrasekar, 2010, p. 463),
- Safer products (Iannuzzi, 2016, p. 6),
- Saving money through energy efficiency.

Benefits for Society

To be green, organizations must implement (Johnson, 2011) reasonable actions, real advertising campaigns, one research in implementing eco-marketing, green labeling for qualitative products, recyclable measures for energy and paper, maintain sustainable ecological optimism, develop online green marketing opportunities, create eco-niche marketing.

Green market and implication of organizations in green marketing will lead to (Ottman, 2011, p. 3):

- Raising organization reputation,
- Raising the degree of sustainable resources consumption,
- Raising the degree of green consumers satisfaction,
- Raising the life cycle of green markets and green products,
- Raising the quality of environment and the concern for the limited resources.

Benefits for Employees

By implementing green strategies, an organization obtains competitive advantage, satisfies better the needs of all stakeholders and implicitly the employees' needs (Kaufmann, 2014, p. 128). Applying green marketing, the organization may attract better employees. Employees feel betters when they know that they are working for an environmentally responsible company. To not take the wrong actions in green marketing, the firms must find a balance between consumers' expectations, government regulations, science, corporate profit, societal long-term welfare, and motivating employees.

Green isn't just about environment; it also represents a way of seeing the business and its facing challenges through a new lens, which can bring risks but also opportunities. This behaviour has impact on microlevel (save money for all stakeholders, cut wastes, reduce use of resources), and also on macrolevel (impact on jobs, economic development, balance of payments, quality of life, improve infrastructure, reduce financial crises) (Friend, 2009, p. ix).

METHODOLOGY

The main objective of this study is to analyse the actual situation of green marketing in Romania and to:

- Analyse the green customers behaviours using probabilities calculations, MATLAB and Markov chains,
- Analyse the impact could have the number of specialists and the surfaces used in ecological agriculture on green production by using a simulation model and Excel program,
- Propose some measures in order to improve the companies' involvement in developing green activities and improve behaviours with green consumers.

Data Presentation and Analysis

Green Marketing in Romania: Initiatives and Opportunities Through the Prism of Green Agriculture

This chapter will analyse the role of green agriculture, its role being to produce cleaner food in correlation with environment preservation and development. Increase of organic farming areas shows that the first European country has almost 19 percent of total utilised agricultural area (in 2005 having almost 17), while Romania has in 2013 a little over 2 percent (in 2005 having under 1 percent) (ec.europa.eu, EU27, RES 2015, p. 42). The total area under organic farming across Europe increased from 5.9 million ha in

2003 to 9.6 million ha in 2011 (63% growth). It is estimated that organic is the fastest growing sector of the food industry, with global revenues increasing from $18 billion in 2000 to $72 billion in 2013, i.e., a fourfold increase in just over a decade (first 2014 estimate being close to $80 billion).

Romania presents some structural characteristics alike with the other agricultural sectors form other EU member countries, but it is unique through the gap between the category of large farms and the small ones, and also through the prevalence of subsistence/semi-agriculture. In 2010, 93% from Romanian exploitations were in these two categories; from these, three quarters were operating on less than 2 hectares and more than a quarter were managed by farmers with age over 65 years (http://www.madr.ro/docs/agricultura/strategia-agroalimentara-2020-2030.pdf). From economical point of view, 73% from the exploitations offered less than 2,000 Euros, which places almost 2.7 mill. exploitations in economic non-viable farms category (being 5% of the surfaces cultivated from EU). Thus, a significant percent of these surfaces from Romania is linked by the agriculture sub-optimal activities, who stay as a barrier in achieving its high potential.

Tough economical conditions after the crisis from 2009 made that 120,000 farms to become farms under 2,000 Euros category (comparing to 2007) and they caused a step back from the condition who limited their percent to two thirds from the total.

A positive aspect is this field is that demographic transition from Romanian agriculture brought positive transformations (http://www.madr.ro/docs/agricultura/strategia-agroalimentara-2020-2030.pdf):

- Between 2005-2010, the number of farms decreased with 400,000 farms,
- The number of young farm managers increased in 2010 (23% of the farmers have less than 45 years comparing with only 17% in 2005).
- Young farm managers contributed more and more to standard agricultural production: 29% in 2010, comparing to just 18% in 2005.
- The average size of the farms grew up modestly (from 3.11 ha in 2002 ha to 3.45 ha in 2010 and to 3.6 ha in 2013), due to the diminishing phenomenon of the used agricultural surfaces.
- The implementation of a life rent schema, favoured a transfer rather through lease (247 thousand ha) then through selling (82 thousand ha), having also a positive role.

The same source (The Romanian Ministry of Agriculture), says that the problems of Romanian agriculture is facing are due to the following factors (www.madr.ro):

- Reluctance to land consolidation,
- Agriculture is still a less attractive field for young entrepreneurs,
- The incomes are too reduced,
- The import of food is growing,
- Agricultural machines are insufficient and under the European standards,
- The agro-food chains are inefficient,
- The access to credits for agricultural investments are deficit areas,
- The conditions for raising animals are poor,
- The promotion of Romanian agricultural and food products is poor,
- A national brand for products is missing,
- The capacity for storage is insufficient.

To show a view regarding the current state of some indicators in this study are presented some surveys results:

- The Resource Efficiency Scoreboard (RES) (EU28, 2015) showed that the most reduces levels of resource productivity/indicator are registered in eastern European countries (Romania, Bulgaria). The same report analyses the recycling rates in 2013; more European countries (EU27) are over 40 percent, Romania being the only one under 10 percent (actually being under 5 percent) (ec.europa.eu/RES, 2015, p. 31).
- Eco-innovation index (ec.europa.eu/RES, 2015, p. 33) shows that Romania obtained a little over 300 (being on the 21th place from 28 European countries), the first having an index of over 700.
- Flash Eurobarometer 367 (25568 respondents) made in 2015 showed that a very high proportion of citizens buy environmentally-friendly products so are classified into the two maintenance categories (80%). More than half of respondents are classified as occasional maintenance (54%) and another quarter as regular maintenance (26%). In total, 15% of EU citizens do not buy environmentally-friendly products (ec.europa.eu/public_opinion /flash/fl_367_sum_en.pdf).

The organic products on the Romanian market are quite reduced. The most food, among canned vegetables, fruits, certain breads, are brought form abroad. The total selling of bio Romanian products are representing less than 1% from the retail market, toward the European average of 5-6% (http://www.infomina.ro). In October 2007, Romania had a production from ecologic agriculture of 7457 thousand tones (only for cereals), and the total surface used for this type of agriculture is of 190129 ha, toward 31.4 mil. ha at global level. The consumption for ecologic products is of 1% against other countries as Germany (5%), England and Austria (3%). Romania is one of the East EU members who grew up at bio production, next to the Czech Republic and Poland, but is important to grow to processing and selling too (http://www.ziare.com). Romania has exported in 2014 agri-food products with 6.1% more than previous year, while the imports have grown in a slower pace, surpassing with 2.6% the value obtained in 2013 (http://www.madr.ro/schimburi-comerciale-cu-produse-agroalimentare.html).

The analyses, surveys, and the trends show that in the next years the green market from Romania has a great potential of development in the European organic industry. The most important issues being for Romanian green market that there are no companies for processing the ecological products, thus the raw materials being exported, and they are coming back (processed, labeled, transported) a few times more expensive.

Green Marketing Evolution in Romania Using Simulation Techniques

To understand better the evolution of green marketing in Romania based on the analyses presented above and past data registered officially at European level are implement some models and are used some simulation techniques.

Case 1: Analysing the Actual Situation of Green Marketing in Romania and Implementing Mathematical Calculation to Measure the Impact of Different Factors on Green Marketing Efficiency

This research is made departing from a survey made by Flash Eurobarometer 367 (2013, pp. 8, 10) on 28 countries from Europe:

- In the first case (Table 1) are extracted from Question 5 data just for four countries from South-East of Europe (Romania, Croatia, Bulgaria, and Hungary, noted as RO, HR, BG, and HU) regarding the fact that choosing a labelled green product will cause less damage to the environment.
- In the second case are extracted from Question 2 and calculations regarding the decisions of respondents on what aspects are important when they are buying a product: the quality, the price, the impact on the environment and the brand (name) of the product.

Departing from these data it is seen in tables data extracted from questions Q2 and Q5, developing some calculations using Markov chains.

And then it is build a matrix formed by four lines and four columns, according to the registered data.

$$\begin{pmatrix} 0.15 & 0.31 & 0.45 & 0.09 \\ 0.16 & 0.52 & 0.24 & 0.08 \\ 0.17 & 0.53 & 0.21 & 0.09 \\ 0.22 & 0.44 & 0.27 & 0.07 \end{pmatrix} \quad (1)$$

It is also taken into account the fact that when the respondents are deciding on what aspects are important when are buying a product; they are taking into account the quality, the price, the impact on the environment and the brand (name) of the product.

Making the calculation, according to the registered data at Q2 presented in Table 2, the following scores are obtained:

Below are calculated the scores obtaining:

- For quality:

$$q = (65\times5+32\times4+2\times3+1\times2+1\times1)\div100 = 4.61 \quad (2)$$

Table 1. Data regarding the confidence that labelled green products cause less damage to the environment

Country/Scale	5	4	3	2 and 1	Total
RO	15	31	45	9	100
HR	16	52	24	8	100
BG	17	53	21	9	100
HU	22	44	27	7	100

Source: data extracted from Flash Eurobarometer 367, 2013, Q5, p. 8.

- For price:

$$p = (40 \times 5 + 47 \times 4 + 10 \times 3 + 2 \times 2 + 1 \times 1) \div 100 = 4.23 \quad (3)$$

- For environment:

$$e = (38 \times 5 + 46 \times 4 + 12 \times 3 + 3 \times 2 + 1 \times 1) \div 100 = 4.17 \quad (4)$$

- For brand:

$$b = (14 \times 5 + 32 \times 4 + 36 \times 3 + 17 \times 2 + 1 \times 1) \div 100 = 3.41 \quad (5)$$

To transform into a stochastic matrix, are made the summing up of the scores, which is 16.42, and then is divided each score to this sum, obtaining the following elements of the line vector:

$$T_0 = \begin{pmatrix} 0.28 & 0.26 & 0.25 & 0.21 \end{pmatrix} \quad (6)$$

It is considered that T_0 is the actual moment, thus it will be used the simulation (using Markov chains) of the actual values for the next three years till 2019.

$$\begin{pmatrix} 0.15 & 0.31 & 0.45 & 0.09 \\ 0.16 & 0.52 & 0.24 & 0.08 \\ 0.17 & 0.53 & 0.21 & 0.09 \\ 0.22 & 0.44 & 0.27 & 0.07 \end{pmatrix} \times \begin{pmatrix} 0.28 & 0.26 & 0.25 & 0.21 \end{pmatrix} \quad (7)$$

Table 2. Factors important when choosing a green product

Analysed Factor/Scale	5 (Very Important)	4 (Fairly Important)	3 (Not Very Important)	2 (Not at All Important)	1 (Don't Know)
Quality	65	32	2	1	1
Price	40	47	10	2	1
Environment	38	46	12	3	1
Brand	14	32	36	17	1

Source: data extracted from Flash Eurobarometer 367, 2013, Q2, p. 10.

Table 3. The trend of QPEB for the next three years

Analysed Elements/T	T_0	T_1	T_2	T_3
Quality	0,28	0,17	0,17	0,17
Price	0,26	0,45	0,48	0,48
Environment	0,25	0,30	0,27	0,27
Brand	0,21	0,08	0,08	0,08

Using MATLAB, are obtained the following results for quality, price, environment and brand for green products (noted as QPEB). It is observed that these results tend to stabilize and are presented in Table 3.

It is observed that in the next three predicted years, the quality is continuing to decline slightly starting from 0.28 and reaching in 2019 at 0.17 being on the third place in a predicted future; the price is continuing to grow in the next year, and then is stabilizing reaching to 0.48; the value for environment is rising from 0.25 to 0.30 in the next year, and then is stabilizing at 0.27; the brand diminish its values from 0.21 in T0 to 0.08 in the next three years, stabilizing itself.

The conclusion of this new matrix, where the respondents from the four analysed South-Eastern European, including Romania, is that the analysed countries will change their vision regarding the four analysed elements of a green product: if in T0 the most important element was the quality in choosing a green product, now remain the second (from 0.28 to 0.17), the price which was on the second preferred element in the predicted future is the first (from 0.26 to 0.48), the environment is gaining preference from 0.25 (the third place) to 0.27 (the second place), and the brand is losing in the predicted future reaching from 0.21 in T0 to 0.008 in T3 being on the last place, far from the other values.

Thus, in the present, a buyer prefers a green product after the quality, the price, the environment, and the brand; into a simulated future the buyers will choose a green product after the price (increasing to 0.48 from 0.28), the environment (increasing from 0.25 to 0.27), the quality (decreasing from 0.28 to 0.17), and then the brand (decreasing from 0.21 to 0.08). So, the future buyer is choosing a green product depending on the price and its impact on the environment, choosing to be aware of the consequences on the health of the environment and the consumption of the resources.

Case 2: Analysing the Green Market From Romania and the Impact It Could Have on the Number of Specialists and the Surfaces Used in Ecological Agriculture on Green Production in Romania Using a Simulation Model and Excel Program

This analysis started from data presented in Table 4, in which are presented three variables, one chosen as being dependent and two independent, and the goal is to see if there is a relationship between them. For this it is applicated the regression function and Excel calculation.

Table 4. Data regarding the ecological Romanian production and the two analysed variables

Years	Production in Ecologic Agriculture in Romania: Cereals (Thousand Tones) (Y)	Total Surface used in Ecologic Agriculture (Ha) (X1)	Nb of Operators Certified in Ecologic Agriculture (X2)
2007	7457	190129	3834
2008	16288	221410	4191
2009	14430	202058	3673
2010	16226	182706	3155
2011	13113	229946	9703
2012	12288	288261	15544
2013	20198	301148	15194
2014	20903	289252	14470

Sursa: www.madr.ro, www.maap.ro.

Pearson correlation coefficient (Table 5) is equal to 0.9779. The coefficient is positive, so the correlation between variables is direct and very strong (close to 1).

The R value (the value of the correlation coefficient) indicates whether or not there is correlation between the dependent variable (Y) and the independent variable (X1 and X2). The R value is equal to 0.9779, so it can be said that there is a very close, positive, and direct connection between the analysed variables.

R^2 means that 95.63% of the variance in the dependent variable Y is predicted or explained by the independent variables X_1 and X_2.

There are obtained in the Table 6 the values of the regression parameters and the values of a and b (Unstandardized Coefficients) (a is 0.0753 and b is – 0.3134).

Lower 95%, Upper 95% – upper and lower limits of the confidence interval for the parameter. The limits for 0.05 are calculated automatically, regardless of the initialization procedure Regression. It could be said that the linear model parameters are within the following ranges: a between 0.0377 and 0.1128 and b between -1.206 and 0.5793.

The estimated model of regression is:

$$y = 0.0753 \times x_1 - 0.3134 \times x_2 \tag{8}$$

From the formula founded by the computer simulation model results that X1 and X2 (the two analyzed variables) are very important factors in the evolution of Y (production in ecologic agriculture). To increase with a monetary unit the X2 will get an increase of 0.0753 monetary units of X1 and an increase with a monetary unit of X1 will get a decrease of 0.3134 monetary units of X2. It must be noted that the value of free term is zero allowing us to conclude that the factors were not taken into account in the model construction have not any material impact on the evolution of the Y.

Correlation table (Table 7) shows the values of correlation coefficients between the variables "total surface" and "nb. of operators".

Table 5. Model summary output

Regression Statistics	Multiple R	R Square	Adjusted R Square	Standard Error	Observations
Values obtained	0.9779	0.9563	0.7824	3776.49	8

Table 6. The parametres of the regression

The Parametres	Unstandardized Coefficients	Standard Errors	T Stat	Sig.	Lower 95%	Upper 95%
Intercept	0	#N/A	#N/A	#N/A	#N/A	#N/A
a (total surface)	0.0753	0.0153	4.9	0.002	0.0377	0.1128
b (nb. of operators)	-0.3134	0.3648	-0.859	0.42	-1.206	0.5793

Table 7. Correlations

	Total Surface	Nb. of Operators
Total surface Pearson correlation Sig. (2-tailed)	1.000	0.9979 0,.42
Nb. of operators Pearson correlation Sig. (2-tailed)	0.9779 0.42	1.000

The T test is applied to check whether there is a significant correlation between the two variables. The Sig Value corresponding of T test is equal with 0,42 so, it can be concluded that it has achieved significant correlation (correlation is significant at the 0.01 level [2-tailed]).

RESULTS, DISCUSSIONS, AND RECOMMENDATIONS

This study aims to highlight the importance of green market in the vision of the green organizations by analysing some important concepts as green strategies, green management and objectives, the four green Ps, green consumers, and green organizations.

The main objectives of this study were to analyse the actual situation of green marketing in Romania by using:

- Probabilities calculations and Markov chains,
- a simulation model (regression function) and Excel program,
- Propose some measures in order to improve the companies' involvement in developing green activities and improve behaviours with green consumers.

Our study reflected that applying a model of linear regression function, one of the most complex procedures of processing and statistical analysis package from Excel, enables statistical and economic analysis, but also builds the necessary fit to the linear model. It was found that by implementing a computer-based simulation model, the two analyzed factors are very important factors in the evolution of the first variable.

After analysing some important green issues in this chapter, some research hypothesis were launched with some recommendations which may help organizations to overcome barriers that stand in front of green consumption and green behaviors/attitudes.

First, this study offers the idea that organizations that are challenged to have a good involvement and a healthy thinking may offer to the new consumers the desired product/service according to the principle of determining the factors which can influence the choosing process.

Thus, we proposed the following recommendations:

1. Proposing a plan and some measures to improve the companies' involvement in developing green activities and improve behaviours with green consumers.

Starting from the idea that analysing customers' needs and making a segmentation of these customers, the organizations could satisfy them by implementing a plan necessary for improving green implementation:

To have a strong and clear green plan the organizations must in have in mind the main objectives of the green marketing:

- **Developing New Green Standards**:
    - Creating differentiations: products, brand and organization image which is greener than the alternatives,
    - Launching new green products.
- **Developing New Green Responsibilities**:
    - The way of using the products of consumers to be greener,
    - The campaigns for encouragement of consuming green and healthy products.
- **Sustaining the Greenest Innovations**:
    - Creating new lifestyles,
    - Creating new business models, normal and acceptable (obtaining green profit).

Thus, we have developed a new marketing style, the niche marketing or the green marketing, which has success with the fulfilment of the following conditions:

- Raising the degree of education of the population in order to understand the impact of the consumption of resources on environment,
- Raising the level of culture,
- Raising the degree of changing the lifestyle,
- Raising the degree of choosing the attractive alternatives: the green alternatives,
- Developing new practices which may substitute the old practices which were based on consumerism and affecting the environment.
    2. Making an analysis of the consumers based on segmentation, analysing the internal and the external factors which may influence the green behaviour of consumers.

To improve the consumption of green products and to make aware the consumers about the firm products, the firm must make a segmentation based on some important factors, internal and external. This segmentation consists in determining the internal and the external factors that influence the consumption of green products:

Internal Factors

- **Contextual Factors:** Availability on shelf, location, the moment of consumption, accessibility, consumption opportunity, the way of use, perceived quality, perceived characteristics (flavor, taste, flavor, nutritional value, texture), past experience with the product/brand/manufacturer.
- **Behavioral Factors:** Searched advantages, the importance given to the shopping, attitude and the status of the user, the frequency of the using/shipping, the loyalty, \the increasing level of consumer needs, the size of the shopping.
- **Physiological Factors:** Health state, metabolism, allergies, genetic factors, fashion, comfort, healing sensation/capacity.
- **Socio-Cultural Factors:** Consumer preference, religion, habits, norms, traditions, lifestyle, personality, personal opinion, and values.

External Factors

- **Technological Factors:** The degree of innovation, R&D, use optimization of resources through human resources quality development.
- **Economic Factors:** Income, price influence, suppliers' attitudes, nature of the competitors, rapid obtaining of profit, continuity of transactions, decision quality in risk conditions, the rapid exchange of goods/services for consumer need satisfaction.
- **Demographic Factors:** Level of education, sex, age, size of the family/house, life cycle of the family, nationality, race, marital status, profession,
- **Political Factors:** Economic politics, legislation, rules, regulations, stability/force of the politic parties.

CONCLUSION AND FUTURE WORK DIRECTIONS

Now, people are living in a new world where they are aware of the impact of their actions on environmental health and also of the consumption of those products that have impact on their health. The goal of this chapter is to implicate all the participants on the market in implementing green issues in business practice to make a difference, so our society will continue to develop in harmony with the nature.

This study presents the role of green issues in our daily lives, such as green strategies, green objectives, green management, green employees, green product, price, place and promotion, green consumers and green organizations. It is known that is difficult for organizations to establish policies and strategies at corporate level who must be in accordance with environmental issues, due to the costs involved (necessary for modifying the marketing process, the way of production, the way of thinking or the attitudes). But trying is not costly, and the results are on long-term, especially for the future generations. It is known from schools that resistance to change is the most important barrier in obtaining performance, so accepting that healthy products, healthy organizations, healthy employees, healthy thinking and attitudes means healthy consumers and environment is the beginning. Changing must start with us, now, and green marketing strategies must be perceived by organizations as a competitive tool that will bring performance on long-term. Everything the organizations and people are doing in present will leave a footprint on the future; thus, they might be responsible of the present actions by implicating in the three Rs actions: reducing, recycling, and reusing.

The strength of this chapter is consisting in using simulation methods (Markov chains, regression function, and IT programs such as Excel and MATLAB) in order to offer for managers and organizations a simple and cost-effective way of analysing the future impact of their actions and decisions on performance and environment, and also on resources consumption. Using such simulation techniques, the managers can see the future trends of green behavior as being a future opportunity for organizations and environment, and the organizations may predict future problems and may solve them in time and with minimum effort.

The limitations of this chapter are the not so very large analyzed period and the analysed data captured in just one moment in time, but this study could offer new opportunities for further research, and a new necessity to investigate the importance of using mathematical simulation in order to determine the future green performance.

As future work directions, it is proposed to use in any field, not only in green marketing, due to their advantages for future prediction and reduced costs. So, this will lead to a green future that will surely consist of developing clear regulations, offering the necessary equipment to transform, produce, and sell green products, and change step-by-step the thinking and the attitudes regarding the behaviour towards the environment.

REFERENCES

Ayuk, E., Oku, E., Asubonteng, K., & Nutakor, P. (2017). *Promoting Green Economy: Implications for Natural Resources Development, Food Security and Poverty Reduction in Africa*. United Nations University Institute for Natural Resources in Africa.

Burke, R. J., & Cooper, C. L. (2005). *Reinventing human resources management:Challenges and new directions*. Routledge.

Chandrasekar, R. S. (2010). *Marketing Management. Text and cases, India*. McGraw Hill.

Chen, T. B., & Chai, L. T. (2010). Attitude towards the Environment and Green Products: Consumers' Perspective. *Management Science and Engineering*, *4*(2), 27–39.

Cohen, N. (2011). *Green business: and A-to-Z guide*. Sage Pub. doi:10.4135/9781412973793

Cook, D. T., & Ryan, J. M. (2015). *The Wiley Blackwell encyclopedia of consumption and consumer*. John Wiley & Sons. doi:10.1002/9781118989463

Cox, R. (2010). *Environmental communication and the public sphere*. Sage.

Danaher, K., Biggs, S., & Mark, J. (2016). *Building the Green Economy: Success Stories from the Grassroots*. Routledge.

Edstrom, A., & Lorange, P. (1984). Matching strategy and HR in multinational corporation. Journal of International Business Studies.

Emmet, S., & Sood, V. (2010). *Green supply chains: an action manifesto*. John Wiley & Sons.

Ferrell, W. P. (2008). *Marketing*. Cengage Learning.

Florea, N. V. (2011). Using branding to attract, recruit and retain talented staff. *Marketing & Management Review*, *9*(2), 283–297.

Florea, N.V. (2013). *Auditul resurselor umane*. Bucuresti, Romania: C. H. Beck.

Florea, N.V. (2014). *Planul de marketing*. Bucuresti, Romania: C. H. Beck.

Florea, N. V., & Florea, D. (2009). *Integrating sustainable development in human resources recruitment and employment processes. In Conferinta Dezvoltarea Durabila şi energii regenerabile, Univ* (pp. 260–264). Spiru Haret.

Friend, G. (2009). *The truth about green business*. Que Publishing.

Gasparatos, A., & Willis, K. (2015). *Biodiversity in the green economy*. Routledge.

Grant, J. (2009). *The green marketing manifesto*. West Sussex, UK: John Wiley & Sons.

Ha, T. (2008). *The Australian green consumer guide: choosing products for a healthier home,planet and bank balance*. UNSW.

Holbeche, L. (2012). *Aligning human resources and business strategy*. Butterworth-Heinemann.

Iannuzzi, A. (2016). *Greener products: the making and marketing of sustainable brands*. CRC Press.

Johnson, F. K. (2011). *Green marketing concepts. How to cash in with ecological Niche marketing*. PLR Rights Marketing.

Kahle, L., & Gurel-Atay, E. (2015). *Communicating sustainabilityfor the green economy*. Routledge.

Kaufmann, H. R. (2014). *Hanbook of reserach an consumerism in business and marketing: concepts and practices*. IGI Global. doi:10.4018/978-1-4666-5880-6

Kirgiz, A. (2016). *Green marketing: a case study of the sub-industry in Turkey*. Springer.

Koester, E. (2016). *Green entrepreneur handbook: the guide to building and growing a green and clean business*. CRC Press.

Management Assoc. Info Ress. (2014). Marketing and consumer behavior: Concepts, methodologies, tools, and applications. IGI Global

Mansvelt, J. (2010). *Green consumerism: an A-to-Z guide*. London, UK: Sage Pub.

Marinova, D., Annandale, D., & Phillimore, J. (2008). *The international handbook on environmental technology management*. Edward Elgar Oublishing.

McKinnon, A., Browne, M., & Whiteing, A. (2015). *Green logistics: improving the environmental sustainability of logistics*. London, UK: Kogan Page Pub.

Megicks, P., Donnelly, R., & Harrison, G. (2009). *The marketing planning process*. Butterworth-Heinemann.

Nhamo, G., & Mjimba, V. (2017). *Sustainability, climate change and the green economy*. Africa Institute of South Africa.

OECD. (2015). *OECD Green Growth Studies Material Resources, Productivity and the Environment*. Paris: OECD Publishing.

Ottman, J. A. (2011). *The new rules of green marketing. Strategies, tools, and inspiration for sustainable branding*. Berrett-Koehler Pub.Inc.

Patil, D. B., & Bhakkad, D. D. (2014). *Redifining management practices and marketing in modern age*. Atharva Pub.

Peiry, K., Ziegler, A., & Baumgartner, J. (2016). *Waste managementand the green economy*. Edward Elgar Pub. doi:10.4337/9781783473816

Polonsky, M. J. (1999). *Greener marketing: a responsible approach to business*. Greenleaf Pub.

Rajagopal & Castano, R. (2015). Understanding consumer behavior and consumption experience. IGI Global.

Roettgers, F. (2011). *Going green together: how to align employees with green strategies*. Environmental Pioneers.

Sahay, B. S., Stough, R. R., Sohal, A., & Goyal, S. (2006). *Green business*. Allied Publishers.

Saxena, R. (2005). *Marketing management*. New Delhi, India: Tata McGraw-Hill Education.

Shmelev, S. (2016). *Green economy reader*. Springer.

Stegaroiu, I., & Florea, N.V. (2013). *Tehnici si instrumente de recrutare si selectie*. C. H. Beck.

Tehrani, N., & Sinha, S. (2011). *Understanding green business*. Bloomington, IN: AuthorHouse.

The John Marshal Review of Intellectual Law. (2010). *The intersection of intellectual property law and the green movement: RPL's Green Issue 2010*. Quid Pro Books.

Unhelkar, B. (2016). *Green IT strategies and applications: using environmental intelligence*. CRC Press.

Universal-Publishers. (2011). *International Journal of Economic and Political Integration, 1*(1).

Vasile, A., & Nicolo, D. (2017). *Sustainable entrepreneurship and investments in the green economy*. IGI Global. doi:10.4018/978-1-5225-2075-7

Wilson, R., & Olson, S. (2004). *Utility green pricing programs: a statistical analysis of program effectiveness*. Diane Pub. Retrieved from http://www.wall-street.ro/articol/Economie/69736/Scadere-de-15-pentru-productia-de-produse-ecologice-in-2009.html

KEY TERMS AND DEFINITIONS

Green Economy: An economy responsible and sustainable who comes with healthy regulations and policies for every stakeholder.

Green Employees: Are those employees who act according to those principles based on social responsibility, sustainable development, ethics, equity and not-discrimination.

Green Marketing: Is an activity who must concern every employee and organization in order to offer an opportunity of development and future performance for future generations.

Green Product: An eco-friendly product who does not affect consumers and environment.

Green Strategy: A planning activity and establishing objectives who are made to be safety and to satisfy stakeholders and environment.

Chapter 6
Driving Green Marketing in a Developing Country:
Reducing the Attitude-Behaviour Gap

Shweta Pandey
International Management Institute, India

Deepak Chawla
International Management Institute, India

ABSTRACT

Despite having a pro-environment attitude, customers may not consistently reflect the same in their behaviour. This chapter explores the applicability of the social-normalisation theory to reduce the attitude-behaviour gap of customers for driving green behaviour in India. The theory argues that green behaviour can be driven by positioning green activities as normal. The chapter details the findings of an empirical study done across 496 customers pan India. Analysis done based on various techniques (Heat maps, factor analysis and regression) indicates that while a broader consensus existed among customers about what is green, the conceptions of normality of the activities vary thereby, corroborating the existence of an attitude-behaviour gap. Results shows that perceptions of what is normal have a significantly higher impact than perceptions of what is green and hence, social-normalisation theory can be applied to drive green marketing in developing countries like India.

INTRODUCTION

Rapid pace of growth and burgeoning population has bought unmindful and irresponsible consumerism leading to several environmental challenges for emerging economies in Asia (Zhao and Schroeder, 2010; Lee, 2009). Asian markets like India and China face growing challenges like resource scarcity, rising consumption levels and fast pace of urbanisation resulting in sustainability issues for both consumers and companies (Accenture and UN Global Compact, 2013). As per World Bank estimates, the cost of environmental degradation from various sources (urban air pollution; inadequate water supply, poor

DOI: 10.4018/978-1-5225-2912-5.ch006

sanitation, hygiene; indoor air pollution, natural resource damage) in India was USD 80 billion or 5.7% of GDP in 2009 (The World Bank, 2013). In a survey conducted across 178 countries by World Bank, India ranked 155th overall and almost last in the level of air pollution exposure (The World Bank, 2014). Greendex 2008 survey findings show that consumer choices have a big role in ensuring sustainable pro-environment practices (phys.org, 2008). For example, customer choices regarding lowering household energy consumption by using energy-efficient devices, reduction of fuel consumption by walking or using public transport instead of individual transport, use of organic or lesser polluting products can impact environment positively. Individuals need to accept pro-environmental products which may impact their lifestyles and beliefs. Thus, many of the environmental issues are embedded in human behaviour and therefore, need to be managed by changing the relevant behaviour (Vlek and Steg, 2009).

While there is an increase in environmental issues in emerging Asian markets like India, yet researchers find a higher proclivity towards the future purchase of sustainable products by customers of these emerging markets (Khare, 2015; Kumar and Ghodeswar, 2015; Accenture and UN Global Compact, 2013). Further, the rising economic and social costs of environmental pollution resulting in business sustenance issues, stricter enforcement of environmental regulations, higher awareness and penchant for customers to adopt pro-environmental practices and have led Indian firms to explore green marketing for sustainable growth (Saxena and Khandelwal, 2012; Mishra and Sharma, 2010; Jain and Kaur, 2004).

Green marketing is the marketing of pro-environment products or products that are presumed to be environmentally preferable (Barbarossa and Pastore, 2015). Green marketing can create value for corporates as it yields a triple bottom-line of social, environmental and financial performance for the firms (Elkington, 1997). It can help companies manage risk of operational disruptions like resource scarcity and climate-change. It can reduce operating costs through better internal resource management like minimisation of energy consumption and higher carbon credits, which can result in improved value propositions for products. Driving green appeal can further mitigate risks, capture opportunities from regulation (Barbarossa and Pastore, 2015) and can drive higher brand equity (Trott and Sople, 2016). Additionally, it can drive sustainable competitive advantage, for example; the 3Ps (polluting prevention pays) program of 3M has been recognised as a significant step in corporate environmental practices.

Indian companies have also been making progressive efforts towards green marketing. Tata Motors has taken steps for introducing alternate fuel based cars like hybrid-electric cars, CNG based Nano and the greener Indigo; ITC is promoting green hotels; Samsung India and LG are building eco-friendly and energy-efficient electronics, etc. (Trott and Sople, 2016; Mishra and Sharma, 2010). Similarly, durable, non-durable and service industries are pursuing green marketing in India to ensure sustainable growth (Saxena and Khandewal, 2012).

RESEARCH CONTEXT: THE ATTITUDE-BEHAVIOUR GAP

Numerous studies done across the world as well as in India indicate that despite having a pro-environment attitude, customers do not consistently reflect the same in their behaviour (Carrington, et al., 2014; Rettie et al., 2014; Black, 2010; Gupta and Ogden, 2009). Similarly, while several pro-environmental products have been introduced to the market by the Indian companies, green product's adoption has often met with more verbal appreciation from stakeholders and customers than actual purchase (Khare, 2015). Nittala (2014) finds that while educated university teachers in India are aware of impact of pro-environment consumption yet their beliefs do not necessarily result in purchase of green products. She states that product recycling has a positive influence while comfort, eco-labelling, and lack of information has a negative influence on the willingness of teachers to purchase green products. Manaktola and Jauhari(2007) find that while Indian consumers show positive attitude towards hotels practising green marketing, they are not willing to pay additional money for the same. Jain and Kaur (2004) find that Indians (sample limited to Delhi) have high willingness towards pro-environment behaviour but feel that individual contribution may not do much towards the cause and therefore, their pro-environment behaviour is confined to themselves. Thus, the attitude-behaviour gap precludes adoption of green practices in India. Marketers need to understand how to bridge this attitude-behaviour gap to ensure sustainability of green marketing.

Several approaches have been explored to address the attitude-behaviour gap. Moser (2015) suggests that green marketing needs a complete blend of economic, technological and cultural adoption to manage the attitude-behaviour gap. Ottman et al. (2006) critique the myopic sense of green marketers and state that marketers focus on the positioning of green products as environmental friendly and do not focus on customer satisfaction resulting in consumers not purchasing green products. Other researcher's highlight issues like high pricing and scarce availability (Eckhardt et al., 2010; Finisterra do Paco and Raposo, 2010; Bhate, 2001), lack of consumer knowledge or information (Ottman et al., 2006) and improper communication (Barbarossa and Pastore, 2015) as reasons for customers not adopting green products. Researchers argue for the need to refocus on consumer value, enhancing consumer knowledge, environmental concern and ensuring credibility of product claims (Ottman et al., 2006; Finisterra do Paço and Raposo, 2010). Social norms i.e. complying with community beliefs and practices are stated to have a significant impact on green behaviour of customers across the world (Fiske and Taylor, 2013; Alcott, 2011; Nolan et al., 2008). However, consumption-practices change over time and are shaped by what is considered normal within a social group or a community or a reference group (Gupta and Ogden, 2009). Thus, an emerging area beyond customer attitudes, knowledge and product characteristics is the process of social-normalisation for driving sustainable green marketing in India (Rettie et al., 2014).

Social-normalisation relates to gradual acceptance of green activities as normal by the consumers leading to better adoption and sustainability of such practices (Rettie et al., 2014). However, conception of what constitutes normal practice changes over times and thus, there is a need to assess them continuously. Diverse cultures, regions and social classes have varied opinion about activities being green versus normal and consequently, the social-normalisation theory needs to be explored across different national and cultural contexts (Rettie et al., 2012). However, the social-normalisation process remains unexplored in the Indian context. Further, social norms may be driven by various factors like gender, marital status, income, region, education, etc. (Uddin and Khan, 2016; Kumar and Ghodeswar, 2015; Khare, 2015; Saxena and Khandelwal, 2012; Jain and Kaur, 2006). Diamantopoulos et al. (2003) suggest that factors like legislative norms, social norms and situational impact factors should be analysed along with socio-demographics to understand the green customer profile. Thus, there is also a need to understand the impact of socio-demographic factors on green behaviour to drive better marketing strategies (Lee, 2009).

Given the above research gaps, this chapter has two objectives:

1. Explore the impact of social-normalisation theory in the Indian green marketing context.
2. Understand the impact of socio-demographic factors on green marketing strategies in India.

This chapter explores the social-normalisation process and its impact on adoption of green practices in India based upon an empirical study.

LITERATURE REVIEW

Social-normalisation is the process of green activities and products being gradually perceived as mainstream or normal over a period resulting in higher acceptance and sustainability of the practices by the customers (Rettie et al., 2014). Researchers argue that green practices, which are considered as normal, become a habit for consumers and are pursued more often than the ones which are positioned on just environment benefit and therefore, such normalisation of practices can lead to reduction in the attitude-behaviour gap in the green marketing context (Shove, 2003).

The impact of social norms on adoption of pro-environment behaviour has been observed in several studies. For example, Barr et al. (2001) state that "putting out recyclable material for collection" is a socially-visible activity and is replicated by others due to it being perceived as a social norm. Social norms are also known as subjective norms. Several studies show that such socially visible subjective norms impact pro-environmental behaviour (Wang et al., 2011; Park & Ha, 2012) like purchase of green products and recycling. Johnstone and Tan (2015) state that making green as the social norm can lead to bridging of the green attitude versus behaviour gap as it leads to the collective goals being prioritised over individual goals. Comparative feedback on energy consumption of oneself versus others in society has been stated to motivate people for energy consumption (Alcott, 2011). Adoption of ecology-friendly practices into the normal routines of consumers impacts their sustainability. For example, Shove (2003) highlights that patterns of consumption of energy and water (depicted through examples of laundering and showering) reflect people normal habits and routines. Some studies done in the Indian context also highlight the impact of social norms on adoption of green practices in India. Khare (2014) finds that normative influences, i.e. compliance to social norms to avoid negative consequences, impact green attitude of Indian consumers. Kumar and Ghodeswar (2015) find that social appeal, environment protection and responsibility, green product experience and environmental friendliness of companies drive green behaviour in India. Consumer conceptions of normality are driven more at a social level than individual (Shove, 2003) and therefore, sustainability of green consumption requires such green practices to be perceived as normal by the individual. These examples indicate that social-normalisation can be extended to pro-environmental behaviour.

However, green practices and their perceptions may vary across countries. For example, people in developed countries use household heating/cooling systems whereas the same is yet to be adopted across larger parts of India. Similarly, tumble drying is a normal practice in the US and UK households whereas Indians practice drying in sunlight as the norm, resulting in different energy consumption requirements. Hence, such changes in social norms needs continued focus and research (Khare, 2015; Varman and Costa, 2008).

Some researchers have explored the impact of socio-demographics on adoption of green practices in India. Saxena and Khandelwal (2010) find that compared to males, females have a higher positive attitude towards green marketing. They also find that married people, people living in metros and big cities, better educated and older people have a more positive attitude toward green marketing. Krishna and Qaim (2008) find that higher level of wealth and education impact sustainable acceptance and consumption of genetically modified crops. However, given the attitude-behaviour gap there is a need to further explore impact of socio-demographics on the actual green behaviour.

RESEARCH METHODOLOGY

A study was conducted to explored customer conceptualisation for some common environment-related activities. These activities consisted of a mix of activities adapted from existing literature (Rettie et al., 2012) and new activities added based on the Indian context and expert opinion. The research steps are explained below.

Step 1: Visualising Consumer Perceptions of Green vs. Normal.

All respondents were asked to rate each pro-environmental activity across green and normal scales. The results were plotted graphically using heat maps to visualise consumer perceptions of activities as being green versus normal and draw insights based on the same.

Step 2: Exploring Perceived Green and Normal Dimensions.

The activities were grouped into green and normal dimensions using exploratory factor analysis to identify the key green and normal perceptions existing in the Indian context.

Step 3: Exploring Actual Green Behaviour Dimensions.

Exploratory factor analysis was done to identify green behaviour dimensions in the Indian context.

Step 4: Impact of Green and Normal Perception Factors on Actual Green Behaviour Dimensions.

Expert opinion was used to identify activities relevant to each of the green behaviour factors found in step 3. Then green and normal perception factors were formed using the average of ratings given on the normal and green scales respectively for the above identified activities. Each green behaviour dimension was regressed upon the green and normal perception factors to assess the impact of green and normal perceptions on the actual green behaviour.

Step 5: Impact of Socio-Demographics on Green Behaviour Dimensions

The detailed methodology and results are discussed ahead.

Survey Development

A quantitative survey was developed containing four key sections. Section I of the questionnaire had items related to socio-demographic data like age, gender, occupation, income, marital status, etc. Section II and III captured customer perceptions of 23 sustainability related activities being normal and being green respectively using a 5-point Likert scale (Strongly disagree = 1; Strongly agree = 5). Section IV captured the level of green behaviour exhibited by customers using 15 items drawn from previous research (Robert, 1996). The questionnaire was rolled out both online and offline across all four regions in India.

Selection of Activities

23 sustainability related activities were selected from a mix of previous studies on sustainability (Rettie et al., 2012) and post discussions with experts. Some activities like "drying clothes in a tumble dryer," "using patio heaters" and "eating meat or fish" (Rettie et al., 2012) were not considered. This was done in consultation with experts as use of tumble dryers or patio heaters is not prevalent across all regions in India due to varying climatic conditions and level of technological acceptance. Further, "eating meat or fish" may be driven by religious beliefs in India and hence, was removed from the list of activities. Some activities like "Showering/bathing on alternate days," "Monitoring electricity consumption," were modified to reflect the Indian context and reworded as "Using a bucket of water instead of a shower while bathing" and "Switching off lights and fans when not in use." In addition, new activities that were not included in the research by Rettie et al. (2012) were added to the study based on expert opinion. These were, "Use of cosmetics made from herbs and plant extracts," "Sometimes using a solar cooker for cooking," "Using both sides of paper and waste envelopes for rough work," "Purchasing lead-free petrol," "Switching-off vehicle ignition at red lights" and "Reusing plastic bags obtained at time of shopping for other purposes." These statements reflect some of the prevalent pro-environment practices, which may be the result of several communication campaigns done by pro-environmentalists in India. Furthermore, some statements depicting anti-green behaviour statements were added. For example, "Use of mosquito repellant liquids at night instead of mosquito nets," "Driving in a self-owned vehicle to the office every day," "Using disposable dishes for picnic/outings" and "Purchase of canned food." This was done to ensure inclusion of activities, which may have been adopted by people in certain regions or areas due to benefits like time-saving and personal convenience, but the level of adoption may differ across regions. These anti-green activities were reverse-coded for factor analysis.

ANALYSIS

Data Profile

Out of the 578 questionnaires collected, 514 were complete and usable. Post removal of outliers, 496 were retained. The data points showed varying levels of socio-demographic factors like age, occupation, income, region, education, etc. as given in Table 1.

Visualising Consumer Perception Gap Using Heat Maps

Heat maps are two-dimensional representation of data, which visually indicate the percentage of customers selecting a level of rating (green/normal) using a continuous range of symbols. Cells with hollow dots and light grey shaded background depict a lower percentage of customers selecting a rating and cells with full black dots and darker grey shade background indicate the highest percentage selecting a rating (Figure I). In addition, mean, standard deviation of each activity is also depicted (Figure I). The grid helps understand the distributional patterns of responses against each activity. A quick look overall shows that there are differences across many activities in terms of being green versus being normal, which points towards differences in the social normalisation process across activities.

Table 1. Sample data socio-demographics

Gender	Male	58.20%
	Female	41.80%
Region	North	33.00%
	South	22.20%
	East	22.20%
	West	22.60%
Age Group (years)	18-25	18.55%
	26-35	49.25%
	36-45	22.10%
	46-55	7.50%
	56 and greater	2.60%
Occupation	Student	25.80%
	Professional	29.40%
	Service	30.90%
	Self-employed/Business	6.00%
	Homemaker/Retired/Others	7.90%
Income (INR)	less than or equal to 5 lacs	13.00%
	5 lacs and above but less than 10 lacs	24.10%
	10 lacs and above but less than 15 lacs	20.50%
	15 lacs and above but less than 20 lacs	9.60%
	equal to or greater than 20 lacs	32.80%
Marital Status	Married	53.50%
	Single	46.50%
No. of people staying in house	1	3.00%
	2	13.40%
	3	21.30%
	4	32.40%
	5	15.80%
	6 and greater	14.10%
No. of children	0	53.70%
	1	24.30%
	2	19.00%
	>2	3.00%

Note: The professional category denotes people who run their own business setup and Service denotes people who work for other organisations.

Green Perceptions

Several activities are perceived as green/very green (Figure 1) by a large percentage of respondent base. This is depicted by the similar dark grey shading with solid dots in the green/very green rating category. This consensus is also confirmed by the fact that these activities have a high mean (showing they are green) and low standard deviation (showing agreement between customers). Such activities include "using

Figure 1. Heat Map showing normal versus green perceptions of consumers

	Normal							Green						
Activity	Mean	Std Dev	Not at all normal	Not normal	Neither	Normal	Very normal	Mean	Std. Dev	Not at all green	Not green	Neither	Green	Very green
1. Use Public Transport	0.32	1.32	12.6	22.0	3.0	45.8	16.6	1.25	0.80	1.3	3.8	3.2	52.2	39.4
2. Switch off lights	1.47	0.77	.6	4.3	.4	37.1	57.6	1.56	0.58	.0	1.1	1.3	38.4	59.3
3. Use bucket not shower	0.54	1.38	10.7	19.8	5.5	33.0	30.9	1.13	0.88	1.1	4.7	12.4	44.1	37.7
4.Use shop plasticbag s	-0.37	1.16	5.1	25.8	10.2	44.6	14.3	-0.54	1.43	33.7	29.4	6.0	18.6	12.4
5. Use organic cosmetics	0.02	1.15	9.8	27.3	22.2	32.8	7.9	0.74	0.96	2.6	7.5	24.7	43.7	21.5
6. Use organic pdts.	-0.02	1.13	9.6	29.0	22.0	32.8	6.6	0.94	0.91	1.9	5.3	16.8	49.0	26.9
7. Use solar cooker	-1.27	1.02	56.3	24.7	10.4	6.4	2.1	1.19	0.93	3.0	3.2	7.9	43.5	42.4
8. Walk for short distance	0.79	1.14	3.8	16.0	6.8	44.3	29.0	1.54	0.67	.9	.9	1.9	36.7	59.7
9. Buy recyclable pdts.	0.23	1.03	4.7	20.9	30.5	34.8	9.2	1.37	0.74	.4	2.6	5.5	42.4	49.0
10. Use energy saving appl.	0.81	0.93	1.1	11.7	12.2	54.8	20.3	1.42	0.69	.6	1.5	3.4	44.3	50.1
11. Plant trees	-0.34	1.33	23.0	32.2	11.1	23.2	10.4	1.55	0.80	1.9	1.5	3.4	25.6	67.6
12. Buy milk in plastic not carton	-0.60	1.22	7.9	14.5	11.7	41.6	24.3	-0.24	1.18	14.7	30.3	28.8	16.8	9.4
13. Buy Canned food	0.71	1.12	25.4	44.1	9.2	18.8	2.6	-0.60	0.99	18.8	36.2	34.5	6.8	3.6
14. Use both papersides	0.92	1.05	2.3	12.6	7.5	45.8	31.8	1.27	0.78	.9	3.8	4.1	50.3	40.9
15. Leave TV on standy	0.46	1.26	22.4	39.0	7.7	24.3	6.6	-0.77	1.11	26.7	44.3	13.0	11.1	4.9
16. Use low phos. Det.	-0.12	0.90	7.0	22.2	50.1	16.8	3.8	0.38	0.88	2.1	9.8	46.1	31.8	10.2
17. Own vehicle to office	-0.42	1.38	13.0	17.5	10.2	33.3	26.0	-0.70	1.13	24.7	44.8	11.7	13.6	5.1
18. Disposable dishes	-0.84	1.03	3.6	9.0	13.0	48.2	26.2	-0.03	1.22	12.6	27.9	19.2	30.1	10.2
19.Reuse plastic bags	1.14	0.96	1.9	7.2	6.6	42.9	41.4	0.86	0.84	1.7	6.0	14.9	59.3	18.1
20. Buy lead-free petrol	0.49	1.14	6.4	12.2	28.1	32.8	20.5	0.76	0.83	1.5	3.6	29.9	47.8	17.3
21. Use repellant liquids	-0.69	1.20	8.1	10.7	11.7	42.9	26.7	-0.23	1.11	12.8	29.9	32.8	16.8	7.7
22. Turn off veh. Ignition	0.43	1.19	6.8	20.3	14.3	40.5	18.1	1.17	0.75	.6	2.1	10.4	53.1	33.7
23. Buy grocery online	0.40	1.32	23.5	35.4	8.1	23.7	9.4	0.17	0.95	6.2	9.6	54.6	20.0	9.6

public transport," "switching off the fans and lights when not in use," "using a bucket of water instead of shower for bathing," "using organic products," "using a solar cooker," "walking for short distances," "buying recycled products," "using energy-saving appliances," "planting a tree," "using both sides of paper" and "switching off vehicle at red lights."

There is another set of activities, which are not perceived as green by customers. These are depicted by the dark grey shading with solid dots in the "not green"/ "not at all green" scale ratings. These include, "using a self-owned vehicle to the office," "using plastic bags given by shopkeepers instead of taking your own" and "leaving TV on standby." The rating on the activity, "buying grocery online," shows that customers have no clarity on it being "green" or "not green." This is visually depicted by the dark grey shading with solid dots in the "neither" rating category. The activity has a mean close to 0 and standard deviation less than one showing that most customers do not know how to rate the activity- green or non-green.

There are some activities where the customers did not seem to have a consensus as a similar percentage of them marked the activity as "green" versus "not-green" (activities like buying milk in plastic pouches, buying canned food and using mosquito repellent liquids instead of nets at night). These activities have negative means close to 0 and high standard deviation. Similarly, another group of activities, like "using low phosphate detergent" and "buying lead-free petrol" has ratings between "neither" to "green," depicting the possibility of multiple groups. The activity "using disposable dishes for picnic/outings" has ratings spread across all categories showing dispersed opinion among customers. This may also indicate the presence of different groups of respondents having divergent views and needs further analysis.

Normal Perceptions

Analysis of the heat map for normal scale for all activities shows that opinion about the 23 activities being normal is dispersed. Only few activities like, "switching off lights and fans when not in use," "using a bucket of water for bathing instead of a shower," "walking short distances," "using both sides of paper," "using energy-saving appliances" and "reusing plastic bags for other purposes" are rated as normal by a high proportion of the customers. These activities are also clearly understood as green by customers indicating that they have gone through the social-normalisation process.

While there is a consensus among customers on the activity "using a solar cooker" being green; yet, it is not rated as normal. Further, "using a self-owned vehicle for office" is understood to be a non-green activity but is rated as normal. This attitude-behaviour difference indicates that perceptions about activities being pro-environment may not result in their being incorporated into the normal routines of consumers and vice versa.

Further, different levels of social-normalisation exist for a larger number of activities as depicted by the variation in customer perceptions of the activities being normal or non-normal. For example, activities like "using public transport," "using plastic bags given by shopkeeper instead of carrying own," "using organic ingredient based cosmetic products," "using organic products," "buying recyclable products," "planting a tree," "leaving TV on standby," "switching off vehicle at red lights" and "buying grocery online" have varying perceptions of normality. Similarly, "buying milk in plastic packets" is rated as a normal activity by most respondents whereas the opinion on it being green/non-green is divided. This is indicative of different levels of social-normalisation process for these activities across diverse groups and therefore, a need for understanding various segments associated with it.

Perceived Green and Normal Dimensions

To explore key green and normal dimensions perceived by the customers, exploratory factor analysis (EFA) was conducted for the 23 activities for green and normal ratings respectively.

Green Dimensions

EFA on the 23 activities (green rating) was done using varimax rotation. KMO (0.694) and Bartlett's test for sphericity ($p < 0.00$) indicated factor analysis was appropriate (Hair et al., 2013). All items with loading < 0.5 or cross-loading on other items, were removed resulting in three dimensions. Each dimension had Cronbach alpha >= 0.6 (Nunnally, 1978) and the overall variance explained was 58.62% (Hair et al., 2013).

The three green dimensions obtained were (Table 2) as follows:

- Using pro-environment packaging
- Saving resources
- Using organic products

While all 23 activities were rated on the green scale by customers, agreement in terms of categorisation of these activities was limited to only three dimensions (Table 2). These groupings can be argued to be driven by the mass pro-environmental campaigns done by various sectors like government and private organisations over time, which have eventually moved people to perceive these as green activities.

Normal Dimensions

EFA was done on the 23 activities (Normal ratings) using varimax rotation. KMO (0.534>0.5) and Bartlett's test for sphericity ($p<0.00$) indicated factor analysis could be conducted for the normal scale items. All items with loading<0.5 or having a cross-loading on other items were removed resulting in

Table 2. Perceived green dimensions, factor loadings for each item and Cronbach alpha values based on EFA on 23 activities (green ratings)

Dimension	Items	Factor Loading	Cronbach Alpha
Use of pro-environment packaging	Using plastic bags given by shopkeeper instead of carrying your own- R	.697	.608
	Buying milk in plastic packets versus cartons- R	.692	
	Use of mosquito repellent liquids instead of mosquito nets-R	.674	
	Purchase of canned food- R	.638	
Saving resources	Using energy saving appliances at home	.771	.632
	Walking instead of using own transport while going for short distance	.764	
	Switching off lights and fans when not in use	.675	
Using organic products	Use of cosmetics and toiletries made from herbs and plant extracts	.860	.742
	Using organic products	.854	

Note: R denotes that the item was reverse coded

two dimensions with a Cronbach alpha >= 0.6 for each dimension and an overall variance explained of 65.55%, which indicated satisfactory results (Hair et al., 2013). The two normal dimensions obtained are given below and shown in Table 3:

- Use of private vehicles.
- Use of organic products.

While the study found three green dimensions (Table 2), only two normal dimensions were found (Table 3). "Use of organic products" was the only common dimension having similar green and normal ratings.

Actual Green Behaviour Dimensions

Next, EFA was done on the 15 green behaviour items using varimax rotation. KMO (0.836 > 0.5) and Bartlett's test for sphericity ($p < 0.00$) indicated appropriateness of factor analysis. All items with loading < 0.5 or having a cross-loading on other items were removed resulting in two actual green behaviour dimensions with a Cronbach alpha >= 0.6 (Nunnally, 1978) for each dimension and an overall variance explained of 61.22%, which indicated acceptable results (Hair et al., 2013). The green behaviour factors are given in Table 4.

- Consumption of pro-environmental products
- Consumption of less electricity

Next, the study analysed the impact of green or normal perceptions on the actual green behaviour.

Impact of Green and Normal Perception Factors on Actual Green Behaviour

Expert opinion was used to identify activities relevant to each of the green behaviour factors found in step 3. Then green and normal perception factors were formed using the average of ratings given on the normal and green scales respectively for the above identified activities. Each green behaviour dimension

Table 3. Perceived normal dimensions, factor loadings for each item and Cronbach alpha values based on EFA on 23 activities (normal ratings)

Dimension	Items	Loading	Cronbach Alpha
Use of Private vehicles	Using public transport wherever possible	.836	.600
	Driving in own vehicle to office everyday- R	.726	
	Walking instead of using own transport while going for short distance	.655	
Use of organic products	Use of cosmetics and toiletries made from herbs and plant extracts	.894	.754
	Using organic products	.890	

Note: R denotes the item was reverse coded

Table 4. Green behaviour dimensions, factor loadings for each item and Cronbach alpha values obtained from EFA done on 15 green behaviour items

Dimension	Items	Loading	Cronbach Alpha
Consumption of pro-environmental products	I avoid products made by those companies which are irresponsible towards keeping ecological balance	.800	.826
	I make every effort to buy paper products, for example, paper napkins, made from recycled paper	.764	
	I do not buy household products that harm environment	.756	
	I have convinced members of my family or friends not to buy some products that are harmful to the environment	.733	
	When I make choice between two similar products, I buy one which is less polluting	.727	
Consumption of less electricity	I conserve energy by turning off lights and electrical appliances when I am not using them	.837	.722
	I try to minimise the use of electricity to save energy	.820	
	I use those bulbs which use very little of electricity	.711	

was regressed upon the green and normal perception factors relevant to it to assess the impact of green and normal perceptions on the actual green behaviour.

Green Behaviour Dimension 1: Pro-Environmental Product Consumption

To understand whether perceptions of green versus normal impact the consumption of pro-environmental products, 10 activities related to green behaviour factor of pro-environmental product consumption were chosen from the list of 23 activities for each of the green and normal scales. The items are listed below.

- Using plastic bags given by shopkeepers instead of carrying own bag
- Use of cosmetics and toiletries made from herbs and plant extracts
- Using organic products
- Sometimes using a solar cooker for cooking
- Using low-phosphate detergent for cleaning clothes
- Not using disposable dishes for picnic/outings
- Buying products that are recyclable
- Not buying milk in plastic packets and using cartons instead
- Not purchasing canned food
- Use of mosquito repellent liquids at night instead of mosquito nets

Ratings of the above activities on the green and normal scales were taken and averages of items for the green and normal scales respectively were done to arrive at the following factors.

- **Normal Pro-Environment Product Consumption:** This indicates the rating of the above stated activities on the normal scale by respondents. The factor reflects the level of normalisation of pro-environment product consumption related activities.

- **Green Pro-Environment Product Consumption:** This indicates the rating related to the level to which the customers assess the above activities to be green.

The pro-environmental product consumption dimension was then regressed upon the green and normal perception factors identified. The regression results are given in Table 5.

The regression is significant with a R^2 value of 0.143 indicating that 14.3 percent of the variation in green behaviour is explained by the two independent variables (green and normal pro-environment product consumption factors). The results show that only the normal pro-environment factor has a significant impact on the pro-environment product consumption behaviour whereas the impact of the green factor is insignificant ($p>0.05$). This supports the social-normalisation theory wherein as green activities become more embedded in the normal routines of society, people have a higher tendency to confirm to the same, even if they do not have very strong pro-green beliefs (Rettie et al., 2014). Hence, marketers can look upon using the social-normalisation theory to drive pro-environment product consumption sustainability behaviour.

The heat map of each of the 10 items forming the normal pro- environment consumption factor shows that there are two items among the ten items for normal pro-environment product consumption (using disposable dishes for picnics and using mosquito repellent liquids instead of nets) on which there is a consensus among a large percentage of customers with respect to the same being normal. For the other 8 items contributing to this factor, there are different groups, which look upon the activity as being normal/non-normal and therefore, there exist groups for which these activities need to be positioned as normal to ensure pro-environment consumption behaviour. Thus, the impact of socio-demographics on pro-environmental product consumption behaviour is analysed later in the chapter.

Table 5. Regression results for green behaviour related to pro-environment consumption

Model Summary						
Model	**R**	**R Square**	**Adjusted R Square**	**Std. Error of the Estimate**		
1	.379[a]	.143	.140	.69392		
ANOVA						
1	Regression	37.578	2	18.789	39.020	.000[a]
	Residual	224.390	466	.482		
	Total	261.968	468			
Variable	**Predictor**	**B coefficient**	**Standard error**	**Std. B coefficient**	**t**	**Sig.**
Pro-environment consumption	**Constant**	0.617	.055		11.173	.000
	Normal pro-environment product Consumption	0.697	.079	.379	8.805	.000

Green Behaviour Dimension 2: Lower Electricity Consumption Behaviour

To understand if attitude towards the activity or normalisation of the activity impacts the lower electricity consumption behaviour, two activities related to lower electricity consumption were chosen from the list of 23 activities for each of the green and normal scales. The activities are:

- Switching off lights and fans when not in use
- Using energy-saving appliances at home,

The average of the ratings of the above two activities on the normal and green scales was done to form the following factors.

- **Normal Lower Electricity Consumption**: This indicates the rating given on the normal scale for the above two activities. The factor reflects the level of normalisation of the above two activities.
- **Green Lower Electricity Consumption:** This indicates the level to which customers assess the above activities to be green.

The lower level of electricity consumption behaviour was then regressed upon these green and normal perception factors. The regression results are given in Table 6.

The regression is significant with a R^2 value of 0.171 indicating that 17.1 percent of the variation in green behaviour is explained by the two independent variables (green and normal lower electricity consumption factors). The results show that both the normal and green lower electricity factors have a significant positive impact on actual lower electricity consumption behaviour. However, the impact of the normal factor is higher than the green factor as indicated by the coefficient values for each. This shows

Table 6. Regression results for green behaviour related to lower electricity consumption

Model Summary						
Model	**R**	**R Square**	**Adjusted R Square**	**Std. Error of the Estimate**		
1	.414[a]	.171	.168	.51815		
ANOVA						
1	Regression	25.888	2	12.944	48.212	.000[a]
	Residual	125.110	466	.268		
	Total	150.998	468			
Variable	**Predictor**	**B coefficient**	**Standard error**	**Std. B coefficient**	**t**	**Sig.**
Lower electricity consumption	Constant	.705	.079		8.944	.000
	Normal lower electricity consumption	.296	.037	.344	8.048	.000
	Green lower electricity Consumption	.196	.047	.179	4.185	.000

that as a green activity becomes a part of the normal routine of people, more people start confirming to it and thus, marketers need to position green activities as normal for them to ensure sustainability of such practices.

Impact of Socio-Demographic Factors on the Green Behaviour Dimensions

Next impact of socio-demographic differences on the green behaviour factors was analysed. The ANOVA results for the same are summarised in Table 7.

- **Gender**: There is no significant difference across gender for each of the two green behaviour factors (Table 7).
- **Marital Status:** There is a significant difference by marital status for each of the green behaviour wherein married people have higher mean scores than singles for both pro-environment product consumption and lower electricity consumption green behaviour factors (Table 7).
- **Income:** The ANOVA result (Table 7) shows that there are significant differences across income categories for green pro-environment product consumption factor. The post-hoc analysis based on mean differences across the two groups (< 15 lacs and >= 15 lacs) reveals that the < INR15 lacs category has higher mean scores than >= 15 lacs income category for pro-environment product consumption behaviour. However, there are no significant differences across income categories for lower electricity consumption behaviour.
- **Region:** The ANOVA result (Table 7) shows that there are significant differences across regions for green pro-environment product consumption factor. The results show that mean green scores across India are in the following order South>East>West>North, i.e. South has the highest score and North the lowest score. The post-hoc results reveal that North is significantly lower on green consumption behaviour as compared to South and East. Further, South and East form one homogeneous subset. However, there is no significant difference across region mean scores on the consuming less electricity behaviour.
- **Occupation:** Although the ANOVA result shows a significant difference in lower electricity consumption behaviour by occupation (Table 7), the post-hoc results show no significant differences among each of the groups. This could also be due to the unequal group sizes.
- **Age Group:** The ANOVA results show that there are significant differences across age groups for both green behaviour factors (Table 7). The post-hoc analysis results reveal that the older age group (>45 years) has significantly higher pro-environment consumption behaviour than the other three age groups (<25 years, 26-35 years, 36-45 years). The age group greater than 45 years forms a subset considerably different than the other three age groups. Further, for the second green behaviour factor related to less electricity consumption, the age groups <25 years and 26-35 years form a homogeneous subset which is significantly different from the other subset consisting of 36-45 years and >45 years wherein the subset 2 mean scores for lower electricity consumption are significantly higher than the score of subset 1 which is similar to findings by Wang et al. (2011) in Beijing.
- **No of Family Members:** There is no significant difference based on family size for both green behaviour factors.

Table 7. Results for ANOVA for green behaviour factors

Factor	Group	Pro-Environment Consumption			Lower Electricity Consumption		
		F value	p value	Mean value	F value	p value	Mean value
Gender	Male	0.419	0.518(ns)	0.479	0.748	0.388(ns)	1.316
	Female			0.524			1.362
Marital Status	Married	3.935	0.048**	0.561	4.856	0.028**	1.389
	Single			0.424			1.273
Income	<INR15 lacs	13.196	0.000***	0.604	0.005	0.944(ns)	1.337
	>= INR15 lacs			0.353			1.333
Region	North	6.031	0.000***	0.309	1.705	0.165(ns)	1.253
	South			0.686			1.394
	East			0.573			1.381
	West			0.515			1.352
Occupation	Student	1.833	0.096(ns)	.413	2.232	0.050**	1.275
	Self-employed			.307			1.309
	Profession			.444			1.289
	Homemaker			.656			1.546
	Service			.622			1.367
	Retired			.583			1.694
Age	<= 25 years	6.602	0.000***	.452	7.981	0.000***	1.222
	26-35 years			.402			1.259
	36-45 years			.561			1.519
	>= 46 years			.910			1.510
Family size (no of members)	1	1.722	0.128(ns)	.328	0.530	0.753(ns)	1.476
	2			.320			1.301
	3			.444			1.373
	4			.510			1.291
	5			.621			1.364
	>= 6			.618			1.476
No. of children	None	7.741	0.006**	0.409	1.941	0.1649(ns)	1.301
	1 or more children			0.600			1.374

Note: For p values *** = 1% significance level, **= 5% significance level

- **Children:** There is a significant difference across the groups having no child versus groups having 1 or more children for the pro-environment consumption green behaviour factor. Here, the mean score for green behaviour is higher for group having 1 or more children as compared to people having no children. However, there is no significant difference between the two groups for the factor of lower electricity consumption behaviour.

The study finds that pro-environment consumption behaviour (Table 7) is higher for people who are married, have less than INR15 lacs income, have children as compared to those who are single, having income of INR15 lacs or more and having no children. Further, the group with age of 45 years and above has higher pro-environment consumption behaviour than lower age groups. In addition, South and East are higher in pro-environment consumption behaviour than North. Therefore, the 10 activities need to be reinforced by positioning them as normal for the following geo-demographics: lower age groups with respondents less than 46 years of age, marital status as single, income greater than or equal to 15 lacs and belonging to the North region.

FINDINGS AND MANAGERIAL IMPLICATIONS

The study finds that there exists a gap between green-attitudes and actual green behaviour of customers.

This gap may be driven by the fact that customers often find it inconvenient to practice pro-environmental behaviour and hence, do not adopt some of these practices (Carrette et al., 2012; Laroche et al., 2001). For example, Rettie et al. (2011) found that although consumers perceived flying for foreign holidays as not green, they regarded it as a normal part of their routine and did not envisage changing it. Conversely, other researchers suggest that customers are driven by social norms for environmentally friendly activities (Barr et al., 2011). For example, this study indicates that while some of the activities like "walking for short distances," "reusing plastic bags for other purposes," etc. may not be convenient, a high proportion of customers rate them as normal. This can be argued to be a result of customer habituation of these activities as depicted by the normal ratings attached to these activities. Such normalisation may have been driven through several initiatives like banning of plastic bags in some parts across the country by the Indian government, routine of collection of garbage by specific people in societies, shortage of water supply in some regions, etc. It could also have been driven by the economic cost of buying garbage bags for the lower-income group and the issue of not getting plastic bags easily for the higher-income groups. Thus, by using varied methods for different target groups, the same activity can be normalised across the society and result in higher green behaviour among customers. Similar results have been found in other research studies as well, for example; Gregory and Leo (2003) found that households with lower water usage show a higher involvement in water conservation issues and tend to form habits associated with lower water usage thereby entering a self-sustained cycle of conservation.

The study also finds that activities, which are perceived as non-green (driving in a self-owned vehicle to the office), are still part of normal activities. This could be driven by the fact that in many cases, people act habitually and may be guided by automated cognitive structures in their mind rather than reasoning (Steg and Vlek, 2009). Such habits can, however, be modified through some interventions. For example, Fujii et al. (2001) found that temporarily forcing car drivers to use alternative travel modes by closing the freeway access, reduced the level of their individual car use by modifying their beliefs about the alternate transport modes.

The study shows that there is a significant and relatively higher impact of normal factors on both the green behaviour dimensions i.e. pro-environment product consumption and lower electricity consumption factors.

The study finds that perceptions of activities being green do not impact pro-environment product consumption whereas perceptions of activities being normal have a significant impact on actual pro-environment product consumption. This corroborates the applicability of social-normalisation for driving green marketing in India. Further, the study finds a higher level of pro-environment product consumption green behaviour for respondents who belong to higher age group, are married and have children. These results corroborate previous findings (Saxena and Khandelwal, 2010; Laroche et al., 2001). This may be driven by the fear of environment degradation impacting the future of their children. Parents may care for their children and therefore, values of family welfare need to be stressed on pro-environment products related communication. Further, people in the lower-income bracket (income of 15 lacs or less) exhibit higher level of pro-environment product consumption. This contrasts with the findings by Khare (2015) who states that higher income positively impacts pro-environment behaviour of the Indian consumers. This can be argued to be a result of unaffordability of products like canned food or disposable dishes and therefore, such activities may not have been adopted by the lower-level income groups. Thus, higher income levels may not automatically drive pro-environmental behaviour and therefore, incorporating green practices into normal routines of people may be a better way to sustain the same. In addition, pro-environment product consumption is highest in South region followed by the Eastern region in India. The same can be correlated with the fact that government in Southern states like Kerala have heavily focussed on driving green behaviour and promoted policies like organic farming. Government, political systems and institutions have a huge impact in emerging markets like India as they can use both direct and indirect measures to drive both demand and supply of green products (Stevens, 2010). Therefore, public-private partnerships can be used to drive green practices, for example, non-governmental organisations have worked with Spice board to enhance organic production of spices in Kerala, Tamil Nadu and Andhra Pradesh apart from North-eastern states. Further, social practice of relying on the Ayurveda treatment is embedded in traditions in these regions making them prone to buying products, which are green. Therefore, marketers need to have their communication and distribution for pro-environment products implemented in a socially embedded manner (i.e. working with the local community, using local human capital and through developing their relationships with government and non-government stakeholders) to ensure that social-normalisation process is faster and easier. This is especially important as people from different strata of society in a developing country like India may not be able to afford organic products, which are priced higher than normal ones but may adopt the practice based on social norms. Environmentally harmful products can be made less feasible (example, by incorporation of higher taxes or through legal prohibitions) and pro-environmental products can be made widely available (example, recycled paper, organic products, etc.). Marketers need to target specific-groups (as highlighted before) to reinforce social-normalisation of green activities resulting in long-term sustainability.

The empirical study results show that lower electricity consumption behaviour is impacted by both green and normal factors with the latter having a higher impact. Thus, the study finds that social-normalisation of green practices like switching off lights and fans when not in use or using energy saving appliances at home can drive lower electricity consumption in India corroborating the results from previous studies (Alcott, 2011; Nolan et al., 2008). Electricity consumption is different from product consumption as electricity is intangible and consumed only indirectly and as a by-product of other practices. It is not easily measurable in comparison to say price of a product and not socially visible as a lifestyle product. Information on social norms and individual electricity consumption can therefore, be given to customers for them to take steps towards meeting the norms and gradually make it part of their routine. On analysing items in the green and normal factors for lower electricity consumption (switching off lights and fans when not in use; purchasing electricity-saving appliances) there seems to be a consensus amongst customers on the same being green and normal respectively (Figure 1). However, comparison of the individual items shows that a lower percentage of customers rate the use of energy-saving appliances as normal. This essentially points to the need for introduction of higher incentives for people to buy such appliances. Companies selling green-rated products can highlight the savings attained by customers through use of lower-energy consumption electrical fittings/ appliances. Further, government can roll out policies, which necessitate the use of lower energy consumption fittings in corporate buildings to make it part of normal course of life. They can also introduce lesser taxes for such appliances, which may lower the prices of such appliances and lead to their adoption by a higher number of individuals. Rewards like incentives for reduced electricity consumption can be launched, and these may be redeemable as points for purchasing lower electricity consumption products. In this way, the lower consumption behaviour will enter a cycle of self-reinforcement. Additionally, people can be showcased as a role model for others (Schultz et al., 2007) or could be given special memberships to socially important societies or clubs so that the behaviour becomes a social norm and over time is incorporated into routine of larger parts of society. Further, lower electricity consumption has a higher score for higher age group (36 years and above) and retired people. This may be driven by prior experience of these higher aged individuals where they have faced higher frequency of electricity shortfalls and therefore, developed a habit of saving electricity. Younger people may have experience of lesser electricity cuts and hence may not be so conscious about saving electricity or using energy-saving devices. Hence, effort should be made to drive awareness of electricity demand-supply gaps. Further, having price variations based on consumption levels can increase the electricity saving behaviour. Special marketing campaigns and events should be targeted towards youth and should stress on the need for saving electricity and purchase of energy-saving appliances.

In summary, the study concludes that as green activities become part of normal routine of customers, they start confirming to them. Hence, social-normalisation theory can be applied to the context of green marketing. Everyone can contribute to the environment by adopting pro-green behaviours as part of their routine life. The challenge for marketers is to facilitate such transition of activities from being construed as only green to becoming green and normal.

FUTURE RESEARCH DIRECTIONS

The empirical study done has used a limited number of activities in context of green marketing resulting in only two green behaviour dimensions. Therefore, future studies can explore other pro-environmental activities relevant to the green behaviour being researched. Social-normalisation is a continuous process and thus, categorisation of the activities as normal can change over a period thereby, necessitating further research. The research was limited to the four regions of India and therefore, needs to be replicated across other contexts- region, nation, society and culture. In addition, qualitative research can be done to corroborate or identify what is conceived as green or normal by consumers. Further, effect of various contextual factors, for example, physical infrastructure, technical facilities, availability of products, product characteristics, etc. in driving green behaviour need to be explored using techniques like experiments to get greater insights into which interventions can drive targeted behaviour.

REFERENCES

Aagerup, U., & Nilsson, J. (2016). Green consumer behavior: Being good or seeming good? *Journal of Product and Brand Management*, *25*(3), 274–284. doi:10.1108/JPBM-06-2015-0903

Accenture, UN Global Compact. (2013). *UN global compact—accenture CEO study on sustainability 2013. Architects of a better world.* Retrieved June 5, 2016, from https://www.unglobalcompact.org/docs/news_events/8.1/UNGC_Accenture_CEO_Study_2013.pdf

Allcott, H. (2011). Social norms and energy conservation. *Journal of Public Economics*, *95*(9-10), 1082–1095. doi:10.1016/j.jpubeco.2011.03.003

Barbarossa, C., & Pastore, A. (2015). Why environmentally conscious consumers do not purchase green products: A cognitive mapping approach. *Qualitative Market Research: An International Journal*, *18*(2), 188–209. doi:10.1108/QMR-06-2012-0030

Barr, S., Gilg, A. W., & Ford, N. J. (2001). Differences between household waste reduction, reuse and recycling behaviour: A study of reported behaviours, intentions and explanatory variables. *Environmental & Waste Management*, *4*(2), 69–82.

Barr, S., Shaw, G., & Gilg, A. W. (2011). The policy and practice of sustainable lifestyles. *Journal of Environmental Planning and Management*, *54*(10), 1331–1350. doi:10.1080/09640568.2011.574996

Bhate, S. (2001). One world, one environment, one vision: Are we close to achieving this? An exploratory study of consumer environmental behaviour across three countries. *Journal of Consumer Behaviour*, *2*(2), 169–184. doi:10.1002/cb.98

Black, I. (2010). Editorial: Sustainability through anti-consumption. *Journal of Consumer Behaviour*, *9*(6), 403–411. doi:10.1002/cb.340

Carrete, L., Castaño, R., Felix, R., Centeno, E., & González, E. (2012). Green consumer behavior in an emerging economy: Confusion, credibility, and compatibility. *Journal of Consumer Marketing*, *29*(7), 470–481. doi:10.1108/07363761211274983

Carrington, M. J., Neville, B. A., & Whitwell, G. J. (2014). Lost in translation: Exploring the ethical consumer intention–behavior gap. *Journal of Business Research*, *67*(1), 2759–2767. doi:10.1016/j.jbusres.2012.09.022

Diamantopoulos, A., Schlegelmilch, B. B., Sinkovics, R. R., & Bohlen, G. M. (2003). Can socio-demographics still play a role in profiling green consumers? A review of the evidence and an empirical investigation. *Journal of Business Research*, *56*(6), 465–448. doi:10.1016/S0148-2963(01)00241-7

Eckhardt, G. M., Belk, R., & Devinney, T. M. (2010). Why dont consumers consume ethically? *Journal of Consumer Behaviour*, *9*(6), 426–436. doi:10.1002/cb.332

Elkington, J. (1997). *Cannibals with forks. The triple bottom line of 21st century*. Mankato, MN: Capstone.

Finisterra do Paço, A. M., & Raposo, M. L. (2010). Green consumer market segmentation: Empirical findings from Portugal. *International Journal of Consumer Studies*, *34*(4), 429–436. doi:10.1111/j.1470-6431.2010.00869.x

Fiske, S. T., & Taylor, S. E. (2013). Social Cognition: From Brains to Culture. *Sage (Atlanta, Ga.).*

Fujii, S., Gärling, T., & Kitamura, R. (2001). Changes in drivers perceptions and use of public transport during a freeway closure: Effects of temporary structural change on cooperation in a real-life social dilemma. *Environment and Behavior, 33*(6), 796–808. doi:10.1177/00139160121973241

Gassler, B., Meyer-Höfer, M., & Spiller, A. (2016). Exploring Consumers' Expectations of Sustainability in Mature and Emerging Markets. *Journal of Global Marketing*, 1–14.

Gregory, G. D., & Leo, M. D. (2003). Repeated behavior and environmental psychology: The role of personal involvement and habit formation in explaining water consumption. *Journal of Applied Social Psychology, 33*(6), 1261–1296. doi:10.1111/j.1559-1816.2003.tb01949.x

Gupta, S., & Ogden, D. T. (2009). To buy or not to buy? A social dilemma perspective on green buying. *Journal of Consumer Marketing, 26*(6), 376–391. doi:10.1108/07363760910988201

Hair, J. F., Jr., Black, W. C., Babin, B. J., & Anderson, R. E. (2013). Multi-variate Data Analysis (7th ed.). Delhi: Dolrling Kindersley(India) Pvt. Ltd.

Jain, S. K., & Kaur, G. (2006). Role of socio-demographics in segmenting and profiling green consumers: An exploratory study of consumers in India. *Journal of International Consumer Marketing, 18*(3), 107–146. doi:10.1300/J046v18n03_06

Johnstone, M. L., & Tan, L. P. (2015). An exploration of environmentally-conscious consumers and the reasons why they do not buy green products. *Marketing Intelligence & Planning, 33*(5), 804–825. doi:10.1108/MIP-09-2013-0159

Khare, A. (2014). Consumers susceptibility to interpersonal influence as a determining factor of ecologically conscious behaviour. *Marketing Intelligence & Planning, 32*(1), 2–20. doi:10.1108/MIP-04-2013-0062

Khare, A. (2015). Antecedents to green buying behaviour: A study on consumers in an emerging economy. *Marketing Intelligence & Planning, 33*(3), 309–329. doi:10.1108/MIP-05-2014-0083

Krishna, V. V., & Qaim, M. (2008). Consumer attitudes toward GM food and pesticide residues in India. *Applied Economic Perspectives and Policy, 30*(2), 233–251.

Kumar, P., & Ghodeswar, B. (2015). Green Marketing Mix: A Review of Literature and Direction for Future Research. *International Journal of Asian Business and Information Management, 6*(3), 42–59.

Laroche, M., Bergeron, J., & Barbaro-Forleo, G. (2001). Targeting consumers who are willing to pay more for environmentally friendly products. *Journal of Consumer Marketing, 18*(6), 503–520. doi:10.1108/EUM0000000006155

Lee, K. (2009). Gender differences in Hong Kong adolescent consumers green purchasing behavior. *Journal of Consumer Marketing, 26*(2), 87–96. doi:10.1108/07363760910940456

Manaktola, K., & Jauhari, V. (2007). Exploring consumer attitude and behavior towards green practices in the lodging industry in India. *International Journal of Contemporary Hospitality Management, 19*(5), 364–377. doi:10.1108/09596110710757534

May, C., Finch, T., Mair, F., Ballini, L., Dowrick, C., Eccles, M., & Rogers, A. et al. (2007). Understanding the implementation of complex interventions in health care: The normalization process model. *BMC Health Services Research, 7*(1), 148. doi:10.1186/1472-6963-7-148 PMID:17880693

Mishra, P., & Sharma, P. (2010). Green marketing in India: Emerging opportunities and challenges. *Journal of Engineering. Science and Management Education, 3*(1), 9–14.

Muralidharan, S., Rejón-Guardia, F., & Xue, F. (2016). Understanding the green buying behavior of younger Millennials from India and the United States: A structural equation modeling approach. *Journal of International Consumer Marketing, 28*(1), 54–72. doi:10.1080/08961530.2015.1056328

Nittala, R. (2014). Green Consumer Behavior of the Educated Segment in India. *Journal of International Consumer Marketing, 26*(2), 138–152. doi:10.1080/08961530.2014.878205

Nolan, J. M., Schultz, P. W., Cialdini, R. B., Goldstein, N. J., & Griskevicius, V. (2008). Normative social influence is underdetected. *Personality and Social Psychology Bulletin, 34*(7), 913–923. doi:10.1177/0146167208316691 PMID:18550863

Nunnally, J. C. (1978). *Psychometric theory*. New York, NY: Mc Graw-Hill.

Ottman, J. A., Stafford, E. R., & Hartman, C. L. (2006). Avoiding green marketing myopia: Ways to improve consumer appeal for environmentally preferable products. *Environment: Science and Policy for Sustainable Development, 48*(5), 22–36.

Park, J., & Ha, S. (2012). Understanding pro-environmental behavior. *International Journal of Retail & Distribution Management, 40*(5), 388–403. doi:10.1108/09590551211222367

Parker, H. (2005). Normalization as a barometer: Recreational drug use and the consumption of leisure by younger Britons. *Addiction Research and Theory, 13*(3), 205–215. doi:10.1080/16066350500053703

phys.org. (2008, May 7). *First-of-its-kind 14-country study ranks consumers according to environmental behavior.* Retrieved June 8, 2016, from http://phys.org/news/2008-05-first-of-its-kind-country-consumers-environmental-behavior.html

Rettie, R., Burchell, K., & Barnham, C. (2014). Social normalisation: Using marketing to make green normal. *Journal of Consumer Behaviour, 13*(1), 9–17. doi:10.1002/cb.1439

Rettie, R., Burchell, K., & Riley, D. (2012). Normalising green behaviours: A new approach to sustainability marketing. *Journal of Marketing Management, 28*(3-4), 420–444. doi:10.1080/0267257X.2012.658840

Robert, J. A. (1996). Green consumers in the 1990s: Profile and implications for advertising. *Journal of Business Research, 36*(3), 217–231. doi:10.1016/0148-2963(95)00150-6

Saxena, R., & Khandelwal, P. K. (2010). Can green marketing be used as a tool for sustainable growth?: A study performed on consumers in India-An emerging economy. *The International Journal of Environmental, Cultural. Economic and Social Sustainability, 6*(2), 277–291.

Saxena, R. P., & Khandelwal, P. K. (2012). Greening of industries for sustainable growth: An exploratory study on durable, non-durable and services industries. *International Journal of Social Economics, 39*(8), 551–586. doi:10.1108/03068291211238437

Schultz, P. W., Nolan, J., Cialdini, R., Goldstein, N., & Griskevicius, V. (2007). The constructive, destructive, and reconstructive power of social norms. *Psychological Science, 18*(5), 429–434. doi:10.1111/j.1467-9280.2007.01917.x PMID:17576283

Shove, E. (2003). Converging conventions of comfort, cleanliness and convenience. *Journal of Consumer Policy, 26*(4), 395–418. doi:10.1023/A:1026362829781

Sooklal, R., Papadopoulos, T., & Ojiako, U. (2011). Information systems development: A normalisation theory perspective. *Industrial Management & Data Systems, 111*(8), 1270–1286. doi:10.1108/02635571111170794

Steg, L., & Vlek, C. (2009). Encouraging pro-environmental behaviour: An integrative review and research agenda. *Journal of Environmental Psychology, 29*(3), 309–317. doi:10.1016/j.jenvp.2008.10.004

Stevens, C. (2010, February). Linking sustainable consumption and production: The government role. [Blackwell Publishing Ltd.]. *Natural Resources Forum, 34*(1), 16–23. doi:10.1111/j.1477-8947.2010.01273.x

The World Bank. (2013, June 5). *India diagnostic assessment of select environmental challenges: an analysis of physical and monetary losses of environmental health and natural resources.* Retrieved June 6, 2016, from http://www-wds.worldbank.org/external/default/WDSContentServer/WDSP/IB/2013/07/16/000442464_20130716091943/Rendered/PDF/700040v10ESW0P0box0374379B00PUBLIC0.pdf

The World Bank. (2014, March 6). *India: Green Growth - Overcoming Environment Challenges to Promote Development.* Retrieved June 5, 2016, from http://www.worldbank.org/en/news/feature/2014/03/06/green-growth-overcoming-india-environment-challenges-promote-development?cid=SAR_TTWB-SAREN_EXT

Trott, S., & Sople, V. V. (2016). Brand Equity: An Indian Perspective. PHI Learning Pvt. Ltd.

Uddin, W., Khan, B., Shaukat, N., Majid, M., Mujtaba, G., Mehmood, A., & Almeshal, A. M. et al. (2016). Biogas potential for electric power generation in Pakistan: A survey. *Renewable & Sustainable Energy Reviews, 54*, 25–33. doi:10.1016/j.rser.2015.09.083

Varman, R., & Costa, J. A. (2008). Embedded markets, communities, and the invisible hand of social norms. *Journal of Macromarketing, 28*(2), 141–156. doi:10.1177/0276146708314594

Wang, Z., Zhang, B., Yin, J., & Zhang, Y. (2011). Determinants and policy implications for household electricity-saving behaviour: Evidence from Beijing, China. *Energy Policy, 39*(6), 3550–3557. doi:10.1016/j.enpol.2011.03.055

Zhao, W., & Schroeder, P. (2010). Sustainable consumption and production: Trends, challenges and options for the Asia-Pacific region. *Natural Resources Forum, 34*(1), 4–15. doi:10.1111/j.1477-8947.2010.01275.x

Chapter 7
Pro-Social Behaviour and Philanthropy in Conflict and Post-Conflict Contexts

Shaza Aldairany
International Business School, Malaysia

Rosmini Omar
International Business School, Malaysia

ABSTRACT

Pro-social behaviour and philanthropy are critical traits to act in a responsible manner towards society and environment through providing money, time and efforts. Most studies have focused on stable locations. However, conflict may still appear as potential places for such behaviour. This chapter raises three major inquiries: Do individuals and corporates perform pro-social behaviour in conflict context? If so, how do they perform such behaviour? How does literature approach specifically consumer pro-social behaviour in conflict and post-conflict locations. This chapter tries to conceptually review recent literature of pro-social practices in conflict contexts. The chapter reveals that no absolute positive impact relating to violence and conflict on pro-social behaviour. The majority of evidence supports the idea that pro-sociality increases during times of war. People exposed to direct violence may participate more in social activities, with early development of environmental and consumer issues. Moreover, entrepreneurship is found to have similar implications on the war-torn society.

1. INTRODUCTION

Pro-social behaviour and philanthropy indicate to actions in the sake of public goods towards society and surrounding environment through participation and contributing money, time and efforts to the society's most important issues (Brown & Ferris, 2007). The core motivation of both practices towards others in society and nature is the individual moral responsibility (Nickel & Eikenberry, 2010). Pro-social behaviours, in general, cover a diverse kind of practices including donating, volunteering, voting and supporting

DOI: 10.4018/978-1-5225-2912-5.ch007

environmental causes (Lay & Hoppmann, 2015). This notion originally signifies to altruistic and empathic giving and was used for the first time before more than one hundred years ago (Penner, Dovidio, Piliavin, & Schroeder, 2005). Consumer pro-social behaviour represents an example of taking care of others while purchasing goods and needs (Small & Cryder, 2016). Consumer pro-social behaviour refers to a broader conception than pro-environmental behaviour, which focuses on environmental issues only.

On the other hand, philanthropy, in its simplicity, refers to courtesy and benevolence (Sulek, 2010). Schervish (1998) identified it as the feeling of care which is managed by moral responsibility beyond self-interest, towards others. Philanthropy is commonly reflected in same aforementioned set of activities including volunteering and donations (Lay & Hoppmann, 2015). Therefore, many literature bring both terms synonymously, especially when discussing individual level of practices such as volunteering, generosity and donations (Lay & Hoppmann, 2015). They are basically the individual responsibility rather than governmental and public ones (Imada, 2010). In order to approach the largest possible number of articles in conflict and post conflict, this chapter uses both terms as keywords in search engines.

From this perspective, most pro-social behaviour and philanthropy studies have focused on stable locations and developed countries like USA and Europe (Mattis et al., 2000; Paxton, Reith, & Glanville, 2014; Schuyt, Bekkers, & Smit, 2010). However, conflict and post conflict contexts may still appear as potential places for such behaviours, especially with evidences that indicate to positive legacies of violence and increasing participation in social involvement (Bauer et al., 2016; Grosjean, 2014). Conflict here refers to a wide-scale violence and armed crisis that caused due to political, religious, economic or ethnic reasons (Brück, Naudé, & Verwimp, 2012). Furthermore, post conflict also presents a fragile place that faces huge challenges despite of it relative stability compared with conflict locations (Santos, 2003). With a world which constantly evolves through cycles of crisis and conflicts (Pirkkalainen & Abdile, 2009), addressing pro-social behaviour and philanthropic issues seems to be crucial in general and with specific emphasizing on corporates and consumers.

Since philanthropy and pro-social behaviour mainly exist as a private and individual intervention, one can except higher importance when the role of government is missing, like in conflict and violence cases. The question here is: has such importance of pro-social behaviour and philanthropy been well reflected in literature and recent knowledge and what are the most evidenced trends and even gaps? This chapter inquisitively endeavours three major inquiries in a conceptual manner: Do individuals and entrepreneurships perform pro-social behaviour in conflict context, and if so, how is this phenomenon implementing within an instable environment? Finally, how does literature approach specifically consumer pro-social behaviour in conflict and post-conflict locations. From existing literature, this chapter tries to bring the current knowledge of actual pro-social and philanthropy practices in the context of conflict. Moreover, with a very limited amount of literature that analyses consumer pro-social behaviour and philanthropy in conflict and post conflict contexts, this chapter puts forward also arguments from a wider perspective of any evidences relevant to pro-social behaviour, sustainable business or philanthropy in such contexts. The main reason is to bring understanding of how people in general, and more specifically consumers and corporates perform these behaviours. This attempt may build a foundation for further researchers and deeper studies. The main focus of this chapter is to map current knowledge on two levels, individual and corporate. In the individual level, an attempt to find evidence about consumer pro-social behaviour is additionally presenting. Hopefully, this chapter would further motivate future work for in-depth empirical investigation, in accumulating a better understanding of meanings of survival and thriving in conflict and post conflict locations. The rest of this chapter is organized as follow: the second section discusses pro-social behaviour and philanthropy issues in general. The third section illustrates conflict and post conflict meanings. The forth section shows the process of data collection. The fifth section argues the main objectives of this chapter, pro-social behaviour and philanthropy in conflict and post conflict contexts, and finally concluding remarks for further possible research are presented.

2. PRO-SOCIAL BEHAVIOUR AND PHILANTHROPY

In general, pro-social behaviour and philanthropy represent a clear trait of the ability to participate in societal problems and act for the public good by showing interest in contributing money, time and efforts to the society' most important issues (Brown & Ferris, 2007). The essential meaning of such pro-sociality is the moral sense of being responsible towards the society, environment and other people. Pro-social behaviours, as well as philanthropy, involve a diverse kind of practices including donating, volunteering, voting and supporting environmental causes (Lay & Hoppmann, 2015). The idea of pro-sociality refers to altruism and empathy which was used for the first time before more than one hundred years ago (Penner et al., 2005). Similarly, philanthropy points to courtesy and benevolence (Sulek, 2010). Schervish (1998) identified it as the feeling of care which is managed by moral responsibility beyond self-interest, towards others. They are basically the individual responsibility rather than governmental and public ones (Imada, 2010). The early definitions of philanthropy were wide and not specific with certain behaviours and only focused on love mankind and behaving well. The latter meanings of philanthropy indicate to charity (Schuyt et al., 2010). From 1988, a clearer understanding referred to not only charity, but volunteering and supporting causes (Sulek, 2010). The contemporary definition of philanthropy includes any form of behaviour that involves participation beyond the classical charity to a wide range of social problem (Schervish, 1998).

One the other hand, while consumer behaviour usually refers to meet self needs (Small & Cryder, 2016), consumer pro-social behaviour represents purchase behaviour that involves in selflessness and helping others. Even pro-social consumer behaviour focuses on consumers perspectives, it is still under the general pro-social behaviour as a human attitude to help others (Small & Cryder, 2016). Other researchers refer it to as ethical consumption (White, MacDonnell, & Ellard, 2012). Consumer pro-social behaviour is wider concept than pro-environmental behaviour, which emphasises on environmental issues only. It is similar to the wide pro-social behaviour, which includes environmental concerns, and also covers abroad sense of responsibility towards society, nature and globe.

In general, Carlo and Randall (2002) state four main forms of pro-social behaviour. First form is altruistic pro-social behaviour, which is the voluntary behaviour of helping. Compliant pro-social behaviour is helping behaviour upon request. Emotional pro-social behaviour is helping behaviour due to emotional pressure. Public pro-social behaviour is helping behaviour in presence of others.

In general, philanthropy and pro-social behaviour exist at many places and levels in the society. As discussed earlier, the most important one is the individual perspective. Moreover, corporate philanthropy and rich philanthropists represent additional players of pro-social behaviour. Figure 1 shows different level of pro-social and philanthropic behaviour.

Corporate philanthropy represents an integral part of corporate social responsibility and sustainable business. Many researchers consider this philanthropy as a representative of corporate social responsibility (Jamali & Karam, 2016). It basically focuses on performing businesses that spread both financial gains and non-financial gains (Shepherd & Patzelt, 2011). Wallace (2005) defines this responsibility as a combination of social entrepreneurship and sustainable one, which produces environmental, economic

Figure 1. Different levels of pro-social and philanthropic behaviour
Source: Authors' self-compilation

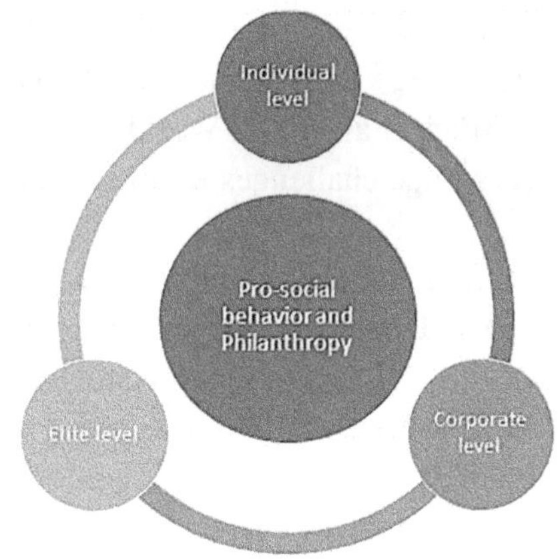

and social responsibility. However, this 'responsibility' of business was debatable long time ago. For instance, Milton Friedman, in his classical view of corporations, emphasised on the maximizing the shareholders' profit as the core responsibility of the managers. He also went far from that to consider the social responsibility as wasting of shareholders' wealth. This view has been later replaced with the wider business responsibilities where it is not enough anymore to only seek for economic profit, and corporations have to extend their benefits to all potential stakeholder and society (Mudrack, 2007). Through the emphasising on what he had termed as "creative destructive", Schumpeter considered the crucial role of entrepreneurship is evolving the wellbeing of people (Schumpeter, 1934). Furthermore, Sarkar and Pansera consider that the social concerns are embedded in the values and impulse of grass-roots entrepreneurship even (2016).

On the other hand, elite or rich philanthropists represent those people who consider social and environmental issues and make generous donations for the sake of society (Nickel & Eikenberry, 2010). These philanthropists usually have great impact on raising awareness of arts and climate change (Harrow, 2010). Basically, this chapter seeks to find evidences from both individual and corporate perspectives.

A diverse range of theories explain the individual pro-social behaviour such as altruistic theory, social cognitive theory and identification theory (Luszczynska & Schwarzer, 2005). Altruistic theory explains philanthropy and prosocial behaviour as the altruistic desire which does not anticipate benefit (P. Schervish & Havens, 1997). Social cognitive theory states that such behaviour is being built on reciprocity where people expect to have benefit (Luszczynska & Schwarzer, 2005). Finally, identification theory combines both altruistic desire with social cognitive (Schervish & Havens, 1997). More specifically, many drivers are said to be crucial in promoting such behaviour such as personal values, reputation, solicitation and altruism (Bekkers & Wiepking, 2011). Philanthropic and responsible corporate are also based on many theories, basically economic, institutional and psychological theories (Shepherd & Patzelt, 2011).

3. CONFLICT AND POST CONFLICT

Conflict and post conflict contexts represent very problematic locations at different level of analysis. In general, conflict here refers to wide-scale violence and armed crisis that caused due to political, religious, economic or ethnic reasons (Brück et al., 2012; World Bank, 2011). Furthermore, post conflict also presents a fragile status that faces huge challenges despite of its relative stability compared with conflict locations (Santos, 2003).

The most apparent features of conflict and post conflict areas are fragility, high levels of poverty, sharp reduction in society's well-being and the missing role of government (Brück, Naudé, & Verwimp, 2011), as well as wide scale destructions and loss in human capital in terms of numbers of dead or at least injured people (Brück et al., 2012; Roberts, 2010). In conflict and post conflict locations, people need help. Nature and infrastructure are often destroyed or at least highly affected (Brück et al., 2011).

While inheritances of conflict and armed strife are represented by wide devastation of society, economic and even people (Bauer et al., 2016), many views consider that such conflict was necessary condition of the recovery and growth of many European countries (Bauer et al., 2016; Blattman, 2009; Grosjean, 2014). This chapter adopts this view in looking for the positive and bright inheritances of conflict in a form of pro-social behaviour as it is discussed in the following section. Actually, addressing such issues in conflict and post conflict contexts may be important more any time before. This is due to the increasing number of conflicts all over the world. Since the Cold War time, new wars occurred and caused by religious, ethical and economic problems (Pirkkalainen & Abdile, 2009). Those wars and conflicts resulted huge number of refugees and migrants, and make the world more risky (World Economic Forum, 2016)

4. DATA COLLECTION

The main objective of this chapter is to review the relevant literature of pro-social behaviour and philanthropy in conflict and post conflict contexts. Generally, literature review method is an attempt to bring the recent knowledge in a research area and define the existing gaps (Petticrew & Roberts, 2008). This review often peruses systematically by identifying relevant literature, synthesising and analysing it (Wright, Brand, Dunn, & Spindler, 2007). The process starts with identifying the study questions and then collecting the literature. The following keywords were used to approach the most relevant articles, pro-social behaviour, philanthropy, consumer pro-social, corporate philanthropy, responsible business, conflict, war, violence and post conflict. Searching was conducted using Emerald, Sage, Google scholar, Wiley online library and Taylor Francis online. The inclusive criteria were any empirical study that addresses research topic with filed work or at least well developed secondary data. It is important to note here that due to the limited literature of corporate philanthropy, this chapter brings the most relevant articles that discussed non-economic role of entrepreneurship in a form of societal implications.

5. DISCUSSION AND FINDING PRO-SOCIAL BEHAVIOUR AND PHILANTHROPY IN CONFLICT AND POST CONFLICT

The earlier two sections argue pro-social behaviour and philanthropy from individual and business perspectives, as well as defining conflict and post conflict contexts. This section attempts to bring these issues contextually and discuss how people, and more specifically consumers and entrepreneurship perform such behaviours. It is worth to mention here again that conflict and violence may not only affect infrastructure or destroy houses, they also have high potential impact of people who are living in the place, their norms and values (Bellows & Miguel, 2009). At this point, one can predict changes in pro-social behaviour and philanthropy of people and corporates, including consumers as well.

After the World War One and the World War Two, as well as different wars in Asia and Europe, a study reveals that conflict and war increased collaboration and pro-social behaviour (Grosjean, 2014). Furthermore, many evidences have been found in Sierra Leone, Uganda, Tajikistan and Nepal that support positive social participation from people who have exposed to war and violence (Bellows & Miguel, 2009). Another study confirms that people who had past experience in being threatened tend to take care more of other people and act more socially towards society (Bauer et al., 2016).

However, some studies found that violence and conflict maybe in stark contrast foster negative behaviour and even support radical perspectives as the case of Nazi in Germany (Grosjean, 2014). Moreover, another study considers that the higher social participations caused by conflict, tend to be limited to certain close groups, rather than to a general society (Cassar, Grosjean, & Whitt, 2013). Here, the type of conflict arises to play decisive role. In civil war, for example, pro-social behaviour may be performed with the same political group (Grosjean, 2014). Such altruistic feelings may be missing towards oppositions (Cassar et al., 2013). It is clear from literature that the impact of civil war may destroy the empathy with people who have different political views.

Furthermore, and as one of individual pro-social behaviour, consumer pro-social behaviour during and after conflict is underdeveloped area in existing literature. While there is significant discussion concerning consumer pro-social behaviour, ethical consumerism and green purchase behaviour, too little articles have approached such issues in unstable locations. Rawwas, Patzer, and Vitell (1998) is one of this limited literature that studies consumer ethical values in two conflict locations, Ireland and Lebanon. In both countries, consumers reveal low tendency and sensitivity towards ethical issues. Examining consumer pro-social behaviour in conflict and post conflict contexts may provide a wide gap than requires deep examining.

On the other hand, business world may also show different shapes of corporate philanthropy. Entrepreneurship in Bosnia and Herzegovina personifies significant role in diminishing poverty and increase employment rates, beside other social effects in a country which had suffered from ethnic tensions (Djip, 2014). In Uganda, more specifically, social entrepreneurship also reveals a crucial role at individual and societal levels in post conflict recovery. An empirical research at Uganda clarifies significance of entrepreneurial heroes of social enterprises, starting from discovering the opportunity and creating "the new idea- innovation" solutions (Sserwanga, Isabella Kiconco, Nystrand, & Mindra, 2014). Another research of the entrepreneurship role in Rwanda after the genocide, focuses on enhancing the intergroup relationship between Hutu and Tutsi, the two conflicting parties, along with the reconciliation policies in the coffee sector after liberalization. The quantitative study reveals positive relationship between entrepreneurship and reconciliation efforts. Both groups accept each other more when they work together and have the profit as a common goal. This study concludes a vital role of business in conflict reduction, which has been tested in one of conflict causes, the coffee sector in Rwanda (Tobias & Boudreaux, 2011). Promoting entrepreneurial efforts does not only lead to economic outcomes, but at the same time produces positive social effects that in turn may reduce conflict possibilities and enhance the intergroup relationship, leading at the end to stability after the horrific genocide (Tobias & Boudreaux, 2011) as well as decreasing the conflict possibilities (Tobias, Mair, & Barbosa-Leiker, 2013). From his perspective, Desai (2011) insists on the role of entrepreneurship in conflict contexts which may surpass the governmental and public function in providing employment opportunities. Through their resilience, entrepreneurs can disseminate the benefits to a particular groups of population (Desai, 2011).

However, and even many researches discuss the positive role of entrepreneurship, this does not implicate undoubtedly positive functions of business in conflict situations. In another place of the world, the positive role of entrepreneurship may be missing. For instance, in Palestine and especially after Oslo Peace Agreement, the relationship between entrepreneurship and economic growth remains in eclipse. This can be demonstrated by the unique status of Palestinian economy as a limited access society to both funds and skills and relies too much on the international aids (Sabella, Farraj, Burbar, & Qaimary, 2014). Probably, a certain potential negativity such as 'destructive entrepreneurships' appears to be a hindrance which means that some parties may benefit from conflicts and contribute in prolonging the violence and in this sense, entrepreneurs may seek profit through undesirable business like drug, weapons and money laundering (Desai, 2011). Moreover, unproductive entrepreneurship, which is defined as neutral case without any positive or negative effects, resists any opportunity due to fear and high risks (Rettberg, Leiteritz, & Nasi, 2011). Such destructive and unproductive entrepreneurship may exist in conflict areas along with the productive entrepreneurship, the wealth creating one (Rettberg et al., 2011). Subedi, in his paper studying a Nepal case, distinguishes between what he calls "conflict profiteers" who may arouse the conflict and "pro peace entrepreneurs" who support peace building process (2013). According to Subedi, it is misleading to consider all private sector under one of the above-mentioned categories. Moreover, an interesting research of Democratic republic of Congo addresses a name of destructive entrepreneur; Laurent Kabila, the former president of Congo. Kabila was destructive entrepreneurs when he recognizes an opportunities and implements his ideas despite the catastrophic social consequences of his child army and squandering the natural resources of the country (Desai, 2016). The following table summarizes all relevant evidences of pro-social behaviour and philanthropy in both individual and corporate levels.

Table 1 shows that social and political perspectives are clear examples of pro-social behaviour and philanthropy in conflict contexts like in Sierra Leone, Uganda, Tajikistan and Nepal. Evidence of environmental responsibility seems to be very rare and provide opportunity to more research. On the other hand, it is important to emphasise that above table includes positive implications of business, regardless if they were performed consciously or unconsciously as an intended philanthropic behaviour from entrepreneurs. This intention may also require further examination in conflict and post conflict contexts.

6. CONCLUSION

Basically, this chapter aims to discuss pro-social behaviour and philanthropy in conflict contexts from individual and corporate point of view. The review of individual level includes consumer as a particular example. This review may provide quick signals and directions for further research opportunities. It was apparent from the reviewed evidences that the effects of conflict and violence on pro-social behaviour and philanthropy are not absolute or positive. This was clear from both perspectives, individual and cor-

Table 1. Individual and corporate pro-social behaviour in conflict and post conflict contexts

Country	Researches	Pro-social behaviour and philanthropy forms	Summary
Individual Level			
Sierra Leone	(Bellows & Miguel, 2009)	Community services and voting	High pro-social behaviour.
Uganda	(Blattman, 2009)	Voting	high political engagement
Tajikistan	(Cassar et al., 2013)	Community services	High social engagement with decline in level of trust.
El Salvador	(Wood, 2003) cited in (Blattman, 2009)	Negative	Foster immoral reactions.
Nepal	(Gilligan, Pasquale, & Samii, 2014)	Social and political involvements	High social and political activities.
Ireland, Lebanon	(Rawwas et al., 1998)	Ethical values	Consumers are less sensitive towards ethical values
Corporate Level			
Bosnia and Herzegovina	(Djip, 2014)	Positive social effects	Positive social effects.
Rwanda	(Tobias & Boudreaux, 2011)	Positive social effects	Improve the intergroup relationship.
Uganda	(Sserwanga et al., 2014).	Positive social effects	crucial role at individual and societal levels in recovery
Palestine	(Sabella et al., 2014)	Missing role	Limited role.
Nepal	(Subedi, 2013)	Negative role	More "conflict profiteers" entrepreneurship

porate since both levels have negative implications as well. Approaching consumer pro-social behaviour is still highly missing in literature. In a particular literature, positive and negative implications can be found converge within a context (Gilligan et al., 2014). A considerable amount of literature indicates that individual pro-social behaviour as well as corporate philanthropy increase in conflict and post conflict contexts. Such implications are crucial for policy makers in conflict and post conflict contexts. This may make the mission of recovery easier by developing and implementing programs and policies that guide and improve this social participating. NGOs and humanitarian may also develop their policy to target and benefit from this pro-sociality trends in people as well as companies. However, the majority of these behaviours appear in forms of social implications and political involvement. Still, the literature gap is obviously obscured. The environmental responsibility seems to be missing in researches. This may be due to the catastrophic situation of conflict and most conflict contexts. Moreover, examining and exploring the consumer perspectives about pro-sociality in conflict and war locations need deep researches. These gaps probably due to the preferences of researchers in studying such phenomenon from the social and political standpoints only. Both contextual in-depth understanding and broad generalizable examinations are needed as pro-social behaviours and philanthropic entrepreneurships emerge as probable solutions to society in crisis and conflict. Along with examining pro-social behaviour from environmental and consumer perspectives, future researches may also explore the attitude or intention of corporate philanthropy in conflict contexts.

REFERENCES

Bauer, M., Blattman, C., Chytilová, J., Henrich, J., Miguel, E., & Mitts, T. (2016). Can war foster cooperation? *The Journal of Economic Perspectives*, *30*(3), 249–274. doi:10.1257/jep.30.3.249

Bekkers, R., & Wiepking, P. (2011). A literature review of empirical studies of philanthropy: Eight mechanisms that drive charitable giving. *Nonprofit and Voluntary Sector Quarterly*, *40*(5), 924–973. doi:10.1177/0899764010380927

Bellows, J., & Miguel, E. (2009). War and local collective action in Sierra Leone. *Journal of Public Economics*, *93*(11), 1144–1157. doi:10.1016/j.jpubeco.2009.07.012

Blattman, C. (2009). From violence to voting: War and political participation in Uganda. *The American Political Science Review*, *103*(02), 231–247. doi:10.1017/S0003055409090212

Brown, E., & Ferris, J. M. (2007). Social capital and philanthropy: An analysis of the impact of social capital on individual giving and volunteering. *Nonprofit and Voluntary Sector Quarterly*, *36*(1), 85–99. doi:10.1177/0899764006293178

Brück, T., Naudé, W., & Verwimp, P. (2011). Small Business, Entrepreneurship and Violent Conflict in Developing Countries. *Journal of Small Business and Entrepreneurship*, *24*(2), 161–178. doi:10.1080/08276331.2011.10593532

Brück, T., Naudé, W., & Verwimp, P. (2012). Business under Fire: Entrepreneurship and Violent Conflict in Developing Countries. *The Journal of Conflict Resolution*, *57*(1), 3–19. doi:10.1177/0022002712464846

Carlo, G., & Randall, B. A. (2002). The development of a measure of prosocial behaviors for late adolescents. *Journal of Youth and Adolescence*, *31*(1), 31–44. doi:10.1023/A:1014033032440

Cassar, A., Grosjean, P., & Whitt, S. (2013). Legacies of violence: Trust and market development. *Journal of Economic Growth*, *18*(3), 285–318. doi:10.1007/s10887-013-9091-3

Desai, S. (2011). A Tale of Entrepreneurship in Two Iraqi Cities. *Journal of Small Business and Entrepreneurship*, *24*(2), 283–292. doi:10.1080/08276331.2011.10593539

Desai, S. (2016). Destructive entrepreneurship and the security context: Program design considerations for disarmament, demobilization and reintegration (DDR) and counterinsurgency. *Journal of Entrepreneurship and Public Policy*, *5*(2), 240–250. doi:10.1108/JEPP-03-2016-0009

Djip, V. (2014). Entrepreneurship and SME development in post-conflict societies: The case of Bosnia & Herzegovina. *Journal of Entrepreneurship and Public Policy*, *3*(2), 254–274. doi:10.1108/JEPP-09-2012-0048

Gilligan, M. J., Pasquale, B. J., & Samii, C. (2014). Civil war and social cohesion: Lab-in-the-field evidence from Nepal. *American Journal of Political Science*, *58*(3), 604–619. doi:10.1111/ajps.12067

Grosjean, P. (2014). Conflict and social and political preferences: Evidence from World War II and civil conflict in 35 European countries. *Comparative Economic Studies*, *56*(3), 424–451. doi:10.1057/ces.2014.2

Harrow, J. (2010). *Philanthropy. In Third sector research* (pp. 121–137). Springer. doi:10.1007/978-1-4419-5707-8_10

Imada, M. (2010). *Civil Society in Japan: Democracy, voluntary action, and philanthropy. In Civic Engagement in Contemporary Japan* (pp. 21–40). Springer. doi:10.1007/978-1-4419-1504-7_2

Jamali, D., & Karam, C. (2016). Corporate Social Responsibility in Developing Countries as an Emerging Field of Study. *International Journal of Management Reviews*. doi:10.1111/ijmr.12112

Lay, J. C., & Hoppmann, C. A. (2015). Altruism and Prosocial Behavior. In N. A. Pachana (Ed.), *Encyclopedia of Geropsychology* (pp. 1–9). Singapore: Springer Singapore. doi:10.1007/978-981-287-080-3_69-1

Luszczynska, A., & Schwarzer, R. (2005). Social cognitive theory. *Predicting Health Behaviour, 2*, 127-169.

Mattis, J. S., Jagers, R. J., Hatcher, C. A., Lawhon, G. D., Murphy, E. J., & Murray, Y. F. (2000). *Religiosity, volunteerism, and community involvement among African American men: An exploratory analysis*. Academic Press.

Mudrack, P. (2007). Individual personality factors that affect normative beliefs about the rightness of corporate social responsibility. *Business & Society*, *46*(1), 33–62. doi:10.1177/0007650306290312

Nickel, P. M., & Eikenberry, A. M. (2010). Philanthropy in an Era of Global Governance. In R. Taylor (Ed.), *Third Sector Research* (pp. 269–279). New York, NY: Springer New York. doi:10.1007/978-1-4419-5707-8_19

Paxton, P., Reith, N. E., & Glanville, J. L. (2014). Volunteering and the dimensions of religiosity: A cross-national analysis. *Review of Religious Research*, *56*(4), 597–625. doi:10.1007/s13644-014-0169-y

Penner, L. A., Dovidio, J. F., Piliavin, J. A., & Schroeder, D. A. (2005). Prosocial behavior: Multilevel perspectives. *Annual Review of Psychology*, *56*(1), 365–392. doi:10.1146/annurev.psych.56.091103.070141 PMID:15709940

Petticrew, M., & Roberts, H. (2008). *Systematic Reviews in the Social Sciences. In Systematic Reviews in the Social Sciences*. Blackwell Publishing Ltd.

Pirkkalainen, P., & Abdile, M. (2009). *The diaspora-conflict-peace-nexus: A literature review*. University of Jyväskylä.

Rawwas, M. Y. A., Patzer, G. L., & Vitell, S. J. (1998). A cross-cultural investigation of the ethical values of consumers: The potential effect of war and civil disruption. *Journal of Business Ethics, 17*(4), 435-448.

Rettberg, A., Leiteritz, R. J., & Nasi, C. (2011). Entrepreneurial Activity in the Context of Violent Conflict: Business and Organized Violence in Colombia1. *Journal of Small Business and Entrepreneurship*, *24*(2), 179–196. doi:10.1080/08276331.2011.10593533

Roberts, N. C. (2010). Entrepreneurship in Peace Operations. *Journal of Civil Society*, *6*(1), 1–21. doi:10.1080/17448689.2010.481908

Sabella, A. R., Farraj, W. A., Burbar, M., & Qaimary, D. (2014). Entrepreneurship and economic growth in West Bank, Palestine. *Journal of Developmental Entrepreneurship, 19*(01), 1450003. doi:10.1142/S1084946714500034

Santos, N. (2003). *Financing small, medium and micro enterprises in post-conflict situations Microfinance opportunities in the Democratic Republic of the Congo.* Paper presented at the OECD Development Centre. Discussion Paper Produced for the Seminar "Public Private Partnership for the Development of the Democratic Republic of Congo", Kinshasa.

Sarkar, S., & Pansera, M. (2016). Sustainability-driven innovation at the bottom: Insights from grassroots ecopreneurs. *Technological Forecasting and Social Change*. doi:10.1016/j.techfore.2016.08.029

Schervish, G. P. (1998). Philanthropy. In R. Wuthnow (Ed.), Encyclopedia of Politics and Religion (Vol. 1, pp. 600-603). Washington, DC: Congressional Quarterly Inc.

Schervish, P., & Havens, J. (1997). Social participation and charitable giving: A multivariate analysis. *VOLUNTAS: International Journal of Voluntary and Nonprofit Organizations, 8*(3), 235–260. doi:10.1007/BF02354199

Schuyt, T., Bekkers, R., & Smit, J. (2010). The Philanthropy Scale: A sociological perspective in measuring new forms of pro social behaviour. *Social Work & Society, 8*(1), 121–135.

Shepherd, D. A., & Patzelt, H. (2011). The new field of sustainable entrepreneurship: Studying entrepreneurial action linking what is to be sustained with what is to be developed. *Entrepreneurship Theory and Practice, 35*(1), 137–163. doi:10.1111/j.1540-6520.2010.00426.x

Small, D. A., & Cryder, C. (2016). Prosocial consumer behavior. *Current Opinion in Psychology, 10*, 107–111. doi:10.1016/j.copsyc.2016.01.001

Sserwanga, A., Kiconco, I., & Rebecca, N. (2014). Social entrepreneurship and post conflict recovery in Uganda. *Journal of Enterprising Communities: People and Places in the Global Economy, 8*(4), 300–317. doi:10.1108/JEC-02-2014-0001

Subedi, D. B. (2013). Pro-Peace Entrepreneur or Conflict Profiteer? Critical Perspective on the Private Sector and Peacebuilding in Nepal. *Peace and Change, 38*(2), 181–206. doi:10.1111/pech.12011

Sulek, M. (2010). On the modern meaning of philanthropy. *Nonprofit and Voluntary Sector Quarterly, 39*(2), 193–212. doi:10.1177/0899764009333052

Tobias, J. M., & Boudreaux, K. C. (2011). Entrepreneurship and Conflict Reduction in the Post-Genocide Rwandan Coffee Industry. *Journal of Small Business and Entrepreneurship, 24*(2), 217–242. doi:10.1080/08276331.2011.10593535

Tobias, J. M., Mair, J., & Barbosa-Leiker, C. (2013). Toward a theory of transformative entrepreneuring: Poverty reduction and conflict resolution in Rwandas entrepreneurial coffee sector. *Journal of Business Venturing, 28*(6), 728–742. doi:10.1016/j.jbusvent.2013.03.003

Wallace, B. (2005). Exploring the meaning (s) of sustainability for community-based social entrepreneurs. *Social Enterprise Journal*, *1*(1), 78–89. doi:10.1108/17508610580000708

White, K., MacDonnell, R., & Ellard, J. H. (2012). Belief in a just world: Consumer intentions and behaviors toward ethical products. *Journal of Marketing*, *76*(1), 103–118. doi:10.1509/jm.09.0581

Wood, E. J. (2003). *Insurgent collective action and civil war in El Salvador*. Cambridge University Press. doi:10.1017/CBO9780511808685

World Bank. (2011). *World development report 2011: Conflict, security, and development*. Retrieved from World Economic Forum: http://wef.ch/risks2016(11th Edition)

Wright, R. W., Brand, R. A., Dunn, W., & Spindler, K. P. (2007). How to write a systematic review. *Clinical Orthopaedics and Related Research*, *455*, 23–29. doi:10.1097/BLO.0b013e31802c9098 PMID:17279036

Section 3

Green Marketing Strategies

Chapter 8
Green Marketing Strategies and Marketing Performance:
The Case of Turkey

Serkan Kılıç
Uludağ University, Turkey

Erkan Özdemir
Uludag University, Turkey

ABSTRACT

Businesses have increasingly paid more attention to the production and marketing of green products. The aim of this study is to establish the marketing mix (4P) strategies that businesses pursuit for their green products and examine the effects of green product, green pricing, green marketing channel and green marketing communication strategies on the marketing performance. The results of the present study are particularly important in terms of shaping the marketing mix strategies of businesses that have already implemented/will implement the production and marketing of green products. The research data were collected by the web based questionnaire method from 258 businesses that operated in Turkey. SPSS 18.0 and AMOS 17.0 softwares were used to conduct the analysis. As a result of multiple regression analysis, it was found that green pricing and green marketing communication strategies had a significant effect on the marketing performance.

INTRODUCTION

Today when environmental interests and awareness of the consumers have come to increase, more and more consumers have started to demand environmentally friendly products and services from the businesses. In addition to the businesses that emphasize the environmental issues, the businesses that have noticed the environmental demands and preferences of the consumers have tended to develop and implement green marketing strategies (Agrawal & Das, 2013) both during the manufacturing processes and in their marketing approaches (Alsmadi, 2007). This particular trend plays various roles such as the creation of legal regulations related to environment, awareness-rising in terms of the costs and the lack

DOI: 10.4018/978-1-5225-2912-5.ch008

of natural resources, increase in the demands by the community and stakeholders and the activities of the pressure groups (Jones, Clarke-Hill, Comfort, & Hillier, 2008). In other words, it is possible to say that businesses turn to green marketing for reasons such as government pressure, cost issue, competitive pressure, increase consumer base, subsidies from government and social responsibility (Pawar & Kamble, 2016). Currently, green marketing strategy is a very important issue and if businesses think that they are responsible for long term, they will be able to use this strategy very effectively. The sustainable marketing strategy, which is an important strategy, is also a requirement in ensuring the consumer confidence.

Green marketing is comprised of activities that are designed to satisfy the wants and needs of the individuals, and have minimal detrimental effect on the natural environment (Nair & Menon, 2008). Green marketing is defined as "the holistic management process responsible for identifying, anticipating and satisfying the requirements of customers and society in a profitable and sustainable way" (El Dief & Font, 2010, p. 158). This definition emphasizes the significance of market orientation in the process of environmental marketing (Nair & Menon, 2008). From the perspective of macro marketing, Mitchell et al. (2010), on the other hand, recommended the sustainable market orientation and emphasized its importance. Terms such as environmental marketing, ecological marketing and sustainable marketing are used to mean the same as green marketing (Garg, 2015). These concepts reflect an environmental approach from the perspective of marketing. However, sustainable marketing represents an integrative approach that emphasizes environmental (green marketing), social value (social marketing) and economic / financial issues in the development of marketing strategies (Bridges & Wilhelm, 2008). While social marketing, on the one hand, includes the green marketing and sustainable marketing issues such as environmental pollution, nutritional aspects of products and consumer health, it also includes other social issues such as reducing smoking and excessive alcohol consumption in general, demotivating the use of harmful drugs, and increasing the public prosperity. Social marketing campaigns are aimed at changing people's consciousness, values, actions or behaviors in a positive manner (Kotler & Keller, 2012, p. 638). Although sustainable marketing currently focuses on consumers and their needs, it includes the consumers of next generation and meeting their needs (Seretny & Seretny, 2012). From this point of view, it can be said that responsive and proactive market orientations (Narver, Slater, & MacLachlan, 2004; Atuahene-Gima, Slater, & Olson, 2005; Tsai, Chou, & Kuo, 2008; Li, Lin, & Chu, 2008; Zhang & Duan, 2010; Zhang & Duan, 2010a; Bodlaj, 2010; Bodlaj, Coenders, & Zabkar, 2012; Yannopoulos, Auh, & Menguc, 2012; Oswald, Brettel, & Engelen, 2012) are closely related to sustainable marketing. Within the framework of sustainable marketing, environmental marketing or green marketing strategy signifies that consumers' needs are met not only through the commercialization of green products and services, but also through making the systems and processes green (Fraj-Andrés, Martínez-Salinas, & Matute-Vallejo, 2009b). The concept of sustainable production (Ali & Suleiman, 2016) can also be considered at this point.

The concept and scope of green marketing, in general, is quite comprehensive within the field of marketing. In this sense, green marketing is not only limited to the communication policies of the operator, but is also associated with all the functional areas of marketing. Furthermore, green marketing should be seen as a philosophy guiding all actions of the business, not just a series of procedures, activities and techniques for the design and commercialization of green products. Green marketing philosophy can be expressed as a way of understanding the exchange relationships that go beyond the current needs of consumers and take into account the social interests of protecting the natural environment (Chamorro & Bañegil, 2006). In this respect, the environmental marketing strategy includes decisions at the operational and functional levels. With the commercialization strategies at the business level, the competitive position of the business develops. Functional strategy, on the other hand, manages the planning and processing procedures between different functions such as marketing and research and development. Businesses should demonstrate environmental proactive behavior. Therefore, businesses can have competitive advantages such as cost minimization, quality improvement, and social image enhancement by reducing the consumption of raw materials and energy resources by environmental management and can pursue more profitable marketing opportunities by targeting the ecological consumer segments (Fraj-Andrés et al., 2009b). In addition, the sectors that produce environmentally-friendly products balancing the technical features, price acceptability and compliance with environmental protection (Pap, Ham, & Turalija, 2015) can be financially supported by the state (Garg, 2015). Tax exemptions may be provided to importers, exporters and green businesses for green applications (Ali & Ahmad, 2012).

When the studies in the literature are examined, though rare, the sustainable and green marketing concept and system (Murphy, 2005; Singh & Pandey, 2012; Paramod, 2016; Antony & Pakutharivu, 2016; Nair & Menon, 2008; Pawar & Kamble, 2016; Phalke & Ranade, 2016) green labeling (Chamorro & Bañegil, 2006), design of environmentally sustainable products (Diego-Mas, Poveda-Bautista, & Alcaide-Marzal, 2016), sustainable production (Ali & Suleiman, 2016), green marketing strategies (Banerjee, Iyer, & Kashyap, 2003; Ginsberg & Bloom, 2004; Fraj-Andrés, Martínez-Salinas, & Matute-Vallejo, 2009a; Leonidou, Katsikeas, & Morgan, 2013; Garg, 2015; Pap et al., 2015; Rastogi & Khan, 2015; Villarino & Font, 2015), sustainable market orientation (Mitchell, Wooliscroft, & Higham, 2010) were investigated by different researchers.

Green marketing strategies and the performance relationship were also addressed in various studies (Chen, Lai, & Wen, 2006; Fraj, Martínez, & Matute, 2011; Leonidou et al., 2013; Fraj-Andrés et al., 2009b). In one of those studies, Chen et al. (2006) found that green product and process innovation of businesses had a positive impact on the performance. Fraj-Andrés et al. (2009b) also found that environmental marketing affected the operational and commercial performance of businesses. In a similar study, Fraj et al. (2011) suggested that the environment-oriented businesses had more superior operational and marketing performance. Leonidou et al. (2013) concluded that green products and green distribution had significant effects on the product-market performance. Wu and Lin (2016) investigated the influence of green marketing strategies on business performance and found that green marketing strategies improved the business performance. Al Khattab and As'ad (2015) found that the elements of the green supply chain management "internal environmental management, green purchasing, green information systems, cooperation with customers, eco-design and packaging, and investment recovery" practices affected the environmental-based marketing performance. Richey et al. (2014) also found that the environmental focus of businesses did not lead to superior performance without the support of senior management.

The businesses that wish to make a difference in the minds of consumers position themselves as socially responsible and environmentally with their advertising activities and competitive prices. Green marketing is comprised of aims such as eliminating the concept of waste rather than getting rid of it, developing the concept of product consistent with the environmental commitment, offering value for money to the consumers by enabling to reflect the true costs of the product, and possessing environmental awareness and converting it into profit (Alsmadi, 2007). In line with these aims, the businesses create their marketing strategies and put them into practice. However, it has become an intriguing issue especially for the businesses that have tended to be involved in green marketing whether the green marketing strategies are effective on the marketing performance of the businesses. This issue is even more important especially in the countries where the adoption of the green marketing philosophy is still an ongoing issue.

The aim of this chapter is to review the relevant literature regarding the green marketing and investigate the effects of green marketing strategies of the businesses operating in various sectors in Turkey on their marketing performances. The study aims to investigate and analyze which factors of the marketing mix (4P) will have an impact on the marketing performance of the businesses. Based on the findings to be obtained, recommendations will be offered to the businesses. This paper is structured as follows: Firstly, the existing literature regarding the green marketing strategies and marketing performance are reviewed. Secondly, the research methodology and the results are shown. Next, conclusions are drawn and the limitations of the research are discussed. Finally, some suggestions for future research are made.

LITERATURE REVIEW

Green Marketing Strategies

Businesses can develop green marketing strategies by focusing on 3Rs (Reduce, Reuse, and Recycle) that help green consumption (Alsmadi, 2007; Phalke & Ranade, 2016) and they can become a green business in three ways such as value-addition processes (firm level), management systems (firm level) and/or products (product level) (Prakash, 2002). First of all, the green consumer segments should be identified and consumers' wants / needs should be investigated. As the number of consumers interested in the environment increase, it is observed that the businesses also turn to these target markets (Singh & Pandey, 2012). Demand for green products should be assessed at this point. If consumers demand green products and are willing to pay more for these products, the consumer-oriented businesses should focus on developing environmentally friendly products and adopting the environmental standards (Bhaskaran, Polonsky, Cary, & Fernandez, 2006).

Green consumer segments, on the other hand, can be classified as true blue greens, greenback greens, sprouts, grousers and basic browns (Ginsberg & Bloom, 2004). The importance of value, consequential belief and sense of responsibility are the main factors that affect the consumer behavior towards green products (Shao, Taisch, & Mier, 2017). Green marketing involves the promotion of environmentally safe and useful products. This, in turn, includes the development of ecologically safe products, recyclable packaging, green marketing channels, green promotional efforts and green labeling (Bati, 2016). However, businesses should create green marketing strategies that are appropriate for themselves. Ginsberg and Bloom (2004), according to marketing mix elements, defined these strategies as the lean green strategy, the defensive green strategy, the shaded green strategy, and the extreme green strategy. At this point, businesses should identify the green marketing as a long-term investment with long-term benefits (Garg, 2015) and change their attitudes to "think green, think clean, and think eco-friendly" (Pawar & Kamble, 2016, p. 154). Green marketing strategies can be examined according to four components of marketing mix such as product, price, distribution and promotion. These components are discussed below.

Green Product Strategies

The green products can be identified as naturally grown, recyclable, biodegradable, reusable, containing natural ingredients, recycled contents and nontoxic chemicals; do not harm or pollute the environment; have eco-friendly packaging i.e. reusable and refillable containers (Phalke & Ranade, 2016). Green product characteristics are also related with the manufacturer's production processes, policies and practices, and the social and ecological nature of the product material. It is especially important to integrate ecological characteristics with the concept of quality in the new product development process (Pap et al., 2015).

The green product strategy requires the businesses to emphasize such subjects as easily recyclable products, products using renewable energy sources such as rechargeable batteries, solar powered machines, recyclable packaging, non-destructive products such as organic foods and materials used throughout the production process, consumed energy and packaging regulations (Alsmadi, 2007). Thanks to the businesses that are interested in these issues, automobiles can be designed with alternative energy sources and furniture can be produced with recyclable materials (Murphy, 2005). For instance, Nike used less glue and recycled materials during the production of Air Jordan XX3 shoes (Leonidou et al., 2013).

Green products can be classified as simple, extended and completely green products (Chamorro & Bañegil, 2006). The ISO 14000 environmental management system helps to improve the environmental performance of the products of the businesses with environmental labeling and instruction standards (Bridges & Wilhelm, 2008). Environmentally conscious consumers also rely on green labels as an indicator of green characteristics (Suki, Suki, & Azman, 2016) and use less packaging (Pinto, Nique, Herter, & Borges, 2016). Packaging is important in terms of attracting attention, enabling effective communication and having a critical role in the decision-making process. For instance, in his study, Jerzyk (2016) examined what the consumers expected of the ecological messages in the packaging of products, the characteristics of sustainable packaging in consumer behavior, and how the consumers made the purchasing decisions based on sustainable packaging. Accordingly, packaging design should be environmentally friendly; emphasizing the nature of the product, or the design process should consider sustainable development principles.

Green Pricing Strategies

In connection with the subject of pricing, some green products can be extra costly for the consumers. Therefore, the environmental characteristics of the products may cause the price of the products to be higher. Nevertheless, in many cases green products can be developed at low cost due to the cost savings associated with materials, energy and even processes in comparison to the non-green products and can be sold at a lower price (Alsmadi, 2007). For instance, the 3M firm has publicly introduced the "Pollution Prevention Pays" program in recent years and obtained significant savings from this program (Murphy, 2005). However, this may not be true for every sector. Many businesses consider that the green policies are expensive and they usually set the price of green products higher (Prakash, 2002). Consumers may want to pay higher prices for products if they perceive that the products offer them higher value (such as higher performance, function, design, visual quality and taste) or the products have environmental characteristics (Antony & Pakutharivu, 2016; Rastogi & Khan, 2015). It has also been observed that consumers can pay 5% to 10% more for environmentally friendly products (Kostadinova, 2016; Bati, 2016). It is also seen that when green products with the same value and quality as non-green products are offered to consumers, they may purchase the green products (Kostadinova, 2016).

Green Marketing Channels

In terms of distribution, businesses want their consumers to easily reach their green products. This position must be consistent with the image the business wants to have and distinguish it from its competitors. For this purpose, in-store promotional activities, visual presentations or recyclable materials that emphasize environmentalism and other benefits can be used (Antony & Pakutharivu, 2016). In other words, the fact that channel members have the image of being environmentally committed in the market, and focusing on recycling or re-using will help green marketing practices (Alsmadi, 2007). Regarding the distribution issue, "reverse channel" issue such as investment costs and transportation costs should also be addressed (Murphy, 2005).

Green Marketing Communication

Sustainable communication has two main points: The first one is to raise awareness on the target consumers by specifying how the product will meet consumer needs and the effects related to economic, social and environmental issues; and the second one is to make the necessary communication about the operations and activities with the stakeholders (Villarino & Font, 2015). The target audience should be reached through the convincing environmental messages and communication strategies. In this sense, there are three types of green advertising. Firstly, advertisements should focus on the relationship between a product / service and the biophysical environment; secondly, advertisements contribute to creating a green lifestyle by highlighting a product or service; finally, advertisements should demonstrate the image that the business has environmental responsibility (Singh & Pandey, 2012, p. 28).

The reliability of the message in green communication is very important. Consumers must trust the content of the advertising message. For this reason, in many cases green advertising should be supported by some government agencies and environmentalists in the community (Alsmadi, 2007; Diego-Mas et al., 2016). It is very important for the businesses with regards to promotion to use ecological messages in the advertisements, educate consumers with special programs and cooperate with environmental organizations in the context of green marketing (Fraj-Andrés et al., 2009b). One of the most important obstacles before the purchase of eco-friendly products is the gap between consumers' product-related expectations and perceptions. Information about the sustainability of the product should be presented to the consumers in the purchasing process (Shao et al., 2017). For instance, the Timberland irm has presented its Green Index rating system to the customers to communicate the effect of each product on the environment (Leonidou et al., 2013).

Businesses can sell green shopping bags under the green environment capital by reducing the use of plastic bags (Antony & Pakutharivu, 2016). Businesses can educate the consumers about green marketing by emphasizing the importance of protecting the environment, the ways of protecting the natural environment, the benefits of protecting the environment and the damages of anti-environmental practices in their advertisements (Ali & Ahmad, 2012). They also maintain eco-friendly communications on their websites (Murphy, 2005). It is important for consumers to recommend environmentally friendly products to one another in the development of environmentally friendly behavior. At this point, word of mouth marketing is effective. Social networks such as Facebook and Twitter can also be used for effective communication (Lee, 2008; Ali & Ahmad, 2012). Green marketing communication, which is a requirement for sustainable development, is an important factor in ensuring the consumer confidence (Garg, 2015).

Marketing Performance

Performance defines the number of new-products, the sales percentage of new-products and the frequency of new products offered relative to competitors by a business (Atuahene-Gima, 2005). New-product performance is to be achieved based on the level of organizational aims in areas such as new-product profitability, sales and market share (Yang & Liu, 2006). Marketing performance characterizes the effectiveness of marketing function used to meet the needs of customers and the expectations of the community. Marketing performance is considered as the important consequence of green marketing strategies of businesses (Fraj et al., 2011, p. 343). Marketing performance measurement provides performance feedback to the businesses regarding the results of marketing efforts (Clark, Abela, & Ambler, 2006) and can be measured with objective criteria such as profitability, sales growth, and market share (Hacioglu & Gök, 2013), and with subjective criteria based on personal opinions such as consumer satisfaction and employee satisfaction. Performance is also evaluated from the perspective of sales, profitability, and consumer awareness, attitudes, commitment and satisfaction by comparison with the competitors (Erdil & Kitapçı, 2007; Ambler, Kokkinaki, & Puntoni, 2004; Lamberti & Noci, 2010; Beukes & Van Wyk, 2016).

When the literature on green marketing is examined, it is seen that the measurement criteria of performance in the measurement of marketing and / or business performance have been addressed in relation to different issues (Fraj-Andrés et al. 2009a; Fraj et al., 2011; Wu and Lin, 2016, Al Khattab, & As'ad, 2015; Leonidou et al., 2013; Richey, Musgrove, Gillison, & Gabler, 2014). The marketing performance criteria are used not just in assessing the results of the operations of the businesses; at the same time, they are used in the strategic decisions and applications of the businesses (Hacioglu & Gök, 2013). Therefore, addressing the objective and subjective marketing performance criteria together may provide more meaningful results. Marketing performance is measured and evaluated from the perspective of objective and subjective criteria in this chapter. Objective scale items are sales growth, market share, level of customer retention (Fraj-Andrés et al. 2009a; Leonidou et al., 2013) and subjective scale items are customer satisfaction, brand image of products, success of the new products offered to the market, level of adoption between businesses' offers and the market expectations (Fraj-Andrés et al. 2009a; Fraj et al., 2011).

Businesses can meet the environmentalist expectations of consumers through specific abilities and resources by focusing on the expectations of the market. Thanks to the development of environmental marketing programs or strategies, some marketing benefits such as better commercial brand image, more satisfied and loyal customers, and removing the negative image can be enabled. Eventually, environmentalist responsibility can generate positive relations in the mind of individuals, develop positive attitudes towards the business and its brands and enhance the perception of consumers about the product quality. Finally, the green marketing strategies enable the optimization of marketing performance of businesses and this contributes to the increase in economic performance (Fraj et al., 2011). Consequently, it is proposed that green marketing strategies have a positive effect on businesses' marketing performances. Following this idea, four hypotheses are stated:

H1: Green product strategy has a positive effect on marketing performance.
H2: Green pricing strategy has a positive effect on marketing performance.
H3: Green marketing channel strategy has a positive effect on marketing performance.
H4: Green marketing communication strategy has a positive effect on marketing performance.

METHODOLOGY

Purpose

The purpose of this paper is to determine the effects of green marketing strategies on marketing performance of businesses. The basic research problem is to determine which strategies have significant effects on marketing performance. Hence, multiple regression analysis was used to fulfill this purpose. AMOS 17.0 software was used to conduct the fitness analysis of research model and SPSS 18.0 software was used to conduct the multiple regression analysis.

Sampling and Data Collection

There is no perfect listing of green businesses that can be used for sampling in Turkey. For this reason, it was decided to reach to Turkish Exporters Assembly (TIM). As the sampling framework, it was decided by the researchers that it would be appropriate to conduct the study on the businesses registered in this assembly thought to implement green marketing applications. Therefore, the judgement sampling method was used in this study. Turkish Exporters Assembly (TIM) is the roof organization of the exporting businesses in Turkey. There are 13 exporting associations under this roof organization. For the study, initially, the exporters' assembly was contacted with. A web-based questionnaire was used in the study. For the study, a link containing the questionnaire form was intermittently sent twice to the registered members of this assembly. However, nearly half of the sent emails bounced back due to various reasons. Totally, 258 businesses replied to the questionnaire.

Questionnaire

Firstly, a literature review was conducted to determine the green marketing strategies and marketing performance. A total of 29 items were found. Secondly, 15 businesses were interviewed to check these factors related to the strategies of green marketing. Seven items were assumed to represent marketing performance and the other twenty two items describe green marketing strategies. All respondents were asked to evaluate the green marketing strategies by using a 5-point Likert scale (1= not at all important, 2= not important, 3= Neutral, 4= important, 5= very important). Marketing performance items were evaluated by using a 5-point Likert scale (1= Not very satisfied, 2= Not Satisfied, 3= Neutral, 4= Satisfied, 5= very satisfied).

RESULTS

Participants' Characteristics

The respondents consisted of owners (42.8%) and managers (57.2%) of the businesses. The participants of the study were composed of 78.3% males and 21.7% females. When the education levels of business owners and managers are examined, it is seen that 2.3% had elementary school degrees, 14.3% high school degrees, 58.9% undergraduate degrees and 24.4% post-graduate degrees. The participants of the study can be divided into 5 groups in terms of experience: Those with 1-5 years of experience, (13.6%), with 6-10 years of experience (12.8%), with 11-15 years of experience (18.6%), with 16-20 years of experience (18.6%) and finally those with 21 years or more experience (36.4%). Sizes of the participant businesses were classified into four groups: 69.7% were small-sized businesses (1-49 employees) 21.7% medium-sized businesses (50-249 employees), and 8.5% large-sized businesses (250 and more employees).

Measures

- **Marketing Performance Scale:** This scale was adopted from Fraj-Andrés et al. (2009a), Fraj et al. (2011) and Leonidou et al. (2013). Marketing performance scale had seven items. Reliability was (Cronbach alpha) 0.882. Validity results indicated a good fit as shown in Table 1. In the literature, the accepted values of these indices were χ^2 / df ≤ 3; GFI ≥ .90; CFI ≥ .90; 0.05 ≤ RMSEA ≤ 0.08 (Baumgartner & Homburg, 1996; Iacobucci, 2010; Weston & Gore, 2006). Scale items were; sales growth, market share, customer satisfaction, level of customer retention, brand image of products, success of the new products offered to the market, level of adoption between businesses' offers and the market expectations.
- **Green Marketing Strategies Scale:** This scale was adopted from Fraj-Andrés et al. (2009a), Banerjee et al. (2003) and Leonidou et al. (2013). Green marketing strategies scale had twenty-two items. The reliability of green marketing strategies items was 0.958, no items were dropped from the list to increase Cronbach alpha. Then, an exploratory factor analysis was conducted to identify the main groups. The Kaiser-Meyer-Olkin (KMO) measure of sampling adequacy was 0.93, which suggested that the data were suitable for factor analysis. Initially, using a scree plot test to determine the factor number, four factors were identified and therefore extracted, accounting for 73.75% of the variance with varimax rotation. As a result, four main factors were maintained in the exploratory factor analysis. Common method bias was examined using Harman's one factor test and was found to be a non-issue in this study. Consequently, the green marketing strategies scale consisted of four main factors and 22 sub-items in total and the factor loadings were strong. Four first- order factor model (correlated) had a good model fit as shown in Table 2. The results of the confirmatory factor analysis showed a good fit.

These factors can be included to the regression analysis. Factor 1 (Green marketing communication) included six items. Factor 2 (Green product strategies) included six items. Factor 3 (Green marketing channels) included six items. Factor 4 (Green pricing) included four items as shown in Table 3.

Table 1. Fit Indices

χ^2 / df	p-value	CFI	GFI	AGFI	RMSEA	RMR
1.32	0.264	0.99	0.99	0.95	0.03	0.008

Table 2. The Fitness Analysis of Model

χ^2 / df	p-value	CFI	GFI	AGFI	RMSEA	RMR
1.74	0.001	0.97	0.90	0.86	0.054	0.08

Table 3. Exploratory Factor Analysis Results

The Statements of Green Marketing Strategies	Green Marketing Communication	Green Product	Green Marketing Channels	Green Pricing
Emphasizing the responsibility regarding the protection of the environment in the business communications	.825			
Informing the customers and institutions about the environmental efforts/management of the business in the promotions	.804			
Supporting or sponsoring the environmental groups or activities	.787			
Efforts to minimize the negative effect of marketing promotions on the natural environment	.774			
Emphasizing the environmental aspect of products in the advertisements	.728			
While positioning the product characteristics and content in branding efforts, communicating the eco-friendly aspect of the product	.594			
Orientation towards eco-friendly product designs		.850		
Developing products with minimal negative effects to the environment		.821		
Pay attention to the content and the raw material of the products are friendly to the environment		.775		
Focusing on environmental benefits in the packaging and labelling decisions (such as ecological and clean materials)		.667		
Maintaining and increasing the recyclable content of product packaging for a long time		.655		
Using recyclable and reusable materials in the products		.546		
Encouraging the suppliers and distributers to establish and demonstrate environmental responsibility and obligations			.722	
Cooperating with the suppliers and distributors to develop eco-friendly marketing programs			.651	
Establishing clear / specific guidelines and specifications to monitor the reactions and environmental responsibilities of the channel members			.630	
Using reusable or recycled containers in logistics			.627	
Working as a team with the members of the channel to improve the product and packaging appropriate to the regulations after use			.599	
Cooperating with the members of the channel to take on responsibility aimed at protecting the environment			.571	
Evaluating the costs of eco-friendliness within the price of the product				.859
Setting higher prices for the eco-friendly versions of products				.804
Evaluating the benefits of eco-friendliness within the price of the product				. 792
Using pricing tactics (such as discounts and product return) to encourage end-users to take environmental actions (reuse and recycling)				.584
Explained variance %	53.41	9.16	6.04	5.14
Cronbach alpha	.934	.895	.918	.885

Research Model

Based on the literature, a research model showing four research hypotheses for empirical testing is shown in Figure 1.

To test the hypotheses, a multiple regression analysis was conducted. Inter-correlations of variables can be seen in table 4. Normality assumption was tested for using the normal probability plot and scatter plot tables to ensure that the score distributions were normal and linear. All variables were distributed as normal according to P-P plot and scatter plot. There was also no evidence of multicollinearity among the independent variables according to inter-correlations and variance inflation factor that did not exceed 5.0 (in this study VIF was found at 1.85 and 3.72 level for each construct).

Table 5 presents the results for the multiple regression analysis for each of the four green marketing strategy factors of businesses on marketing performance. The regression coefficients, p values for the significance of the relationships and the associated coefficients of determination were reported. The sign and the statistical significance, rather than the magnitude, of each regression coefficient were of primary interest here. For each of the green marketing strategy measures, the final model p value, the

Figure 1. Research model

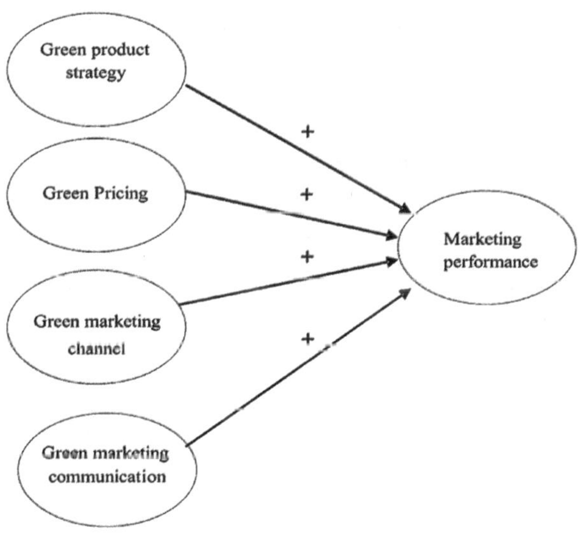

Table 4. Intercorrelations of variables

		1	2	3	4	5
Green Product Strategy	1	1.00				
Green Pricing Strategy	2	.482*	1.00			
Green Marketing Channel	3	.659*	.705*	1.00		
Green Marketing Communication	4	.624*	.636*	.798*	1.00	
Marketing Performance	5	.331*	.206*	.374*	.406*	1.00

Note: Significant at *p < 0.01

Table 5. Multiple regression analysis results

	Unstandardized Coefficients		Standardized Coefficients	
Factors	β	SE	β	Sig.
Green product strategy	.080	.061	.102	.189
Green pricing strategy	-.096	.048	-.161	.047*
Green marketing channel strategy	.108	.066	.179	.102
Green marketing communication strategy	.174	.056	.303	.002*

Dependent variable = Marketing performance; *p < 0.05
Adjusted $R^2 = .178$; $F = 14.86$; $p < 0.05$

model R^2, the independent variables entered in the model, their beta coefficients and the p values for the independent variables were listed.

Two factors were significant at $p < 0.05$ and two independent variables did not meet this significance level. Multiple regression analysis showed that green pricing strategy ($\beta = -.161$, $p < 0.05$) and green marketing communication ($\beta = .303$, $p < 0.05$) factors had a positive effect on marketing performance at a significance level of 0.05. Green product strategy and green marketing channel factors did not have a significant effect on marketing performance. As a result, H2 and H4 hypotheses were accepted, but H1 and H3 hypotheses were rejected.

CONCLUSION AND MANAGERIAL IMPLICATIONS

This study focused on the effects of the green marketing strategies on marketing performance of businesses. The research was conducted with the businesses which were the members of Turkish Exporters Assembly and the basic research problem was to determine which green marketing strategies had a significant effect on marketing performance. Although some studies were conducted on green products in Turkey (Daştan & Gürler, 2016; Tayfun & Öçlü, 2016), little attention was given to the green marketing strategies of Turkish businesses. The findings of this study will give valuable insights to businesses to learn the effects of manufacturing these products on marketing performance. It was found that two main green marketing strategy (green pricing strategy and green marketing communication strategy) factors had a significant effect on marketing performance. This result is not compatible with the results of the study conducted by Leonidou et al. (2013) in England. In their study, Leonidou et al. (2013) concluded that green products and green distribution had significant effects on the product-market performance. It is possible to think that this different result might be due to the different sampling in both studies. Especially the fact that the income capita per consumer in a developing country like Turkey is low in comparison to the developed countries may cause the price flexibility to be high. This particular result might be due to the fact that the consumers paid more attention to the price of eco-friendly products. At this point, the communication strategies of businesses also played an important role in specifying the price and eco-friendly characteristics of the products.

The fact that businesses are green oriented may provide the businesses with higher financial gains, market share and business performance, and help their abilities to increase. At this point, implementing the right green marketing strategies is a crucial factor for businesses in green competition. Consumers are inquisitive to know "the true" green businesses. Therefore, the green marketing strategies of businesses aimed at reluctant customers are critically important. In order to overcome the reluctance and skepticism of consumers, the businesses should focus on sustainable activities more, be more transparent and minimize the environmentally threatening wastes (Cronin, Smith, Gleim, Ramirez, & Martinez, 2011). Therefore, marketing managers should be more aware of the increasing environmental responsibility of businesses and implement the green marketing strategies in a way to secure their reliability from the perspective of shareholders without sacrificing the profitability (El Dief & Font, 2010). In fact, as also stated by Fraj et al. (2011), green marketing strategies contributed to the optimizations of businesses' marketing performance and enhanced their profitability by reducing the production costs. One of the most important results revealed by the present study was that environment-oriented businesses had more superior operational and marketing performance. Businesses should continuously improve their values that they offer to meet the mixed needs of consumers and consumer-oriented benchmarking approach should be adopted (Shamma & Hassan, 2013). Chen et al. (2006) also found that the green product and process innovation of businesses had a positive impact on the performance and competitive advantage. Banerjee et al. (2003), on the other hand, found that competitive advantage affected the environmental marketing strategies of businesses. In their study, Fraj-Andrés et al. (2009b) also found that environmental marketing affected the operational and commercial performance of businesses and this, in turn, was reflected on the economic results of the businesses. Environmental marketing positively influenced competitiveness of businesses and benefited them in gaining competitive advantage and product differentiation.

For the creating of marketing strategies, food safety, health information and environmental values should be emphasized. It is because, as Juwaheer et al. (2012) also stated, there is a relationship between the green marketing strategies of businesses and the purchasing decisions of consumers. For instance, Saba and Messina (2003) concluded in their study that consumers found the organic products healthier, more eco-friendly, more delicious and more nutritious in comparison to the traditional products. It is clearly observed that especially the health and environmental-related benefits (Gracia & Magistris, 2007) and economic benefits (Maniatis, 2016) are the most important factors in consumers' purchasing decisions of green and organic products. Accordingly, businesses should develop their green products considering their target markets, their characteristics and preferences of this market (Vernekar & Wadhwa, 2011). For instance, marketing managers should carefully consider all the information that the green consumers look at before purchasing the product and the factors that demonstrate the reliability of all information products (Maniatis, 2016).

Businesses should also adopt an appropriate pricing strategy for green products, considering the issues related to the quality and product category. In fact, Hughner et al. (2007) found that consumers integrated high price with high quality and taste. It should be aimed to protect the products from the chemicals and save the costs by using as few channel member as possible for the distribution of the green products. Offering the green products to consumers at more affordable or lower prices and through more efficient distribution channels may increase the demand for green products. In the promotion of green products, businesses need to attend training courses and fairs in order to inform the consumers, implement promotional and advertising efforts, arrange the sections in the store together with the retailers to make it easy for the consumers to compare the green products, and organize in-store promotions of the green products and showcase them in the best possible way. In this respect, it is also important to provide the seller support in marketing the green products (Vernekar & Wadhwa, 2011). In this regard, Richter and Hempfling (2003) stated that organic products should be displayed on the shelves separately from the traditional products, so consumers should be able to find organic products more easily by showing them with different signs and colors in the product classification. Similarly, La Via and Nucifora (2002) also stated that consumers should be better informed about product certification and quality issues and that advertising should be regulated in such a way to increase the demand for organic products. In this regard, Tayfun and Öçlü (2016) also demonstrated that consumers received information about products' level of environmentalism more through advertisements.

Green marketing involves proactive activities in the management of business resources. For instance, it is possible to reduce consumption by designing and producing environmentally friendly products, using recyclable materials or by implementing efficient systems. The integration of environmental issues into distribution reduces the production costs of businesses by helping the economic and environmental objectives. For this reason, businesses can reduce their costs and improve their efficiency with some process-oriented activities such as eco-design, reverse logistics or by using the clean materials in their products and packaging, and clean transportation systems. For instance, they can improve their products and packaging with cheaper and alternative raw materials. Integrating the green values with marketing strategies will contribute to the development of corporate reputation and image as well as helping to use the resources effectively. All these affect the operational results of the businesses positively and enable the business to be more economical and have better performance results (Fraj et al., 2011).

LIMITATIONS AND DIRECTIONS FOR FUTURE RESEARCH

The present study has some limitations. Firstly, only the opinions of businesses' managers who were members of the Turkish Exporters Assembly were considered. In future studies, certain green product categories can be selected and consumers' reactions to the marketing applications of these green products can be investigated. Therefore, if the present study conducted on the businesses in different sectors is carried out on the businesses operating in the same sector, more in-depth results can be obtained. Another limitation is the analyses of data from only one country. In this context, a cross-cultural study might be conducted to analyze the structure of businesses and their reactions to environmental issues.

In future studies, it would be beneficial to consider the opinions of businesses about the green marketing strategies and make a comparison of the businesses according to their size and experiences. Again, in future studies, the effect of green marketing strategies on the marketing performance can be examined within the framework of a model together with the moderating effect of idle resources and competitive intensity.

REFERENCES

Agrawal, A. D., & Das, M. (2013). Green marketing: Sustainable marketing strategy. *Indira Management Review*, *7*(1), 17–31.

Al Khattab, S. A., & Asad, H. (2015). The Impact of the Green Supply Chain Management on Environmental-Based Marketing Performance. *Journal of Service Science and Management*, *8*(4), 588–597. doi:10.4236/jssm.2015.84059

Ali, A., & Ahmad, I. (2012). Environment Friendly Products: Factors that influence the green purchase intentions of Pakistani consumers. *Pak. J. Eng. Technol. Sci.*, *2*(1), 84–117.

Ali, M. H., & Suleiman, N. (2016). Sustainable food production: Insights of Malaysian halal small and medium sized enterprises. *International Journal of Production Economics*, 1–12.

Alsmadi, S. (2007). Green marketing and the concern over the environment: Measuring environmental consciousness of Jordanian consumers. *Journal of Promotion Management, 13*(3-4), 339–361. doi:10.1080/10496490802306905

Ambler, T., Kokkinaki, F., & Puntoni, S. (2004). Assessing marketing performance: Reasons for metrics selection. *Journal of Marketing Management, 20*(3-4), 475–498. doi:10.1362/026725704323080506

Antony, T. K., & Pakutharıvu, D. N. (2016). Go green and save green (Issues faced by green marketing). *Indian Journal of Applied Research, 6*(5), 191–193.

Atuahene-Gima, K. (2005). Resolving the capability—rigidity paradox in new product innovation. *Journal of Marketing, 69*(4), 61–83. doi:10.1509/jmkg.2005.69.4.61

Atuahene-Gima, K., Slater, S. F., & Olson, E. M. (2005). The contingent value of responsive and proactive market orientations for new product program performance. *Journal of Product Innovation Management, 22*(6), 464–482. doi:10.1111/j.1540-5885.2005.00144.x

Banerjee, S. B., Iyer, E. S., & Kashyap, R. K. (2003). Corporate environmentalism: Antecedents and influence of industry type. *Journal of Marketing, 67*(2), 106–122. doi:10.1509/jmkg.67.2.106.18604

Bati, U. (2016). Green marketing activities to support corporate reputation on a sample from Turkey. *International Journal of Marketing Studies, 8*(3), 189–201. doi:10.5539/ijms.v8n3p189

Baumgartner, H., & Homburg, C. (1996). Applications of structural equation modeling in marketing and consumer research: A review. *International Journal of Research in Marketing, 13*(2), 139–161. doi:10.1016/0167-8116(95)00038-0

Beukes, C., & Van Wyk, G. (2016). An investigation of the marketing performance measurement practices in Hatfield Volkswagen group. *African Journal of Business Management, 10*(6), 131–139. doi:10.5897/AJBM2015.7772

Bhaskaran, S., Polonsky, M., Cary, J., & Fernandez, S. (2006). Environmentally sustainable food production and marketing: Opportunity or hype? *British Food Journal, 108*(8), 677–690. doi:10.1108/00070700610682355

Bodlaj, M. (2010). The impact of a responsive and proactive market orientation on innovation and business performance. *Economic and Business Review for Central and South-Eastern Europe, 12*(4), 241–261.

Bodlaj, M., Coenders, G., & Zabkar, V. (2012). Responsive and proactive market orientation and innovation success under market and technological turbulence. *Journal of Business Economics and Management, 13*(4), 666–687. doi:10.3846/16111699.2011.620143

Bridges, C. M., & Wilhelm, W. B. (2008). Going beyond green: The why and how of integrating sustainability into the marketing curriculum. *Journal of Marketing Education, 30*(1), 33–46. doi:10.1177/0273475307312196

Chamorro, A., & Bañegil, T. M. (2006). Green marketing philosophy: A study of Spanish firms with ecolabels. *Corporate Social Responsibility and Environmental Management*, *13*(1), 11–24. doi:10.1002/csr.83

Chen, Y. S., Lai, S. B., & Wen, C. T. (2006). The influence of green innovation performance on corporate advantage in Taiwan. *Journal of Business Ethics*, *67*(4), 331–339. doi:10.1007/s10551-006-9025-5

Clark, B. H., Abela, A. V., & Ambler, T. (2006). An information processing model of marketing performance measurement. *Journal of Marketing Theory and Practice*, *14*(3), 191–208. doi:10.2753/MTP1069-6679140302

Costa, Pinto, D., Nique, W. M., Herter M., M., & Borges, A. (2016). Green consumers and their identities: How identities change the motivation for green consumption. *International Journal of Consumer Studies*, 1–12.

Cronin, J. J. Jr, Smith, J. S., Gleim, M. R., Ramirez, E., & Martinez, J. D. (2011). Green marketing strategies: An examination of stakeholders and the opportunities they present. *Journal of the Academy of Marketing Science*, *39*(1), 158–174. doi:10.1007/s11747-010-0227-0

Daştan, İ., & Gürler, C. (2016). Yeşil bilgi teknolojileri ürün tercihinde tüketici satın alma niyetlerini etkileyen faktörlerin tespiti. *Atatürk University Journal of Economics & Administrative Sciences*, *30*(1), 173–186.

Devi Juwaheer, T., Pudaruth, S., & Monique Emmanuelle Noyaux, M. (2012). Analysing the impact of green marketing strategies on consumer purchasing patterns in Mauritius. *World Journal of Entrepreneurship. Management and Sustainable Development*, *8*(1), 36–59.

Dief, M. E., & Font, X. (2010). The determinants of hotels marketing managers green marketing behaviour. *Journal of Sustainable Tourism*, *18*(2), 157–174. doi:10.1080/09669580903464232

Diego-Mas, J. A., Poveda-Bautista, R., & Alcaide-Marzal, J. (2016). Designing the appearance of environmentally sustainable products. *Journal of Cleaner Production*, *135*, 784–793. doi:10.1016/j.jclepro.2016.06.173

Erdil, O., & Kitapçı, H. (2007). TKY araçlarının kullanımı ve firma yenilikçiliğinin yeni ürün geliştirme hızı ve işletme performansına etkisi. *Atatürk Üniversitesi İktisadi ve İdari Bilimler Dergisi*, *21*(1), 233–145.

Fraj, E., Martínez, E., & Matute, J. (2011). Green marketing strategy and the firms performance: The moderating role of environmental culture. *Journal of Strategic Marketing*, *19*(4), 339–355. doi:10.1080/0965254X.2011.581382

Fraj-Andrés, E., Martinez-Salinas, E., & Matute-Vallejo, J. (2009a). A multidimensional approach to the influence of environmental marketing and orientation on the firms organizational performance. *Journal of Business Ethics*, *88*(2), 263–286. doi:10.1007/s10551-008-9962-2

Fraj-Andrés, E., Martínez Salinas, E., & Matute Vallejo, J. (2009b). Factors affecting corporate environmental strategy in Spanish industrial firms. *Business Strategy and the Environment*, *18*(8), 500–514. doi:10.1002/bse.611

Garg, A. (2015). Green marketing for sustainable development: An industry perspective. *Sustainable Development, 23*(5), 301–316. doi:10.1002/sd.1592

Ginsberg, J. M., & Bloom, P. N. (2004). Choosing the right green-marketing strategy. *MIT Sloan Management Review, 46*(1), 79–84.

Gracia, A., & de Magistris, T. (2013). Organic food product purchase behaviour: A pilot study for urban consumers in the South of Italy. *Spanish Journal of Agricultural Research, 5*(4), 439–451. doi:10.5424/sjar/2007054-5356

Hacioglu, G., & Gök, O. (2013). Marketing performance measurement: marketing metrics in Turkish firms. *Journal of Business Economics and Management, 14*(sup1), 413-432.

Hughner, R. S., McDonagh, P., Prothero, A., Shultz, C. J., & Stanton, J. (2007). Who are organic food consumers? A compilation and review of why people purchase organic food. *Journal of Consumer Behaviour, 6*(23), 94–110. doi:10.1002/cb.210

Iacobucci, D. (2010). Structural equations modeling: Fit indices, sample size, and advanced topics. *Journal of Consumer Psychology, 20*(1), 90–98. doi:10.1016/j.jcps.2009.09.003

Jerzyk, E. (2016). Design and communication of ecological content on sustainable packaging in young consumers opinions. *Journal of Food Products Marketing, 22*(6), 707–716. doi:10.1080/10454446.2015.1121435

Jones, P., Clarke-Hill, C., Comfort, D., & Hillier, D. (2008). Marketing and sustainability. *Marketing Intelligence & Planning, 26*(2), 123–130. doi:10.1108/02634500810860584

Kostadinova, E. (2016). Sustainable consumer behavior: Literature overview. *Economic Alternatives*, (2), 224-234.

Kotler, P., & Keller, K. L. (2012). *Marketing Management* (14th ed.). Boston: Prentice-Hall.

La Via, G., Antonio, & Nucifora, M. D. (2002). The determinants of the price mark-up for organic fruit and vegetable products in the European Union. *British Food Journal, 104*(3/4/5), 319-336.

Lamberti, L., & Noci, G. (2010). Marketing strategy and marketing performance measurement system: Exploring the relationship. *European Management Journal, 28*(2), 139–152. doi:10.1016/j.emj.2009.04.007

Lee, K. (2008). Opportunities for green marketing: Young consumers. *Marketing Intelligence & Planning, 26*(6), 573–586. doi:10.1108/02634500810902839

Leonidou, C. N., Katsikeas, C. S., & Morgan, N. A. (2013). Greening the marketing mix: Do firms do it and does it pay off? *Journal of the Academy of Marketing Science, 41*(2), 151–170. doi:10.1007/s11747-012-0317-2

Li, C. R., Lin, C. J., & Chu, C. P. (2008). The nature of market orientation and the ambidexterity of innovations. *Management Decision, 46*(7), 1002–1026. doi:10.1108/00251740810890186

Maniatis, P. (2016). Investigating factors influencing consumer decision-making while choosing green products. *Journal of Cleaner Production, 132*, 215–228. doi:10.1016/j.jclepro.2015.02.067

Mitchell, R. W., Wooliscroft, B., & Higham, J. (2010). Sustainable market orientation: A new approach to managing marketing strategy. *Journal of Macromarketing, 30*(2), 160–170. doi:10.1177/0276146710361928

Murphy, P. E. (2005). Sustainable marketing. *Business & Professional Ethics Journal, 24*(1/2), 171–198. doi:10.5840/bpej2005241/210

Nair, S. R., & Menon, C. G. (2008). An environmental marketing system–a proposed model based on Indian experience. *Business Strategy and the Environment, 17*(8), 467–479. doi:10.1002/bse.586

Narver, J. C., Slater, S. F., & MacLachlan, D. L. (2004). Responsive and proactive market orientation and new product success. *Journal of Product Innovation Management, 21*(5), 334–347. doi:10.1111/j.0737-6782.2004.00086.x

Oswald, M., Brettel, M., & Engelen, A. (2012). How departments decision-making influence and interdepartmental dynamics relate to two facets of strategic market orientation. *Journal of Strategic Marketing, 20*(6), 483–507. doi:10.1080/0965254X.2012.711346

Pap, A., Ham, M., & Turalija, A. (2015). Product policy management as part of sustainable marketing strategy. *Interdisciplinary Management Research, 11*, 131–140.

Pawar, R., & Kambale, R. N. (2016). Green marketing-future challenges and opportunities. *Asian Journal of Multidisciplinary Studies, 4*(3), 149–155.

Phalke, V., & Ranade, A. (2016). Green marketing: Complementing Swachh Bharat mission (SBM). *Asian Journal of Multidisciplinary Studies, 4*(4), 167–173.

Prakash, A. (2002). Green marketing, public policy and managerial strategies. *Business Strategy and the Environment, 11*(5), 285–297. doi:10.1002/bse.338

Pramod, V. (2016). Green marketing -an eco-friendly revolution. *Indian Journal of Applied Research, 6*(1), 594–596.

Rastogi, E., & Khan, M. S. (2015). An analytical study of online advertising and its co-relationship with green marketing for facilitating sustainable marketing effectiveness. *International Journal of Applied Research, 1*(5), 182–184.

Richey, R. G. Jr, Musgrove, C. F., Gillison, S. T., & Gabler, C. B. (2014). The effects of environmental focus and program timing on green marketing performance and the moderating role of resource commitment. *Industrial Marketing Management, 43*(7), 1246–1257. doi:10.1016/j.indmarman.2014.06.014

Richter, T., & Hempfling, G. (2003). Supermarket study 2002: Organic products in European supermarkets. *FiBL*, 1-182.

Saba, A., & Messina, F. (2003). Attitudes towards organic foods and risk/benefit perception associated with pesticides. *Food Quality and Preference, 14*(8), 637–645. doi:10.1016/S0950-3293(02)00188-X

Seretny, M., & Seretny, A. (2012). Sustainable marketing -a new era in the responsible marketing development. *Foundations of Management, 4*(2), 63–76. doi:10.2478/fman-2013-0011

Shamma, H., & Hassan, S. (2013). Customer-driven benchmarking: A strategic approach toward a sustainable marketing performance. *Benchmarking: An International Journal*, *20*(3), 377–395. doi:10.1108/14635771311318144

Shao, J., Taisch, M., & Mier, M. O. (2017). Influencing factors to facilitate sustainable consumption: From the experts viewpoints. *Journal of Cleaner Production*, *142*(1), 203–216. doi:10.1016/j.jclepro.2015.12.111

Singh, P. B., & Pandey, K. K. (2012). Green marketing: Policies and practices for sustainable development. *Integral Review*, *5*(1), 22–30.

Suki, N. M., Suki, N. M., & Azman, N. S. (2016). Impacts of corporate social responsibility on the links between green marketing awareness and consumer purchase intentions. *Procedia Economics and Finance*, *37*, 262–268. doi:10.1016/S2212-5671(16)30123-X

Tayfun, N. Ö., & Öçlü, B. (2016). Çevreci ürünlerin tüketicilerin satın alma kararlarındaki yeri üzerine bir uygulama. *Ömer Halisdemir Üniversitesi İktisadi ve İdari Bilimler Fakültesi Dergisi*, *9*(3), 185-198.

Tsai, K. H., Chou, C., & Kuo, J. H. (2008). The curvilinear relationships between responsive and proactive market orientations and new product performance: A contingent link. *Industrial Marketing Management*, *37*(8), 884–894. doi:10.1016/j.indmarman.2007.03.005

Vernekar, S. S., & Wadhwa, P. (2011). Green consumption: An empirical study of consumers attitudes and perception regarding eco-friendly FMCG products, with special reference to Delhi and NCR Region. *Opinion*, *1*(1), 64–74.

Villarino, J., & Font, X. (2015). Sustainability marketing myopia: The lack of persuasiveness in sustainability communication. *Journal of Vacation Marketing*, *21*(4), 326–335. doi:10.1177/1356766715589428

Weston, R., & Gore, P. A. Jr. (2006). A brief guide to structural equation modeling. *The Counseling Psychologist*, *34*(5), 719–751. doi:10.1177/0011000006286345

Wu, S. I., & Lin, S. R. (2016). The effect of green marketing strategy on business performance: A study of organic farms in Taiwan. *Total Quality Management & Business Excellence*, *27*(1-2), 141–156. doi :10.1080/14783363.2014.959256

Yang, J., & Liu, C. Y. (2006). New product development: An innovation diffusion perspective. *The Journal of High Technology Management Research*, *17*(1), 17–26. doi:10.1016/j.hitech.2006.05.002

Yannopoulos, P., Auh, S., & Menguc, B. (2012). Achieving fit between learning and market orientation: Implications for new product performance. *Journal of Product Innovation Management*, *29*(4), 531–545. doi:10.1111/j.1540-5885.2012.00923.x

Zhang, J., & Duan, Y. (2010). The impact of different types of market orientation on product innovation performance: Evidence from Chinese manufacturers. *Management Decision*, *48*(6), 849–867. doi:10.1108/00251741011053433

Zhang, J., & Duan, Y. (2010a). Empirical study on the impact of market orientation and innovation orientation on new product performance of Chinese manufacturers. *Nankai Business Review International*, *1*(2), 214–231. doi:10.1108/20408741011052609

KEY TERMS AND DEFINITIONS

Green Marketing: Green marketing is the marketing of products that satisfy the wants and needs of the consumers, and have minimal detrimental effect on the natural environment.

Green Marketing Mix: Green marketing mix can be defined as the creation of the traditional marketing mix, known as 4P, as being environmentally friendly.

Green Marketing Strategy: The Green Marketing Strategy is a set of marketing strategies that are environmentally friendly.

Marketing Performance: Marketing performance is marketing outputs compared to the determined marketing objectives of the businesses.

Strategy: Strategy is the way to reach the aims and objectives of the businesses in an uncertain environment.

Sustainable Marketing: Sustainable marketing is an integrative approach that emphasizes environmental, social value and economic issues in the development of marketing strategies.

Turkey: Turkey is a developing country with a democratic, secular, unitary, parliamentary republic and various cultural heritages in Eurasia.

Chapter 9
Green Brand Personality:
Its Relevance to the Green Marketing Practices

Anitha Acharya
ICFAI Foundation for Higher Education (IFHE), India

Manish Gupta
ICFAI Foundation for Higher Education (IFHE), India

ABSTRACT

The main purposes of this chapter are to define a green brand, describe its characteristics, and outline its implications. This chapter would help readers understand the need for studying green brand personality and appreciate its importance in the current market scenario. Moreover, it provides a detailed outline of the ways and means that companies can use to market such brands. It highlights the steps companies can take to increase the sales of green brands and get an edge over non-green brands. In addition, it explores certain best practices in the industry to illustrate how well green products can be sold without compromising on sales targets.

INTRODUCTION

Marketing strategists have long achieved competitive advantage by assigning a set of personality characteristics to their brands (Aaker, 1997). Conventional brand-personality strategies focus on products or services and their corresponding utilitarian benefits. However, a recent sharp rise in the number of similar brands coupled with globalization has made it difficult for the marketers to distinguish their brands on the basis of functional attributes alone.

Therefore, the marketers are increasingly realizing the need of attaching symbolic meanings to their brands to achieve brand distinction. One of the emerging ways to fulfill the need for brand distinction is by promoting green marketing – a set of activities to generate and facilitate an exchange to satisfy human needs or wants so that the products cause minimal damage to the environment (Acharya & Gupta, 2016; Polonsky, 1994). Marketers need to know when and how do customers relate themselves to green

DOI: 10.4018/978-1-5225-2912-5.ch009

brand personality and its impact on the purchase decision. The objective of this chapter is to identify the benefits of green brand personality on companies marketing practices. It helps the companies to promote their products and also attracts new customers to switch to products which are environmental friendly. This will benefit the company in the long run by way of profits and also helps them to distinguish their products from that of their competitors.

The six dimensions of green brand personality proposed by Acharya and Gupta (2016) were security, sincerity, competence, sophistication, compassion, and excitement. Dimensions sincerity, competence, and excitement, capture the innate part of human personality, whereas sophistication, security, and compassion tap a dimension that individual's would like to have.

NEED FOR GREEN MARKETING

Companies are now getting inclined to green marketing mainly because of four reasons. These include rise of green consumers, government initiatives, thrust by non-governmental organizations (NGOs), and change of lifestyle. Each of these has been detailed below:

- **Rise of Green Consumers:** Consumers are aware of the environmental degradation that can happen if they use non-green products (Zhu & Sarkis, 2016). Not surprisingly, according to a survey conducted by Cone Communications in 2013, as much as 71% of Americans are inclined to buy green product (Walker, 2013). More recently, Nielsen global online study reported that almost three out of four respondents were willing to pay extra price for buying green products in 2015 (Global, 2015). It was also found that Millennials were also particularly passionate about sustainability while shopping and were interested in buying green products in order to save the environment.
- **Government Initiatives:** Governments around the world are responding positively to the call of the United Nations (UN) for taking green initiatives to control global warming (Bhattacharya, 2016). Indeed, the main agenda for the UN conference in September, 2015 in Paris was to give countries an opportunity to join Paris Agreement to overcome climate change. A major decision was that developed countries would share a major chunk of monetary cost relating to supporting green initiatives (Davenport, Gillis, Chan, & Eddy, 2015). Countries have already started providing funding for this purpose. For example, the Federal Government of Canada offers incentives and funding to boost research and development in Canada. These are relating to conducting research on those products that run on clean energy (Natural Resources Canada, 2016).
- **Thrust by Non-Governmental and Non-Profit Organizations:** NGOs and nonprofit organizations have come forward in support of going green (Kleindorfer, Singhal, & Wassenhove, 2005). These organizations are popularly termed as green NGOs (Herrera, 2010). For example, Carbon Trust, a nonprofit organization based in UK helps companies in formulating strategies with respect to overcome climate change. It had worked with product carbon footprinting which contributed to PAS 2050, a standard for product life cycle. Similarly, Conservation International a NGO advises Starbucks on issues relating to sustainability. EarthShare, another NGO, is famous for developing package of services which helps its clients in implementing green activities in their organizations. Rainforest Alliance has been working with leading brands which produces chocolate, coffee, and tea in sourcing raw materials which are sustainable.

- **Lifestyle Change:** Consumers feel that the presence of green element in an ordinary product makes it extra-ordinary because of the uniqueness it involves (Rao & Bhargav, 2016). These consumers are labeled as 'eco-fashion' consumers. Marketers have started capturing the pulse of these 'eco-fashion' consumers. They do not use raw materials which are hazardous to the health of their workers and the environment. They also ensure that the working conditions of the workers are good (Chan & Wong, 2012). Popular brands which incorporate these strategies are study NY, Alabama Chanin, Titania Inglis, Feral Childe, Awamaki Lab, Carrie Parry, Loomstate, M. Patmos, 100%NY, And Elroy (Phelan, 2012).

WHAT IS GREEN MARKETING

According to researchers Kärnä, Hansen, & Juslin (2003), the definition of marketing considers a utilitarian approach to social responsibility by emphasizing on maximizing the shareholders wealth. Several, marketing epitomizes voracity and they are responsible for the consequences which is arising from over development and over-consumption, where the main motive is to maximize their personal wealth instead of society's welfare and good quality of life. However, marketing helps in promoting consumption which is environment friendly as well they help consumers in leading a better life. Since the scope of marketing is very vast it helps consumers in finding a suitable trade-off between economy and environment. According to (Charter, 1992) the objective of a green marketing philosophy is long term sustainability and for those companies whose main objective is to create sustainable businesses, then green marketing is the way ahead. Peattie (1995) defined green marketing as management practices which considers satisfying the needs of the consumers and the society in such a way that it is profitable and sustainable in the long run. In similar terms, Charter (1992) conceptualized green marketing as management practices that fulfills the needs of the stakeholder and also considers the safety of the consumers and the environment. The supporters of green marketing and sustainability thinking actively take part in wide range of activities in which the company is involved. Holistically, the process of green marketing should not be concerned merely about the end product they should also place more emphasis on activities like developing new products, logistics planning, packaging of the products, etc. (Ottman & Books, 1998; Wasik, 1996). According to Fuller (1999) green marketing must consider the impacts of the entire product life cycle on the environment, because how a product is produced cannot be secluded from how it is consumed and its impact on the environment. If such a vision is lacking, the company can be accused of greenwashing. Its portrayal of a green image will backfire, and this might harm the environment (Grant, 2007; Peattie, 1999).

EMERGENCE OF GREEN BRAND PERSONALITY

Marketing practitioners and advertisers are the first ones to coin the term 'brand personality', much before the concept was studied and accepted by academics. Martineau (1958) used the word brand personality to refer to the dimension which is not materialistic and which makes the store special — its character. According to King (1970) consumers do not look for physical characteristics in a brand but they like brands as people and they choose their brands the same way they choose their friends.

The notion of brand personality can be traced back to its origins through the theory of symbolism (Smith, Graetz, & Westerbeek, 2006; Sirgy, 1982). It is argued that consumers view their preferred products as an extension of themselves, and therefore they purchase only those products which have symbolic value (Elliott, 1994). The self-esteem of the consumers is enhanced when they use products which have symbolic value (Hong & Zinkhan, 1995). The self-concept theory elucidates the motives behind consumers buying products which have symbolic value (Sirgy, 1982). While making a purchase decision consumers try to appraise the degree of similarity between the personality traits communicated by a particular product and the personality which they want to project themselves (Dobni & Zinkhan, 1990).

Though consumers have difficulty in assigning human personality traits to inanimate objects, the theoretical explanation of product personality is relatively underdeveloped (Allen & Olson, 1995). Theories from anthropomorphism (Boyer, 1996) help us to understand why people endow brands which are inanimate objects with qualities of human personality. To interpret the outside world people use their own self-schema as a basis for concepts and labels. Sparks & Guthrie (1998) argued that humans do not want to be associated with objects which are non-human. Prior studies have given evidence that in social gatherings, people are attracted to those who possess similar personality because they feel that it is emotionally rewarding. Emotional and cognitive needs motivate humans to form humanlike models to understand and mitigate events. According to Blackstone (1993), consumers form relationships with brands based on their symbolic value, which results in brand becoming alive and it is no longer considered as a passive object but an active partner in the minds of the consumer.

In practice, celebrity endorsements have helped brands in being personified. With the aid of celebrities and their personalities marketers position their brands in such a way that they can attract consumers who can identify themselves with these celebrities. In other words, consumers perceive a fit between their ideal or actual perceived selves and that of the celebrity, and get attracted towards the brand (Sirgy et al., 1997). According to Levy (1959) this personality endowment gives the brand a meaning in the eyes of the consumer. In fact, consumers perceive brands as having personality traits. In a study conducted by Kapferer (1998) on medical doctors, the results revealed that medical doctors had no difficulty in attributing personality traits to pharmaceutical brands; in addition, the results also revealed that these traits were actually significantly correlated to medical prescription itself. Due to which brand personality has an important role to play in managing the brands.

According to Geuens et al. (2008) brand personality forms a major component of brand identity. Brand identity is defined as a brand's meaning as put forward by the firm (Kapferer, 2008). In other words it is defined as how the company wants to present its brand to its target customers. Customers who give importance to branded possessions value their relationships with companies that own and manage the brand (Alexander, Schouten, and Koenig, 2002). The brand identity of a company needs to focus on differentiating their products from that of their competitors so that they are able to attain sustainable competitive advantage (Aaker & Joachimsthaler, 2000). A thorough understanding of competitor, environment, and customers can form the base for companies brand identity. The brand identity should reflect that the brand will live up to the promise it has made to the customers. The benefits of building strong brand identity are greater customer satisfaction, greater share of customer's wallet, and brand equity (Aaker & Joachimsthaler, 2000). Brand image is defined as the consumer's perception and interpretation of the brands identity (Geuens, Weijters, & De Wulf, 2009). Researchers have conceptualized brand identity and brand image as a multidimensional construct with brand personality as one of the important component. According to Keller, Apéria, & Georgson (2008) brand image consists of: (a) values and personality, (b) profile of the user, (c) history, heritage and experiences of the consumers, and

(d) consumers purchase and usage situations. Aaker & Joachimsthaler (2000) identified four elements of brand identity namely: (1) the brand as a symbol (2) the brand as an organization, (3) the brand as a product, and (4) the brand as a people. Building on prior research Kapferer (2012) developed a brand identity prism in which brand was considered as a message flowing from the sender to the receiver. The dimensions of brand identity prism were physique, personality, reflection, self-image, culture, and relationship. He further stated that brand identity dimension physique which is defined as physical features and qualities and personality which means human personality traits depict the sender. Whereas the brand identity dimensions reflection which focuses on the image of the target group and self-image which refers to how the brand makes consumers feel depict the receiver. The dimension culture which refers to values and relationship forms the link between the sender and receiver.

To date, the focus on the application of the brand personality scale on management was only on restaurant settings (Siguaw, Mattila, & Austin, 1999), consumer goods (Kim, 2000), and web sites (Müller & Chandon, 2003). However, green brand personality has recently evolved as an emerging area of research in the field of brand management (Acharya & Gupta, 2016; Goh & Wahid, 2015).

THE KEY CHARACTERISTICS OF GREEN BRANDS

Before elaborating the characteristics of green brands, it is important to know the characteristics of a brand personality in general that include sincerity, excitement, competence, sophistication, and ruggedness (Aaker, 1997); (a) Sincerity which represented attributes like wholesome, honest, cheerful, and down-to-earth; (b) Excitement which consisted of attributes like spirited, up-to-date, daring, and imaginative; (c) Competence which represented attributes like successful, reliable and intelligent; (d) Sophistication consisted of charming and upper class; and (e) Ruggedness comprised of outdoorsy and tough. The innate part of human personality is captured by dimensions Competence. Sincerity, and Excitement. Whereas Sophistication and Ruggedness tap a dimension that individual's desire but do not necessarily have.

However, these dimensions do not refer to the way consumers relate to a brand but rather how consumers view the brand (Brakus, Schmitt, & Zarantonello, 2009). Of these dimensions, excitement and sincerity are fundamental to the marketing landscape because these comprise two of the three partner ideals in intimate personal relationships (Aaker, Fournier, & Brasel, 2004). In a study conducted by Aaker et al. (2004) it was found that consumers form stronger relationships with sincere brands such as Ford and Coca-Cola than exciting brands such as Yahoo and Virgin. The rationale is that for short-term relationships exciting brands are more suitable, whereas for long-term relationships sincere brands are more useful (Aaker, 1997). Sincere brands are considered warmer such as Gateway and more down to earth such as MetLife, Coke, whereas exciting brands are related with a younger demographic such as Mountain Dew and are viewed as possessing cultural vitality such as BMW. Interestingly, exciting brands are often considered as appealing, attractive, and capable of bringing about interest and trial (Altschiller, 2000). In quintessence, a brand's personality influences how its actions and behaviors are professed by the consumers. Such consumer actions can be inferred from consumer reviews, company advertisement, and prior experiences.

According to Acharya and Gupta (2016) the dimensions of green brand personality are: security, sincerity, competence, sophistication, competence, and excitement. In comparison to the original brand personality dimensions, 'security' and 'compassion' emerged as new dimensions in their study. These new dimensions require confidence and protection (security) and concern and humanity (compassion).

ADVANTAGES OF GREEN MARKETING

Some of the advantages of green marketing that are listed below include customer betterment, innovative products, and customer participation.

- **Customer Betterment:** Marketer should give the best to customers; this is possible only if they use green marketing strategy. They can use environmental friendly packages to pack their products and if they are into manufacturing food product they can give more attention to consumer health benefits. This will help them to attract more customers through positive word-of-mouth. According to Carrie Walsh, Marketing Director, Frito-Lay: "Our customers are consumers who care about their personal health and planetary health".
- **Innovative Products:** Marketers can come out with innovative green products to attract customers. Successful product innovation can lead not just to products that satisfy the existing needs of customers; the company can be the market leaders and have a competitive advantage compared to the other players in the market. Some of the benefits of product innovation are
- **Increased Market Share:** An innovative product that satisfy the needs of the customer and which disrupts the target market can greatly enhance market share, which in-turn can lead to economies of scale and augment a company's market power.
- **Increased Profit:** According to Forbes report (2015) developing an innovative product that's exceptional and of better-quality to what the competition offers can lead to profit growth. In fact, more than 90% of the world's 100 most innovative companies have experienced increased profit due to innovation.
- **Customer Participation:** Green marketing activity campaign by the marketers will allow the customers to participate in the campaigns. There are very few people who realize the importance of safeguarding the environment, this opportunity can be used by marketers by providing them a platform which will allow them to work directly in preserving the environment, for example use of social media like Facebook, Twitter are some of the medium which are considered to be more effective than any other medium.

ROADMAP FOR GREEN MARKETERS

The green marketers need to generate convincing, pertinent, and efficient messaging that differentiates a company and its products and services from its competitors. As Gbadamosi (2016) points out, the first and foremost thing is to include the green elements in the business strategy such as striving hard to achieve sustainability goals, believing integrated thinking, taking a long-term orientation, relying on mutual responsibility, and accounting ecological costs. In all these efforts, the marketers need to convey a message which is convincing, pertinent, efficient, and different (Ottman, Stafford, & Hartman, 2006), as detailed below:

- **Convincing:** Companies need to provide convincing messages by supporting their statements with appropriate facts and figures. The level of information may depend on the image or environmental history of their sector and the target audience. One of the best ways is by using eco-labeling schemes. A product with an eco-label is a product that is proven environmentally preferable. It shows that the manufacturer is adhering to the guidelines that are required to manufacture an eco-friendly product. Marketers need to highlight the eco-friendly benefits that the product has on the consumers as well as on the society.

- **Pertinent:** A pertinent message reports sustainability success that is in line with the company's impacts. For instance, if a pharma company focuses on advertising its efforts to green its facilities while not delivering on quality of its medicines then its green message is not relevant to its key environmental impacts. If a company, markets its strong community benefit programs but does not provide good working condition for its employees then its advertising message will be misleading.
- **Efficient:** An efficient message translates the sustainability information to make sense of the extent of your achievements. For example, a company may have used its limited resources in an efficient manner then the same has to be communicated in such a way that it is easily understood. The efficiency of the message also depends on how the message is communicated to the intended audience.
- **Differentiate:** Companies often strive hard to make their message unique and distinct from competing products and services. Since their target segment is limited to the green consumers. They often face the challenge of differentiating their products not only from the producers of green products but also from their non-green counterparts. For this, the marketers are required to highlight the uniqueness of their products both in terms of the benefits it promises for the environment and in creating brand value by placing their brand as an in thing.

ALIGNING GREEN MARKETING WITH BUSINESS STRATEGY

In order to shift its focus from conventional marketing to green marketing, companies need to align their new business strategy with that of the existing one. It can be done in several ways including reducing greenwashing, increasing transparency, promoting green culture, assisting other environmental causes, and getting into third party collaborations. Each of these is elaborated in the subsequent sections.

- **Greenwashing:** It is a technique in which an organization spends more money on advertising green, sustainable behaviors instead of putting them into practice. For example an automotive company may call itself environmental friendly since it uses battery to run the car. But they might dispose their waste in sea, by doing that they are harming the environment, consumers, and finally their business.
- **Environment**: Greenwashing is bad for the environment because it can promote consumers to do the opposite of what's good for the environment. Greenwashing makes claims that are neither good nor bad for the environment. In order to increase their sales company makes false promises.
- **Consumers**: When it comes to money consumers do not like to be cheated and taken for granted. They avoid spending more money on a product or service which they believe is going to harm the environment.
- **Businesses**: Companies have realized that by being environmental friendly does increase their profits. Even though there are many ways to produce goods and use processes that do not harm the environment, it is saddening to know that the companies still do not do it. It is even worse when they don't make changes and claim to be a green company only to push their products in the market. Environment friendly consumers can see right through their green screen. It backfires and harms the company's reputation and profits.

- **Transparency:** In order to gain the trust of the consumers, companies should conduct their business in an open way. Being transparent is the new goal for many businesses, which will help them to win over shareholders, employees, and the general public. If a business is open about its operations, it can earn a level of trust that it wouldn't have established otherwise. For example Starbucks company prides itself as the world's largest environment friendly company by proving it in the marketing campaign 'Transparency'. For Starbucks, 'Transparency' is a company-wide philosophy in which customers are treated honestly and where prices are actually low.
- **Green Culture: "**Going green" motto should be practiced and embedded in the organization's culture. For example, Go Lite, an outdoor clothing and equipment maker in Boulder, CO which was founded in the year 1998 by Kim and Demetri, the company specializes in ultra-light packs, sleeping bags and down jackets. The main objective of the company is to mitigate 100% of its environmental footprint. To do this, it uses so-called Environmentally Preferred Materials" (EPMs) like recycled nylon and polyester, instead of newly-produced petro-chemical-based fabrics and parts. Till date, 67% of its materials are EPMs and it is aiming for 100% by 2016. It also encourages customers to return their old clothes where it pledges to recycle and reuse items returned by its customers. The company is also trying to make its headquarters a zero waste facility, where it composts or recycles all of its garbage. Some of the strategies which the companies can follow are:
- **Sustainability***:* Companies should identify sustainability as a core corporate value. Companies should carry this theme through all of their communication and environmental activities.
- **Company Tradition**: It should be company's tradition of encouraging and constantly pursuing environmental programs. As a result, it will be well ingrained in the company's operations and understandings. For example, Aeon has been running programs for 25 years.
- **Founder's Philosophy**: Some companies, such as IKEA and LUSH, have imbued their employees with the founder's long-held ethical thinking.
- **Engaging Employees**: More recent adopters of environmental best practices create a sustainability culture in their organization. For example, Wal-Mart and Sam's club have introduced Personal Sustainability Projects (which is now called as My Sustainability Plan) which encourages employees to develop goals to improve their health and also the health of the environment.
- **Communication**: Companies can communicate their sustainability goals to every employee to develop a common understanding and a culture of sustainability.
- **Amenities to Encourage Employee Participation:** Companies should actively encourage and facilitate sustainable practices for employees. For example, Mountain Equipment Co-op (MEC) provides change rooms, showers and lockers for their employees, and currently 82 per cent of their employees use alternative transportation to travel to work every day.
- **Assist Other Environmental Causes:** Organizations should give back to the community. This helps the organizations in building a good overall image of caring for the betterment of society and the environment in the eyes of the consumer. For example Patagonia, Inc. headquartered in Ventura, California, is an American clothing company founded by Yvon Chouinard in the year 1973 it sells and showcases mainly sustainable outdoor clothing with more than 1,300 employees. The company uses organic raw materials which are environmentally preferred. The company also set asides 1% of their profits to environmental preservation groups. It also encourages its employees to volunteer for an environmental organization with two months full pay. It also buys wool only from farmers who use sustainable gazing practices.

- **Collaborating:** Collaborating with third parties is a good way. For example Adobe developed a Green Team that works on corporate sustainability initiatives. They came out with a project which allowed its employees to volunteer to help with the solar installation process for a low-income family. There are several other examples (Makower, 2014) that follow such as (1) General Motors working with Honda to develop cars that can run on hydrogen fuel, (2) Nestle joined hands with beverage company Coca-Cola and other beverage companies to form an alliance of Bioplastics Feedstock that encourages formation of plastic material from plants. Universities are also taking collaborative route to promote green activities. It includes 'Penn Green Campus Partnership' in which Penn has collaborated with a number of organizations such as Delaware Valley Green Building Council. The students have formed a group called Student Sustainability Association at Penn for spreading awareness among students and teach them sustainable practices (Penn, 2016).

LEARNING FROM THE BEST PRACTICES

Starbucks has extensively used green marketing campaign to defeat its competitors. Starbucks Corporation is an American coffee company and coffeehouse chain. Starbucks was founded in Seattle, Washington in the year 1971. The company believes in the importance of caring for the planet and working with and encouraging others to do the same. Some of the strategies which they follow include recycling, energy saving, water conservation, making green building, and addressing climate change issues. All these are discussed below:

- **Recycling:** The organization is trying to develop more environmentally friendly cups, and is working hard to expand their recycling program in an effort to reduce the waste they create. A lot of their customers are also working to reduce their own environmental impact. The company offers 10-cent discount to the US and Canada customers to encourage them to use their own reusable mugs or tumblers for their beverages. Customers staying in a store are also encouraged to use ceramic mug for their beverage. By doing this they are helping in keeping the natural resources i.e forest intact.

The company also introduced Grounds for Your Garden in 1995, which offers customers' complimentary five-pound (2.27-kilogram) bags of used coffee grounds to enrich garden soil. And where commercial composting is available, many stores are able to divert other food waste and coffee grounds from the landfill as well.

- **Energy Saving:** The organization has minimized their energy consumption by using renewable sources of energy to lower their impact on the planet. They have installed Energy Management Systems in approximately 4,000 stores. Energy Management Systems optimize heating and cooling and they enable the company to identify additional opportunities for savings going forward. They are also continuing to focus on driving energy savings in their stores through optimization of equipment and lighting specifications.

- **Water Conservation:** Since water is one of the most valuable natural resources, Starbucks understands its responsibility of preserving it. The company is evaluating their store design, equipments, and operations to identify ways to continue to reduce the amount of water they use. The company installs efficient fixtures, monitors consumption to identify spikes in water usage and targeting leak repairs, and upgrades the water filtration systems in the stores.
- **Green Building:** Starbucks is making its stores as green as they can by using responsible building materials and energy efficient designs to reduce their environmental footprint. It is often termed as the 'green building leader'. It employs around 300 Leadership in Energy and Environmental Design (LEED) certified designers. LEED is given by US Green Building Council to the organizations that follow its rules for green construction and design (GBES, 2015).
- **Addressing Climate Change Issues:** Because climate change poses a serious threat to the world's coffee-growing regions, the company is aggressively pursuing strategies to address this problem and help farmers mitigate the impact. It encourages programmes that facilitate farmers' right to use to carbon markets. It allows them to make additional income while helping to prevent deforestation.

CONCLUSION

Due to the increased awareness of the people toward environment, the growing inclination of consumers to green products is apparent. The emergence of green marketing is all set to modify the existing norms of the marketing strategies. It not only has the ability to address the profitability concern of the companies but also has the potential to attract the society to opt for green solutions and participate in this movement. Governments across the globe are increasingly taking steps to promote eco-friendly products. However, the marketers need to take the lead and innovate ways or follow existing best practices to promote green brands. The private players are also expected to collaborate with the local governments to ensure a greener future for the next generation.

Future studies can investigate whether culture has any impact on green brand personality. In addition future work can investigate the antecedents and consequences of green brand personality. They can also investigate the moderating role of relationship length.

REFERENCES

Aaker, D. A., & Joachimsthaler, E. (2000). The brand relationship spectrum: The key to the brand architecture challenge. *California Management Review*, *42*(4), 8–23. doi:10.2307/41166051

Aaker, D. A., & Joachimsthaler, E. (2012). *Brand Leadership*. New York: Free Press.

Aaker, J., Fournier, S., & Brasel, S. A. (2004). When good brands do bad. *The Journal of Consumer Research*, *31*(1), 1–16. doi:10.1086/383419

Aaker, J. L. (1997). Dimensions of brand personality. *JMR, Journal of Marketing Research*, *34*(3), 347–356. doi:10.2307/3151897

Acharya, A., & Gupta, M. (2016). An Application of Brand Personality to Green Consumers: A Thematic Analysis. *Qualitative Report*, *21*(8), 1531–1545.

Allen, D. E., & Olson, J. (1995). Conceptualizing and creating brand personality: A narrative theory approach. *Advances in Consumer Research. Association for Consumer Research (U. S.)*, *22*(1), 392–393.

Altschiller, D. (2000). Do Dot-Coms' Ads Reveal a More Basic Flaw? *Brandweek*, *41*(12), 32.

Banytė, J., Brazionienė, L., & Gadeikienė, A. (2010). investigation of green consumer profile: A case of lithuanian market of eco-friendly food products. *Economics & Management*, *15*, 374–383.

Bhattacharya, C. B. (2016). Responsible Marketing: Doing Well by Doing Good. *GfK Marketing Intelligence Review*, *8*(1), 8–17. doi:10.1515/gfkmir-2016-0002

Blackston, M. (1993). Beyond brand personality: Building brand relationships. In D. Aaker & A. Biel (Eds.), *Brand equity and advertising: Advertising's role in building strong brands* (pp. 113–124). Hillsdale, NJ: Erlbaum.

Boyer, P. (1996). What makes anthropomorphism natural: Intuitive ontology and cultural representations. *Journal of the Royal Anthropological Institute*, *2*(1), 83–98. doi:10.2307/3034634

Brakus, J. J., Schmitt, B. H., & Zarantonello, L. (2009). Brand experience: What is it? How is it measured? Does it affect loyalty? *Journal of Marketing*, *73*(3), 52–68. doi:10.1509/jmkg.73.3.52

Chan, T. Y., & Wong, C. W. (2012). The consumption side of sustainable fashion supply chain: Understanding fashion consumer eco-fashion consumption decision. *Journal of Fashion Marketing and Management: An International Journal*, *16*(2), 193–215. doi:10.1108/13612021211222824

Charter, M. (1992). *Greener marketing: A responsible approach to business*. Greenleaf Publishing.

Crane, A. (2000). Facing the backlash: Green marketing and strategic reorientation in the 1990s. *Journal of Strategic Marketing*, *8*(3), 277–296. doi:10.1080/09652540050110011

Davenport, C., Gillis, J., Chan, S., & Eddy, M. (2015). Inside the Paris Climate Deal. *The New York Times*. Retrieved from http://www.nytimes.com/interactive/2015/12/12/world/paris-climate-change-deal-explainer.html?action=click&contentCollection=earth&region=rank&module=package&version=highlights&contentPlacement=1&pgtype=collection&_r=0

De Boer, J. (2003). Sustainability labelling schemes: The logic of their claims and their functions for stakeholders. *Business Strategy and the Environment*, *12*(4), 254–264. doi:10.1002/bse.362

Dobni, D., & Zinkhan, G. M. (1990). In search of brand image: A foundation analysis. *Advances in Consumer Research. Association for Consumer Research (U. S.)*, *17*(1), 110–119.

Elliott, R. (1994). Exploring the symbolic meaning of brands. *British Journal of Management*, *5*(s1), S13–S19. doi:10.1111/j.1467-8551.1994.tb00126.x

Fuller, D. A. (1999). *Sustainable marketing: Managerial-ecological issues*. Sage Publications.

Gbadamosi. (2016). *Handbook of Research on Consumerism and Buying Behavior in Developing Nations*. IGI Global.

GBES. (2015). Starbucks: The World's Greenest Retailer. *Green Building Education Services(GBES)*. Retrieved from http://www.gbes.com/blog/starbucks-the-worlds-greenest-retailer/

Geuens, M., Weijters, B., & De Wulf, K. (2009). A new measure of brand personality. *International Journal of Research in Marketing*, *26*(2), 97–107. doi:10.1016/j.ijresmar.2008.12.002

Global. (2015). Green generation: Millennials say sustainability is a shopping priority. *Nielsen*. Retrieved from http://www.nielsen.com/in/en/insights/news/2015/green-generation-millennials-say-sustainability-is-a-shopping-priority.html

Goh, Y. N., & Wahid, N. A. (2015). A Review on Green Purchase Behaviour Trend of Malaysian Consumers. *Asian Social Science*, *11*(2), 103–110.

Grant, J. (2007). *Green is a principle, not a proposition: a review of the green marketing manifesto*. Academic Press.

Herrera, T. (2010). 10 Green NGOs Businesses Should Know About. *GreenBiz*. Retrieved from https://www.greenbiz.com/blog/2010/06/14/10-green-ngos-businesses-know-about

Hong, J. W., & Zinkhan, G. M. (1995). Self-concept and advertising effectiveness: The influence of congruency, conspicuousness, and response mode. *Psychology and Marketing*, *12*(1), 53–77. doi:10.1002/mar.4220120105

Kapferer, J. N. (1998). *The role of branding in medical prescription: An empirical investigation*. HEC working paper. Jouy en Josas, France.

Kapferer, J. N. (2012). *The new strategic brand management: Advanced insights and strategic thinking*. Kogan Page Publishers.

Kärnä, J., Hansen, E., & Juslin, H. (2003). Social responsibility in environmental marketing planning. *European Journal of Marketing*, *37*(5/6), 848–871. doi:10.1108/03090560310465170

Keller, K. L., Apéria, T., & Georgson, M. (2008). *Strategic brand management: A European perspective*. Pearson Education.

Kim, H. S. (2000). Examination of brand personality and brand attitude within the apparel product category. *Journal of Fashion Marketing and Management: An International Journal*, *4*(3), 243–252. doi:10.1108/eb022593

King, S. (1970). *What is a Brand?*. London: Walter Thompson Company Limited.

Kleindorfer, P. R., Singhal, K., & Wassenhove, L. N. (2005). Sustainable operations management. *Production and Operations Management*, *14*(4), 482–492. doi:10.1111/j.1937-5956.2005.tb00235.x

Levy, S. J. (1959). Symbols for sales. *Harvard Business Review*, *37*(Summer).

Makower. (2014). *State of Green Business: Collaboration becomes an accelerator*. Retrieved from https://www.greenbiz.com/blog/2014/01/27/state-green-business-collaboration-becomes-accelerator

Martineau, P. (1958). The personality of a retail store. *Harvard Business Review, 36*(Nov–Dec).

McAlexander, J. H., Schouten, J. W., & Koenig, H. F. (2002). Building brand community. *Journal of Marketing, 66*(1), 38–54. doi:10.1509/jmkg.66.1.38.18451

Müller, B., & Chandon, J. L. (2003). The impact of visiting a brand website on brand personality. *Electronic Markets, 13*(3), 210–221. doi:10.1080/1019678032000108301

Muntean, A., & Stremtan, F. (2010). Green marketing: A new challenge for Romanian organisations. *Journal of Environmental Protection and Ecology, 11*(4), 1472–1474.

Natural Resources Canada. (2016). Funding Programs. *Natural Resources Canada*. Retrieved from http://www.nrcan.gc.ca/energy/funding/programs-funding/12400

Needle, D. (2010). *Business in context: An introduction to business and its environment*. Cengage Learning EMEA.

Ottman, J., & Books, N. B. (1998). Green marketing: opportunity for innovation. *The Journal of Sustainable Product Design, 60*.

Ottman, J. A., Stafford, E. R., & Hartman, C. L. (2006). Avoiding green marketing myopia: Ways to improve consumer appeal for environmentally preferable products. *Environment: Science and Policy for Sustainable Development, 48*(5), 22–36.

Peattie, K. (1995). *Environmental marketing management: Meeting the green challenge*. Financial Times Management.

Peattie, K. (1999). Trappings versus substance in the greening of marketing planning. *Journal of Strategic Marketing, 7*(2), 131–148. doi:10.1080/096525499346486

Penn. (2016). Collaborative Efforts. *Penn*. Retrieved from http://www.facilities.upenn.edu/sustainability/collaborative-efforts

Phelan, H. (2012). 10 Eco-friendly fashion brands we can get behind. *Fashionista*. Retrieved from http://fashionista.com/2012/04/10-eco-friendly-fashion-brands-we-can-get-behind

Polonsky, M. J. (1994). Green marketing regulation in the US and Australia: The Australian checklist. *Greener Management International, 5*(January), 44–52.

Rao, P. K., & Bhargav, V. R. (2016). A Study on Green Packaging-A Case Study Approach With Reference To Dell Inc. *International Educational Scientific Research Journal, 2*(7), 83–84.

Reinhardt, F. (1999). Market failure and the environmental policies of firms: Economic rationales for beyond compliance behavior. *Journal of Industrial Ecology, 3*(1), 9–21. doi:10.1162/108819899569368

Sharma, A., Iyer, G. R., Mehrotra, A., & Krishnan, R. (2010). Sustainability and business-to-business marketing: A framework and implications. *Industrial Marketing Management, 39*(2), 330–341. doi:10.1016/j.indmarman.2008.11.005

Sheth, J., & Parvatiyar, A. (1995). Ecological imperatives and the role of marketing. *Environmental marketing: Strategies, practice, theory and research*, 3-20.

Siguaw, J. A., Mattila, A., & Austin, J. R. (1999). The brand-personality scale. *The Cornell Hotel and Restaurant Administration Quarterly*, *40*(3), 48–55.

Sirgy, M. J. (1982). Self-concept in consumer behavior: A critical review. *The Journal of Consumer Research*, *9*(3), 287–300. doi:10.1086/208924

Sirgy, M. J., Grewal, D., Mangleburg, T. F., Park, J. O., Chon, K. S., Claiborne, C. B., & Berkman, H. et al. (1997). Assessing the predictive validity of two methods of measuring self-image congruence. *Journal of the Academy of Marketing Science*, *25*(3), 229–241. doi:10.1177/0092070397253004

Smith, A. C., Graetz, B. R., & Westerbeek, H. M. (2006). Brand personality in a membership--based organisation. *International Journal of Nonprofit and Voluntary Sector Marketing*, *11*(3), 251–266. doi:10.1002/nvsm.51

Sparks, P., & Guthrie, C. A. (1998). Self--Identity and the theory of planned behavior: A useful addition or an unhelpful artifice? *Journal of Applied Social Psychology*, *28*(15), 1393–1410. doi:10.1111/j.1559-1816.1998.tb01683.x

Tureac, C. E., Turtureanu, A. G., Bordean, I., Grigore, A., Modiga, G., & Pripoie, R. (2010). Ecological food products-general considerations on green marketing. *10th International Multidisciplinary Scientific GeoConference SGEM2010, 2*, 529-537.

Violeta, S., & Gheorghe, I. G. (2009). The green strategy mix–a new marketing approach. *Knowledge Management and Innovation in Advancing Economics–Analysis and Solutions*, *1*, 1344–1347.

Walker, L. (2013). 71% of Consumers Think Green When Purchasing. *Environmental Leader.* Retrieved from http://www.environmentalleader.com/2013/04/03/71-of-consumers-think-green-when-purchasing/

Wasik, J. F. (1996). *Green marketing and management: A global perspective*. Wiley.

Zhu, Q., & Sarkis, J. (2016). Green marketing and consumerism as social change in china: Analyzing the literature. *International Journal of Production Economics*, *181*, 289–302. doi:10.1016/j.ijpe.2016.06.006

Chapter 10
Marketing Strategies for Trendy Animal Products:
Sustainability as a Core

Alfredo J. Escribano
Independent Researcher, Spain

ABSTRACT

There is increasing pressure on companies to follow more strict practices along the whole supply chain regarding sustainability and health. However, consumers' knowledge on nutrition, labelling and on the impacts of the agri-food system is scarce. In this sense, it is particularly interesting to analyse consumers' behaviour towards a family of products coming from one of the most controversial sectors due to both past health hazards and its high environmental impact: the livestock sector. This sector constitutes itself one of the Global issues' bottlenecks that call for urgent action. The present study reviews consumers' behaviour towards meat and dairy products claiming different attributes related to sustainability. Therefore, this chapter reviews, synthesize and discusses the existing knowledge on the topic with an integrative-interdisciplinary approach. Finally, marketing strategy recommendations are provided.

INTRODUCTION

Public's opinion and advertising are increasingly internalizing sustainability attributes (health included) as not only desirable ones but also as companies' musts regarding CSR. Due to this, there is increasing pressure on companies to follow more strict practices along the whole supply chain. However, research shows scarce level of consumers' knowledge of agricultural, manufacturing and marketing practices (i.e. regulations and standards), as well as their consequences on the agri-food system sustainability. In this sense, it is particularly interesting to analyse consumers' behaviour towards a family of products coming from one of the most controversial and sometimes negatively sectors due to both not forgotten past health hazards and its high environmental impact: the livestock sector.

There is increasing pressure from stakeholders around the social and environmental responsibilities of companies, including how products are sourced and manufactured, and marketed to consumers. This

DOI: 10.4018/978-1-5225-2912-5.ch010

poses a challenge for stakeholders in terms of understanding and incorporate sustainability in their every day practices (Oates, Alevizou, & McDonald, 2016).

In line with this contextualization, the present chapter is aimed at: (a) reviewing and synthesizing consumers' behaviour towards products of animal origin claiming different sustainability attributes; (b) discussing on the interplay among: (i) the need to feed a global growing population, while reducing livestock sector's environmental impact and; (ii) the lack of knowledge and response from consumers towards more sustainable animal products; (c) providing with marketing strategies to align the abovementioned interplay, in order to feed the global growing population by means of more sustainable agri-food chains and products (market support/approval).

CONSUMPTION TRENDS

After the great process of industrialization and urbanization of societies during the 20th century, the food security approach lead the industry to focus on producing larger amounts of food at affordable prices. Nowadays, the predictions in growth of global population led to again work on this approach. However, this now must be also compatible with stricter consumers' demands, especially in the areas of health (nutrition), animal welfare and convenience. Consumers themselves are faced with a bewildering range of product choices and increasing information, which raises questions about links between sustainability in production and consumption. The main aspects will be discussed. In order to continue being competitive and sustainable, the meat industry must continually respond to consumer and market-lead quality ques (Troy & Kerry, 2010).

Food Safety

Food safety is an essential pillar of social sustainability, and as a leading cause of foodborne illnesses, meat products have received special attention from consumers, stakeholders and policy makers. Consumers feel that consumers are not satisfied that the current food system is adequately attending to threats (providing sufficient protection from) of foodborne contamination (Tobin, Thomson, & LaBorde, 2012).

Particularly, cattle and beef markets have suffered from these safety concerns mainly as a consequence of the discovery of cattle infected with bovine spongiform encephalopathy (BSE). The impact of this issue was so important that some countries have lost their access to key markets (such as North America into the Japanese market) (Schroeder, Tonsor, Mintert, & Pennings, 2007).

From the industry and producers' perspective, it is necessary to have a clear understanding of consumer produce safety perceptions and preferences, in order to make better-informed decisions regarding their food safety practices. In this sense, Tobin et al. (2012) studied how consumer demographics, along with their preferences for specific attributes in fresh produce, such as local, organic and inspected for food safety (GAP), affect their produce safety perceptions. These authors found that consumers perceive that produce inspected for GAPs offers enhanced safety. In this sense, O'Donovan and McCarthy (2002) found that increasing awareness of food safety and pollution issues are important determinants in the purchase of organic meat.

Environmental Sustainability

Food consumption is associated with various environmental impacts, and consumers' food choices therefore represent important environmental decisions (Tobler, Visschers, & Siegrist, 2011). Ethical food choices result from a desire to sacrifice some of one's consumption benefits out of consideration for other stakeholders. Ethical motivations thus derive from altruistic concerns for other living things. Other people are impacted by our consumption behaviours in a variety of ways (McEachern & Schröeder, 2002).

Unlike intensive production systems, low-input ones are sometimes supported as ones with lower carbon footprint (Escribano, 2016b). From marketing side, Midmore et al. (2005) reviewed consumers' attitudes towards the quality and safety of organic and low input foods.

Meat consumption also presents consumers with a basic moral dilemma, namely the fact that the life of another sentient being is sacrificed for the benefit of the consumer (McEachern & Schröeder, 2002). In this sense, livestock has a bad public image with regard to their impact on environmental sustainability. Production methods (intensive production systems) and their impacts on animal welfare (whose negative perception have been increasing by media) constitutes a great and growing concern by consumers with regard to how meat is produced. Due to this, the meat industry must take into account how this information will influence the perception of meat quality by the consumer.

This trend is increasing, as there is a growing availability of information regarding environmental costs of producing livestock. However, meat production is a traditional farming practice and often contributes to the preservation of traditional grasslands and biodiversity. In this sense, it is important to be aware of the fact that an important part of the negative externalities do not depend on the production itself but on the supply chain (FAO, 2016). Due to these environmental concerns, consumers are taking more active responsibility as citizens and evaluating lifestyle choices. Citizen- consumerism is a concept which refers to how consumers apply their political values to decisions in the shopping arena. In this sense, Dobson (2003) defines 'ecological citizenship' as a shared personal commitment to sustainability and suggests that it can be viewed as a driving force for the practice of sustainable consumption. Despite science (through Life Cycle Analysis assessments) indicates that lowering meat consumption is very environmentally relevant (Jungbluth et al., 2007), consumers assessed reducing meat consumption as the least environmentally friendly of all consumption patterns, which reflect a lack of knowledge also found by researchers (Mesías, Escribano, Gaspar, & Pulido, 2008). Few respondents always looked at the label before purchase. This may be an indication that most consumers do not understand what the labels mean. Consequently, this lack of awareness and knowledge regarding meat production and processing has resulted in greater reliance and trust in grocery multiple stores (McEachern & Schröeder, 2002). This supports consumers' lack of awareness towards the environmental impact associated with meat production mentioned by Tobler et al. (2011).

Animal Welfare

Animal welfare is an ethical concern of growing importance for consumers. Clark, Stewart, Panzone, Kyriazakis and Frewer (2016) reviewed public attitudes towards farm animal welfare, founding that the public are concerned about it in modern production systems. Concern varied in relation to age, gender, education and familiarity with farming. Naturalness and humane treatment were central to what was considered good welfare. They also found that consumers adopted a number of dissonance strategies to enable guilt free meat consumption.

McEachern and Schröder (2002) also studied ethical concerns when purchasing/consuming meat products. They examined the specific values held by consumers towards organic and conventionally produced meat, with particular reference to moral issues surrounding food animal production. A sample of 30 females from both a rural and an urban area of Scotland (UK), were interviewed. Overall, there was low commitment towards the purchase of organic meats and little concern for ethical issues, which appeared to be delegated by the consumer to the meat retailer or government. One justification perhaps offered for respondents' lack of consideration is that there is no moral stigma attached to purchasing meat that is legally sold as it already conforms to minimum welfare standards.

Lifestyles, Convenience and Predicted Age Profiles

Our changing lifestyle and the demand for convenience of the western world will require the meat industry to be more innovative. In this sense, packaging formats and sizes are essential. Moreover, health pre-cooked foods (or fast foods) are still not developed so much as it is necessary. It seems that most of fast food are less healthy, which make no sense. In this sense, there is room for improvement.

The predicted ageing profiles technologies of the future such as nutrigenomics (the impact of foods on genes), personalised food for health, exploitation of animal derived bioactive components must be explored in order to design tailor-made animal products suitable for specific groups of consumers. However, for any new technology or process, consumer trust is paramount (Troy & Kerry, 2010). In this sense, with the rise in diseases such as obesity, diabetes, cancer and heart disease, which are linked to Western diets and lifestyles, consumers are becoming motivated by personal health.

THE COMPLEX CONCEPT OF QUALITY AND PURCHASING BEHAVIOR IN ANIMAL PROCUCTS

Many attributes and standards could be associated to sustainability and quality, and consumer preferences depend on a multitude of factors. For animal products, besides the more traditional aspects related to 'quality,' differential aspects play an important role, which makes the preferences for meat products even more complex, generally in the case of meat products.

Meat

In this sense, extrinsic and personal values, such as the attitude towards animal welfare and the environment, political views, and income levels (especially in meat premium products) are of great importance. Unlike product quality characteristics, consumer value is subjective and depends on the context of consumption. Grocery shoppers today have the choice of a vast diversity of protein products and meat cuts. From the farmer point of view, and especially from the beef farmer, fast changes in consumers' preferences hinder their competitiveness, as their production cycle (dependent on animal physiology) is quite large.

Aspects surrounding the process of meat production are important in the determination of the purchasing behaviour, although some of them do o not influence meat's intrinsic quality). According to Grunert, Bredahl and Brunsø (2004), there have been three broad areas of interest:

- Interest in organic production
- Interest in animal welfare
- Interest in products manufactured in a 'natural' way, i.e. without the use of advanced technology. This group includes the use of genetically modified organisms (GMOs) in food production.

Beef

In general terms, consumer preferences for beef are mainly guided by personal benefits, followed by health and societal concerns (Philipp, Popp, Rumley, Savin, & Coffey, 2015). In addition, personal likings, and particularly the habit of preparing beef at home, were more willing to pay a premium for certain quality aspects.

Regarding labelling strategies (claims), the study of Umberger, Boxall and Lacy (2009) may be of help especially for ruminant products. These authors found that attributes like "grassfinished," "certified organic," or "grazing managed to preserve streams" were much less important than "high nutritional content," "tested for mad cow disease," or "good value for the price," which was the highest-ranking attribute available for selection, while attributes such as "animals treated humanely" and "no antibiotics" ranked in the middle consumers with less income were also less likely to spend more money on beef labelled as "natural," "grass-fed," or similar. However, these finding can vary spatially. Thus, other studies reported that the majority of US consumers did not prefer grass-fed over conventional beef based on taste although grass-fed beef had some visual appeal (Umberger, Feuz, Calkins, & Killinger, 2002; Xue, Zartarian, Wang, & Georgopoulos, 2010). Again, socioeconomic factors played a relatively minor role in assessing the "willingness-to-pay", in this case, for grass-fed beef. However, the education level must be taken into consideration as the knowledge that the interviewed consumers had about health and alternative food protein sourcing influenced their buying decisions (Xue et al., 2010).

A significant hurdle is beef storage for the consumer expected to buy in larger quantity given the lack of cost-effective transportation for this marketing channel. Multi-faceted consumer preferences will make it relatively difficult to lay out a long-term business strategy (Philipp et al., 2015; Escribano, 2016b). With regard to local economy and environmental protection, alternative food networks (local food) has been greatly investigated. In this sense, direct marketing of beef to consumers is scarce, and requires high level of knowledge and implication in the whole agri-food chain. Moreover, also the level of association plays an important role, as the bargaining power is essential (A. J. Escribano, M. Escribano, Gaspar, Mesías, & Pulido, 2015, Escribano 2016a, Escribano 2016b). Also, direct marketing pertain to access to slaughtering facilities (Philipp et al., 2015), which are scarce (Escribano et al., 2015) and developing forage production and grazing strategies allowing year-round beef supply if possible (Philipp et al., 2015).

Eggs

Consumption trends towards healthier animal products and animal welfare make it interesting to study consumers' perception of eggs because of their strong negative association with cholesterol levels and their extremely intensive systems of production. Thus, Mesías, Martínez-Carrasco, Martínez and Gaspar (2011) investigated the preferences of Spanish consumers for alternative types of egg (organic, omega-3-enhanced, free-range eggs and conventional battery cage ones). Authors found that price is the most important attribute determining consumer preferences, followed by the hens' feed and their rearing conditions. It was also found that only some groups of consumers are willing to pay the premium necessary for alternative methods of production. In particular, these attributes were price (30.14%), rearing conditions (19.68%), feed (19.20%), and the choice between different egg sizes (14.41%).

PERCEPTIONS AND ATTITIDES TOWARDS SUSTAINABLE ATTRIBUTES IN ANIMAL PRODUCTS

Organic Products

One of the most common quality standards or production systems related to sustainability attributes is 'organic' production. There has been a huge increase in demand for organic food products during the last decade in many countries (FiBL & IFOAM, 2016). In the following figure, the main countries in the organic market can be observed. Regarding animal products, food scandals often sensationalised by the mass media played a powerful role in influencing people and their food habits, especially with regard to BSE crisis or the scandal surrounding eggs and the risk of salmonella in the late 1980's helps to increase the preferences towards organic beef and free range or organic eggs (Ayers, 2008).

There are many publications focusing on diverse aspects of marketing research for organic products. It has been suggested that there are two major motives for choosing organic products, namely health and environmental concerns. Understanding of "organic" differs from consumer to consumer. Thus, Aarset et al. (2004) found in different groups and countries the following meanings:

- **France:** Natural, limited human intervention.
- **Germany:** High welfare, natural, environmentally kind.
- **Norway:** Characterized by confusion and ambivalence natural.
- **Spain:** Synonymous with ecological and natural non-use of pesticides, not environmentally damaging. Throughout the Ecomarket project, González and Calatrava (2009) found the following motivations and their importance for organic consumers in Spain (perhaps making a figure of bars in descending order of ranking type): Food quality (66.95%, much importance); Freshness, healing; Dietary value (low fat, cholesterol, sugar, salt, etc.); Low content of additives and chemicals; Nutritional value (proteins, vitamins, etc.); Price (33.62%); External appearance (21,88%); Respect for the environment when producing (21.76%); Brand of the product (13.19%); They are healthier 43.49%; They are more natural 22.28%; They do not contain chemical residues 13,57%; They are better for the environment 13.48%; Its flavour is better 5.21%; Other reasons 1.98%.
- **UK:** Freedom from artificial inputs, limiting environmental damage.

The main attributes of importance for consumers with regard to organic food are summarized on the basis of Annunziata and Vecchio (2016), where the authors reflected the level of agreement with regard to such attributes.

Trust on organic certification and the benefits of this product with regard to others, poses doubt among many profiles of consumers. Taste is also central in the development of loyalty for an organic food product. Most regular consumers in our sample were found to be relaxed about their loyalty towards organic products and were willing to substitute organic milk for conventional milk when the former was unavailable. Treason in these instances was directly related to issues of convenience. Occasional consumers generally do not have loyal organic habits, however, some 'supermarket orientated' occasional

Table 1. Respondents' perception of organic food. Source: Annunziata & Vecchio (2016)

	Totally Disagree (%)	Totally Agree (%)
Environmental protection	-	40
Better for my health	-	42
Better taste	12	16
Rigorous safety control	2	38
Biodiversity preservation	7	30
Distrust if conventional	18	25
Modern and trendy	31	6
To support rural farmers	7	19
Fresher products	2	35
Curiosity	3	9
Respect for animal welfare	9	14
Prices too high	15	21
Not available	6	15
Little difference with conventional	32	4
No trust in certification body	18	12
Too many label	16	23
Insufficient information	5	18

Table 2. Motives and deterrents of buying organic food. Source: Aarset et al. (2004), Shaw Hughner et al. (2007), Bellows et al. (2008); EcoMarket project

Promotors	Deterrents
Health and nutritional concern	High price premiums
Superior taste	Lack of organic food availability, poor merchandising
Concern for the environment	Scepticism of certification boards and organic labels
Food safety, lack of confidence in the conventional food industry	Insufficient marketing
Concern over animal welfare	Satisfaction with current food source
Support of local economy	Sensory defects
More wholesome	Higher price
Nostalgia	Less attractive aspect
Fashionable/Curiosity	"I have to trust label"
Neotribalism: connection among people, bargaining to groups of common interest	Inexistent or non-continuous supplying in most of the points of sale
Animal welfare	Difficult to identify
Food safety	Not enough knowledge and information
Freshness	

consumers tend to be loyal to a specific organic product such as milk or eggs which they try to always buy as organic (Ayers, 2008).

Despite these increase in preference towards organic food, there is an attitude-behaviour gap between qualitative findings (consumers have a preference for organic food products) and quantitative ones (i.e. organic food only accounts for 3.5% of the total food market in Germany) (Aarset et al., 2004). One of the reasons for such gap is the unrealistic expectations that some consumers have about the better taste of organic products; a disconfirmation of this expectation could constitute a barrier to organic demand. The range of barriers to consumption reported by consumers is wide. However, some of them al almost reported by all consumers. In general terms, they could be divided into those related to intrinsic values and trust, on the one hand, and those related to external factors such as availability, convenience and price; on the other hand (Grunert et al., 2004). Although barriers vary depending among ranges of products, price strategies, and the point of sale (size, type and merchandising), there are some common/main barriers to consumption of organic products that are summarized in below (Grunert et al., 2004; Ayers, 2008):

- Type 1 (practical barriers):
    - Price differences
    - Availability in supermarkets, convenience
    - Range of organic products is limited
- Type 2 (emotional or cognitive):
    - Trust
    - Belief that organic fulfil certain credentials

Price and Point of Sale in Organic Products: Different Aspects but Greatly Interrelated

Price

The price difference between organic and conventional products is a recurring topic (Table 3 shows such differences in USA).

Ayers (2008) found that regular organic consumers opt to choose specific organic products where the price premium is not particularly large and where they believe the benefits to health will be most notable, are considered worth paying the extra for. Also, this report shows that the price premium of organic food for some regular consumers is to shop in places that are perceived to be the most competitively priced,

Table 3. Average prices of some organic and conventional products of animal origin in the USA. Source: extract of V. Falguera, Aliguer and M. Falguera (2012), based on USDA-ERS (2009) data

Product	Source	Unit	Price (US $)	
			Conventional	Organic
Milk	Retail	Half gallon	2.28	4.43
Eggs	Retail	Dozen	1.35	3.99
Poultry	First receiver	Pound	0.80	2.37

which tend to be large chain supermarkets. At this point, consistency of the organic agri-value chain takes place in consumers' mind, which will be discussed later.

In general terms, organically oriented consumers are less price-sensitive (Enneking, 2002; Mondelaers et al., 2009; Stolz, Stolze, Hamm, Janssen, & Ruto, 2010) who showed that consumers with strong preferences for organic food are not affected by higher prices, while non-users of organic food display a very price-sensitive reaction. As pointed out by Stolz et al. (2009), this probably holds true as long as the price levels do not exceed acceptable and common market prices such as those used in the purchase simulations. However, price elasticity depends on the product itself, on the type of consumer (regular, occasional, supermarket oriented, etc.), and on the supply chain, as well as on the comparison consumers carry out in the point of sale: i.e. either organic products are together with conventional ones or separated (Stolz, Stolze, Janssen, & Hamm, 2011). Only dedicated consumers do not perceive price as a barrier/concern.

For many consumers, high prices are seen as indicating profiteering in the industry, which reinforces an existing lack of trust for the authenticity of organic food, which has to do with the process of conventionalization of the organic supply chain. Rödiger and Hamm (2015) reviewed consumers' behaviour regarding the price of organic food, and found that deep knowledge on this topic is reduced, as very few studies exist on price learning and price knowledge of consumers, while there was a lack of studies regarding affective processes of consumer behaviour about price. Moreover, those studies on price elasticity and on willingness-to-pay are contradictory.

Point of Sale

Dedicated organic consumers tend to shop in specialist outlets where the premium for organic food is often above competitive market value. They differ from other consumers in their relationship to the price of organic food. Large chain supermarkets are perceived to be the most competitively priced, (Ayers, 2008).

Regarding meat, the store type also influences the purchasing behaviour, so that marketing strategies must focus on market share data according to store types (Table 4). Moreover, store type choice is not necessarily generally applicable for all groceries, but can depend on single commodity groups. The sequence of possible shopping trips can be from product type to store type and vice versa (Staus, 2011). Besides, the type of store influences loyalty, which is important in animal food products due to the mistrust from consumers towards these products. In the case of meat products, loyalty is strongest towards discounters, followed by large hypermarkets and supermarkets, specialised stores and small hypermarkets (Staus, 2011).

Moreover, the different store types are correlated to different attributes (Table 5).

Table 4. Grocery store type choices of the estimation sample for meat. Source: Staus (2011)

	Meat (%)
Discounter	41.55
Supermarket	13.90
Small hypermarket	13.56
Large hypermarket	16.32
Specialized store	14.67

Table 5. Relationship between meat attributes, sociodemographic variables and store type. Source: Staus (2011)

Attributes and Sociodemographic Variables	Supermarket	Small	Large	Specialized
Age	+		-	+
Gender		-		
Income	+			
Environment	-			
Freshness		+		+
Genetically Modified Food		+	+	+
Organic				+
Price	-	-		
Quality				+

At the point of sale, some meat attributes must be taken into account. In this sense, Troy and Kerry (2010) examined the main elements of consumer perception of meat with focus on the red meat sector, placing special emphasis on perception at point of sale and the intrinsic quality cues of colour, packaging and degree of visual fat. Consumers still have difficulty in accurately predicting experienced quality by perception at the point of purchase (Grunert et al., 2004), which poses a real challenge for the meat industry in order to understand consumers attitudes and then adapt to them. Moreover, consumers lack understanding of the science behind the meat products, and many times they show contradictory attitudes (such as wishing more naturally reared animals while preferring white fat and more tender meats). From the industry point of view, the know-how in modulating meat products intrinsic quality (tenderness, nutritional profile, etc.) is high, so that the challenge remains on the side of communication. Thus, the industry must train consumers and learn how to communicate them correctly the quality attributes present in the meat products it sells. All this, must be also be combined with consumer's behaviour towards organic products (and/or sustainability-labelled), which make the design of marketing strategies even more complex.

Consumers' Behaviour Towards Organic Animal Products

In order to provide with solutions for the industry and global society, it is first need it to understand consumers' perceptions towards meat. Perception has been defined as the act of apprehending by means of the senses and/or the mind. Hence, perception not only relates to basic senses such as visual, flavour

Table 6. Consumer cues for selecting fresh meat. Source: Modified from Troy & Kerry (2010)

At the Point of Sale	At the Point of Consumption	Background Cues
Meat colour	Tenderness	Safety: zoonotic pathogens, chemical contaminants, traceability, biotechnology
Packaged meat colour	Flavour	Nutrition: composition and health implications
Visible drip	Juiciness	Sustainability: greenhouse gas emissions, local economy
Visible fat	Succulence	Ethics: fairness, animal welfare, environment, biotechnology

and taste attributes, but also to formed learning or experiences. Some of our non-cognitive learning mechanisms such as conditioning and imitation are predominant in the early formation of food habits. Therefore, perception incorporates complex aspects of consumer behaviour such as learning, motivational and contextual factors (Troy & Kerry, 2010; Köster & Mojet, 2007). This concept along is dynamic and evolves according to consumers' context does it. This is why the concept of quality must be understood and constantly defined in order to be oriented to the market. Thus, meat quality has evolved from security and safety to ethics, sustainability and convenience. In the present work, the author focuses on the extrinsic attributes of the concept of quality.

Organic products positioning must be different depending on consumers' profile, as they have different attitudes, values and practices relating to food shopping. Three main groups of consumers identified with regard to organic food could be summarized as follows: 'non-consumers,' 'alternatively orientated,' 'supermarket orientated,' 'regulars,' 'skeptical,' 'occasional' and 'committed.'

McEachern and Schröeder (2002) found that price and product appearance were the primary meat selection criteria. These authors also found that there is a situational attribution (attitude-behaviour anomalies), which means that consumers think purchasing organic meat in special moments, such as guests coming to dinner. This has an impact on how to design the products (in terms of packaging, signalling, labels, etc.).

According to these researchers, cognitive dissonance results from a discrepancy between beliefs and behaviour. Respondents' dissonance towards animals and meat was justified using defences such as "... organic meat is too expensive, especially when you have a family to feed"; "it's far too confusing to know what all the labels mean"; or "no-one has time to study the labels on meat..."

Verhoef (2005), after analysing Dutch consumers of organic meat, came to the conclusion that purchase of organic meat is based on both 'rational' economic (quality, price, and distribution) and emotional motives (fear, empathy, and guilt). The emotional motives as well as the rest of extrinsic cues of meat are possibly more important for consumers in the case of organic meat.

Beef

Red meat is particularly a noteworthy case, as it combines concerns on safety, health and environment. Despite the amount of scientific literature, there is no unique recipe, as consumer perception of meat is both dynamic and difficult to define. This is partly due to the increased public knowledge on the relationship between nutrition and health (especially in developed countries) and the variety of meat products regarding consumers' perception of their healthiness.

The perception of a negative impact of agricultural production on the environment and health concerns are having a major impact on the food consumer purchasing decisions for beef. However, most consumers are not willing to pay a price premium for labelled beef (Angulo, Gil, & Tamburo, 2008). Part of the lack of willingness to pay higher prices for organic beef could be due to the fact that consumers do not clearly perceive the differences between organic and conventional meat (Krystallis, Arvanitoyannis, & Chryssohoidis, 2006; Krystallis & Chryssohoidis, 2005). In this sense, Nunes, Bennett and Júnior (2014) showed that there is a clear need to excel in organic meat products, quality, and environmental contribution. However, it is can be complex to define and evaluate the quality characteristics of a meat product, especially when the benefits of organic meat over conventional are not clear from the sensory, nutritional, and health aspects (Krystallis et al., 2006; Krystallis & Chryssohoidis, 2005), particularly when they are compared with conventional extensive systems, such as those present in the pasture (Escribano, 2016b).

However, the same does not occur in all countries. In 2003, Corsi and Novelli found that consumers' WTP was quite high, thus suggesting that organic beef meat might gain an appreciable market share. Authors in fact stated that production of organic meat could be a viable option to compensate the likely increase in production costs with a substantial premium for the new good.

Later, Mesías et al. (2008) evaluated the results obtained from surveying 535 meat consumers in SW Spain in order to determine their attitudes towards organic meat with Protected Geographical Indication (IGP) and conventional meat. Key messages: (i) consumers did not really distinguish between organic and IGP meats (even higher recognition of PGI meat in some cases), while it was found poor consumer education about organic meat; (ii)greater appreciation of women over men; (iii) there was a clear relationship between the evaluation of quality meats and the level of studies, which also influences the understanding the externalities of facts such the use of foreign substances on health, etc.; (iv) consumers of lesser age and the sons of smaller families, re those who most appreciate organic meat; (v) family size.

Later, García-Torres, López-Gajardo and Mesías (2016) evaluated consumer liking and preferences towards organic beef from two production systems: i) free-range and ii) intensive (fattened in feedlot with organic feedstuff) as compared with conventionally produced beef. A sample of 150 regular beef consumers who completed two tasks: Firstly, a sensory test where consumers tasted and rated the meats, and secondly the beef purchasing preferences were analysed, as well as willingness-to-pay. Results showed that consumers preferred organic-from-concentrate beef at sensory level while organic beef from animals fed on grass was preferred when process characteristics (i.e. farming system) or attributes perceived at the point of purchase (i.e. colour) were evaluated. It was also found that the price-premium for organic beef is over 40%, with organic-fed-on grass beef preferred slightly over that fed-on-concentrate.

Pork

For both the British and Danish respondents, there seem to be at least four different reasons for choosing or not choosing organic pork: Animal welfare, budgetary restraints, health, and enjoyment with different across countries (Grunert et al., 2004). Concerns for animal welfare seem to be more important to British consumers than to the Danish. Budgetary restraints seem to be important both in Great Britain and in Denmark. This is by far the most important motive for not eating organic pork. The means-end study shows two important things. Firstly, consumers make a whole range of positive inferences from the label 'organic,' and these refer not only to concern for the environment and health, but also to animal welfare and better taste.

Dairy

Products that rank highly on the organic list for regular consumers are dairy products such as milk and yoghurt. Organic dairy is a gateway product category for organic food (Chang, Hooker, & Sam, 2011). For such products, the premium price is viewed as marginal and they are generally considered worth paying extra for due to perceived rewards such as health benefits and safety from possible pesticides (Ayers, 2008).

Regarding personal ecological norms, it has been observed that consumers with strong personal norms use "organic production", the "EU-BIO-Label" and "ingredients" as additional criteria during their decision process. For people with strong ecological norms the price difference between organic and conventional milk, the lack of knowledge about organic milk, and convenience are less important constraints.

Klöckner and Ohms (2009) applied a structured approach to understand the importance of personal ecological norms in purchasing organic food, predicting the self-reported and observed purchase behaviour of organic milk of 63 customers of a German supermarket. The self-reported and the observed purchase of organic milk was predicted by personal ecological norms, social norms, and perceived behavioural control. Personal norms are activated by awareness of need, awareness of consequences, perceived behavioural control, and social norms. People with strong personal norms use "organic production", the "EU-BIO-Label" and "ingredients" as additional criteria during their decision process. For people with strong ecological norms the price difference between organic and conventional milk, the lack of knowledge about organic milk, and convenience were less important constraints. People with strong personal norms reacted more sensitively to proposed norm-centred interventions.

Later, Akaichi, Nayga and Gil (2012) assessed the determinants of consumers' willingness to pay (WTP) for organic milk in a multiunit shopping scenario, as well as the effect of positive and negative information about organic farming on WTP. Results suggested that consumers were willing to pay a premium for organic milk but that this WTP decreases with the number of units purchased. Besides, health issues, high price of organic foods, taste, and lack of information on organic foods were factors that influence WTP for organic milk.

More recently, in 2015, Amirnejad and Tonakbar studied the factors that determine the consumers' willingness to pay for organic milk in Tehran. Results showed that variables such as income, family's illness history, age, educational level, distance to the shopping centre, apprising respondents, organic milk quality, and the offered price had a significant effect on consumers' willingness to pay for organic milk. Overall, 80.3% of the respondents were willing to buy organic milk, being the estimated average of consumers' willingness to pay at 28,600 Rials per litre of organic milk.

Rabbit

Villanueva, López and De Dios (2015) studied consumer preferences and WTP for food safety, freshness, organic and price for rabbit meat, as well as preferences. The most favourite attributes, in order of importance, were the organic, safety, freshness, and the price of meat. The "organic" attribute was highly preferred by 64% of the sample, followed by safety. The reasons to prefer organic meat were health and social responsibility. The socio demographics variables schooling, household income from, knowledge about organic food, and the safety attribute were significant. This reveals the importance of income level and formal education in the consumer's decision of paying a premium for the organic attribute. The price premium that consumers would pay per kilogram of organic rabbit meat was 15% of the average price ($13.50 more per kilogram) charged to consumers.

Origin: Belonging, Trust, Loyalty and Health – Local vs Organic

Origin is an important attribute for many consumers due to several reasons which respond to the different meanings and implications that the term 'local' has for them (see figure 1).

Local food systems have approached as a potential solution to problems in the globalized food system, and the promotion of agriculture and urban sustainability (Kremer & DeLiberty, 2011). According to the study carried out by Tobin et al. (2012), local food products are desired for their perceived superior

Figure 1. (Adapted from Escribano, 2016a)

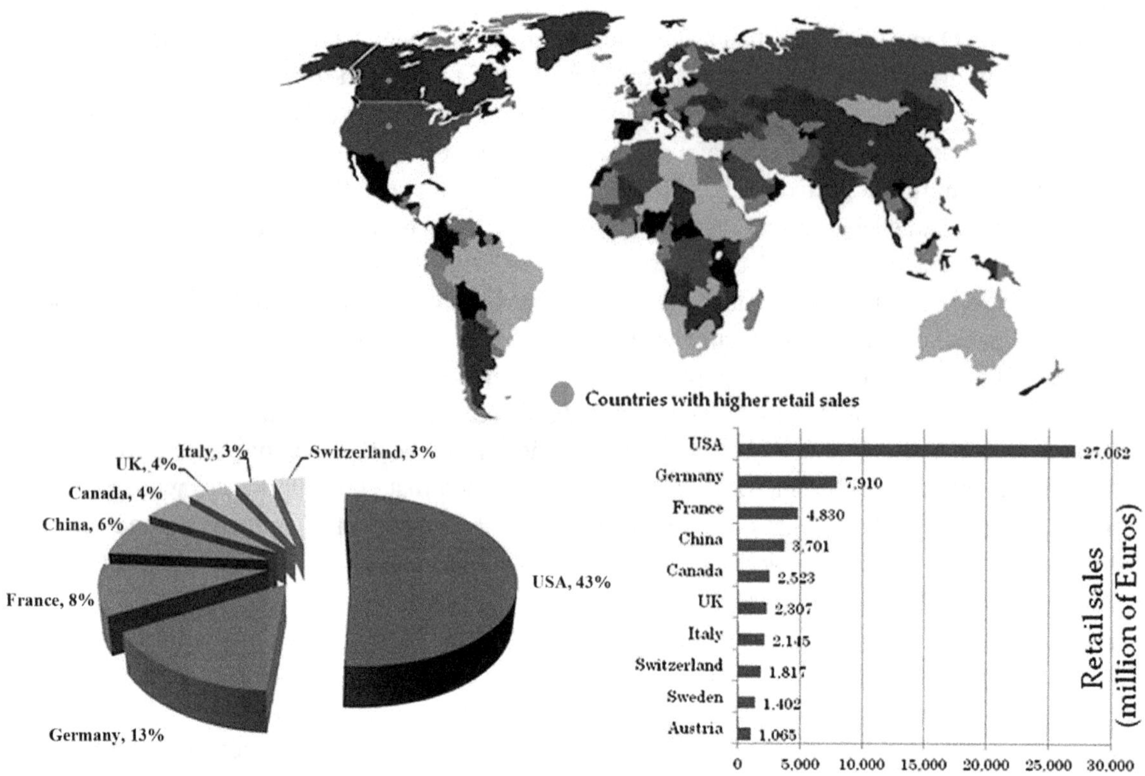

attributes such as quality (Pirog, 2004; Yiridoe, Bonti-Ankomah, & Martin, 2005; Carpio & Isengildina-Massa, 2009; Fotopoulus

& Krystallis, 2002a, 2002b; Scarpa & Del Giudice, 2004) and benefits for the environment, local economy, and the preservation of farmland, as well as enhanced freshness, taste, nutrition, and eating quality (Roininen, Arvola, & Lähteenmäki, 2006; Bond, Thilmany, & Bond, 2008; Carpio & Isengildina-Massa, 2009; Yue & Tong, 2009; Onozaka, Nurse, & McFadden, 2010). Food safety has also been listed as an important reason that consumers prefer locally and organically grown produce (Berlin, Lockeretz, & Bell, 2009; Bond et al., 2008; Onozaka et al., 2010; Yue & Tong, 2009). It appears that knowing the origin of the particular of beef product will probably override or soften other concerns such as health attributes (Philipp et al., 2015).

However, a large share of organic animal products is being produced with imported protein feedstuffs, and products labelled as 'local' are also often produced with imported feed. Then, at the point of purchase, animal products are not usually labelled with any information on the feed that was used to produce it. Therefore, it remains unclear what consumers think about the use of imported feed, in particular in the case of products labelled as 'local' (Wägeli, Janssen, & Hamm, 2015).

Moreover, the 'food miles' (Denver and Jeansen, 2014) and rural depopulation concerns (and its consequences: i.e. landscapes degradation) have led to an increased interest of local food, even higher than organic food for some consumers. Then, there is an open debate regarding the integrity and sustainability of organic versus locally produced foods, which has implication in consumers' behaviour. In this

Figure 2. Meanings and concepts elicited by the 'local' term in food
Source: own elaboration

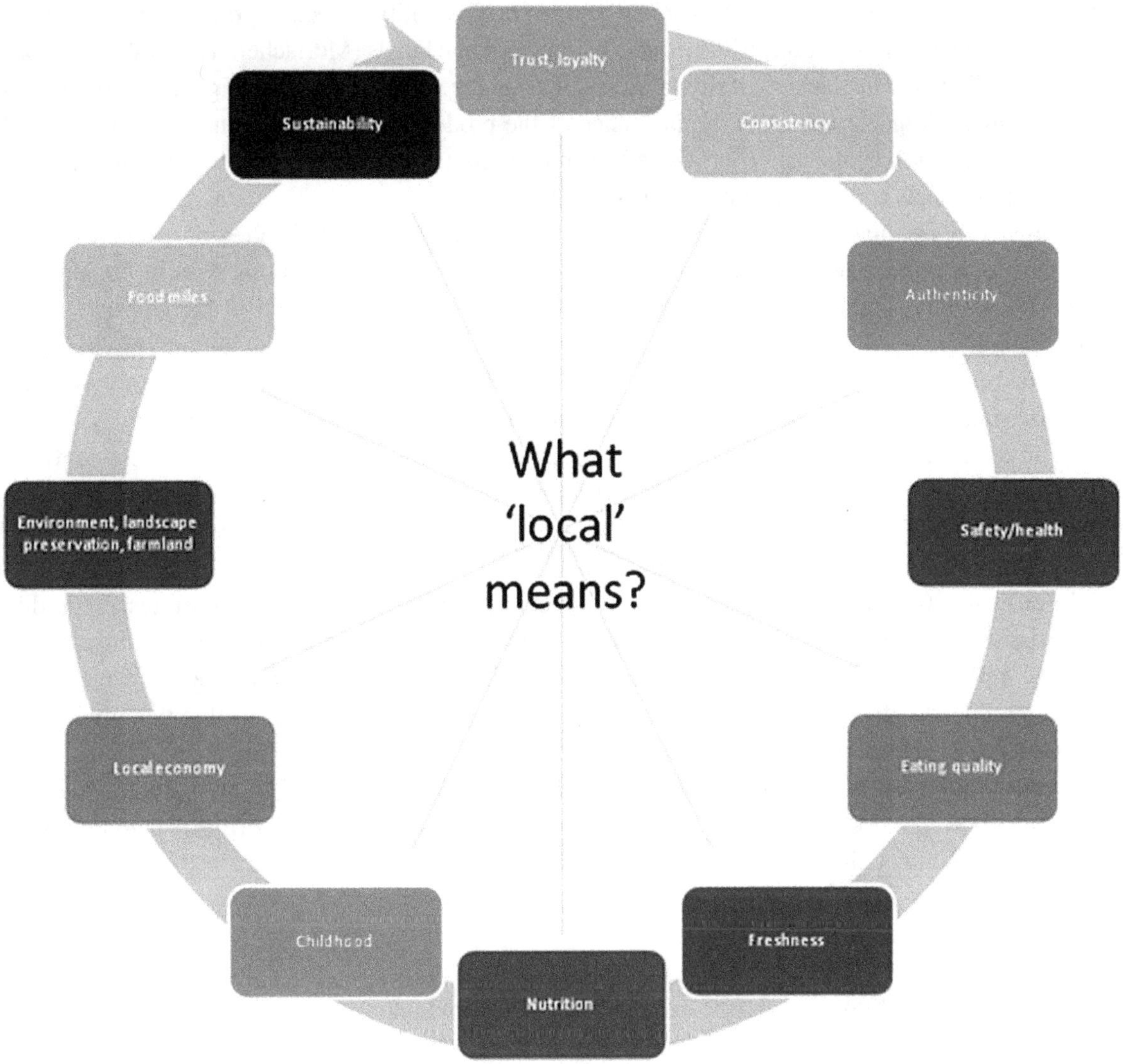

sense, imported organic produce are viewed as environmentally unsustainable because they have been air freighted into the UK and have incurred a high number of food miles. The importance consumers give to this quality cue is also linked to consumers' regional identity that is the value of 'locality' or the 'sense of belonging' (Bernués et al., 2003a, b). In response to this dissatisfaction, consumers will often employ treason and buy locally produced food that isn't organic (Ayers, 2008). Then, local food has been suggested as a model of sustainable consumption for a range of economic, social and environmental reasons (Seyfang, 2006; Stagl, 2002). Seyfang (2006) indicated that in 2003, 65% of organic produce eaten in the UK was imported. In light of consumer concern about 'food miles' for distribution, climate threat may also constitute a barrier to increasing demand of imported organic food as consumers prioritise local, non-organic food if they cannot source a local organic option.

In other researches, it was found that organic and local product attributes could serve as substitutes (Costanigro, McFadden, Kroll, & Nurse, 2011). Another reason for rural respondents' non-purchase of organic meats was that they were perceived as being of equal quality to locally produced meat, indicating a lack of understanding of the criteria underpinning organic labels (McEachern & Schröeder, 2002), which is also linked to the lack of clarity for consumers on the reason behind the higher quality of some organic products (organic per se vs the influence of the production system: extensive, pasture-based, etc.). Moreover, rural citizens are more linked to animal production, which also modifies their perception of meat products and their quality (Escribano, 2016b).

'Alternatively orientated' regular consumers believe that organic food supplied by a supermarket is inauthentic, constituting an emotional barrier to organic consumption within this domain. In fact, consumers prefer buying organic food from smaller, alternative locations, despite their higher price (Ayers, 2008). For consumers, this poses contradictions between the ideal 'organic' and 'natural' products, and the sustainability of their supply chain (some of them think about food miles and local economy, while others also state that the efficiency of the mainstream value chain can make it more sustainable). Related to this, products labelled or certified by foreign organic standards make consumers feel less confident as they do not trust nor know if all organic certifications are equal and trustworthy. This business model and supply chain within the organic sector (called ('conventionalization' of the organic production) have been analysed and discussed by several authors (i.e. Escribano, 2016b).

Wägeli et al. (2015) analysed whether the use of local feed represents an option for successful product differentiation in the organic animal products market, based on a sample of 597 organic consumers in Germany. Authors investigated consumers' preferences and willingness-to-pay for local organic animal products produced with local feed. The outcome of our investigation also shows that the provision of information on feed imports into Germany can be an important tool for promoting organic animal products produced with local feed. The results suggest the use of local feed could be an option for successful product differentiation in the organic animal products market, especially if effort is put into raising consumer awareness of current organic feed importation practices.

Lamb as Example

Font i Furnols et al. (2006) studied the consumers acceptance of lamb from their own country (Germany, Spain or UK; at two ageing times, 7 and 20 d) in comparison with lamb from Uruguay (light and heavy lambs aged 20 d), and regarding tenderness, flavour and overall acceptability. German and British consumers showed higher acceptability for heavier animals and aged 20 d. Spanish consumers, however, preferred lighter lambs. Production systems, cultural aspects and consumption habits also seemed to affect the acceptability of the lamb to the consumers. Later, Font i Furnols et al. (2011) studied the effect of three extrinsic cues (country of origin, price and feeding system) on consumer's purchasing decisions making process for lamb meat in three European countries: Spain, France and United Kingdom. Four countries were considered for evaluating the effect of the country of origin (local, Argentina, Switzerland and Uruguay), three feeding systems (grain-fed, grass-fed and grain + grass-fed) and different price levels. In this second study, authors found that the country of origin of the meat has a great influence in the purchasing intention, thus being local meat the most preferred and Uruguayan lamb the least preferred, which has implication for exports of lambs from Uruguay to the European market. However, there were no clear differences with regard to the feeding system. Price was the most important attribute in the purchase decisions (being low prices the most preferred) and men were more influenced by this attribute than women.

Bernués, Olaizola and Corcoran (2003b) found that in all European regions studied, the type of information most in demand with regard to lamb and beef were the origin or region of production of meat, along with the deadline or 'consume by' information.

Fair Trade

It is important to note that dedicated organic consumers are not representative of the general population but instead they can be described as a highly motivated group of citizen consumers who are conversant in discourses of sustainable consumption. Therefore, for the rest of consumers' profiles there is some competition/substitution between organic and fair-trade products. In this sense, Van Herpen, Van Nierop and Sloot (2012) studied the relationship between in-store marketing and observed sales for organic versus fair trade products, finding that the effect of these variables differs between organic versus fair trade products, as buying motives might differ. Thus, organic buyers tend to be more loyal, and price is a more informative signal of quality for organic products.

The same holds for the price difference with the leading brand, which is important for fair trade brands but not for organic brands. In contrast, an arrangement of the product category by brand is associated with higher market share for organic brands but not for fair trade brands. Additionally, placement at eye level and clustering of items benefits both types of sustainable brands, whereas they appear to be not very sensitive to price promotions. Finally, higher sales of sustainable products are found in areas where the customer base is older and has a higher education level.

Green Labelling

The addition of a "green" or environmentally friendly product feature is often assumed to elevate consumer involvement in the choice of the product, which if true, could be then useful to shape consumers' decisions. However, the complexity in purchasing decisions make this feature not to be always enough to shape consumers choices. Moreover, the consequences of such strategy vary depending on the nature of the product.

Beef

Even specific environmental sustainability attributes (such as water use) has been evaluated. Thus, White and Brady (2014) developed a model estimating consumer willingness to pay (WTP) for environmental meat attributes and used a multi-objective nutritional optimizer to explore the extent to which WTP can offset on-farm costs of reducing water use. As environmental attributes, WTP for 'organic,' 'grass-fed,' and 'natural' were used. A case study is conducted to identify the expected reduction in water use that can be funded from capturing WTP through labelling. Authors found that a 10% premium ideal WTP, resulting in water use reductions between 24.4 L and 41.4 L.

Dairy

Thøgersen, Jørgensen and Sandager (2012) investigated whether adding such a "green" product attribute actually made any difference to how consumers make choices. The study was based on observation and follow-up interviews of consumers at the milk counter in two supermarkets which stock both organic (a "green" attribute) and conventional milk. Authors concluded that, rather than changing the way consumers make decisions when buying this type of product, the availability of a "green" alternative seems to make "green" consumers develop a new, simple choice heuristic that allows them to do their shopping as effortless and time-efficient as consumers buying conventional products. Thus, the "green" attribute increase consumer involvement in the decision-making among consumers choosing organic than among consumers choosing conventional milk. However, the difference in stated involvement is not reflected in the amount of time and effort spent on choosing the product in the store.

Fish

Aquaculture products have been predicted to be the source of protein of the future, in face of the predicted coming demand for animal protein. Moreover, there is a global concern on oceans and fisheries sustainability, so that companies have started to produce aquaculture products under more sustainable standards of production. In this context, Zander, Bürgelt, Christoph-Schulz, Salamon and Weible (2015) conducted a study with fish consumers in different German cities. The results showed that consumers expect sustainable fisheries to avoid by-catches, overfishing and not to use dynamite. Moreover, participants were skeptical about food labelling and standard setting in general. Accordingly, many participants stated not to look for sustainability labels when purchasing fish products. In order to tackle with consumers' limited knowledge of fish and low interest in additional information, communication of sustainability in fisheries must be improved (easier to understand and clearly different from conventional fisheries).

Participants' knowledge on sustainability labels was again low. Participants assessed the credibility of the labels as low, were unsure about the meaning of the certification and argued about missing controls. The low perception of the labels and the importance of other issues like time constrain and taste result in a low relevance for consumer's purchase decision (Buergelt, Christoph-Schulz, Salamon, & Weible, 2013).

Animal Welfare

As discussed above, animal welfare is an important aspect shaping consumers' purchase decisions. In order to illustrate this aspect with a specific example, it is timely to mention the study published by Gerini, Alfnes and Schjøll (2016). These researchers, in an attempt to understand the market for sustainable foods, explored the preferences for various types of premium eggs across three consumer segments (900 Norwegian consumers) by means of choice experiment and behavioural segmentation based on the frequency of organic food purchase. As expected, the authors found that the segment purchasing the most organic food was willing to pay a significant premium for organic eggs over eggs displaying only enhanced animal welfare. However, most consumers, who only occasionally purchase organic products, were unwilling to pay more for organic eggs than for enhanced animal welfare eggs, suggesting diminishing marginal utility for additional attributes. A third consumer segment attempted to avoid organic eggs, even when their cost the same as other eggs.

Organic and Conventional-Plus Products

Due to the differences between the organic standards, the lack of precise (and credible, for some customers) claims in organic products, many consumers have stated their preference for organic-plus (not only organic but also with other sustainability attributes such as fair trade) and conventional-plus) (not organic but in line with specific concerns: animal welfare, antibiotic-free, etc.).

In this sense, betting on conventional-plus products can be also interesting, as they have particular attributes in line with consumers' trends ('no artificial additives or flavours,' 'from pasture-raised cows,' 'no preventive use of antibiotics,' 'no use of genetically modified organisms,' 'domestic production') and that, in fact, convey more clear and concrete attributes than the 'organic' pool of products and standards. Moreover, these specific claims are more attractive for consumers than generic umbrellas (such as 'organic'). In this sense, Stolz et al. (2009) found that organic consumer perception is selective and focused on individual criteria of organic production, and often these individual criteria refer to the final stage of the production process. Additionally, it must be noted that the relevance of attitudes as determinants for preferences varies between the products. Thus, Stolz et al. (2011) found that organic yoghurt was chosen if a consumer believed that organic yoghurt was free from artificial additives and flavours and thus being healthier than yoghurt with artificial additives and flavours. This corresponds to findings from previous research on health claims on food products showing that food products with health claims are more preferred by consumers and that consumers who rated the products with claims as relatively healthier had a higher likelihood of choosing these products (Aschemann-Witzel & Hamm, 2010). Interestingly, consumer attitudes towards the criterion 'from pasture-raised cows' was significant in relation to organic milk choice, however, not in relation to organic yoghurt choice, given that yoghurt is more processed than milk (Stolz et al., 2009).

As example of this, McEachern and Schröeder (2002) found that as organic meat was thought to be very expensive, when individuals considered moral choices, they were more interested in conventionally produced meats with added-value features (e.g., animal welfare).

In parallel, it is necessary to say that food products with health claims are more preferred and chosen by consumers (Aschemann-Witzel & Hamm, 2010). Moreover, trust and loyalty play a great role, so that these aspects must be well understood in order to increase consumers' engagement, and then propose marketing strategies to achieve this.

MARKETING STRATEGIES AND CONCLUDING REMARKS

In recent times, consumers are active agents in the food chain aware of costs associated with production, so that they not only consume nutritional content of food. This leads to marketing strategies of different type that must include also differential aspects such as sustainability and social belonging ("*societing* or *tribal marketing*"), where the link is more important than the thing.

In this sense, consumers are supportive of sustainably produced foods but not highly confident on them and on their ability to recognize and purchase them. Due to this, the present study may be useful for professionals implied in the supply chain of foods of animal origin as it critically reviews consumers' attitudes and behaviours. This provides an insight into the processes of motivating behaviour and can therefore be used to design intervention and marketing strategies. Such interventions and strategies must be focused in all steps playing a role in the process between consumers' perception and final purchase (see figure 3).

The Problem of Consumer Acceptance Towards Innovate Foods

There is ample room for the development of differentiated products, both in terms of improved eating quality, positive health effects, added convenience and desirable process characteristics. However, innovations are not always accepted by consumers. For example, Almli et al. (2011) found that consumers did not show the same willingness to pay for all innovations presented in traditional cheeses in France and Norway. The innovations presented varying according to six factors: pasteurisation, organic production, omega-3, packaging, price and appropriateness. Well-accepted innovations in traditional cheese are those that reinforce the traditional and authentic character of the product (traditional, Omega-3 and finally UHT, organic). The authors also found that consumers' willingness to buy traditional cheese is highly driven by price, appropriateness and pasteurization in both countries. However, on average consumers in the French sample preferred buying raw milk cheese, while consumers in the Norwegian sample preferred buying pasteurized cheese (the same for the milk is also found in these countries). In addition, the context of consumption had an important effect on the acceptance of innovations in traditional cheese.

It is needed to take into account that the changes in the adoption of patterns with regards to food is, in most of the cases, gradual, as is the process of changing habits (Ayers, 2008). Therefore, before introducing disruptive innovations responding to sustainability attributes in every aspect (i.e. packaging and labelling), sustained but gradual changes ('sustaining innovations') must be introduced (Christensen, 2011).

Figure 3. Steps and processes to address by marketing strategies of sustainable food products
Source: own elaboration

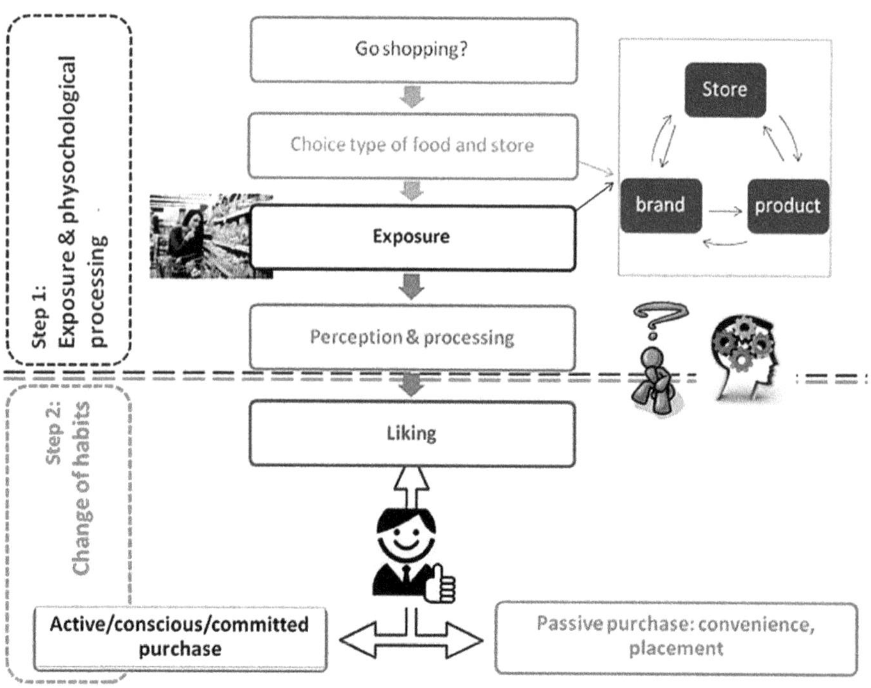

Comments of the Growth of Sustainable Foods of Animal Origin

It is necessary to note that the demand for 'sustainable' food of animal origin could stagnate in certain segments (not advocated consumers) once they face with the product and do not really find differential aspects. Moreover, price differential with conventional products, inelasticity of demand for products such as meat, and limited knowledge and awareness about these sustainable products by consumers play against market growth and, more importantly, stability. Fortunately, there are strategies that could solve this.

The Importance of Segmentation

Most studies of consumer preferences for sustainable foods only investigate average consumer preferences. However, it is important to allow for heterogeneous preferences (Gerini et al., 2016). Consumers vary greatly in their stated preferences and attitudes across countries and cultures. This makes implementing broad supply chain management strategies challenging as no single strategy will effectively hit the target for all consumers in a particular country, let alone across countries. Hence, it is important to consider the differences between consumers when a market study is to be carried out, because consumers from neighbouring countries, as well as consumers in a variety of regions within the same country, could have differences in preferences. Breeds, live weights and ageing time must also be considered, as they influence the intrinsic quality of the product. Due to this, Martínez-Cerezo, Sañudo, Medel and Olleta (2005) proposed that meat quality labels in this species should include them in their specifications.

In view of the diversity of profiles, the delivery of consumer-led designed meat products than can be appropriately labelled to target various consumer types, could constitute an opportunity for the industry to better access different segments of the market (Bernués et al., 2003b). Based on the differences found according to sociodemographic characteristics of the consumers, supermarkets and produce growers should consider the income, gender, and age profiles of their client base when making decisions regarding their produce safety policies and practices.

Health is the Core Attribute

Despite all the aspects commented above, it is clear that consumers also take into account safety in their purchasing decisions. This is particularly true for consumers concerned about safety and nutrition/health issues, who generally demanded more information and tended to rely on and use labels more. Thus, quality attributes relating to system of production, traceability and quality control of both animals and products are recognised as indicators for credence quality and therefore reliable and credible information cues on these aspects are increasingly in demand. Hence, marketing strategies will be more successful when health claim are used.

Food safety has also been listed as an important reason that consumers prefer locally and organically grown produce (Berlin, et al., 2009; Bond et al., 2008; Onozaka et al., 2010; Yue & Tong, 2009). These findings indicate that growers and supermarkets can position themselves advantageously by meeting consumer demands for produce that is local, organic and safe. Thus, the consumption of organic and local products is inspected to verify compliance with on-farm food safety standards to provide enhanced safety (Pirog & Larson, 2007; Bond et al., 2008; Berlin, et al., 2009; Yue & Tong, 2009; Onozaka et al., 2010).

Freshness, Origin and Shelf-Life: A Particularity (and Issue) of Many Animal Origin Products

With regard to fresh meat, perishability is a bottleneck (Escribano, 2016b). However, the vast majority of consumers in all studies indicate product freshness is the single most important trait when considering fresh meat, especially beef (Schroeder et al., 2007). In this sense, the use of natural antioxidants in animal nutrition could be beneficial in order to both increase shelf-life, reduce cost derived from loss of meat, and use it as a marketing strategy in labelling claiming higher 'antioxidant content' and 'natural Feeding'.

The origin/region of production and deadline (consume by) information for beef and lamb were the most important informational cues for consumers to appear in the label. This was for example found in all European regions considered in the study published by Bernués et al. (2003a, b). Information on 'deadline' is directly related to the freshness of meat, which constitutes a major cue when searching for quality in the shop and anticipating and the quality controls put in place by the industry (quality assurance systems).

In other cases, the origin has not been evaluated *per se* (a sensory analysis of the meat was carried out). In any case, the locality of this products plays a role in the preference (ethically, rationally, emotionally, or sensorially) so that this attribute must be taken into account for product development and design marketing strategies. The combination of territorial origin labelling and quality certification (i.e. organic), have a positive impact on the perception of consumers (Annunziata & Vecchio, 2016).

Main Attributes for Meat Products

The identification that the type of information that is most demanded by consumers is essential, as well as the analysis of the relationships between the importance of informational cues and other aspects concerning consumer attitudes towards meat consumption and meat quality, and socio-demographic characteristics. Also, identifying groups of consumers according to their labelling preferences is needed.

In this sense, Bernués et al. (2003b) identified European consumer profiles with regard to labelling of beef and lamb, classifying them into: 'quality/safety orientated,' 'traditional,' 'quality unconcerned/ convenience-driven,' and 'origin motivated' consumers.

Regarding production of quality in lamb meat either at the farm level or at the time of purchase, the aspects highlighted by Sepúlveda, Maza and Pardos (2011) are worthy to be taken into account for the design of marketing strategies:

- **At the Farm Level**:
  - Feeding
  - Breed
  - Production system: level of intensification
  - Environmental respect
  - Correct disease control
  - Animal welfare
  - Hygiene practices

- **At The Time of Purchase**:
    - Price
    - Quality label (Protected Geographical Indication)
    - Animal welfare
    - Feeding
    - Environmental respect
    - Direct appraisal (colour, freshness, fat, etc.)

For lamb meat, both consumers and industrials coincided in considering animal feeding to be most important in terms of lamb's quality in relation to animal production. In addition, for both consumers and producers, environmentally friendly production and production methods that respect animal welfare are amongst the aspects that are least valued. However, there is a segment of consumers for whom these aspects deserve a higher rating. Given that this segment is comprised of younger persons, attention should be paid changes this trend may undergo in the future (Sepúlveda et al., 2011).

Communication and Labelling: A Matter of Clarity, Education and Credibility – Producer vs. Consumer Perceptions

Companies have to communicate to be noticed on the market, to promote their services and products, and to give assurances that they are a credible partner in the relationship with stakeholders (Jianu, Ţurlea, & Guşatu, 2016). For companies, conveying credible sustainability principles has been showing to increase their financial performance. Even, companies promoting business in accordance with the principles of sustainability have become a hot spot in the global economy (Jianu et al., 2016). Research on communication (especially on how unlike what to say) must be increased.

Communicating consumer perceptions of produce safety to growers is especially important, for lack of interaction among different stakeholders in the food system often hamper efforts for improvement (Sobal, Khan, & Bisogni, 1998). Supermarkets will not increase consumer confidence and loyalty if their customers are unaware of their efforts to assure safety (Tobin et al., 2012; Tobin, Larkin, & Moane, 2011).

It is essential to understand the communications gap and misunderstanding between farmers and consumers. These are two distant points of the agro-food chain that, many times, they do not communicate the same way, do not speak the same language nor have the same level of knowledge. An important part of market asymmetry stems from this. Many attitude-behaviour anomalies were identified, mainly as a result of respondents' cognitive dissonance and lack of understanding regarding meat production criteria underpinning meat quality marks (McEachern & Schröder, 2002). Borkfelt, Kondrup, Röcklinsberg, Bjørkdahl and Gjerris (2015) illustrated the tensions between paradigms of animal welfare and concepts of naturalness as these are used in animal product marketing, discusses the ethical implications of this type of marketing communication, and stresses the need for transparency in the area of animal welfare

Also, simplification of logos is important, as well as the unification of messages (claims or benefits) because depending on the consumers interviewed, the attributes related to organic production are quite variable. Thus, Tobler et al. (2011) found that consumers strongly associate environmental friendliness with organic production, while in more recent studies they found that organic food consumption was not assessed as a very environmentally beneficial consumption pattern, and that consumers also found buying organic food and reducing meat consumption least environmentally relevant and reported having adopted these behaviours least frequently. According to the authors, a possible explanation for this discrepancy might be that there is a large variety of organic labels in Switzerland.

Clearer labelling about regulations and certification procedures, and the inclusion of information regarding the grower and its agricultural practices, may be interesting (Ayers, 2008). In line with the some of conclusions of Philipp et al.'s (2015) study, the authors highlight the necessity to use tools (mainly through labelling) that inform consumers about sustainability of animal production (such as carbon footprint), as well as, the provision of unbiased information by universities and extension can serve to alleviate the misunderstanding and lack of knowledge about animal production and their products. In this sense, more than CO2 meq there are claims with probably higher impact that can be used. Thus, according to Umberger et al. (2009), Attributes like "grassfinished," "certified organic," or "grazing managed to preserve streams" were much less important than "high nutritional content," "tested for mad cow disease," or "good value for the price," which was the highest-ranking attribute available for selection, while attributes such as "animals treated humanely" and "no antibiotics" ranked in the middle.

Organic Products

Organic products should try to be linked to other quality standards. The products with more added value (they would be more than organic) and the growing consumer preferences towards them have both been called 'organic-plus,' and have been described by some authors. Within this trend, health is key, as abovementioned. Thus, products caliming organic and residues or antibiotic-free will probably more attractive for consumers.

Moreover, environmental sustainability, freshness, and local economy are attributes of relevance. In other words, the consequences of the agrifood system (marketing channels, distribution) are becoming important for a growing number of consumers (Escribano, 2016b).

Finally, and in line with the language gap and misunderstanding mentioned in the communication section, it is timely to mention that there are differences in in understandings about concepts of organic food and perspectives about rewards or benefits relating. The majority of consumers have a limited knowledge and understanding of organic farming practices and even less about food processing conventions. The common view is that organic production methods involve the use of less harmful pest control and fertilization methods than conventional food production. Looking at price, organic food benefits are not believed to exist in relation to health and better taste or is not considered significant enough to be worth paying extra money for (Ayers, 2008).

Supply Chain: Externalities and Consistency

This is one of the main constraints of the sector, especially in organic products, and it is the point where there are more possibilities for improvement (Escribano, 2016b). A large share of organic animal products is being produced with imported protein feedstuffs, and products labelled as 'local' are also often produced with imported feed. Then, at the point of purchase, animal products are not usually labelled with any information on the feed that was used to produce it. Therefore, it remains unclear what consumers think about the use of imported feed, in particular in the case of products labelled as 'local'. The provision of information on feed imports can be an important tool for promoting organic animal products produced with local feed. The results suggest the use of local feed could be an option for successful product differentiation in the organic animal products market, especially if effort is put into raising consumer awareness of current organic feed importation practices (Wägeli et al., 2015).

Point of Sale and Merchandising

Moreover, knowledge on the effects of merchandising (point of sale) must be also improved. Tailor-made strategies for each points of sale must be implemented. Here, placement strategies have a great impact.

Meat is preferred at supermarkets or specialised stores. With increasing age, more local (compared to large hypermarkets) store types are favoured for fresh food. With increased age, specialised stores and supermarkets are preferred. Females avoid small supermarkets, while these store types are preferred for consumers with increasing income. Loyalty is an important attribute for meat products (especially for fresh and red meat). In this sense, discounters and local groceries would be the preferred ones.

Placement must be also considered as physical differentiation can lead to easier identification of sustainable products which, on the one hand could facilitate consumer identification of them, but on the other hand, many of them could not be interested in go shopping to those specific places. Results show that the number of facings has a positive relationship with the market share of fair trade brands, but not with the market share of organic brands. Consumers use very little time and effort on decision making in the buying situation when buying an everyday repeat-purchase product, such as milk, and it extends this finding to cases where the product has a "green" attribute Thøgersen et al. (2012). Merchandising, labelling and claims are very important aspects because consumers are not willing to spend time evaluating labels, and they do not understand them properly. This should therefore be taken into account in stores merchandising.

Modern-Urban Lifestyle: Convenience

Certain meat products (mainly beef and lamb) do not fit with modern lifestyle and family size. According to Schroeder et al. (2007), nowadays consumers have limited time for food preparation, which has resulted in large increases in consumption of food prepared away from home, as well as increases in meal packages that are highly processed and microwaveable. However, this is not a valid solution for all consumers, as consumers have less confidence in the safety of food that is prepared or highly processed by others (Schroeder et al., 2007).

There is an interesting point for retailers to bear in mind: starting to buy an everyday product with a "green" attribute is hardly the haphazard or random process that is often assumed for common everyday products (Hoyer, 1984), which could discourage conventional (non-regular or occasional organic) consumers, and even green consumers, as they are motivated (as everybody else) to minimize time and effort at the point of purchase (Hoyer, 1984; Payne, Bettman, & Johnson, 1988). This responds to time that it takes for consumers to adopt a new product (see Thøgersen, Haugaard, & Olesen, 2010).

Stakeholders' Collaboration: Marketing People and Farmers– Animal Production Professionals – Marketing People – They Cannot Forget Each Other in This Project

Both farmers and the industry should adopt more sustainable practices to produce products demanded by the consumer. However, farmers are not really willing to adopt such practices for several reasons: McEachern and Willock (2004) identified British livestock producers' motivations towards converting to organic systems of production as being environmental concern, market demand, and policy factors (e.g., government support). In the UK during 1997, there were only 800 organic farms and less than 0.3% of the total agricultural area used for organic production. In 2000, the number of organic farms had risen to 2865 and the area of certified production increased to just over 2.3%. Fifty-five percent of all organically managed land is in Scotland due to its predominant areas of rough grazing and land of low productive capacity (Soil Association, 2000). Consequently, the most common farm types that have converted to organic systems in Scotland are those that might be regarded as those already farming under extensive production techniques (e.g., beef and sheep). However, despite the ease of conversion for conventional Scottish beef and sheep producers, imports of organic meat into the UK rose from 5% in 1999 to 30% in 2000 (Soil Association, 2000).

Packaging

Consumers believed avoiding excessive packaging had the strongest impact on the environment (Tobler et al., 2011). Apart from sustainability issues, also preferences for packaging in animal products due to other attributes (such as convenience, aspect, or taste) must be taken into account (see studies published by different authors, such as Mesías et al., 2013; Eldesouky, Pulido, & Mesías, 2015; Eldesouky, Mesías, Elghannam, Gaspar, & Escribano, 2016).

Price Strategy

Price strategies must be adopted according to seller goals. In this sense, one must decide the segments to address (i.e. committed consumers are less price sensitive, while those who are less committed may think one of these options: that high prices are profiteering the industry, or that this higher price as a cue of quality). This must be also related to the type of store, as each profile is usually associated to store types (i.e. committed consumers frequently buy in specialised stores).

Therefore, prices strategies must be applied to both the products themselves and the store types. It must be reminded that small hypermarkets are rather at the upper and large hypermarkets at the lower level of prices. Specialised stores offer prices between hybrid and high. The associated price order beginning with the lowest priced store type is discounter, large hypermarket, supermarket, small hypermarket and specialised store. Price- and very price-conscious consumers prefer stores types with a lower price image. For meat, small hypermarkets and supermarkets are less preferred compared to discounters by price- or very price-conscious consumers (Staus, 2011).

Further Research

There are many publications focusing on diverse aspects of marketing research for organic products. Nevertheless, there are still many aspects within these research areas that have not (or almost not) yet been addressed, such as ecological packaging, price knowledge and price processing (Hemmerling, Hamm, & Spiller, 2015).

Hence, there is a need for greater innovation and knowledge utilisation to enhance consumer perception (both expected and experienced) by the meat industry. The authors believe there has been much research carried out at various institutes and universities which has not transferred or been adopted by the industry. This is why the need for increased partnering and collaboration (e.g. along the supply chain, developing relationships between producers, processors and retailers) is necessary (Troy & Kerry, 2010). In this sense, Tarrant (1998) pointed out a number of research priority areas for the meat industry in product safety, product quality and product development. In this sense, packaging formats and sizes are essential. Moreover, health pre-cooked foods (or fast foods) are still not developed so much as it is necessary. It seems that most of fast food are less healthy, which make no sense. In this sense, there is room for improvement. The meat industry needs to invest in and embrace an innovation agenda in order to be sustainable. It must utilise emerging scientific knowledge and take a more proactive role in setting out a research agenda (Troy & Kerry, 2010).

Extension services are important in order to communicate consumers' perceptions. More joint research (private company-academic research) must be carried out in order to orientate academic research to solve market needs and research outcomes are used to improve the competitiveness of the industry. These studies must address the financial field, as the industry will probably not change their structure and production cost if they do not know the return on such changes.

REFERENCES

Aarset, B., Beckmann, S., Bigne, E., Beveridge, M., Bjorndal, T., Bunting, J., & Young, J. et al. (2004). The European consumers understanding and perceptions of the organic food regime: The case of aquaculture. *British Food Journal, 106*(2), 93–105. doi:10.1108/00070700410516784

Akaichi, F., Nayga, R. M. Jr, & Gil, J. M. (2012). Assessing consumer's willingness to pay for different units of organic milk: Evidence from multiunit auctions. *Canadian Journal of Agricultural Economics, 60*(4), 469–494. doi:10.1111/j.1744-7976.2012.01254.x

Almli, V. L., Næsa, T., Enderli, G., Sulmont-Rossé, C., Issanchou, S., & Hersleth, M. (2011). Consumers acceptance of innovations in traditional cheese. A comparative study in France and Norway. *Appetite, 57*(1), 110–120. doi:10.1016/j.appet.2011.04.009 PMID:21550369

Amirnejad, H., & Tonakbar, P. (2015). The willingness to pay for organic milk by consumers in Tehran. *Journal of Agricultural Science and Technology, 17*, 1685–1694.

Angulo, A. M., Gil, J. M., & Tamburo, L. (2008). Food safety and consumers willingness to pay for labelled beef in Spain. *Journal of Food Products Marketing, 11*(3), 89–105. doi:10.1300/J038v11n03_06

Annunziata, A., & Vecchio, R. (2016). Organic farming and sustainability in food choices: An analysis of consumer preference in Southern Italy. *Agriculture and Agricultural Science Procedia*, *8*, 193–200. doi:10.1016/j.aaspro.2016.02.093

Aschemann-Witzel, J., & Hamm, U. (2010). Do consumers prefer foods with nutrition and health claims? Results of a purchase simulation. *Journal of Marketing Communications*, *16*(1-2), 47–58. doi:10.1080/13527260903342746

Ayers, N. (2008). *Consumption of Organic Foods from a Life History Perspective: An Exploratory Study among British Consumers*. Aberystwyth: University of Wales, School of Business and Management.

Bellows, A. C., Onyango, B., Diamond, A., & Hallman, W. K. (2008). Understanding Consumer Interest in Organics: Production Values vs. Purchasing Behavior. *Journal of Agricultural & Food Industrial Organization*, *6*(2), 1–28.

Berlin, L., Lockeretz, W., & Bell, R. (2009). Purchasing foods produced on organic, small and local farms: A mixed method analysis of New England consumers. *Renewable Agriculture and Food Systems*, *24*(04), 267–275. doi:10.1017/S1742170509990111

Bernués, A., Olaizola, A., & Corcoran, K. (2003a). Extrinsic attributes of red meat as indicators of quality in Europe: An application for market segmentation. *Food Quality and Preference*, *14*(4), 265–276. doi:10.1016/S0950-3293(02)00085-X

Bernués, A., Olaizola, A., & Corcoran, K. (2003b). Labelling information demanded by European consumers and relationships with purchasing motives, quality and safety of meat. *Meat Science*, *65*(3), 1095–1106. doi:10.1016/S0309-1740(02)00327-3 PMID:22063692

Bond, C. A., Thilmany, D. D., & Bond, J. K. (2008). What to choose? The value of label claims to fresh produce consumers. *Journal of Agricultural and Resource Economics*, *33*(3), 402–427.

Borkfelt, S., Kondrup, S., Röcklinsberg, H., Bjørkdahl, K., & Gjerris, M. (2015). Closer to nature? A critical discussion of the marketing of ethical animal products. *Journal of Agricultural & Environmental Ethics*, *28*(6), 1053–1073. doi:10.1007/s10806-015-9577-4

Buergelt, D., Christoph-Schulz, I. B., Salamon, P., & Weible, D. (2013). Impacts of sustainability labels on consumers' purchasing decisions for fish. In H. Röcklinsberg & P. Sandin (Eds.), *The ethics of consumption. The citizen, the market, and the law* (pp. 39–46). Wageningen: Wageningen Academic Publishers. doi:10.3920/978-90-8686-784-4_5

Carpio, C. E., & Isengildina-Massa, O. (2009). Consumers willingness to pay for locally grown products: The case of South Carolina. *Agribusiness*, *25*(3), 412–426. doi:10.1002/agr.20210

Chang, C. H., Hooker, N. H., & Sam, A. (2011). Organic and conventional milk purchase behaviors in Central Ohio. *Agribusiness*, *27*(3), 311–326. doi:10.1002/agr.20269

Christensen, C. M. (2011). *The innovators' dilemma: The revolutionary book that will change the way you do business*. New York, NY: Harper Collins Publisher Inc. doi:10.15358/9783800642816

Clark, B., Stewart, G. B., Panzone, L. A., Kyriazakis, I., & Frewer, L. J. (2016). A systematic review of public attitudes, perceptions and behaviours towards production diseases associated with farm animal welfare. *Journal of Agricultural & Environmental Ethics*, *29*(3), 455–478. doi:10.1007/s10806-016-9615-x

Corsi, A., & Novelli, S. (2003). Measuring quantity-constrained and maximum prices consumers are willing to pay for quality improvements: the case of organic beef meat. In *Proceedings of the 25th International Conference of Agricultural Economists (IAAC)*. Durban, South Africa: Document Transformation Technologies.

Costanigro, M., McFadden, D. T., Kroll, S., & Nurse, G. (2011). An in-store valuation of local and organic apples: The role of social desirability. *Agribusiness*, *27*(4), 465–477. doi:10.1002/agr.20281

Denver, S., & Jensen, J. D. (2014). Consumer preferences for organically and locally produced apples. *Food Quality and Preference*, *31*, 129–134. doi:10.1016/j.foodqual.2013.08.014

Dobson, A. (2003). *Citizenship and the environment*. Oxford, UK: Oxford University Press. doi:10.1093/0199258449.001.0001

Eldesouky, A., Mesías, F. J., Elghannam, A., Gaspar, P., & Escribano, M. (2016). Are packaging and presentation format key attributes for cheese consumers? *International Dairy Journal*, *61*, 245–249. doi:10.1016/j.idairyj.2016.06.011

Eldesouky, A., Pulido, A. F., & Mesías, F. J. (2015). The role of packaging and presentation format in consumers preferences for food: An application of projective techniques. *Journal of Sensory Studies*, *30*(5), 360–369. doi:10.1111/joss.12162

Enneking, U. (2002). Analysis of food preferences using discrete choice modelling – The case of organic sausages. *Agrarwirtschaft*, *52*(5), 254–267.

Escribano, A. J. (2016a). Beef cattle farms conversion to the organic system. Recommendations for success in the face of future changes in a global context. *Sustainability*, *8*(6), 572. doi:10.3390/su8060572

Escribano, A. J. (2016b). Organic livestock farming: Challenges, perspectives, and strategies to increase its contribution to the agrifood system's sustainability. In P. Konvalina (Ed.), *Organic Farming—A Promising Way of Food Production* (pp. 229–260). Rijcka, Croatia: InTech; doi:10.5772/61272

Escribano, A. J., Escribano, M., Gaspar, P., Mesías, F. J., & Pulido, F. (2015). Comparative sustainability assessment of extensive beef cattle farms in a high nature value agroforestry system. In V. R. Squires (Ed.), *Rangeland ecology, management and conservation benefits* (pp. 65–85). Lanzhou, China: Nova Publishers.

Falguera, V., Aliguer, N., & Falguera, M. (2012). An integrated approach to current trends in food consumption: Moving toward functional and organic products?. *Food Control*, *26*(2), 274–281. doi:10.1016/j.foodcont.2012.01.051

Font i Furnols, M., Realini, C., Montossi, F., Sañudo, C., Campo, M. M., Oliver, M. A., & Guerrero, L. et al. (2011). Consumers purchasing intention for lamb meat affected by country of origin, feeding system and meat price: A conjoint study in Spain, France and United Kingdom. *Food Quality and Preference, 22*(5), 443–451. doi:10.1016/j.foodqual.2011.02.007

Font i Furnols, M., San Julián, R., Guerrero, L., Sañudo, C., Campo, M. M., Olleta, J. L., & Montossi, F. et al. (2006). Acceptability of lamb meat from different producing systems and ageing time to German, Spanish and British consumers. *Meat Science, 72*(3), 545–554. doi:10.1016/j.meatsci.2005.09.002 PMID:22061739

Food and Agriculture Organization of the United Nations (FAO). (2016). FAO's work on climate change: Livestock and climate change. In *United Nations Climate Change Conference 2016*. Marrakech, Morocco: FAO.

Fotopoulos, C., & Krystallis, A. (2002b). Purchasing motives and profile of the Greek consumer: A country-wide survey. *British Food Journal, 104*(9), 730–765. doi:10.1108/00070700210443110

Fotopoulus, C., & Krystallis, A. (2002a). Organic product avoidance. Reasons for rejection and potential buyers' identification in a countrywide survey. *British Food Journal, 104*(3/4/5), 233-260. doi:10.1108/00070700210425697

García-Torres, S., López-Gajardo, A., & Mesías, F. J. (2016). Intensive vs. free-range organic beef. A preference study through consumer liking and conjoint analysis. *Meat Science, 114*, 114–120. doi:10.1016/j.meatsci.2015.12.019 PMID:26771143

Gerini, F., Alfnes, F., & Schjøll, A. (2016). Organic- and animal welfare-labelled eggs: Competing for the same consumers? *Journal of Agricultural Economics, 67*(2), 471–490. doi:10.1111/1477-9552.12154

González-Roa, M. C., & Calatrava, J. (2009). *El comportamiento del consumidor español respecto a los alimentos ecológicos: Algunos resultados del proyecto Ecomarket II*. Paper presented at the Congreso Nacional de Economía Agraria, Almería, Spain.

Grunert, K. G., Bredahl, L., & Brunsø, K. (2004). Consumer perception of meat quality and implications for product development in the meat sector—a review. *Meat Science, 66*(2), 259–272. doi:10.1016/S0309-1740(03)00130-X PMID:22064127

Hemmerling, S., Hamm, U., & Spiller, A. (2015). Consumption behaviour regarding organic food from a marketing perspective—a literature review. *Organic Agriculture, 5*(4), 277–313. doi:10.1007/s13165-015-0109-3

Hoyer, W. D. (1984). An examination of consumer decision making for a common repeat purchase product. *The Journal of Consumer Research, 11*(3), 822–829. doi:10.1086/209017

Hughner, R. S., McDonagh, P., Prothero, A., Shultz, C. J. II, & Stanton, J. (2007). Who are organic food consumers? A compilation and review of why people purchase organic food. *Journal of Consumer Behaviour, 6*(2-3), 94–110. doi:10.1002/cb.210

Jianu, I., Ţurlea, C., & Guşatu, I. (2016). The reporting and sustainable business marketing. *Sustainability*, *8*(1), 23. doi:10.3390/su8010023

Jungbluth, N., Tietje, O., & Scholz, R. W. (2000). Food Purchases: Impacts from the Consumers Point of View Investigated with a Modular LCA. *The International Journal of Life Cycle Assessment*, *5*(3), 134–142. doi:10.1007/BF02978609

Klöckner, C. A., & Ohms, S. (2009). The importance of personal norms for purchasing organic milk. *British Food Journal*, *111*(11), 1173–1187. doi:10.1108/00070700911001013

Köster, E. P., & Mojet, J. (2007). Boredom and the reasons why some new products fail. In H. J. H. MacFie (Ed.), Consumer-led food product development (pp. 262-280). Abington, UK: Woodhead Publishing. doi:10.1533/9781845693381.2.262

Kremer, P., & DeLiberty, T. L. (2011). Local food practices and growing potential: Mapping the case of Philadelphia. *Applied Geography (Sevenoaks, England)*, *31*(4), 1252–1261. doi:10.1016/j.apgeog.2011.01.007

Krystallis, A., Arvanitoyannis, I., & Chryssohoidis, G. M. (2006). Is there a real difference between conventional and organic meat? Investigating consumers attitudes towards both meat types as an indicator of organic meats market potential. *Journal of Food Products Marketing*, *12*(2), 47–78. doi:10.1300/J038v12n02_04

Krystallis, A., & Chryssohoidis, G. (2005). Consumers willingness to pay for organic food: Factors that affect it and variation per organic product type. *British Food Journal*, *107*(5), 320–343. doi:10.1108/00070700510596901

Martínez-Cerezo, S., Sañudo, C., Medel, I., & Olleta, J. L. (2005). Breed, slaughter weight and ageing time effects on sensory characteristics of lamb. *Meat Science*, *69*(3), 571–578. doi:10.1016/j.meatsci.2004.10.009 PMID:22062998

McEachern, M. G., & Schröeder, M. J. A. (2002). The role of livestock production ethics in consumer values towards meat. *Journal of Agricultural & Environmental Ethics*, *15*(2), 221–237. doi:10.1023/A:1015052816477

McEachern, M. G., & Willock, J. (2004). Producers and consumers of organic meat: A focus on attitudes and motivations. *British Food Journal*, *106*(7), 534–552. doi:10.1108/00070700410545737

Mesías, F. J., Escribano, M., Gaspar, P., & Pulido, F. (2008). Consumers' attitudes towards organic, PGI and conventional meats in Extremadura (Spain). *Archivos de Zootecnia*, *57*(218), 139–146.

Mesías, F. J., Martínez-Carrasco, F., Martínez, J. M., & Gaspar, P. (2011). Functional and organic eggs as an alternative to conventional production: A conjoint analysis of consumers preferences. *Journal of the Science of Food and Agriculture*, *91*(3), 532–538. doi:10.1002/jsfa.4217 PMID:21218489

Mesías, F. J., Pulido, F., Escribano, M., Gaspar, P., Pulido, A. F., Escribano, A., & Rodríguez Ledesma, A. (2013). Evaluation of new packaging formats for dry-cured meat products using conjoint analysis: An application to cry-cured Iberian ham. *Journal of Sensory Studies*, *28*(3), 238–247. doi:10.1111/joss.12040

Midmore, P., Naspetti, S., Sherwood, A.-M., Vairo, D., Wier, M., & Zanoli, R. (2005). Consumer attitudes to quality and safety of organic and low input foods: a review. Aberystwyth: University of Wales. Retrieved from https://www.researchgate.net/publication/265191937_CONSUMER_ATTITUDES_TO_QUALITY_AND_SAFETY_OF_ORGANIC_AND_LOW_INPUT_FOODS_A_REVIEW

Mondelaers, K., Verbeke, W., & Van Huylenbroeck, G. (2009b). Importance of health and environment as quality traits in the buying decision of organic products. *British Food Journal*, *111*(10), 1121–1140. doi:10.1108/00070700910992952

Nunes, B., Bennett, D., & Júnior, S. M. (2014). Sustainable agricultural production: An investigation in Brazilian semi-arid livestock farms. *Journal of Cleaner Production*, *64*, 414–425. doi:10.1016/j.jclepro.2013.07.023

O'Donovan, P., & McCarthy, M. (2002). Irish consumer preference for organic meat. *British Food Journal*, *104*(3/4/5), 353-370. doi:10.1108/00070700210425778

Oates, C., Alevizou, P., & McDonald, S. (2016). Challenges for Marketers in Sustainable Production and Consumption. *Sustainability*, *8*(1), 75.

Onozaka, Y., Nurse, G., & McFadden, D. T. (2010). Local food consumers: how motivations and perceptions translate to buying behavior. *Choices: The Magazine of Food, Farm and Resource Issues*, *25*(1).

Payne, J. W., Bettman, J. R., & Johnson, E. J. (1988). Adaptive strategy selection in decision making. *Journal of Experimental Psychology. Learning, Memory, and Cognition*, *14*(3), 534–552. doi:10.1037/0278-7393.14.3.534

Philipp, D., Popp, M. P., Rumley, E. R., Savin, M. C., & Coffey, K. P. (2015). Regulatory, production, and consumer based challenges of forage-based cattle production systems in the southeastern United States. *Animal frontiers*, *5*(4), 24–31. doi:10.2527/af.2015-0043

Pirog, R. (2004). Eco-label value assessment phase II: consumer perceptions of local foods. *Leopold Center Pubs and Papers, 140*. Retrieved from www.leopold.iastate.edu/pubs/staff/ecolabels2/ecolabels2.htm

Pirog, R., & Larson, A. (2007). Consumer perceptions of the safety, health and environmental impact of various scales and geographic origin of food supply chains. *Leopold Center Pubs and Papers, 169*. Retrieved from http://lib.dr.iastate.edu/leopold_pubspapers/169

Research Institute of Organic Agriculture (FIBL) & International Federation of Organic Agriculture Movements (IFOAM). (2016). *The world of organic agriculture. Statistics & emerging trends*. Rheinbreitbach, Germany: Medienhaus Plump. Retrieved June 16, 2016, from: https://shop.fibl.org/fileadmin/documents/shop/1698-organic-world-2016

Rödiger, M., & Hamm, U. (2015). How are organic food prices affecting consumer behaviour? A review. *Food Quality and Preference*, *43*, 10–20. doi:10.1016/j.foodqual.2015.02.002

Roininen, K., Arvola, A., & Lähteenmäki, L. (2006). Exploring consumers perceptions of local food with two different qualitative techniques: Laddering and word association. *Food Quality and Preference, 17*(1-2), 20–30. doi:10.1016/j.foodqual.2005.04.012

Scarpa, R., & Del Giudice, T. D. (2004). Market segmentation via mixed logit: Extra-virgin olive oil in urban Italy. *Journal of Agricultural & Food Industrial Organization, 2*(1), 141–160. doi:10.2202/1542-0485.1080

Schroeder, T., Tonsor, G., Mintert, J., & Pennings, J. M. E. (2007). *Consumer risk perceptions and attitudes about beef food safety: implications for improving supply chain management.* Kansas State University.

Sepúlveda, W. S., Maza, M. T., & Pardos, L. (2011). Aspects of quality related to the consumption and production of lamb meat. Consumers versus producers. *Meat Science, 87*(4), 366–372. doi:10.1016/j.meatsci.2010.11.013 PMID:21167649

Seyfang, G. (2006). Ecological Citizenship and Sustainable Consumption: Examining local food networks. *Journal of Rural Studies, 22*(4), 383–395. doi:10.1016/j.jrurstud.2006.01.003

Sobal, J., Khan, L. K., & Bisogni, C. (1998). A conceptual model of the food and nutrition system. *Social Science & Medicine, 47*(7), 853–863. doi:10.1016/S0277-9536(98)00104-X PMID:9722106

Soil Association. (2000). *The organic food and farming report.* Bristol: Soil Association.

Stagl, S. (2002). Local organic food markets: Potentials and limitations for contributing to sustainable development. *Empirica, 29*(2), 145–162. doi:10.1023/A:1015656400998

Staus, A. (2011). Which household attitudes determine the store type choice for meat? *Journal of Retailing and Consumer Services, 18*(3), 224–234. doi:10.1016/j.jretconser.2010.11.003

Stolz, H., Bodini, A., Stolze, M., Hamm, U., & Richter, T. (2009). Lebensmittelqualität aus der Verbraucherperspektive - eine Synthese qualitativer Studien zur Wahrnehmung und Beurteilung verschiedener Qualitätskriterien bei Öko-Produkten. *Berichte über Landwirtschaft, 87*(1), 153–182.

Stolz, H., Stolze, M., Hamm, U., Janssen, M., & Ruto, E. (2010). Consumer attitudes towards organic versus conventional food with specific quality attributes. *NJAS – Wageningen. Journal of Life Science, 58*(3/4), 67–72. doi:10.1016/j.njas.2010.10.002

Stolz, H., Stolze, M., Janssen, M., & Hamm, U. (2011). Preferences and determinants for organic, conventional and conventional-plus products – The case of occasional organic consumers. *Food Quality and Preference, 22*(8), 772–779. doi:10.1016/j.foodqual.2011.06.011

Tarrant, P. V. (1998). Some recent advances and future priorities in research for the meat industry. *Meat Science, 49*, S1–S16. doi:10.1016/S0309-1740(98)90035-3 PMID:22060702

Thøgersen, J., Haugaard, P., & Olsen, A. (2010). Consumer responses to ecolabels. *European Journal of Marketing, 44*(11/12), 1787–1810. doi:10.1108/03090561011079882

Thøgersen, J., Jørgensen, A. K., & Sandager, S. (2012). Consumer decision making regarding a green everyday product. *Psychology and Marketing, 29*(4), 187–197. doi:10.1002/mar.20514

Tobin, D., Thomson, J., & LaBorde, L. (2012). Consumer perceptions of produce safety: A study of Pennsylvania. *Food Control*, *26*(2), 305–312. doi:10.1016/j.foodcont.2012.01.031

Tobin, R., Larkin, T., & Moane, S. (2011). The Irish organic food market: Shortfalls, opportunities and the need for research. *Journal of the Science of Food and Agriculture*, *91*(12), 2126–2131. doi:10.1002/jsfa.4503 PMID:21751220

Tobler, C., Visschers, V. H. M., & Siegrist, M. (2011). Eating green. Consumers willingness to adopt ecological food consumption behaviors. *Appetite*, *57*(3), 674–682. doi:10.1016/j.appet.2011.08.010 PMID:21896294

Troy, D. J., & Kerry, J. P. (2010). Consumer perception and the role of science in the meat industry. *Meat Science*, *86*(1), 214–226. doi:10.1016/j.meatsci.2010.05.009 PMID:20579814

Umberger, W. J., Boxall, P. C., & Lacy, R. C. (2009). Role of credence and health information in determining US consumers willingness-to-pay for grass-finished beef. *The Australian Journal of Agricultural and Resource Economics*, *53*(4), 603–623. doi:10.1111/j.1467-8489.2009.00466.x

Umberger, W. J., Feuz, D. M., Calkins, C. R., & Killinger, K. (2002). U.S. consumer preference and willingness-to-pay for domestic corn-fed beef versus international grass-fed beef measured through an experimental auction. *Agribusiness*, *18*(4), 491–504. doi:10.1002/agr.10034

United States Department of Agriculture. Economic Research Service (USDA-ERS). (2009). *Organic prices. Data Sets.* Retrieved from https://www.ers.usda.gov/data-products/organic-prices/

Van Herpen, E., Van Nierop, E., & Sloot, L. (2012). The relationship between in-store marketing and observed sales for organic versus fair trade products. *Marketing Letters*, *23*(1), 293–308. doi:10.1007/s11002-011-9154-1

Verhoef, P. C. (2005). Explaining purchases of organic meat by Dutch consumers. *European Review of Agriculture Economics*, *32*(2), 245–267. doi:10.1093/eurrag/jbi008

Villanueva, J. L. J., López, S. V., & De Dios Guerrero Rodríguez, J. (2015). Behavior of consumers and willingness to pay for quality attributes of organic meat rabbit. *Revista Mexicana de Ciencias Pecuarias*, *6*(2), 221–232.

Wägeli, S., Janssen, M., & Hamm, U. (2015). Organic consumers preferences and willingness-to-pay for locally produced animal products. *International Journal of Consumer Studies*, *40*(3), 357–367. doi:10.1111/ijcs.12262

White, R. R., & Brady, M. (2014). Can consumers willingness to pay incentivize adoption of environmental impact reducing technologies in meat animal production? *Food Policy*, *49*, 41–49. doi:10.1016/j.foodpol.2014.06.007

Xue, J., Zartarian, V., Wang, S. W., Liu, S. V., & Georgopoulos, P. (2010). Probabilistic modeling of dietary arsenic exposure and dose and evaluation with 2003–2004 NHANES data. *Environmental Health Perspectives*, *118*(3), 345–350. doi:10.1289/ehp.0901205 PMID:20194069

Yiridoe, E. K., Bonti-Ankomah, S., & Martin, R. C. (2005). Comparison of consumer perceptions and preferences toward organic versus conventionally produced foods: A review and update of the literature. *Renewable Agriculture and Food Systems*, *20*(4), 193–205. doi:10.1079/RAF2005113

Yue, C., & Tong, C. (2009). Organic or local? Investigating consumer preference for fresh produce using a choice experiment with real economic incentives. *Horticultural Science*, *44*(2), 366–371.

Zander, K., Bürgelt, D., Christoph-Schulz, I., Salamon, P., & Weible, D. (2015). Consumers' response to sustainability labeling in wild caught fish. In *EAFE 2015 XXII Conference of the European Association of Fisheries Economists*. Salerno, Italy: EAFE.

KEY TERMS AND DEFINITIONS

Brand Green Washing: Market/advertising strategy looking for projecting a better image of the company without really looking for (and achieving) a higher environmental sustainability performance.

Food Safety: This term is related to the that prevention of foodborne illness. This includes a number of routines that should be followed to avoid potentially severe health hazards. This includes the origins of food including the practices relating to food labeling, food hygiene, food additives and pesticide residues, etc.

Food Security: This concept is related, in summary, to the supply of food, and individuals' access to it. In other words, food availability (of enough quality and safety) to meet all humans' dietary needs for a healthy life.

Green Marketing: Green marketing consists of marketing products and services with a focus on CSR, trying to reduce the environmental impact of the whole supply chain (before and after) of the product/service. It must be differentiated from *green washing* or *brand green washing*.

Organic Food: Organic food is a regulated system of food production looking for a higher sustainability and based on four principles: a) Principle of Health: Healthy soil, plants, animals, humans = a healthy Planet; b) Principle of Ecology: Emulating and sustaining natural systems; c) Principle of Care: Care for the generations to come; d) Principle of Fairness: Equity, respect and justice for all living things.

Sustainable Food Production: Sustainable agricultural production is that which is economically viable (profitable), socially just (fair and equitable distribution of the wealth generated), and environmentally friendly (compatible with the maintenance of natural ecosystems). Moreover, it must be low-input and regenerative, and has to make good use of a farm's internal resources through the incorporation of natural processes, knowledge, and improved production practices.

Section 4
Sustainability Paradox

Chapter 11
Sustainable Development Values:
What Do We Know From Developing Country Perspective?

Farzana Quoquab
Universiti Teknologi Malaysia, Malaysia

Fong Teng
Universiti Teknologi Malaysia, Malaysia

Jihad Mohammad
Universiti Teknologi Malaysia, Malaysia

Ramayah Thurasamy
Universiti Sains Malaysia, Malaysia

ABSTRACT

There is a great difference between developed and developing nations' perception about sustainability development values. As such, it is expected that the current sustainable development value facets might not represent the developing country needs as well. Therefore, there is a necessity to define sustainable development value and its dimension based on developing country perspective. The present study is such an attempt to fill this gap in the literature. 16 in-depth interviews were carried out to gain in-depth understanding about the phenomenon. Transcriptions were made and thematic analysis was utilized to analyse the qualitative data. It is crucial in order to achieve the nations' vision and its future sustainable development goals according to the nations need and demand.

INTRODUCTION

Sustainable development value is a set of fundamental values that drive individual's attitude and behaviour in a way that enables the sustainability for the present and future generation. The notion of sustainable development value (SDV) originated after World War II. It was based on a study from the U.S. National

DOI: 10.4018/978-1-5225-2912-5.ch011

Academy of Sciences to collect aspirations and desire of people around the world. At that point, only human value was identified and not sustainable development value. The identified values are peace, freedom, development, and environment. Peace was identified since the whole world was threatened by the nuclear arms race. The war had been sustained during the cold war and finally ceased and thus peace was difficult to achieve especially in Middle East and Africa. Desire for freedom also continued after World War II in order to end imperialism and totalitarian oppression and to extend the rights of women, indigenous peoples, and minorities (Leiserowitz et al., 2006). Indeed, economic development was the focus after the postcolonial world to ensure that basic necessities are provided to the poorest two thirds of the world. Following this, a global value for the nature and environment finally emerged after a quarter of century (Leiserowitz et al., 2006).

On 8 September 2000, to mark the new millennium, the General Assembly of the United Nations adopted a set of fundamental values such as freedom, equality, solidarity, tolerance, respect for nature, and shared responsibility. These fundamental values are known as 'sustainable development value' (SDV). These values are essential to international relations in the 21st century since they are likely to guide policy decisions (by international bodies and national governments), organizational actions, as well as customer and user behavior, which subsequently impact the quality of life throughout the world and the preservation of the social and natural environment (Shepard et al., 2009). These sustainable development values underlie 60 millennium development goals regarding peace, development and environment, human rights, vulnerability, hunger, and poor.

Need for Sustainable Development Value

Sustainable development values support sustainable development by translating these values into sustainable development goals according to country needs. As mentioned above, on 2000 the General Assembly of the United Nations adopted a set of fundamental values which are known as sustainable development values such as: freedom, equality, solidarity, tolerance, respect for nature, and shared responsibility.

Although these values have been discussed extensively by researcher, nevertheless there is a lack of studies that address these values from developing countries perspective. Therefore, not all citizens of the developing countries are fully aware of the notion of sustainable development value. Furthermore, the notion of sustainable development values greatly varies from country to country, culture to culture. Indeed, there are differences in perceiving these values from developed country and developing country perspective as well.

As such, there is a need to provide a holistic definition on SDV and its dimension based on developing country perspective. This is because the current conceptualization provided by United Nation is defined based on developed country perspective which may not fully represent the developing countries' needs and demand. Moreover, since economic aspect, technological aspect and socio-cultural aspects differ from developed countries to developing countries, the value, belief, norms also greatly vary among these countries. Therefore, there is a necessity to define sustainable development value and its dimension based on developing country perspective. Accordingly, there are two questions need to be answered by this study:

- How to define SDV from the developing country perspective?
- What are the relevant dimensions of sustainable development value that suit developing country perspective?

Methodology

Choosing the right research paradigm is important as it shows how a research result could be affected and guided by a certain research paradigm. Present study requires an in-depth understanding about the definition of sustainable development value and its relevant facets tailored to developing country perspective. As such, qualitative approach found most suitable to answer the research questions. The sample of questions that were asked to the participants is as follows:

- In your opinion, how should sustainable development value be defined from developing country perspective?
- What are the relevant dimensions of sustainable development value that suit developing country's need and demand and why?
- Do you suggest for inclusion of any additional aspect in the existing set of value dimensions? Please explain your view more detail.
- Is there any dimension that you think does not fit in the developing country perspective? If so, why? Please explain.

All together 16 interviews were conducted. Each interview lasted for 1 to 2 hours. Interviewees' age ranged between 18 years to 41 years. This age range was highly preferred as they were financially independent. Hence, it is expected that their feedback was not constrained and influenced which provide more insight on how to define SDV and its dimension according to developing country perspective.

The participants were from different industry background; some of them were entrepreneur, educator, and lawyer whereas, some others were marketers and accountant. It is believed that this diversity would allow more input to consider the issue from different perspectives. Contacts have been made through email correspondence and personal telephone calls. All participants had sufficient experience in handling customer social responsibility and other social causes.

Among 16 interviewees, 3 of them were male and 13 were female. Working professionals were invited due to their expertise on the topic of sustainable development value that could be categorized under opinion leaders. In addition, they were also interested in sustainability of future generation and SDV.

Qualitative Data Analysis and Its Findings

All interviews were transcribed in order to proceed to further analysis. Thematic analysis has been utilized by reading all transcriptions individually. The qualitative data analysis results are discussed in brief below.

Defining Sustainable Development Value Based on Developing Country Perspective

Based on the analysis of the interview transcriptions, it is realized that, all 16 interviewees believed that SDV should be defined differently for developing country aspect than the definition given by UN. Some of them have commented that the SDV should define according to developing country perspective in order to better reflect on the developing nations' needs and demand. The definition of these values will translate into key objective of sustainable development goals desired by developing countries. The main concern of the participants was that the six facets of SDV which are proposed by developed nation do not reflect the developing nations' nature and requirement.

Some other respondents have suggested to include 'integrity' and 'care for future generation' since these two are related to a nations' long term sustainability. Following participants' feedback and suggestion (Table 1), the SDV is re-defined as "…a set of values that drives individuals' attitude and behavior towards the sustainable development in environmental, economic and social aspects which are crucial for present and future generation. These values include freedom, equality, solidarity, tolerance, respect for nature, shared responsibility, concern for future generation and integrity."

Sustainable Development Value Dimensions

All participants commented that some of the SDV dimensions should define according to developing country perspective as it requires to reflect the developing nations' needs and demand. The definitions provided by UN and the definition and facets suggested by the participants are showed in the Table 2.

Although most of the interviewees expressed their agreement on the existing sustainable development value dimensions but they also felt these values are unrealistic and it will only reflect the developed country perspective. They have suggested to incorporate Integrity and Concern for future generation since these two values deemed suitable for the developing country perspective. The notion of these two additional dimensions is as follows:

- **Integrity:** This value refers to individual's ability to adhere to moral and ethical principles.
- **Concern for Future Generation:** This value highlights one's sense of accountability to consider the right of the future generation. It also emphasizes on the consumption pattern of individuals. The current care-free pattern of production and consumption must be changed for the sake of future generation.

Among 16 participants, 9 of them mentioned that when individuals suffer from hunger and are afraid of security (be it job or shelter), they tend to overlook the other values such as tolerance, solidarity or respect for nature. Therefore, they suggested that, 'freedom' and 'equality' are two most important values. Based on the in-depth interviews, it is realized that the sustainable development values should be clustered into three different levels, as it is showed in the Figure 1.

Freedom and equality are considered as the core, whereas, solidarity, tolerance and shared responsibility are considered as the secondary values. Conversely, respect for nature, integrity and concern for the future generation are suggested to be considered as the tertiary values:

- **Core Values**: 'Freedom' and 'equality'
- **Secondary Values**: 'Solidarity', 'tolerance' and 'shared responsibility'
- **Tertiary Values**: 'Respect for nature', 'integrity' and 'concern for the future generation'

Table 1. Experts' feedback about SDV definition

Expert 1	A set of fundamental values that drive individuals' attitude and behavior in such a way that enables the sustainability of the world for the current and future generation.
Expert 2	Sustainable Development values refers to a set of values that drives individuals' attitude and behavior towards the sustainable development for present and future generation. The values include freedom, equality, solidarity, tolerance, and respect for nature, shared responsibility and integrity
Expert 3	Sustainable development value consists of six fundamental values which are freedom, equality, solidarity, tolerance, and respect for nature, shared responsibility and integrity. These values drive people's attitude and behavior towards the sustainable development of the world.

Table 2. Modified SDV Dimensions and their Definitions

Sustainable Development Value Dimensionww	Definition provided by United Nation	Definition based on developing country perspective
Freedom	Men and women have the right to live their lives and raise their children in dignity, free from hunger and from the fear of violence, oppression or injustice. Democratic and participatory governance based on the will of the people best assures these rights.	This value emphasizes on all human being regardless of their age, gender, race, ethnicity have the right to live their lives and raise their children in dignity, free from hunger and from the fear of violence, oppression or injustice.
Equality	No individual and no nation must be denied the opportunity to benefit from development. The equal rights and opportunities of women and men must be assured.	This value refers to all individual and nation must have the equal opportunity to benefit from the output of development. The equal rights and opportunities of women and men must be assured.
Solidarity	Global challenges must be managed in a way that distributes the costs and burdens fairly in accordance with basic principles of equity and social justice. Those who suffer or who benefit least deserve help from those who benefit most.	This value refers to the feeling of unity among individuals in order to gain sustainable development. In this regard, global challenges must be managed in such a way that the advantageous parties should help the disadvantageous parties.
Tolerance	Human beings must respect one or another, in all their diversity of belief, culture and language. Differences within and between societies should be neither feared nor repressed, but cherished as a precious asset of humanity. A culture of peace and dialogue among all civilizations should be actively promoted.	This value emphasizes on human beings must respect each other regardless of their diversity of belief, culture and language'. Differences within and between societies should be neither feared nor repressed, but cherished as a precious asset of humanity. A culture of peace and dialogue among all civilizations should be actively promoted.
Respect for nature	Prudence must be shown in the management of all living species and natural resources, in accordance with the precepts of sustainable development. Only in this way can the immeasurable riches provided to us by nature be preserved and passed on to our descendants. The current unsustainable patterns of production and consumption must be changed in the interest of our future welfare and that of our descendants.	This value represents care for the nature. It emphasizes on wise management of all living species and natural resources, in accordance with the precepts of sustainable development. It will help to keep the environment sound and will ensure healthy living.
Shared responsibility	Responsibility for managing worldwide economic and social development, as well as threats to international peace and security, must be shared among the nations of the world and should be exercised multilaterally. As the most universal and most representative organization in the world, the United Nations must play the central role.	Responsibility for managing worldwide economic and social development, as well as threats to international peace and security, must be shared among the nations of the world and should be exercised multilaterally.
Integrity	It was not suggested by UN	This value refers to individual's ability to adhere to moral and ethical principles.
Concern for future generation	It was not suggested by UN	This value highlights one's sense of accountability to consider the right of the future generation. It also emphasizes on the consumption pattern of individuals. The current care-free patterns of production and consumption must be changed for the sake of future generation.

Theoretical and Practical Contribution

This study provided significant theoretical contribution to the existing body of the knowledge. The sustainable development value construct is redefined based on qualitative interviews from developing country perspective. The new sustainable development values define how is the future of Malaysia are build. The definition supports vision2002 of Malaysia plan to preserve the beauty of the land, to ensure valuable natural resources are not wasted and the lands must remain productive and fertile, our atmosphere clear and clean, our water unpolluted, and our forest resources capable of regeneration, able to yield the needs of our national development and must not be desecrated for its own sake and for our economic advancement. Furthermore, the dimensions of sustainable development value also redefined based on experts interview. There are two SDV dimension added for developing country perspective. These values are Integrity and Concern for Future Generation. Practically, this study draw the attention

Figure 1. The three layers of the sustainable development values

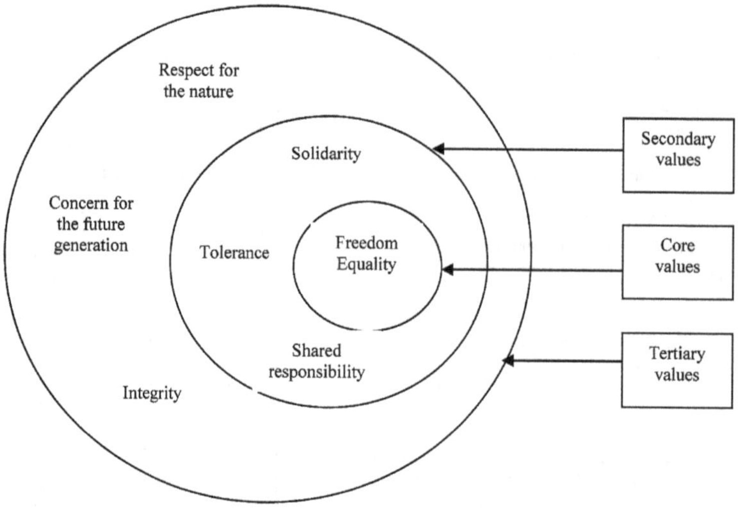

of policy maker and decisionmaker about the importance of creating awareness among the public about SDV which can be achieved through education system. More clearly SDV can be introduce in primary, secondary and tertiary education especially for Master student specializing in entrepreneurship.

CONCLUSION

Based on interviewees' opinion, this study concludes that there is a need to provide a new theoretical and operational definition for sustainable development value from developing countries perspective. In a nutshell, it is expected that the findings of this study contribute significantly to the existing body of knowledge in regard to sustainable development values. The findings revealed that the perception about SDV and its dimensions varies from developed country to developing country perspective. It is hoped that the future studies will consider this difference and carry out further studies to address the need of developing nations.

REFERENCES

Conway, G. R. (1987). The properties of egroecosystem. *Agricultural Systems*, *24*(2), 95–117. doi:10.1016/0308-521X(87)90056-4

Kates, R., Parris, T. M., & Leiserowitz, A. A. (2005). What is Sustainable Development? Goals, Indicators, Values, and Practice. *Environment*, *47*(3), 9–21.

Leiserowitz, A. A., Kates, R. W., & Parris, T. M. (2006). Sustainability values, attitudes and behaviors: a review of multi-national and global trends. *Annual Review of Environment and Resources*, *31*(1), 413–444. doi:10.1146/annurev.energy.31.102505.133552

Schwartz, S. H. (1994). Are there universal aspects in the content and structure of values? *The Journal of Social Issues*, *50*, 19–45. doi:10.1111/j.1540-4560.1994.tb01196.x

Shepherd, D. A., Kuskova, V., & Patzelt, H. (2009). Measuring the values that underline sustainable development: The development of a valid scale. *Journal of Economic Psychology*, *30*(2), 246–256. doi:10.1016/j.joep.2008.08.003

Thøgersen, J., & Ölander, F. (2002). Human values and the emergence of a sustainable consumption pattern: A panel study. *Journal of Economic Psychology*, *23*(5), 605–632. doi:10.1016/S0167-4870(02)00120-4

Turner, R. K. (Ed.). (1988). *Sustainable Environmental Development. Principles and Practice*. London: Belhaven Press.

UN. (2000). *The United Nations Millennium Declaration*. New York: United Nations.

World Commission on Environment and Development. (1987). *Our Common Future*. New York: Oxford University Press.

KEY TERMS AND DEFINITIONS

Concern for Future Generation: This value highlights one's sense of accountability to consider the right of future generation. It also emphasizes the consumption pattern of individuals.

Equality: The equal rights and opportunities of women and men must be assured.

Freedom: Men and women have the right to live their lives and raise their children in dignity, free from hunger and from the fear of violence, oppression or injustice.

Integrity: This value refers to individuals' ability to adhere to moral and ethical principles.

Respect for Nature: Prudence must be shown in the management of all living species and natural resources, in accordance with the precepts of sustainable development.

Shared Responsibility: Responsibility for managing worldwide economic and social development, as well as threats to international peace and security, must be shared among the nations of the world and should be exercised multi-laterally.

Solidarity: Global challenges must be managed in a way that distributes the costs and burdens fairly in accordance with basic principles of equity and social justice.

Sustainable Development: It refers to social movement i.e., a group of people with a common ideology who try together to achieve certain general goals.

Sustainable Development Value: It refers to a set of fundamental values that drive individuals' attitude and behaviour in a way that enhance the sustainability for the present and future generation.

Tolerance: Human beings must respect one other, in all their diversity of belief, culture and language.

Chapter 12
Sustainable Software Lifecycle for Green Consumerism

Shah Muhammad Nazmus Saquib
Technical University Munich, Germany

ABSTRACT

In recent years, consumers are very concerned about environmental issues. However, they often face difficulties to regard this during purchase. This more preponderant domain of ICT includes the scopes of digital media consumption and e-platforms. Cell phones outfitted with sustainability software can be profitable for the marketers by considering consumers' choices in regard to their environmental and biodiversity impacts. This chapter seeks to address the accountability of the digital consumers who care to keep the earth green through their purchases and simultaneously those who design and administrate these digital products that include senior and mid-level professionals from industries and from government authorities.

INTRODUCTION

Sustainability and green development, have turned out to be the prime issue during the most recent quite a few years. Software lifecycles firmly influence our regular daily existences in numerous viewpoints and in differing settings. Therefore, supporting sustainability in software architecture building unequivocally is probably going to substantially affect making our planet greener over the long haul and enhancing our society and additionally our surroundings. Essentially, "Green and Sustainable" applications ought to be as sustainable as would be prudent. This implies financial, societal, environmental effects, and effects on individuals that outcome from the product over its entire lifecycle, ought to be as limited as it could be expected under the circumstances.

It was conferred in Rio+20 UN Conference entitled "The future we want" on Sustainable Development in June 2012, the world pioneers affirmed green economy policies in the context of sustainable development and poverty eradication (Green economy - The Future We Want, 11 September 2012) (United Nations General Assembly, 2012). The outcomes and synopsis of the Rio+20 Conference were numbered in 283 points that became the accountability of Governments to ensure within their reach of

DOI: 10.4018/978-1-5225-2912-5.ch012

governance. It simply illustrates to monitor and motivate the business plan and strategies, supply chain and marketing policies of Software development industries, IT services related companies and startups to follow the minimal conventions, that turns out their product to be green for the consumers as well as for the earthly atmosphere. Consequently, gaining proper knowledge based on practical research over the topic is highly appreciable and brings significance to departments and individuals from both ends (Government departments and company policy makers). Let's proceed with this drive to move on with this chapter, henceforth it will put on some lights on the facts and methodologies to its readers. The potential objectives are-

1. To explain the underlying obscure phenomenon of a digital application, that could consequently affect the earth
2. To provide indications on the measures that could be taken to counterpart the global sustainability flaws of web and digital apps
3. To inspire researchers digging deep to set optimal standards for the cross disciplinary approach of sustainable IT product development and green marketing

A large amount of existing mobile applications was reviewed for sustainable consumption to evaluate their straightforwardness, their legitimacy, regardless of whether the associations amongst utilization and biodiversity effects are accessible to consumers, and whether sustainability appraisals are steady. The survey found a few applications that met the hunt criteria. Sustenance and administration items were the most ordinarily evaluated, the supportability assessment criteria were not openly available for a significant number of apps, and few connections amongst utilization and biodiversity preservation were made.

An ideal software would have the transparency and should overcome these lacking to conquer the authority legitimacy and need to utilize straightforwardness, sustainable evaluations. This leads to several obvious concerns. In which extent, web-applications, e-media giants are committed to their users' data privacy? Is it safe to apportion an individual's location with Google Maps? Or is it tracking down their each and every daily real-life activity? Does Amazon really keep consumers' credit card data safe? Who else can reach the user's shared pictures and life events on Facebook? These questions could relate the 3.6 billion consumers all over the world, who have access to the internet. Therefore, software industries and even small IT startups ought to take account of the sustainability and data transparency issues to mitigate this sort of questions which may eventually popup in consumers' mind.

The fast industrialization in Asian market and the consequent rapidly elevating utilizations of software, desktop applications, web applications and mobile apps needs to care differently than the more stable market of America and Europe. As of late, the improvement of open arrangements and the resultant industrializations in Asia's significant economies have started to react to worldwide issues. For example, environmental change, notwithstanding nearby concerns relating to territorial contamination and administration of information exchange policies. These patterns mirror the expanded awareness in Asia of the interdependence on long term monetary prosperity of the area being dependent upon utilizing ecological and human assets admirably and economically by enhancing IT applications. Which requires applying Empirical Studies in advance to research this issue from the view of global media as well.

The globalization of agricultural supply moves the production model into one overwhelmed by multinational organizations, customer practices are progressively applicable as a potential answer for relieving the ecumenical sustainability crisis. In a more extensive setting, political consumerism as a method for communicating one's political position through selections of producers and items has been picking up drive, particularly among the young by means of online and app based shopping platforms. To practice moral utilization, consumers need to overcome information asymmetries in the market. There are faulty knowledge branches not just from information asymmetries in the market additionally from the ascent of vertical specialization among nations in various phases of assembling procedures. Therefore, end clients are physically and candidly disconnected from the ecological consequences of their shopping choices. Such as, it would be troublesome for a novice dwelling in Germany to link the choice to purchase Shampoo of a specific brand to biodiversity cuts in Malaysia. It is currently apparent that oil-palm supplication, which gives palm oil as a part in many toiletries, is a noteworthy operator of desertification in Southeast Asia.

Next section of this chapter will explore this in relation to the digital media advances, internet applications, more specifically mobile applications as the chosen criteria of software application reviewed and the versatile types of information trade and consumers' behavioral activities it brings about. Later, on this chapter an ideal model of Sustainable software will be illustrated and discussed. Additionally, at the end of this chapter, how Empirical Methodologies could be applied to improve the existing software systems in terms of green consumerism will be covered precisely.

Methodology

It is obvious to clarify here two important terms already mentioned in the introduction, sustainable consumption, and data transparency. Sustainable consumption is the utilization of products and services that minimally affect the echo system thus future eras can continue living without being affected. Where data transparency is the guarantee that data being accounted are authentic and are originating from the official source.

New Internet-related innovations may exhibit a chance to build the familiarity with worldwide ecological issues. In particular, cellphone applications offer various potential outcomes for individuals to survey the connections amongst conduct and welfare or to connect people and science. Portable applications that connect consumption to impact on biodiversity could give an approach to illuminate consumer buying decisions continuously and prompt reinforcement for sustainable consumption. Notwithstanding the capability of ecolabeling and the utilization of advanced mobile phone applications in boosting shopper hones that support the preservation of biodiversity, there is very few research done here. A pursuit of academic publications in the most recent 15 years in Web of Science with the keyword "ecolabel" brought about 152 publications, of which just 2.1% were in the field of biodiversity protection.

To help fill this information lack, (i) A survey was run on the current sustainability consumption applications to evaluate their legitimacy, straightforwardness, and whether the links between individual consumption and weight on nature and biodiversity are accessible to consumers and (ii) evaluate the consistency in sustainability appraisals among these applications.

The assessment constrained to applications that notified end users on the sustainability of their acquiring alternatives. Applications that notified clients of the natural effects of their activities that did not include purchases (e.g., giving advices to limit water or energy usage at home units, mentoring solar powered energy utilization and so on.) were avoided.

A methodical audit was completed for medium of language applied as English applications in the Apple and Google Play stores, following the Preferred Reporting Items for Systematic Reviews and Meta-Analyses (PRISMA) guidelines (Moher et al., 2009) Illustrated in Figure 1. It constrained the quest to the virtual stores in Europe. Identification of methodologies and primary data acquiring was done over

Figure 1. Preferred Reporting Items for Systematic Reviews and Meta-Analyses: The PRISMA Statement

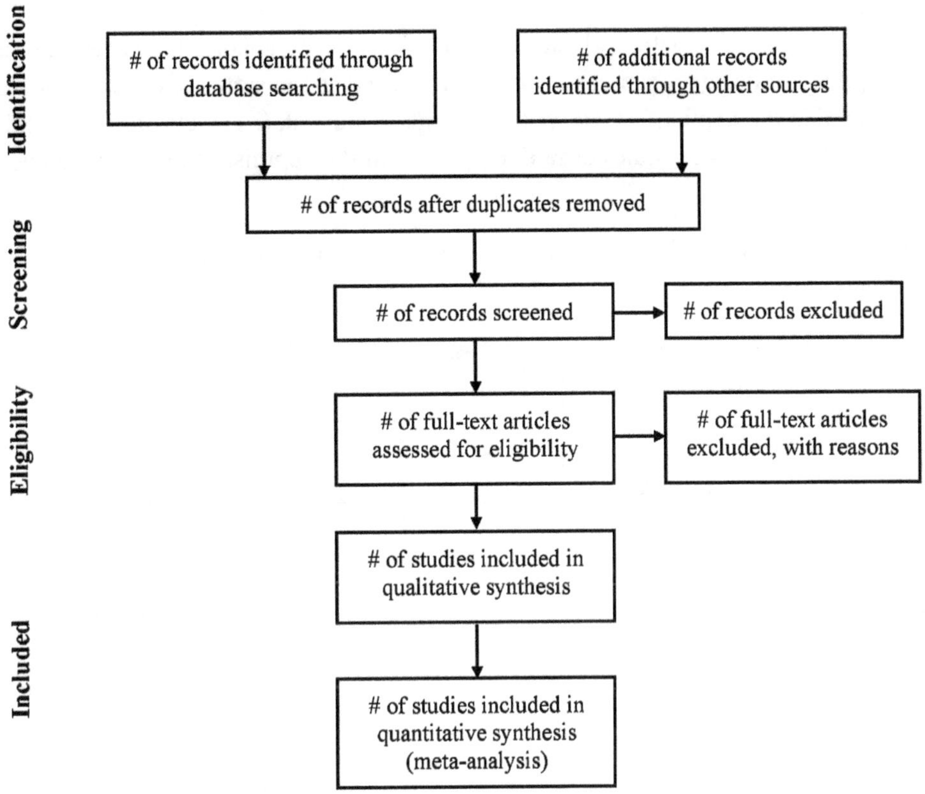

a duration of three months in early 2016. Data synthetization on the survey of applications substance and final inquiries to conclude reports were directed from 11 November 2016 to 25 November 2016. The search words "sustainable" or "green" were utilized, leading to 824 possibly pertinent applications. Apps were constrained to the following classes as referred in Table 1.

The inquiry was supplemented by a different screening of the 407 worldwide sustainability applications aggregated by the UN Sustainable Development Knowledge Platform – STI (Science, Technology, and Innovation; https://sustainabledevelopment.un.org/TFM/STIForum2017). When both results were merged, 31 substantial applications were distinguished. The study played out another step of screening of the applications identified with these 31 applications using the customers also bought and similar sections in iPhone and Android, resulting in 8 extra applications included in the survey. A sum of 39

Table 1. App classes assessed from different app stores

Google Play Store	Apple Store
Education and book	Education
Lifestyle	Lifestyle
-	Food and drink
Shopping and tools	Health and fitness

applications were chosen. The app filtration flow in action by the application of PRISMA guidelines referring to the Figure 2.

Aside from using the information given in the application metaphors, the survey led a different sweep of the application designer's sites that were announced in the stores to confirm the information or capacities offered in the application: (i) writes of items evaluated, (ii) assets of the item advanced by the application, (iii) whether the values or ranking plans and the appraisal strategy were unequivocally

Figure 2. The Preferred Reporting Items for Systematic Reviews and Meta-Analyses: The PRISMA flowchart in application

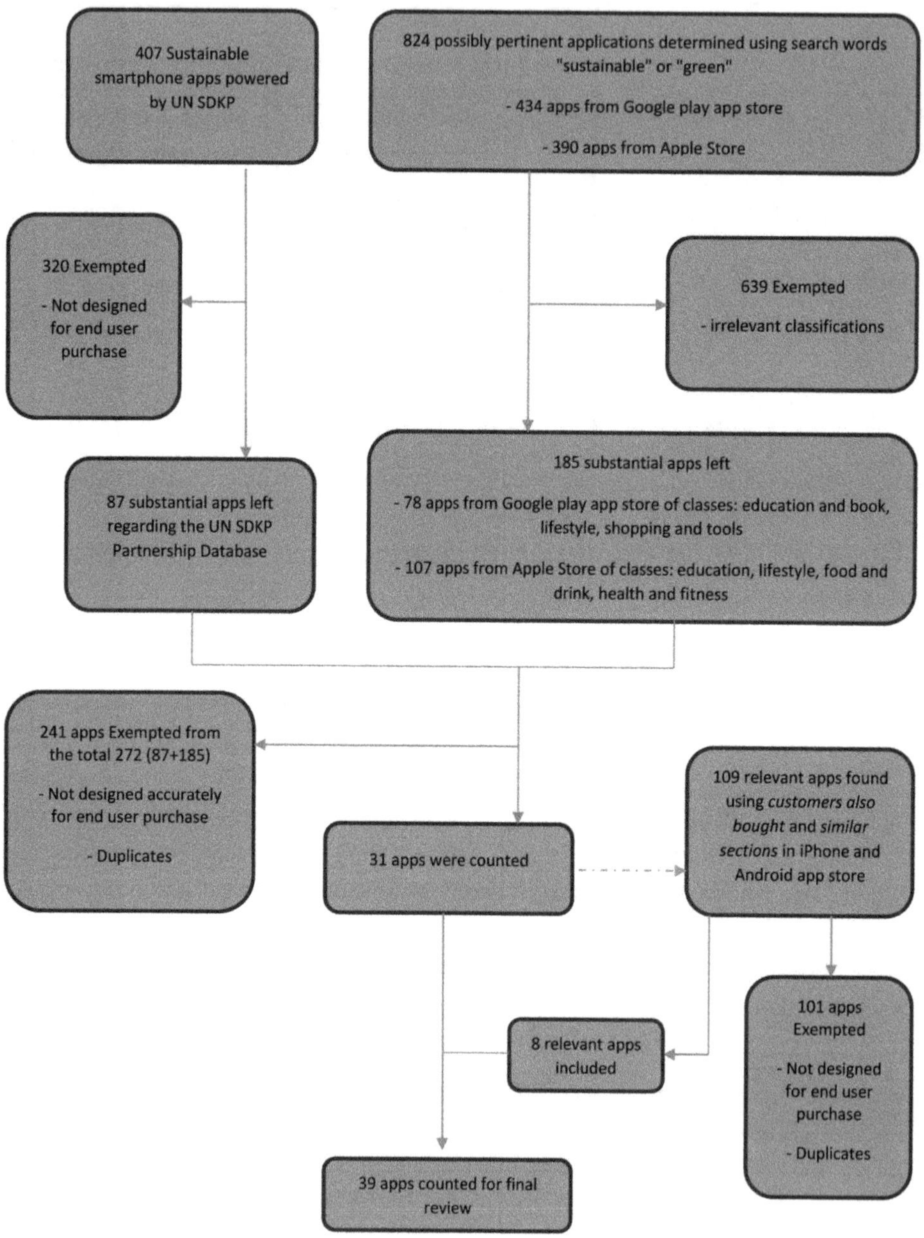

supplied and whether the producer was involved in the review, (iv) how the evaluation results were introduced to the applications clients, and (v) whether ecological indicators or biodiversity affect indicators were incorporated in the evaluation class or standards. Regression analysis was applied to evaluate the consistency between the sustainability scores or ratings. To have the capacity to play out the relationship tests on unqualified factors, the function "str2num()" was applied in the Matlab environment to change over straight out factors into numerical factors. Additionally, the European Commission Technical Report 2012 determined the measures and standards (European Commission: Technical Report, 2012) that was applied during the assessment.

Analysis

From the assessment, 39 applications were discovered that met the hunt criteria in the phone app stores of Apple and Android stands, of which 27 and 21 (same apps in both platforms along with different apps) were offered in the Android and Apple stores, separately. These applications were available to download free of cost.

The items advanced in the applications were evaluated using sustainability indicators that could be characterized in two main classes: moral and social (24 applications) and/or ecological (15 applications). All applications depicted subjectively the sustainability indicators utilized. Among moral and social indicators, the portrayal enveloped items not tried on wildlife (8 applications), items conforming to reasonable exchange standards (6 applications, e.g., The Good Shopping Guide), organizations against value fixing, organizations encouraging nearby and/or bio items, the reasonable treatment of laborers, organizations against hereditarily adjusted life forms, and socially dependable items. Moral and social indicators were related to nonfood items. Among natural sustainability indicators, these included items from sustainably oversaw sea-food stocks or ranches, that advanced preservation of tropical timberlands (3 applications), that minimized effects on marine life and coral reefs, that diminished greenhouse gas emanations, that advanced recycling and that minimized rackful chemicals.

13 applications (33%) if binary yield information, for example, whether the item was sustainable in a certain angle (e.g., whether it contained palm oil; Palm Oil Shopping Guide, Palm Oil Guide and Scanner) or whether it was licensed by the application supplier. 9 applications (24%) displayed sustainable evaluations in an ordinal scale, for the most part using the movement light framework. 6 applications (Climate Count, Ethical Barcode, GoodGuide, The Good Shopping Guide) doled out unequivocal "sustainable scores" to the evaluated items. Scores were all the more normally connected with food-related items. 6 applications (Audubon Gulf Seafood Guide, Conscious Consumers, Cruelty-Free, Ethical Eats!, Noshplanet) represented considerable authority in presenting to clients their prescribed businesses/items. EcoDirectory was the main application providing general information about the items. 8 applications likewise incorporated a route work for clients to find their suggested businesses (generally eateries) or gave clients a rundown of their "best" or "accomplice" brands other than giving ratings of other brands. Add up to 13 applications (33%) had the capacity to work as a marketing stage for businesses. Of these 13 applications, just Certified Humane and Non-GMO Project Shopping Guide clearly broadcasted both their standards/rating plans and appraisal methodology. In these two cases, the application suppliers work as certifying associations that liaise with the businesses who apply to get their items/administrations approval. This could explain the relationship between open sustainability criteria and the advertising of other items.

To distinguish which particular associations with biodiversity effects are available in the improvement of the accessible applications, the accessible rating plans was examined and found that exclusive 6 applications (EcoDirectory, Audubon Gulf Seafood Guide, GoodGuide, Seafood Finder, Seafood Watch, and Sustainable Seafood Guide) incorporated contemplations of effects on biodiversity. Aside from GoodGuide, the preservation related rating criteria were centered around marine biological communities. Other applications, for example, Palm Oil Shopping Guide, that concentrated on the preservation of tropical woodlands and backwoods dwelling species (e.g., the orangutan) had inaccessible rating criteria.

Detailed description of the linear regression analysis how it was performed in Matlab environment is excluded here and that is beyond the scopes of this chapter. Table 2. illustrates the converted and aggregated sustainability rankings of the main 20 family unit brands in The Good Shopping Guide, Climate Counts, and Shop Ethical applications.

The sustainability appraisals of the applications for the worldwide top ranked 20 brand organizations was cross verified. Just three of the chosen applications—The Good Shopping Guide, Climate Counts, and Shop Ethical—served sustainability appraisals of the selected brands. It was discovered both textures and inconsistencies in the ranking of sustainability between brands referring to the Table

Table 2. The sustainability rankings of the main 20 family unit brands in The Good Shopping Guide, Climate Counts, and Shop Ethical applications

No.	Business title	The good shopping guide	Climate Counts	Shop Ethical
1	Nestlé	42-55	83	5
2	P&G	18-41	61	5
3	PepsiCo	40-58	68	5
4	Uniliver	45-68	94	2
5	Coca-Cola	29	78	5
6	Anheuser-Busch	Na	66	5
7	Mars	38	Na	5
8	L'Oréal	49	89	5
9	Danone	51	83	3
10	Kimberly-Clark	Na	66	2
11	Kraft Foods	Na	76	5
12	General Mills	Na	58	2
13	Colgate-Palmolive	51-64	74	2
14	SABMiller	Na	58	2
15	Diageo	38	Na	2
16	Reckitt Benckiser	54	87	2
17	Kao	53	Na	2
18	H. J. Heinz	55	62	2
19	Avon	51	70	3
20	LG	71	86	2

Hint: Scaling from 0 - 100, higher numeric scores indicate more sustainable items; on the scale from 1 to 5, number of lower order indicate more sustainable brands. Abbreviation: Na, Not Available, data absent

1. In the examination of family brands, Climate Counts positioned most brands positively, though the other applications seemed to apply stricter standards and therefore gave distinctive ratings for general brands. Using Linear relationship coefficient, no correlation was found between the scores for The Good Shopping Guide and Climate Counts (connection coefficient = 0.19, p= 0.41). Converting the scores of Shop Ethical into a numeric scale and running relationship tests demonstrated a critical negative connection with The Good Shopping Guide (connection coefficient = –0.48, p < 0.02). For this situation, this outcome indicates predictable scores since Shop Ethical takes after the in-order position (e.g., 1 is more sustainable than 2; table 2). No connection was found, nonetheless, with Climate Counts (relationship coefficient = –0.055, p= 0.81). These outcomes were validated with the relapse examination in which the scores by Shop Ethical were kept as absolute (scores 2, 3, and 5 introduced coefficients of –29, –26 and –35, with p < 0.055 when The Good Shopping Guide was utilized as reliant variable).

To simplify the results of the analysis in plain words, it was clearly observed that even well-known brands rarely follow the transparency of their product lifecycle through the app based marketing which relates the obscured transparency of the app's itself. The materials and source used to produce the product often kept in vague. Web based marketing scopes are also countable among these trends, while e-commerce and app-based purchasing is uprising as a parallel stream. On the other hand, the underlying IT industries working behind the e-commerce systems are not that much of concern about the echo sustainability issues that they are bringing to the doors of their consumers. Distributed web applications are no more bounded to one's desktop only, they are much more of device and platform independent and thus span of their lifecycle grew just massive. Lack of accountability and inadequate knowledge of green consumerism can push the world to an unsustainable situation, where software production managers and IT policy makers show less enthusiasm over these topics. Hence, let's move forward to the next section which must benefit to understand what is a sustainable software model really is.

Sustainable Model

It is observed that these apps rarely meet the sustainability standards and could solve the sustainability issues, what can be done to lessen the environmental impacts of ICTs? To boost the green consumption from consumer's point? There are several models and methodologies that can be applied to avail the continuity of sustainable software lifecycle and green consumerism. Researchers and engineers have instead of esteem changes stressed the specialized conceivable outcomes of a move to less asset intensive sorts of utilization and to keep the earth green. One arrangement they supported is the idea of administration proficiency, which might be defined as providing a most extreme of valuable end-administrations to consumers using the minimum of materials and energy use. There is a broad writing on this idea and many endeavors to plan new sorts of benefit producing applications that convey energy administrations using innovative combinations of market products and services and household work.

But there is only one approach in software engineering that explicitly addresses sustainability. It is a reference framework with specific application in web engineering. Customary software engineering methods and domain-categorical procedures and techniques was discovered from other disciplines. The idea of sustainability is utilized by a wide range of groups, frequently in vague ways. At the point when connected to a product framework, the term typically indicates to an item's potential for life span within a given field. Over the following decades, the product development group has fulfilled noteworthy advances in the regions of software maintenance, program understanding, reverse engineering, reengineering, mining software stores, software relocation, and application platforms. This approach has consequently been to cull as rudimental a definition as would be prudent (e.g., "the competency to persist"), and base instead on an ascertained structure for thinking about sustainability and a course of action of estimations by which to approach it.

The center issue can be represented as far as an inclination more than one or other of the charts appeared in Figure 3. Figure 3(a) demonstrates a typical representation of sustainability as far as three separate concerns. The key thought is that human culture is just maintainable in the event that it can be supported in each of the three measurements: social, monetary and ecological. This view is consolidated into the triple bottom line approach, where organizations account for budgetary returns, as well as for advantages and effects in the social and ecological circles (Elkington, 2004).

This approach is dismissed as feeble maintainability by the individuals who contend that it's a mistake to look to adjust the three concerns. As indicated by this view in Figure 3(a) is deluding, as the economy is truly just a subsystem of society, which thus is a subsystem of the ecology (Figure 3(b)). To accomplish solid sustainability, we need to recognize that there are central biophysical limits that oblige the streams of normal assets on the environment, and no course of action of society can be viewed as economical

Figure 3a. Competing visualizations of sustainability: Weak sustainability

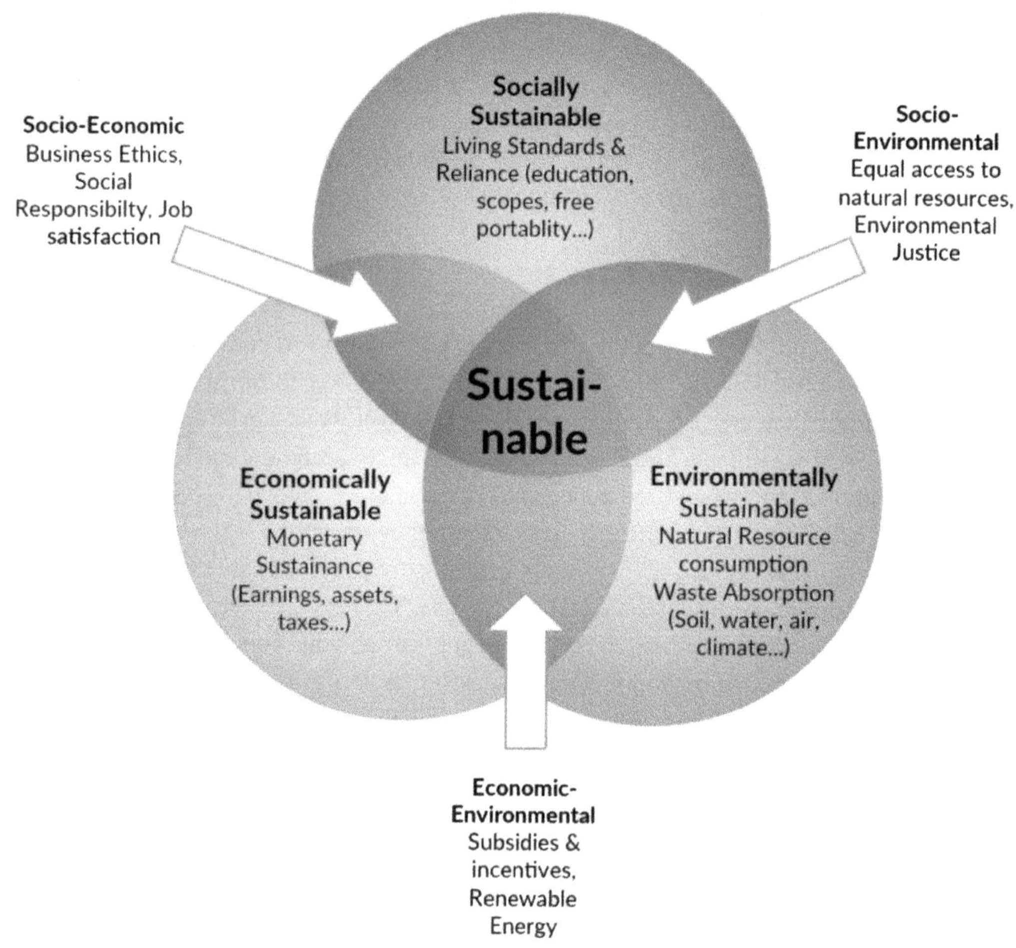

Figure 3b. Competing visualizations of sustainability: Strong sustainability

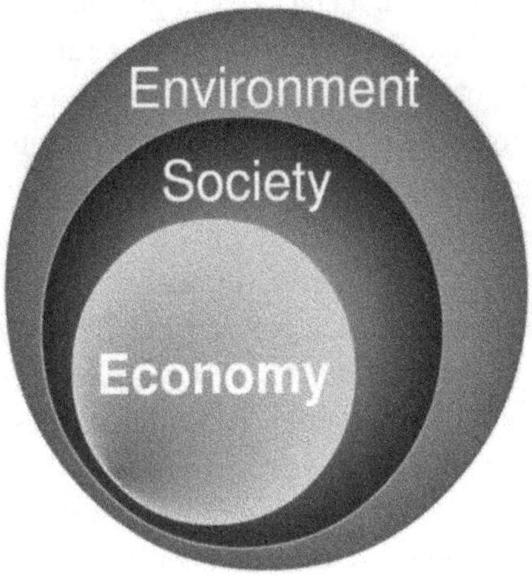

unless it lives inside these points of confinement (Neumayer, 2003). In this view, it isn't right to discuss sustainability regarding an arrangement of 'dimensions', as the uncertainties are entirely progressive.

The contention between these two perspectives plays out distinctively in various orders. In financial matters, it lays on the topic of substitutability. Numerous financial analysts accept that common capital is limitlessly substitutable with human capital (e.g., human resourcefulness). In the event that they are, then monetary development requires not be compelled by biophysical limits. Nonetheless, natural fi-

Figure 3c. Competing visualizations of sustainability: A more practical view for software research

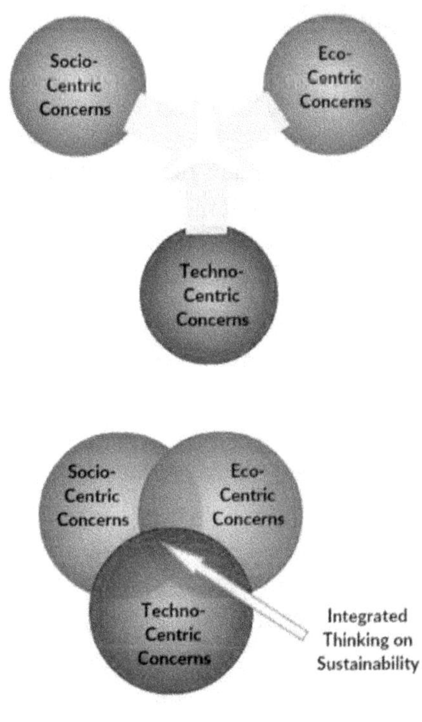

nancial specialists debate this, and contend that there are firm points of confinement to substitutability, which suggests there are cutoff points on monetary development. For social issues, the debate focuses on whether all parts of social maintainability follow in the long run to inquiries of distributional equity over access to characteristic assets, or whether there are different parts of social maintainability (e.g., human rights) that emerge freely from the topic of how we allot assets.

While these inquiries are trusted as critical, there is no certainty that they offer a valuable beginning stage for software specialists and analysts battling with the topic of what sustainability implies for them. A more practical view is appeared in Figure 3(c), where sustainability is portrayed as a learning procedure by which it moves towards coordinated considering. Software specialists tend to treat techno-driven concerns (e.g., programming qualities and the monetary esteem they make) independently from socio-driven concerns (how applications can improve individuals' lives) and eco-driven concerns (securing the earth). As opposed to asking whether it is proper to adjust these worries, it is ought to rather be asking What techniques and instruments are expected to investigate between conditions amongst these doubts, and to cultivate more coordinated and long haul considering.

Programming frameworks, specifically, assume a transformative part, as they empower dematerialization, drive utilization designs for items, administrations, materials, and energy, and encourage auxiliary changes from devouring material products towards expending immaterial services, for example, the switch from tuning in to music online rather to buying and disposing of printed copies. They likewise gather, oversee and appropriate data expected to see long-running complex marvels extending from atmosphere information to individual wellbeing records and measurements of worldwide value and capital. In that capacity, the product business progressively speaks to a focal driver for development and financial success, however all the while expands social imbalance, as individuals without access and specialized abilities are abandoned, and causes ecological harm, as utilization of technology develops.

The approach has been accepted is to concentrate on how we comprehend and assume liability for the different interfacing openings and effects of software innovation, including to start with first, second and third order impacts. In the first order impacts are effects and openings made by the quick presence of a software architecture, emerging from its outline elements and blemishes. Second order impacts are those made by the continuous utilize and utilization of the product, for example, how it changes what we do and what we're able to do. Third order impacts are the progressions that happen through the collected practices of extensive quantities of individuals utilizing the application over the medium to long term (e.g., energy requisition, mass reconnaissance, and so forth). These impacts play out crosswise over numerous areas. Taking after Goodland (Goodland, 2002) and Penzenstadler and Femmer (Penzenstadler & Femmer, 2013), it is distinguished by five sustainability measurements:

1. **Environmental:** Looks to enhance human welfare by ensuring natural capital. The measurement incorporates biological communities, crude assets, environmental change, nourishment generation, water, contamination, squander, and so on.
2. **Social:** Goes for protecting the societal groups (gatherings of individuals, associations) in their solidarity and administrations. This incorporates social value, equity, business, majority rule government, etc.
3. **Economic:** Goes for keeping up resources regarding capital and included esteem. This incorporates riches creation, success, productivity, capital venture, salary, etc.

4. **Technical:** Alludes to life span of data, frameworks, and foundation and their sufficient development with changing encompassing conditions. It incorporates support, development, out of date quality, information trustworthiness, and so forth.
5. **Individual:** Alludes to keeping up individual human capital. This incorporates mental and physical prosperity, instruction, sense of pride, aptitudes, versatility, and so on.

A comprehension of these short and long-term impacts of software innovation and how they play out over different measurements can then prompt to a thought of use focuses: where are the best places to mediate to accomplish sustainability? Such mediations may be changes in the way it is been dissected and planed software frameworks, or they may change by the way of trying to apply software resolutions for societal issues.

Empirical Methodology

To wind up distinctly a genuine building discipline it is ensured that Web and Software designing need to receive and adjust study techniques from different disciplines. One empowering agent for doing this is estimation. Web and Software estimation frame the premise; however, they are not adequate. Empirical methods, for example, controlled tests, contextual investigations, overviews and post-mortem examinations are expected to progress assess and approve the inquire about outcomes. These techniques are required with the goal that it is conceivable to deductively state whether a system is superior to some other system. Accordingly, observational techniques give one vital logical premise to both Web and Software development. For some kind of issues different strategies, for instance the utilization of scientific models for anticipating software reliability, are more qualified, however the best strategy is to apply empiricism. The principle reason being that Web and programming advancement are human concentrated, and consequently they don't borrow themselves to solely scientific methodologies. This implies exact strategies are fundamental to the analyst.

The empirical methods are however likewise essential from a modern perspective. Organizations trying to wind up learning associations, need to consider the accompanying meaning of a learning association:

A learning organisation is an organisation skilled at creating, acquiring, and transferring knowledge, and at modifying its behavior to reflect new knowledge and insights… (Garvin, 1998)

Garvin proceeds with expressing that learning associations are great at five exercises: methodical critical thinking, experimentation, gaining from past encounters, gaining from others, and exchanging information. This incorporates depending on logical strategies instead of guessing. From the point of view of this chapter section, the key issue is the use of a logical technique and the utilization of empirical methods as a transport for precise change when designing Web applications and Software. The quote from Garvin is in-accordance with the ideas of the Quality Improvement Paradigm and the Experience Factory (Basili, Caldiera, & Rombach, 2002) that are regularly utilized as a part of a software designing setting.

In rundown, the above implies that Web and software designing specialists and learning associations both have a need to grasp empirical strategies. The primary goal of this section is to give a prologue to four exact research strategies and to place them into an engineering framework.

There are two primary sorts of research ideal models having diverse ways to deal with experimental reviews. Qualitative research is related with examining objects in their regular setting. A qualitative specialist endeavors to decipher a wonder in light of clarifications that individuals convey to them (Creswell, 1994). Qualitative research starts with approaching that there is a scope of various methods for elucidation. Quantitative research is for the most part concerned with evaluating a relationship or to look at least two gatherings (Denzin, & Lincoln, 1994). The point is to distinguish a cause-impact relationship. The quantitative research is regularly led through setting up controlled tests or gathering information through contextual investigations. Quantitative examinations are suitable when testing the impact of some control or action. Flexibility is that quantitative information advances correlations and factual examination.

It is workable for qualitative and quantitative research to examine the same points yet each of them will address an alternate kind of question. For illustration, a quantitative examination could be propelled to research how much another investigation technique diminishes the quantity of deficiencies found in tests. To answer inquiries regarding the wellsprings of varieties between various examination bunches, it requires a qualitative examination.

When all is said in done, any observational review can be mapped to the accompanying principle consider steps: Definition, Planning, Operation, Analysis and translation, Conclusions and Presentation and bundling. The work inside the means varies extensively relying upon the kind of experimental review. Nevertheless, rather than attempting to present four distinctive research techniques as per this general procedure, we have highlighted the fundamental parts of enthusiasm for the diverse sorts of studies. Contingent upon the motivation behind the assessment, regardless of whether it is procedures, techniques or apparatuses, and relying upon the conditions for the exact examination, there are four noteworthy diverse sorts of systems that are tended to here:

Experiment: Examinations are now and then alluded to as research-in-the-small (Kitchenham, Pickard, & Pfleeger, 1995), since they are related to a restricted extension and regularly are keep running in a lab setting. They are regularly exceedingly controlled and thus likewise every so often alluded to as controlled analysis, which is utilized in the future. When testing, subjects are appointed to various treatments indiscriminately. The goal is to control at least one factors and control every single other variable at settled levels. The impact of the control is measured, and in light of this, a factual investigation can be performed. At times, it might be difficult to utilize genuine experimentation; we may need to utilize semi tests. The last term is regularly utilized when it is difficult to perform arbitrary task of the subjects to the distinctive treatments. A case of a controlled test in Web building is to look at two changed strategies for creating web applications (e.g. REST versus SOAP). For this sort of studies, techniques for factual derivation relate to the reason for appearing with statistical centrality that one strategy is superior to the next (Montgomery, 1997).

Case study: Case examine research is now and again alluded to as research-in-the-average (Kitchenham, Pickard, & Pfleeger, 1995). It is depicted along these lines in light of the fact that a contextual investigation ordinarily concentrates a genuine venture and subsequently the circumstance is "common". Contextual investigations are utilized for observing tasks, exercises or assignments. Information is gathered for a particular reason all through the review. In light of the information gathering, measurable examinations can be done. The contextual analysis is typically gone for following a particular property or building up connections between various properties. The level of control is lower for a situation examined than in an investigation. A contextual analysis is an observational review while the investigation is a controlled review (Zelkowitz, & Wallace, 1998). A case study may, for instance, be gone for building a model to foresee the quantity of issues in testing. Multivariate measurable investigation is regularly connected in this kind of studies. The examination techniques incorporate linear regression and primary segment examination (Manly BFJ, 1994).

Survey: The survey is by (Kitchenham, Pickard, & Pfleeger, 1995) alluded to as research-in-the-large (and past), since it is conceivable to send a survey to or meet a huge number individuals covering whatever objective populace it has. Hence, a review is regularly an examination performed all things considered, when e.g. an instrument or strategy, has been being used for some time. The essential method for social occasion subjective or quantitative information are meetings or surveys. These are done through taking an example that is illustrative from the populace to be examined. The outcomes from the study are then broke down to infer clear and illustrative conclusions. They are then summed up to the populace from which the test was taken. Overviews are talked about further in.

Post-mortem analysis: This kind of analysis is likewise led in the past as showed by the name. Be that as it may, it ought to be deciphered somewhat more extensive than abstract as an after death. For instance, a venture does not need to be done to dispatch a post-mortem analysis. It is conceivable to concentrate any part of a venture reflectively utilizing this kind of analysis. Along these lines, this kind of analysis may, in the distinct route utilized by (Kitchenham, Pickard, & Pfleeger, 1995), be depicted as being examination in-the-past-and-typical. It can subsequently be seen as identified with both the study and the contextual investigation. The postmortem might be directed by taking a gander at venture documentation or by meeting individuals, separately or as a gathering, who have taken an interest in the protest that is being broke down in the post-mortem analysis.

An experiment is a formal, thorough and controlled examination. In a try the key variables are recognized and controlled. The partition between contextual analyses and trials can be spoken to by the thought of a state variable. In an investigation, the state variable can accept diverse qualities and the goal is ordinarily to recognize two circumstances, for instance, a control circumstance and the circumstance under examination. Cases of a state variable could be, for instance, the examination strategy or experience of the Web engineers. For a situation ponder, the state variable just accepts one esteem, administered by the real venture under review.

Case study is a method where key components that may have any effect on the result are recognized and after that the movement is reported. Contextual analysis research is an observational technique, i.e. perception of an on-going task or movement finishes it.

Surveys are extremely basic inside sociologies where, for instance, outlooks are surveyed to decide how a populace will vote in the following race. A study gives no control of the execution or the estimation, however it is conceivable to contrast it and comparative ones, yet it is unrealistic to control factors as in the other examination techniques.

At last, a post-mortem analysis might be seen as acquiring properties from both studies and contextual investigations. A posthumous may contain overview components, however it is typically worried about a case. The last could either be a full Web extend or a particularly focused activity.

For all four techniques, it is vital to consider the number of inhabitants in intrigue. It is from the populace that an example ought to be found. The specimen ought to ideally be picked arbitrarily from the populace. The specimen comprises of various subjects, for instance much of the time people taking an interest in a review. The real populace may differ from an aspiration to have an overall public, as is ordinarily the target in tests where we might want to sum up the outcomes, to a tighter view, which might be the situation in post-mortem investigations and contextual analyses.

It has been introduced a synopsis of the decisions required in selecting fitting observational techniques for programming architectural examination. The point in this section was not given a detailed portrayal of every technique, but instead to cover the issues that a researcher must face when choosing how to address a given research issue. Additional reading (Conradi & Wang, 2003), and perhaps some particular preparing might be fundamental before an analyst can finally apply on a picked technique.

CONCLUSION

Expanding consideration is being paid to the more extensive impacts of Software on society and the need to typify long term considering moral duty, and a comprehension of maintainability into the outline of application frameworks. In any case, the software professionals do not have a shared belief that explains its part in sustainability outline, and a steady arrangement of misperceptions continue in research, hypothesis, and practice. To genuinely gain ground on comprehension the part programming plays in the decisions are taken by the originators of the core works at the foundation of our civilization, it must be comprehended the way of sustainability and locate a shared conviction for a calculated system.

Early of this chapter a large number of applications have been assessed and has taken as case study to serve an applied mitigation. The audit of sustainable utilization of applications demonstrated a few exemplary techniques. It was found that apps, for the most part, centered around sustenance related consumption. This concurs with the remarkable quality of Purchase between worldwide nourishment utilization and the preservation of natural assets or sustainable use. It is found that a significant extent of the applications recommended organizations to clients, demonstrating the capability of the applications to buyers' choices. This could be a type of promotion and a potential approach to financial application improvement, represented that moral issues identified with incompatible situation can be dodged. Albeit such a special component of applications could work as a source of perspective to empower the buys from feasible organizations/benchmarks, the suggestions ought to in a perfect world outcome from evident and transparent criteria. In this regard, one principle finding of the review is the way rarely the application engineers promote their judgement forms.

These outcomes may be useful while arranging the product improvement group in an organization. Making little groups concentrated on building up a specific part or administration may prompt to less malformations once the part hits production. Setting up a procedure for enduring commitments from new colleagues or partners from another group may prompt to less deformities underway.

It is withal paramount to capitalize on software implements that monitor resources in an energy efficient manner and take part in renewable power scheme features. Here green and sustainable software model have been demonstrated that can be applied during software development procedures. Green computing and programming ideas can be utilized and alluded to in the phases of a product designing procedure to help yield a green and feasible programming environment and have a green advancement process. Permitting business specialists, clients, and software architects to cooperate all guide in having a green and reasonable software building process.

The chapter depicted the key components of empirical research plan: An unmistakable research address gives a concentration to the review. An unequivocal philosophical position helps to comprehend the reader's exploration objectives and select a fitting examination strategy. An exploration technique helps to outline a review, and choose what sorts of information to gather and how to gather it. A hypothesis helps to clarify the information and relate it to the examination address and to past reviews in the writing. A fitting arrangement of criteria for evaluating legitimacy enhances the review plan and clear up the way of the conclusions.

From the review, even the pronounced green shoppers are not prepared or propelled enough to settle on choices on which issue is the most significant for each purchase and change their buy in like manner (Göran Bolin, 2011). Moreover, they don't have time for research, data illumination and item search required for green acquiring. Along these lines, it is stressed that any administration approach that exclusively depends on green customers as specialists of progress for shopping items are misinformed. The outcomes demonstrate that green purchasers can utilize their purchasing energy to have any kind of effect, yet at a high cost regarding exertion and time, which is a critical boundary. These customers require assistance from governments as motivators and single-issue marks to demonstrate to them where they ought to think their restricted endeavors. More in a general sense, 'being green' needs time and space in people groups' lives that is not accessible in progressively bustling ways of life. Subsequently, there should be intelligent practical creation and utilization approaches crosswise over government offices, not simply 'green exhortation' to the customers.

REFERENCES

Basili, V. R., Caldiera, G., & Rombach, H. D. (2002). Experience Factory. In J. J. Marciniak (Ed.), *Encyclopaedia of Software Engineering*. Hoboken, NJ: John Wiley & Sons, Inc. doi:10.1002/0471028959.sof110

Bolin, G. (2011). *Value and the Media: Cultural Production and Consumption in Digital Markets*. Ashgate Publishing, Ltd.

Conradi, R., & Wang, A. I. (Eds.). (2003). Empirical Methods and Studies in Software Engineering. Berlin, Germany: Academic Press.

Creswell, J. W. (1994). *Research Design, Qualitative and Quantitative Approaches*. Sage Publications.

Denzin, N. K., & Lincoln, Y. S. (1994). *Handbook of Qualitative Research*. London, UK: Sage Publications.

Elkington, J. (2004). Enter the triple bottom line. In The triple bottom line: Does it all add up?. Routledge.

European Commission. (2012). *Technical Report section 061: Policies to encourage sustainable consumption*. Retrieved from http://ec.europa.eu/environment/eussd/pdf/report_22082012.pdf

Garvin, D. A. (1998). Building a Learning Organization. Harvard Business Review on Knowledge Management, 47-80.

Goodland, R. (2002). *Sustainability: Human, social, economic and environmental*. John Wiley & Sons.

Kitchenham, B., Pickard, L., & Pfleeger, S. L. (1995, July). Case Studies for Method and Tool Evaluation. *J IEEE Software*, 52-62.

Manly, B. F. J. (1994). *Multivariate Statistical Methods - A Primer* (2nd ed.). London: Chapman & Hall.

Moher. (2009). *Preferred Reporting Items for Systematic Reviews and Meta-Analyses: The PRISMA Statement*. Available at: http://journals.plos.org/plosmedicine/article?id=10.1371/journal.pmed.1000097

Montgomery, D. C. (1997). *Design and Analysis of Experiments* (4th ed.). New York: John Wiley & Sons.

Neumayer, E. (2003). *Weak Versus Strong Sustainability: Exploring the Limits of Two Opposing Paradigms*. Edward Elgar.

Penzenstadler, B., & Femmer, H. (2013). A generic model for sustainability with process-and product-specific instances. *Proceedings of the 2013 workshop on Green in/by software engineering*, 3–8. doi:10.1145/2451605.2451609

United Nations General Assembly. (2012). *A/RES/66/288 - The Future We Want*. Available at: http://www.un.org/ga/search/view_doc.asp?symbol=A/RES/66/288&Lang=E

Zelkowitz, M. V., & Wallace, D. R. (1998). Experimental Models for Validating Technology. *J IEEE Computer*, *31*(5), 23–31. doi:10.1109/2.675630

KEY TERMS AND DEFINITIONS

Data Transparency: The guarantee that data being accounted are authentic and are originating from the official source.

Green Consumption: It is a form of consumption that is well-suited with the safety measure of the environment for the present and for the next generations.

Green Innovation: Hardware or software innovation that is related to green products or processes, including the innovation in technologies that are involved in energy-saving, pollution-prevention, waste recycling, green product designs, or corporate environmental management.

ICT: Information and Communication Technology.

Software Sustainability: A long-living software system which can be cost-efficiently maintained and evolved over its entire life-cycle.

Sustainable Consumption: The utilization of products and services that minimally affect the echo system thus future eras can continue living without being affected.

Sustainable Production: The creation of goods and services using processes and systems that are non-polluting, conserving of energy and natural resources, economically viable, safe and healthful for workers, communities, and consumers.

Chapter 13
A Conceptual Model of Green HRM Adoption Towards Sustainability in Hospitality Industry

Yusmani Mohd Yusoff
Universiti Sains Malaysia, Malaysia

Mehran Nejati
Edith Cowan University, Australia

ABSTRACT

This chapter seeks to provide a better understanding on the predictors of green human resource management which can result in improved environmental and financial performance across hospitality industry. The proposed model has been constructed from the perspective of external pressure (i.e., normative) and internal pressure (manager's environmental concerns) by using the Institutional Theory and Resource Based View Theory. The chapter examines the antecedents of sustainability in hospitality industry in terms of improved financial and environmental performance. It therefore expands the level of understanding on mechanisms which leads to corporation sustainability. While the chapter is written with a focus on hospitality industry, the proposed model is applicable to corporations across other sectors.

INTRODUCTION

Since the late 1980s, in western economies, there has been increasing concern about the impact of business on the environment (Gadenne, Kennedy, & McKeiver, 2009). This concern spread among various stakeholders such as legislators, employees, customers, local communities, business suppliers, financial institutions and public authorities; therefore, companies in contemporary eras face mounting pressure from shareholders and stakeholders to develop activities related to environmental performance (López-Gamero, Molina-Azorín, & Claver-Cortés, 2009). Besides, companies implement programs and policies

DOI: 10.4018/978-1-5225-2912-5.ch013

to execute the environmental performance programs and perform in compliance with the environmental regulations (Yadav, Han, & Rho, 2015).

At present, one of the main industries mostly affecting the environment is hospitality industry. In recent years, the global hospitality industry has been growing rapidly. The global income generated from international tourists in 2014 was US$ 1,245 billion (Tourism & Unwto, 2015). In the same year, Europe's hospitality industry earned US$ 509 billion, while Asia Pacific earned US$ 337 billion (Tourism & Unwto, 2015). Due to the accelerated growth of this sector, hospitality industry has become one of the major contributors to the source of income for most of the countries such as Malaysia (Inside Malaysia, 2012; Chan & Wong, 2006).

Hospitality industry contributes to the GDP, hence is associated with employment prospects, the growth of secondary activities, and providing substitute earnings (Awang, Ishak, Radzi, & Taha, 2008). However, the industry also consumes substantial amounts of natural resources such as energy and water, leading to several damaging impacts such as excessive volumes of waste and environmental problems (Nabiha et al., 2011). For instance, the generation of wastes in this industry was estimated as 1 kg per customer per day (Bohdanowicz, 2005). Additionally, a large number of unwelcome emissions such as CFCs, CO2, smell and smoke, and industry waste are generated by the hospitality industry (Kirk, 1995).

Closely related to the environmental issues, the hospitality industry has been facing the increasing pressure by many stakeholders to implement the environmental performance programs (Erdogan & Baris, 2007). As shifting in consumer demand, pressure from NGOs, government regulations, and shifting professional ethics have become the main forces developing pressure on the hospitality industry (Erdogan & Baris, 2007). As regard to these environmental issues, companies in the hospitality industry has been recognizing environmental issues as one of the significant element needs specific attention in their business activities (Erdogan & Baris, 2007). Therefore, making the decision to include the environmental performance programs in the company's strategy is the outcome of complex decisions that is influenced by many factors within and outside of the hospitality industry (Lülfs & Hahn, 2015). Environmental performance programs contain the organizational and technical activities take on by the company for the purpose of decreasing environmental effects and lessening their impacts on the natural environment (Cramer, 1998).

One of the organizational activities that has a significant impact on company's operations and performance (both financial and environmental performance) is human resource management (HRM). According to Rani and Mishra (2014), many scholars in the field of HRM believe that the success of innovation management and strategy of a company depends on the quality of facilities and human resources. It has been reported that HRM practices influence individuals and companies to switch their forms of thinking and behaviour into environmental approaches. Therefore, HRM will support to cope with the issues of environmental change over transformative learning and knowledge-sharing (McGuire & Garavan, 2010). Furthermore, Boselie, Paauwe and Jansen (2001) demonstrated that accessibility and ability of human resources engaged in the strategic conducts, called green HRM, is essential to become more competitive in the hospitality industry. Green HRM involves practices that encourage every employee to support environmental activities, and improve employee's commitment and response to environmental issues (Rani & Mishra, 2014). Therefore, green initiatives in the HRM become part of environmental performance programs. It is believed that green HRM practices will bring many benefits to the hospitality industry, such as increased customer loyalty, reduced turnover rate from employees, being a leader in the industry and gaining competitive advantage, improved image and brand value, and compliance to regulations (Graci & Kuehnel, 2010).

Research Motivation

With increasing pressure from stakeholders and concerns about environmental issues, companies develop policies and programs to conduct environmentally sustainable business activities and act in accordance with the environmental regulations (Yadav et al., 2015). Hospitality industry is one of the sectors largely affecting the environment. Hospitality industry is one of the main compositions of the tourism industry and the impact of the tourism industry on the hospitality industry is very important as incomes generated from international tourists in 2014 were US$ 1,245 billion. Furthermore, United Nations World Tourism Organization reported (Tourism & Unwto, 2015), in 2014, the revenue from hospitality industry achieved US$ 1,245 billion (Euro 937 billion). This trend has kept growing, and the number of international tourist arrivals was grew between 3 per cent and 4 per cent in 2015, and in Asia Pacific by +4 per cent to +5 per cent (Tourism & Unwto, 2015).

In Malaysia, the hospitality industry is a result of the rapid pace of tourism industry as in 2007, the total number of foreign tourists who visited Malaysia were more than 20 million (Arokiasamy, 2013) and the revenue was RM 46.1 billion. Additionally, in 2009, the tourism industry contributed RM 36.9 billion to the gross national income (GNI), and this makes it among the five largest industries in Malaysia other than oil, gas, and energy; wholesale and retail trade; financial services and palm oil. Besides, the hospitality industry has contributed several benefits to the national economy such as employment opportunities and it complements the growth of the tourism industry in Malaysia (Awang et al., 2008). Hence, the Malaysian government is willing to expanding the hospitality industry.

On the other hand, the hospitality industry consumes valued raw materials such as energy, water, wood, food and plastics as well as produced numeral of unwanted emissions, for instance chlorofluorocarbons (CFCs), carbon dioxide (CO2), smells, smoke, and noise along with the industry wastes such as water, energy, food and packaging (Kirk, 1995; Nabiha, George, Abdul Wahid, Amran, Abustan & Mahadi, 2011). Furthermore, there are three main areas of hospitality industry's environmental impact; water, energy, and waste (Graci & Kuehnel, 2010). According to night Gössling, Peeters, Ceron, Dubois, Patterson and Richardson (2005), the hospitality industry uses an excessive energy; 130 Megajoules per bed per night in a hotel and releases an average 20.6 kg of CO2 per hotel per night. Therefore, this situation has caused energy consumption by this industry annually is US$3.7 billion (Bruns-smith, Choy, Chong & Verma, 2015). Then again, in the hospitality industry, the generation of waste is undeniably the ultimate obvious outcome from this industry on the environment as estimated at least 1 kg of waste is generated per day per customer (Bohdanowicz, 2005).

In term of the water impact, 218 gallons of water per room per day usage of water in a typical hotel (Bruns-smith et al., 2015). Additionally, the average water consumption in Malaysia's hotel industry, especially in hotels more than 200 rooms, the average water consumption is 5,250,000 to 9,750,000 litres per month (Tang, 2012). This indicator rate as "very poor" according to the standard agreed by International Tourism Partnership (Tang, 2012). Hence, extreme water usag by hotel industry has been claimed as a cause of water usage conflicts globally (Kasim, 2007). Therefore, due to the massive number of environmental issues as discussed above that hospitality industry has encountered, there is increasing the force to pay a correct reaction to environmental issues (Erdogan & Baris, 2007). Consequently, the hospitality industry has an important role in protecting the environment and established the environmental programs to create awareness about the importance of protecting the environment.

As regard to the environmental performance programs, green HRM practices become one of the significant programs because this environmental performance program refers to the effort of the company in converting normal employees into green employees by entire activities involved in the development, execution and on-going maintenance of a system, later, to end create an important impact on environmental sustainability (Opatha & Arulrajah, 2014). However, before the company in the hospitality industry engage with green HRM practices, there is need to identify what are the predictors behind the adoption of green HRM practices that have an influence on environmental and financial performance in the hospitality industry. All these predictors determined the companies' reaction to societal expectation by implementing or increasing environmental performance programs and reporting their performance (Herremans, Herschovis, & Bertels, 2009).

With regard to these factors, DiMaggio and Powell (1991) identified institutional pressures that lead to structural similarity and homogenisation in management practices, and this institutional pressure contains three main pressures; coercive, mimetic and normative. Furthermore, Resource Based View (RBV) theory also emphasized that to satisfy the stakeholders' pressure and market rivalry can be determined by company's capabilities and internal resources (Barney, 1991). In term of the adoption of green HRM practices that lead to the environmental and financial performance in the hospitality industry, these two theories will be able to explain further the predictor behind this adoption from the context of internal and external perspective of a company (Sharma, 2000; Dolores Lopez-Gamero, Claver-Cortes, & Francisco Molina-Azorin, 2011). Take into account these two internal and external factors, companies in the hospitality industry have better opportunities to develop and enhance their environmental performance programs (Dolores Lopez-Gamero et al., 2011). Therefore, it is important to identify the external factor (normative pressures) and internal factor (manager's environmental concerns) that expedite the adoption of green HRM practices in the hospitality industry.

The purpose of this chapter is to provide a fundamental understanding of normative pressure and managers' environmental concerns as predictors of green HRM adoption in the hospitality industry that lead to their sustainability in terms of environmental and financial performance. Specifically, the chapter attempts to answer the following interrelated questions:

1. What is the importance of normative pressure in the hospitality industry?
2. How does manager's environmental concern influence the adoption of environmental performance programs in the hospitality industry?
3. What are green HRM practices and are they important to the environmental and financial performance across the hospitality industry?
4. What is the relationship between green HRM and organization sustainability in terms of environmental and financial performance across the hospitality industry?

Methodology

To achieve the stated objectives and answer the research questions, a systematic review of literature was conducted by using an archival method. This research is grounded on a solid theoretical framework combined the secondary data. This study employs a methodology to review the articles cited in the databases such as Taylor and Francis Online, Sage, ScienceDirect, Springerlink, Emerald, Wiley Online Library and JSTOR with the current topic of green HRM practices, normative pressure and hospitality industry, manager's environmental concerns and hospitality industry, environmental performance and hospitality industry, financial performance and hospitality industry. The secondary data analysis of current literature was studied in order to construct a solid theoretical structure as a foundation for this study (Harkonen, 2012).

Underlying Theories

This study uses Institutional Theory to identify the external predictors that stimulate a company in the hospitality industry to engage with environmental performance program; green HRM and whether this green HRM practices enhance the environmental performance and financial performance in Malaysia's hospitality industry. As regard to the environmental issues, especially in the critical industry such as the hospitality industry, institutional theory is had been expending to investigate the systems covering as of "micro interpersonal interactions to macro global frameworks" (Scott, 2004, p.2). Hence, institutional theory determined how social options are shaped, intervened and directed by the institutional environment (Hoffman, 1999). According to DiMaggio and Powell (1983), there are three pressures in institutional setting that build and diffuse a collective set of norms, values, and rules to create alike structures and practices across companies sharing an organizational field; mimetic, coercive and normative.

On the other hand, Scott (2008) argued that the external forces in the institutional theory encourage companies to accomplish alike strategic actions. As mentioned by DiMaggio and Powell (1983), companies sharing the same environment will employ alike practices over legitimate motives and hence turn into "isomorphic" with each other (Dacin et al., 2008). Furthermore, in general, institutional theory shows how companies behave and react not merely to market forces but also to the pressure of formal and informal institutions such as regulatory agencies; domestic or international, the action of the leading companies and from the general social expectations (Greenwood & Hinings, 1996).

In the hospitality industry, the institutional perspective proposes that companies may perhaps search for social endorsement or ''legitimacy'' over conformity by the ''isomorphic'' pressures from stakeholders to be environmentally responsible, specifically in ambiguous and unsteady circumstances (Shah, 2011). The hospitality industry is characterized by direct customer interface and high visibility, therefore, their survival be determined by their perceived legitimacy relative to the institutional anticipations in which they operate (Davidsson, Klofsten, & Hunter, 2006). Therefore, the green HRM practices possibly will build such legitimacy using outlining a set of main beliefs to guide a company and provided that a standard for continuous improvement (Azzone & Noci, 1996). In addition, by implementing the green HRM practices possibly will damp down coercive pressures put forth by regulators; normative pressures (stakeholders pressure) from NGOs and local communities and who can openly humiliate hospitality industry; and mimetic pressures from industry peers and hotel associations who are environmentally concern market leaders (Shah, 2011). Other study by Jennings and Zandbergen (1995) on ecologically sustainable companies, found that institutional pressures; coercive (regulatory), mimetic (competitor) and normative (customer) are the significant drivers of company sustainability.

Therefore, the conceptual framework of this study is based on one of institutional pressures; normative pressures. As stated by DiMaggio and Powell (1983), normative pressures are represented by the pressures from professionalization, which socializes stakeholder from the external and internal of the company to view certain types of process and structure as legitimate. Therefore, this study analyse the pressure from stakeholders encourage the hospitality industry to engage with green HRM and lead to the environmental performance.

The other significant factors that stimulate the companies to adopt the green HRM practices that lead to environmental performance is the manager's environmental concerns. For that reason, this study focus on the factors of the sufficient resources help the hospitality industry to engage those green HRM practices to build the environmental performance programs in Malaysia's hospitality industry. this study uses the Resource Based View (RBV) theory as a fundamental behind the adoption of green HRM practices in the Malaysia's hospitality industry. According to Barney (1991), the resources of company can be categorized into three types; that is human capital resources, physical capital resources, and organizational resources. As regard to RBV theory by Barney (1991), this study emphasizes on human capital resources as internal predictors of the green HRM practices adoption in Malaysia's hospitality industry to enhance its environmental performance. Barney (1991, pp.101) stated that "human capital resources include the training, experience, judgment, intelligence, relationships and insight of individual managers and workers in a firm". Accordingly, this chapter focuses on individual manager's experience, judgement, and insight towards environmental issues as the effective delivery environmental performance that depends on employees' responsiveness (Bansal & Roth, 2000).

Review of Literature

Hospitality Industry

Since 1950, global tourism industry keeps growing every year with the global tourist visited the foreign countries have improved by 6.5 percent in 2007 (Zein, Wazner Semlali, & Meylan, 2008). Therefore, as tourism industry keeps increasing, hospitality industry also facing the same phenomena; globally the hospitality industry has over 300,000 facilities and lodging to partially of international and national tourists, and in Europe alone, 160 to 200 million international tourists per year (Paulina Bohdanowicz, Simanic, & Martinac, 2005). Thus, currently, tourism industry represents 35 percent of the world's service industry and over 70 percent in several developing countries (Zein et al., 2008).

In the context of Malaysia, the total number of foreign tourists who visited Malaysia were more than 20 million in 2007 as the revenue was RM46.1 billion (Arokiasamy, 2013). Additionally, the tourism industry contributed RM36.9 billion to the gross national income (GNI) in 2009, therefore, tourism industry is the five largest industries in Malaysia other than oil, gas and energy; wholesale and retail trade; financial services and palm oil (Inside Malaysia, 2012). In 2012, Tourism and Hospitality Report stated that the tourism industry is the third largest source of Malaysia's revenue derived from foreign exchange, and in 2010, 24.6 million tourists visited Malaysia, making Malaysia the ninth most visited in the world, with the majority of tourists from China and India (Inside Malaysia, 2012).

Consequently, the hospitality industry is a result of the rapid pace of tourism industry in Malaysia, as tourism industry becomes backbone to the hospitality industry in Malaysia as well as one of the contributor of the country's GDP in term of service sector, which is 50 percent of GDP (Awang et al., 2008). In addition, hospitality industry in Malaysia has contributed a lot of advantages to the national economy such as employment opportunities and support the growth of secondary activities such as suppliers of materials and equipment, (Awang et al., 2008). In line with the potential prospect of the hospitality industry in the emergent of the service industry, Malaysian government is keen to expanding the tourism industry (Arokiasamy, 2013).

Environmental Performance

Presently, many companies in most of the industries are executing a proactive and strategic environmental performance programs to gain competitive advantage (Rodríguez-Antón, del Mar Alonso-Almeida, Celemín, & Rubio, 2012). End to end with this trend of environmental concerns, the hospitality industry has focused increasing interest in environmental performance programs (Kang, Lee, & Huh, 2010). Moreover, environmental performance in the hospitality industry led to the quite a lot of benefits for instance more well-organized business practices, operational cost savings, increasing image, comply with the regulations, and improved competitiveness (Quazi, 1999). On the other hand, the implementation of environmental performance programs supports several industries in term of activities such as reducing their emissions, reduce their hazardous waste, reduce their greenhouse gasses and decreases their solid waste (Daily et al., 2012). Therefore, numerous companies in the hospitality industry manage to execute the environmental performance programs to achieve environmental performance due to the awareness of the environmental issues (Mensah, 2006).

Then again, a broad range of corporate stakeholders such as shareholders, consumers, creditors, regulators, investors, employees and public more aware and keep stress on the environmental performance of the company (Ilinitch, Soderstrom &Thomas, 1998). Furthermore, type of service and product offered were the key influence behind the environmental performance as the impacts of these services and products on environmental will affect the company's environmental risk (Epstein & Roy, 1998). Therefore, the efforts and commitment of the company to protect the environment can be seen through the output of environmental performance (Gadenne et al., 2009). To meet the increased response for environmental performance information in company from all those stakeholders, government, supervisory body groups, entrepreneurs, and companies themselves have established a variety of measures that include the several basics of environmental performance (Ilinitch et al., 1998). In addition, many measurement systems were introduced for instance, the corporate environmental scorecard, environmental rating matrices and corporate environmental reports by the companies (Ilinitch et al., 1998).

A study by Milliman & Clair (1996) discussed there are numerous methods that can be used to measure environmental performance. It involves of adopting corporate-wide metrics for measuring resource acquisition, usage and waste; executing information systems to track resource movements; and conducting field audits to make available opportunities for employees to identify problems while gaining information and response about the environmental performance of the company. Besides, environmental performance can be measured by a set of indicators such as low environmental emissions, pollution prevention, waste minimization and recycling activities (Lober, 1996). In addition, it can also be improved by the implementation of EMS such as ISO 14001 certification, a tool that requires high interaction between HRM and environmental management (Brio, Fernandez, & Junquera, 2007).

Green Human Resource Management Practices

According to Arulrajah, Opatha and Nawaratne (2015) HRM practices are the actual human resource techniques, processes and programs that performed in the company. Likewise, green HRM practices are the techniques, processes and programs that get performed in the company to reduce negative environmental impacts or rise positive environmental impacts of the company (Arulrajah et al., 2015). Furthermore, conventional HRM practices for instance recruitment and selection, training and development, performance appraisal and compensation generally known as essential to the achievement of proactive environmental performance programs, nevertheless, HRM practices have to deliver the competences required for the continuous improvement of the company's environmental performance (Jabbour & Santos, 2008) for instance green recruitment and selection, green training and development, green performance appraisal and green compensation (Opatha & Arulrajah, 2014).

Besides, green HRM practices is diverse from conventional HRM because it has unique characteristics (Fayyazi, Shahbazmoradi, Afshar, & Shahbazmoradi, 2015). Green HRM practices involve the investment of people who are concerned in environmental issues (Renwick, Redman, & Maguire, 2013a) while conventional HRM practices emphasis on great performance workplaces, talent management and knowledge management and for the company's success (Davidson, Mcphail, & Barry, 2011). Hence, green HRM can be demarcated as portion of the sustainable human resource management to deal with the requirements related with environmental sustainability. Also, green HRM is a subset of sustainable human resource management; also, a part of corporate social responsibility (CSR) (Wagner, 2013). In addition, Mampra (2013) stated green HRM is the practice of HRM policies to reassure the sustainable use of resources in business and encouraging ecological aspects that will continue to expand morale and employee satisfaction.

With regards to the environmental issues, companies highly focus on the integration of a company's corporate strategy by establishing green HRM practices into their environmental performance (Marcus & Fremeth, 2009). The extant literature shows that there has been a growing attention on green accounting, green marketing and green management. However, research on green HRM is relatively fractional and diverse (Renwick, Redman, & Maguire, 2013b). Additionally, as mentioned earlier, green HRM practices are innovative management techniques since the "green" concept is embedded in the field of human resource management. Thus, it is defined as systems, policies and practices that encourage employees in companies to implement green practices which can result in positive outcomes for the society, environment, individuals, and businesses (Opatha & Arulrajah, 2014). Furthermore, Zoogah (2011) defined green HRM as the use of policies, philosophies, and practices of HRM to promote the use of sustainable business and prevent any unintended harm that may arise out of environmental concerns in the company.

Based on some evidences, environmental friendly HR initiatives increase employees' engagement, reduce costs, and enhance efficiency. Additionally, HR initiatives help companies to reduce carbon footprint of employees by car-pooling, job-sharing, teleconferencing and online interviews, virtual training, and recycling (Mandip, 2012). With regards to these initiatives, green HRM practices must be implemented into HR practices. For example, as recruitment and selection; training and development; performance management and appraisal; pay and reward system; employee involvement and others, are the practices that should be carried out by a company to form green HRM through HR processes (Mandip, 2012). Overall, this chapter defines green HR as the use of policies, philosophies, and practices of HR (recruitment and selection, training and development, performance management and appraisal, pay and reward systems, and employee involvement) to promote the use of sustainable business. This is beneficial to the society, environment, individuals, and businesses, which is in line with conceptualizations proposed by Opatha and Arulrajah (2014), and Mandip (2012).

On the other hand, an analytical focus on the relationship between the green HRM practices and environmental performance in Malaysia's hospitality industry is still lacking as green HRM practices still at emerging stage in Malaysia and gain minor attention (Aragon-Correa et al., 2015). Alternatively, most of the current research is focused on analyzing the possible relationship between environmental performance programs and company performance. For instance, Guerci, Longoni, and Luzzini (2015) found that green training and involvement are significantly positive to environmental performance; green performance and compensation are significantly positive to environmental performance; and green hiring is not significantly positive to environmental performance. A study by Jabbour (2011) suggested recruitment and selection and financial reward should be incorporated into the green HRM practices to support environmental performance. A different study by Jabbar and Abid (2014) found that green rewards positively impact the employee motivation towards eco-initiatives. Based on above empirical evidences, the hospitality industry needs to engage with green HRM practices in order to response to the stakeholder pressures and gain competitive advantage. Other industries for example manufacturing, small and medium industry, oil industry and health and community services industry are now engaged with green HRM practices, and they recognized that green HRM practices at the workplace possibly will promote social responsibilities among employees and help to retain top talent (Sawang & Kivits, 2015; Jose et al., 2015; Yusoff, Othman, Fernando, & Amran, 2015).

Normative Pressure in Hospitality Industry

This study has adapted institutional theory because as suggested by Bansal (2005), companies need to take basic necessities of national institutions into account in order to remain competitive. This allows companies to obtain a "license to operate" and gain legitimacy through external agents. In the context of hospitality industry, management characteristics namely trust, norms, values, attitude of the owner / manager, and the mental model have been proven to influence companies' strategic choices and behaviours (Banerjee, 2002; Hambrick, 2007). Roxas and Coetzer (2012) pointed out that if the owner / manager of a company perceives institutional environment is supportive of the environmental performance programs, they would be more willing to develop a positive attitude towards issues and concerns of natural environment.

As stated by Scott (2008), institutional level analysis consists of three pillars such as: normative, mimetic, and coercive. However, to determine the institutional level that leads to green HRM practices in the hospitality industry, this study concentrates on one institutional pressure which is normative pressure. Furthermore, as mentioned by Dacin et al. (2008), normative pressure is the main national pressure that evidently describes how different countries regard and react to environmental. Normative pressure reflects cultural values, beliefs, and objectives of the public that define legitimacy of the presented organizational behaviour (Kostova & Roth, 2002). According to DiMaggio and Powell (1983), normative pressure refers to internal and external stakeholders' view about whether certain types of process and structure of companies are legitimate. As such, this study analyses stakeholders' pressure (external factor) that encourages hospitality industry's engagement with green HRM leading to environmental performance.

Normative pressure consists of "social norms, values, beliefs and assumptions about human nature and human behaviour that are socially shared and carried by individuals" (Kostova, 1997, p. 180). According to Marcus and Fremeth (2009), environmental sustainability is absolutely mandatory for a company from the perspective of normative pressure. It is believed that those people who are seriously worried about environmental issues entirely motivate their agents (government, non-governmental organization (NGO), organizations, suppliers, and other stakeholders) to become more responsive towards environmental issues (Aguilera-Caracuel & Ortiz-de-Mandojana, 2013). With the increase in awareness about environmental issues, many stakeholders such as consumers and NGOs expect companies to speed up implementation of environmental performance programs (Brockhoff, Chakrabarti, & Kirchgeorg, 1999).

These stakeholders would force companies to follow the standards and laws of environmental protections (Carmona-Moreno, Céspedes-Lorente, & De Burgos-Jiménez, 2004). Thus, environmental pressure is the best way for companies to enhance their operational efficiency, design new products and services, improve their corporate image, and become competitive (Taylor, 1992).

Suppliers and customers are the most expected groups to persuade hospitality industry owners on the economic impact of environmental-friendly activities (Williamson, Lynch-Wood & Ramsay, 2006). Thus, customers can have a direct economic impact on the business through their expenditure. However, suppliers can spread the knowledge of enhanced environmental practices in the industry (Gadenne et al., 2009). Supporting environmental activities, and having environmental performance programs are compulsory in producing products upon customers' request (Day & Cai, 2012). According to Kirk (1995), many hospitality industry owners react to the pressure from customers and society. The present trend shows that customers are more concerned with the environment. Therefore, they choose green hotel and eco destination. If the hospitality industry fails to embrace this new trend, it may lose its prospective customers (Butler, 2008).

Given stakeholders' pressure, the hospitality industry needs to react to the environmental issues by engaging in the environmental performance programs such as green HRM that can lead to environmental performance. Therefore, pressure from stakeholders is one of the factors that encourage the hospitality industry to be engaged in green HRM resulting in the environmental performance. Therefore, it is proposed that:

Proposition 1: Normative pressure positively influences the adoption of Green HRM practices.

Manager's Environmental Concerns

This chapter uses RBV Theory as a fundamental theory to explain the internal predictor of green HRM adoption to enhance the environmental performance of the hospitality industry. According to RBV theory, companies' ability in facing environmental concerns from their stakeholders and market rivalry depends on their internal resources (Barney, 1991). In addition, Barney (1991) also identified the resources that could be categorized into three types; human capital resources, physical capital resources, and organizational resources. A study on the green practice adoption by Lee et al. (2012) revealed that there is a need to consider physical capital resources (i.e. company infrastructure and its location), human capital resources (i.e. top management commitment, teamwork, and flexibility), and organizational capital resources (i.e. organizational structure, organizational culture, and organizational policies). According to Barney (1991) this strategy (RBV) can exploit environmental opportunities and minimize outside threats by maximizing internal strength that can lead to reducing company's weaknesses. Hence, the paradigm theory has the potential to be applied in the context of environmental issues. Since green HRM practices require use of unique and different resources to achieve competitive advantage (which derives from the use of environmentally friendly practices), it can increase company's performance (Sharma & Aragòn-Correa, 2007).

Barney (1991, pp.101) stated that "human capital resources include the training, experience, judgment, intelligence, relationships and insight of individual managers and workers in a firm". Accordingly, this chapter focuses on individual manager's experience, judgement, and insight towards environmental issues as the effective delivery environmental performance that depends on employees' responsiveness (Bansal & Roth, 2000). However, this chapter summarizes individual manager's experience, judgement, and insight towards the environmental issues as managers' environmental concerns. Gill, Crosby and Taylor (1986) defined environmental concerns as a common attitude related to a person's behavioural intentions.

A number of earlier studies have established a positive relationship between environmental concerns and pro-environmental behaviour and intentions (Pierce, Lovrich, & Dalton, 2000; Stern, Dietz, & Kalof, 1993). Based on a study of environmental education, Pooley and O'Connor (2000) indicated positive relationship between environmental behaviour and environmental attitude. Therefore, environmental knowledge, concern, and awareness are the most important factors to enhance ecological behaviour among employees. As highlighted by Bohdanowicz (2005), managers who are responsible for an aspect of the environmental issues have the chance to enhance their companies' commitment. Managers can significantly encourage and influence their companies' commitment through their concerns towards environmental impacts. This depends on the opportunity of gaining competitiveness by environmental performance programs (Miles & Covin, 2000). Furthermore, Bansal and Roth (2000) pointed out individual concern is the major motivation for environmental responsiveness.

According to Ajzen and Fishbein (1980), an individual's beliefs and attitudes about environmental performance programs as an ethical issue could be the major factor contributing to individual's behaviour. Therefore, people who are concerned with environmental issues and impact of their business on the environment would be more likely to reduce the impact of their business activities (Gadenne et al., 2009). Based on a study by Chan et al. (2014), environmental concern, environmental awareness, and environmental knowledge are the significant factors for employees in the hospitality industry to implement green practices. Hence, hospitality industry might select to implement environmental performance programs regardless of the need for complying with the regulations or increasing their return. In the hospitality industry, hotel managers' attitude towards change and environment and their knowledge about the main output of the environmental performance are considered as the main drivers of environmental concerns (Erdogan & Baris, 2007). It was shown in a study by Chan et al. (2014) that managers need to boost their own and individuals' ecological behaviour to implement the favourable environmental programs in the hospitality industry. To establish the ecological behaviour, managers must have environmental awareness, concern and knowledge, as well as understanding of the entire system (Chan & Hawkins, 2010).

Top management should design the hiring and selection process by selecting people with good environmental concern, knowledge, awareness, and behaviour. Constant environmental training to hotel staff could be a potential resolution to enhance environmental image and performance in a hospitality industry (Chan et al., 2014). Moreover, Day and Cai (2012) mentioned that for implementing green activities and environmental performance programs, participation and support from managers and staffs is necessary. Therefore, the success of these activities depends on the belief systems, importance of environmental protection, and readiness for adoption of environmental behaviours. However, environmental concern is not prevalent feature of every single individual. As mentioned by Barney (1991), it is rather gained through experience, judgment, intelligence, relationships, and insight towards the environment. Thus, managers' environmental concern is a crucial factor in implementing green HRM practices as an environmental performance programs in the hospitality industry. Therefore, we propose that:

Proposition 2: Managers' environmental concern positively influences the adoption of green HRM practices.

Green HRM Practices, Environmental Performance and Financial Performance

The importance of HRM in the implementation of a company's environmental programs has generated universal agreement (e.g. Jabbour & Santos, 2008; Teixeira, Jabbour, & Jabbour, 2012; José, Jabbour, Beatriz, & Sousa, 2015). However, the developments are still disintegrating (Aragon-Correa, Martin-Tapia, & de la Torre-Ruiz, 2015) since some studies have analysed the implication of environmental strategy in specific HRM practices including learning, perception, training, performance work system, and employee motivation strategies (Aragon-Correa et al., 2015).

Since environmental concerns were not a significant cost factor in the past, green HRM was not considered important compared to the present time. However, by emphasizing strict regulations, many companies began to adopt the environmental performance programs (Wagner, 2014). It has been reported that HR functions had limited roles in addressing the issue because its contribution to value creation for companies was not clear (Wagner, 2014). According to Christmann (1999), green HRM has become more prevalent when companies started improving their environmental performance and contending for the best talents with skilled labour shortage. In addition, employees have become progressively more concerned with environmental issues. Therefore, they demand employers to integrate corporate social responsibility concerns in companies' activities (Crane, Matten, & Moon, 2008). Paillé, Chen, Boiral, and Jin (2013) identified environmental performance as the reflection of outcome when companies are dedicated to protecting the natural environment.

A wide range of business stakeholders such as employees, shareholders, creditors, investors, consumers, regulators, and public are further conscious and put pressure on companies' environmental performance (Ilinitch, Soderstrom & Thomas, 1998). This is because the environmental impacts of services and products offered by companies can have an affect companies' environmental risk (Epstein & Roy, 1998). As a result, companies' commitments and efforts to protect the environment can be seen over the output of environmental performance (Gadenne et al., 2009). Several measurement systems were introduced by the companies namely; the corporate environmental scorecard, environmental rating matrices, and corporate environmental reports (Ilinitch et al., 1998). There are also a number of methods that can be used to measure companies' environmental performance. Some of these measures include, (a) implementing corporate-wide metrics for determining resource acquirement, usage and waste; (b) performing information systems to track resource activities; and (c) conducting ground audits to make accessible opportunities for employees to recognize problems while gaining data and reaction towards companies' environmental performance (Milliman & Clair, 1996).

According to Banerjee (2002), environmental performance has been also evaluated using assessing the attitudes, beliefs and values. Jabbour and Santos (2008) measured environmental performance using the right HRM practices at every phase of the manufacturing processes. In addition, environmental performance has been assessed via measuring the beliefs, values, and attitudes of the company members (Banerjee, 2002). In a study by Jabbour and Santos, (2008), environmental performance was assessed through the use of appropriate HRM practices at each stage of the manufacturing processes. There are several studies that have confirmed HRM practices play significant roles in managing environmental performance programs (Jabbour & Santos, 2008; Jose et al., 2015; and Teixeira et al., 2012). As such, green HRM practices (recruitment and selection, training and development, performance management and appraisal, pay and reward systems, and employee involvement) are considered as vital to improve companies' environmental performance. Hence, it is proposed that:

Proposition 3: Green human resource management practices positively influence the environmental performance.

When companies decide to implement environmental performance programs, they do not merely focus on the ethical and social values in the implementation of these programs but rather they ensure their financial growth (Molina-Azorín, Claver-Cortés, López-Gamero, & Tarí, 2009). Therefore, Bansal and Gao (2006) highlighted that environmental performance program is one of the significant factors affecting quality of life, environmental sustainability, and financial growth. Given stakeholders' pressure on reducing companies' harmful impacts on the environment and society, implementation of any environmental performance programs is an integral part of company activities (Molina-Azorín et al., 2009). Companies could enhance their financial benefits by preventing pollutant activities (one of the components of the environmental performance programs), because these activities might help companies especially the hospitality industry to save costs, energy, and water consumption (Bruns-smith et al., 2015). As such, by implementing environmental performance programs, not only consumers' environmental concerns would be met, but also companies could increase their sales (Aguilera-Caracuel & Ortiz-de-Mandojana, 2013).

Companies in the hospitality industry can increase their financial benefit by embedding green HRM practices as one of the environmental performance programs into their company's strategy and culture. This would lead to providing competitive advantages for companies in term of delivering environmental capabilities (Russo & Fouts, 1997). Mehta and Chugan (2015) pointed out that green HRM practices could have economic impact on companies since these practices increase the sales. Good environmental performance management can also reduce costs and improve sales. Therefore, this study proposes that:

Proposition 4: Green human resource management practices positively influence the financial performance.

Proposed Framework

Based on the above discussion, this chapter proposes a conceptual framework as depicted in Figure 1.

DISCUSSION

In the Corporate Social Performance model by Wood (1991), she stated that the motivation for a company's environmental performance programs might stem from the principle of legislation for the institutional level. In addition, according to Williamson (1998), the institutional environments perspective

Figure 1. Conceptual framework

of a company was shaped by stakeholders' pressure and exogenous regulative. In addition, using institutional theory as a reference as mentioned by Bansal (2005), to remain competitive, companies need to take into account the basic national institutions necessities to permit the companies obtain a "license to operate" and also gain legitimacy through external agents. According to DiMaggio and Powell (1983), institutional pressures driven by legitimacy motives, therefore, company that sharing the same environment will engage with similar practices with the other company in the industry. It has been reported that the increasing awareness of environmental performance programs among companies and managers in line with the market pressure and growing number of environmental laws and policies (Jones, Hillier, & Comfort, 2014). Furthermore, Kesidou and Demirel (2012) claims that stringent regulation is the top influence on the progresses of environmental performance program; green HRM practices. In line with this, we assume that companies can use green HRM practices for responding to stakeholder pressures on environmental issues.

On the other hand, awareness of environmental performance programs among companies and managers is increasing due to the pressure of the market and increase the number of environmental laws (Jones et al., 2014). Therefore, to implement the environmental performance programs in a company is depends on manager's concern (Bansal and Roth, 2000). Manager with highly environmental concern because of their knowledge towards the environmental issues usually will show the environmental responsiveness behaviour (Mostafa, 2006). Consequently, environmental concern among the managers play an important role in establishing environmental performance programs (Gill et al., 1986). Jose et al. (2015) concludes that to establish green HRM practices in a company, HR manager's concern on environmental issues and their behaviour towards the environmental performance programs is very crucial.

CONCLUDING REMARKS

This chapter seeks to provide an expanded understanding about factors that stimulate a company in the hospitality industry to practice green HRM which could result in sustainability in terms of improved environmental and economic performance. This included focusing on green HRM in terms of external and internal pressures, and establishing a better insight on how green HRM can enhance hospitality environmental performance. Environmental issues in hospitality industry deserve further consideration since they are getting more extreme and widespread through increase in industrial and human activities.

Several multidisciplinary literatures are concentrated on the relationship between company's environmental management and natural environmental protection (Shwom, 2009). However, the current study shed some light on the external and internal pressure of the adoption of environmental performance programs (green HRM) by using Institutional Theory and Resource Based Theory. Therefore, this chapter provides fresh insights on the factors that can improve development of green HRM practices since there are limited studies in the extant literature on green HRM in the hospitality industry (Moorthy, Yacob, Chelliah & Arokiasamy, 2012).

FUTURE RESEARCH DIRECTION

This research has proposed a model for understanding the predictors of green human resource management which can result in improved environmental and financial performance across hospitality industry based on the perspective of external pressure (i.e. normative) and internal pressure (manager's environmental concerns). In addition, the chapter examines the antecedents of sustainability in the hospitality industry in terms of improved financial and environmental performance. There exist many different antecedents of sustainability in the hospitality industry such as stakeholder pressures, organization's resources and organizational environmental culture. This chapter has identified the 2 main antecedents that place pressure on companies to implement the green HRM practices to achieve environmental and financial performance. Therefore, the chapter proposes this model as a starting point for future empirical research to enhance the environmental and financial performance in the hospitality industry.

REFERENCES

Aguilera-Caracuel, J., & Ortiz-de-Mandojana, N. (2013). Green Innovation and Financial Performance: An Institutional Approach. *Organization & Environment*, *26*(4), 365–385. https://doi.org/10.1177/1086026613507931 doi:10.1177/1086026613507931

Ajzen, I., & Fishbein, M. (1980). *Understanding attitudes and predicting social behavior.* Englewood Cliffs, NJ: Prentice Hall.

Aragon-Correa, J. A., Martin-Tapia, I., & de la Torre-Ruiz, J. (2015). Sustainability issues and hospitality and tourism firms strategies. *International Journal of Contemporary Hospitality Management*, *27*(3), 498–522. doi:10.1108/IJCHM-11-2014-0564

Arokiasamy, A. R. a. (2013). *A Study on Employee Satisfaction Perspectives in the Hotel*. Academic Press.

Arulrajah, A. A., Opatha, H. H. D. N., & Nawaratne, N. N. (2015). *Green Human Resource Management Practices: A Review Literature Review on Green HRM Practices*. Academic Press.

Awang, K. W., Ishak, N. O. R. K., Radzi, S. M., & Taha, A. Z. (2008). Environmental Variables and Performance : Evidence from the Hotel Industry in Malaysia. *International Journal of Economics and Management*, *2*, 59–79.

Azzone, G., & Noci, G. (1996). Measuring the environmental performance of new products: an integrated approach. *International Journal of Production Research*, *34*(11), 3055–3078. https://doi.org/10.1080/00207549608905077

Banerjee, S. B. (2002). Corporate environmentalism: The construct and its measurement. *Journal of Business Research*, *55*(3), 177–191. doi:10.1016/S0148-2963(00)00135-1

Bansal, P., & Roth, K. (2000). Why Companies Go Green: A model of Ecological Responsiveness. *Academy of Management*, *43*(4), 717–736. https://doi.org/10.2307/1556363

Bansal, P. (2005). Evolving sustainably: A longitudinal study of corporate sustainable development. *Strategic Management Journal, 26*(3), 197–218. doi:10.1002/smj.441

Bansal, P., & Gao, J. (2006). Building the Future by Looking to the Past: Examining Research Published on Organizations and Environment. *Organization & Environment, 19*(4), 458–478. doi:10.1177/1086026606294957

Barney, J. (1991). Firm Resources and Sustained Competitive Advantage. *Journal of Management, 17*(1), 99–120. doi:10.1177/014920639101700108

Bohdanowicz, P. (2005). European Hoteliers Environmental Attitudes: Greening the Business. *The Cornell Hotel and Restaurant Administration Quarterly, 46*(2), 188–204. https://doi.org/10.1177/0010880404273891 doi:10.1177/0010880404273891

Bohdanowicz, P., Simanic, B., & Martinac, I. (2005). Article. *Sustainable Hotels, 2005*(September), 1–8.

Boselie, P., Paauwe, J., & Jansen, P. (2001). Human resource management and performance: Lessons from the Netherlands. *International Journal of Human Resource Management, 12*(7), 1107–1125. doi:10.1080/09585190110068331

Brockhoff, K., Chakrabarti, A. K., & Kirchgeorg, M. (1999, July). *Corporate Strategies in Environmental Management. Research-Technology Management.*

Bruns-smith, A., Choy, V., Chong, H., Ph, D., Verma, R., & Ph, D. (2015). Cornell Hospitality Report Cornell Hospitality Report Environmental Sustainability in the Hospitality Industry: Best practices. *Guest Participation, and Customer Satisfaction, 15*(March), 6–16.

Butler, J. (2008). The Compelling Hard Case for Green Hotel Development. *Cornell Hospitality Quarterly, 49*(3), 234–244. doi:10.1177/1938965508322174

Carmona-Moreno, E., Céspedes-Lorente, J., & De Burgos-Jiménez, J. (2004). Environmental strategies in spanish hotels: Contextual factors and performance. *Service Industries Journal, 24*(3), 101–130. doi:10.1080/0264206042000247786

Chan, E. S. W., & Hawkins Rebecca, R. (2010). Attitude towards EMSs in an international hotel: An exploratory case study. *International Journal of Hospitality Management, 29*(4), 641–651. doi:10.1016/j.ijhm.2009.12.002

Chan, E. S. W., Hon, A. H. Y., Chan, W., & Okumus, F. (2014). What drives employees intentions to implement green practices in hotels? The role of knowledge, awareness, concern and ecological behaviour. *International Journal of Hospitality Management, 40*, 20–28. doi:10.1016/j.ijhm.2014.03.001

Chan, E. S. W., & Wong, S. C. K. (2006). Motivations for ISO 14001 in the hotel industry. *Tourism Management, 27*(3), 481–492. doi:10.1016/j.tourman.2004.10.007

Christmann, P. (1999). Forthcoming in the Academy of Management Journal Effects Of "Best Practices" Of Environmental Management On Cost Advantage: The Role Of Complementary Assets. Academy of Management Journal.

Cramer, J. (1998). Environmental management: From fit to stretch.. *Business Strategy and the Environment, 7*(3), 162–172. doi:10.1002/(SICI)1099-0836(199807)7:3<162::AID-BSE149>3.0.CO;2-Q

Crane, A., Matten, D., & Moon, J. (2008). Ecological Citizenship and the Corporation: Politicizing the New Corporate Environmentalism. *Organization & Environment, 21*(4), 371–389. doi:10.1177/1086026608326075

Dacin, M. T., Kostova, T., & Roth, K. (2008). Institutional Theory in the Study of Multinational Corporations : A Critique and New Directions. *Academy of Management Review, 33*(4), 994–1006. doi:10.5465/AMR.2008.34422026

Daily, B. F., Bishop, J. W., & Massoud, J. (2012). The role of training and empowerment in environmental performance: A study of the Mexican *maquiladora* industry. *International Journal of Operations & Production Management, 32*(5), 631–647. doi:10.1108/01443571211226524

Davidson, M. C. G., Mcphail, R., & Barry, S. (2011). *Hospitality HRM: past, present and the future.* Retrieved from https://doi.org/10.1108/09596111111130001

Davidsson, P., Klofsten, M., & Hunter, E. (2006). Institutional Forces: The Invisible Hand that Shapes Venture Ideas? *International Small Business Journal, 24*(2), 115–131. doi:10.1177/0266242606061834

Day, J., & Cai, L. (2012). Environmental and energy-related challenges to sustainable tourism in the United States and China. *International Journal of Sustainable Development and World Ecology, 19*(5), 379–388. doi:10.1080/13504509.2012.675600

Del Brio, J. A., Fernandez, E., & Junquera, B. (2007). *Management and employee involvement in achieving an environmental action-based competitive advantage: an empirical study. The International Journal of Human Resource Management, 18.* https://doi.org/10.1080/09585190601178687

Dimaggio, P., & Powell, W. (1991). The New Institutionalism in organizational analysis. *The International Encyclopedia of Organization Studies*, 144–145. Retrieved from http://web.stanford.edu/group/song/papers/NewInstitutionalism.pdf

DiMaggio, P. J., & Powell, W. W. (1983). The Iron Cage Revisited: Institutional Isomorphism and Collective Rationality in Organizational Fields. *American Sociological Review, 48*(2), 147. doi:10.2307/2095101

Dolores Lopez-Gamero, M., Claver-Cortes, E., & Francisco Molina-Azorin, J. (2011). Environmental Perception, Management, and Competitive Opportunity in Spanish Hotels. *Cornell Hospitality Quarterly, 52*(4), 480–500. doi:10.1177/1938965511420694

Epstein, M., & Roy, M.-J. (1998). Managing corporate environmental performance. *European Management Journal, 16*(3), 284–296. doi:10.1016/S0263-2373(98)00005-X

Erdogan, N., & Baris, E. (2007). Environmental protection programs and conservation practices of hotels in Ankara, Turkey. *Tourism Management, 28*(2), 604–614. doi:10.1016/j.tourman.2006.07.003

Fayyazi, M., Shahbazmoradi, S., Afshar, Z., & Shahbazmoradi, M. R. (2015). Investigating the barriers of the green human resource management implementation in oil industry. *Management Science Letters, 5*(1), 101–108. https://doi.org/10.5267/j.msl.2014.12.002

Gadenne, D. L., Kennedy, J., & McKeiver, C. (2009). An empirical study of environmental awareness and practices in SMEs. *Journal of Business Ethics, 84*(1), 45–63. doi:10.1007/s10551-008-9672-9

Gill, J. D., Crosby, L. A., & Taylor, J. R. (1986). Ecological concern, attitudes, and social norms in voting behavior. *Public Opinion Quarterly*. https://doi.org/10.1086/269002

Gössling, S., Peeters, P., Ceron, J. P., Dubois, G., Patterson, T., & Richardson, R. B. (2005). The eco-efficiency of tourism. *Ecological Economics, 54*(4), 417–434. doi:10.1016/j.ecolecon.2004.10.006

Graci, S., & Kuehnel, J. (2010). How to increase your bottom line by going green. *Green Hotels & Responsible Tourism Initiative*, 1–28.

Greenwood, R., & Hinings, C. R. (1996). Understanding radical organizational change: Bringing together the old and the new institutionalism. *Academy of Management Review, 21*(4), 1022–1054. https://doi.org/10.5465/AMR.1996.9704071862

Hambrick, D. C. (2007). Upper Echelons Theory: An Update. *Source: The Academy of Management Review, 32*(2), 334–343. https://doi.org/10.5465/AMR.2007.24345254

Herremans, I. M., Herschovis, M. S., & Bertels, S. (2009). Leaders and laggards: The influence of competing logics on corporate environmental action. *Journal of Business Ethics, 89*(3), 449–472. doi:10.1007/s10551-008-0010-z

Hoffman, A. J. (1999). Institutional evolution and change: Environmentalism and the U.S. chemical industry. *Academy of Management Journal, 42*(4), 351–371. doi:10.2307/257008

Ilinitch, A. Y., Soderstrom, N. S., & Thomas, E. T. (1998). Measuring corporate environmental performance. *Journal of Accounting and Public Policy, 17*(4–5), 383–408. https://doi.org/10.1016/S0278-4254(98)10012-1

Jabbour, C. J. C., & Santos, F. C. A. (2008). The central role of human resource management in the search for sustainable organizations. *International Journal of Human Resource Management, 19*(12), 2133–2154. doi:10.1080/09585190802479389

Jennings, P. D., & Zandbergen, P. (1995). Ecologically Sustainable Organizations : An Institutional Approach. *Academy of Management Review, 20*(4), 1015–1052. https://doi.org/10.5465/AMR.1995.9512280034

Jones, P., Hillier, D., & Comfort, D. (2014). Sustainability in the global hotel industry. *International Journal of Contemporary Hospitality Management, 26*(1), 5–17. doi:10.1108/IJCHM-10-2012-0180

José, C., Jabbour, C., Beatriz, A., & De Sousa, L. (2015). Green human resource management and green supply chain management: Linking two emerging agendas. *Journal of Cleaner Production*, 1–10. https://doi.org/10.1016/j.jclepro.2015.01.052

Jose, C., Jabbour, C., Jugend, D., Beatriz, A., De Sousa, L., Gunasekaran, A., & Latan, H. (2015). Green product development and performance of Brazilian fi rms : Measuring the role of human and technical aspects. *Journal of Cleaner Production*, *87*, 442–451. doi:10.1016/j.jclepro.2014.09.036

Kang, K. H., Lee, S., & Huh, C. (2010). Impacts of positive and negative corporate social responsibility activities on company performance in the hospitality industry. *International Journal of Hospitality Management*, *29*(1), 72–82. doi:10.1016/j.ijhm.2009.05.006

Kasim, A. (2007). Towards a Wider Adoption of Environmental Responsibility in the Hotel Sector. *International Journal of Hospitality & Tourism Administration*, *8*(2), 25–49. doi:10.1300/J149v08n02_02

Kesidou, E., & Demirel, P. (2012). On the drivers of eco-innovations: Empirical evidence from the UK. *Research Policy*, *41*(5), 862–870. doi:10.1016/j.respol.2012.01.005

Kirk, D. (1995). Environmental management in hotels. *International Journal of Contemporary Hospitality Management*, *7*(6), 3–8. doi:10.1108/09596119510095325

Kostova, T. (1997). Country institutional profiles: concept and measurement. *Academy of Management Best Papers Proceedings*, *8*(1), 180–184. https://doi.org/10.5465/AMBPP.1997.4981338

Kostova, T., & Roth, K. (2002). Adoption of an Organizational Practice By Subsidiaries of Multinational Corporations: Institutional and Relational Effects. ^. *Academy of Management Journal*, *45*(1), 215–233. doi:10.2307/3069293

Lee, C. H., Wahid, N. A., & Goh, Y. N. (2012). Assessing determinants of green practices adoption : A conceptual framework. *Elixir Marketing Mgmt*, *45*, 7760–7766.

Lober, D. D. J. (1996). Evaluating the environmental performance of corporations. *Journal of Managerial Issues*, *8*, 184–205.

López-Gamero, M. D., Molina-Azorín, J. F., & Claver-Cortés, E. (2009). The whole relationship between environmental variables and firm performance: Competitive advantage and firm resources as mediator variables. *Journal of Environmental Management*, *90*(10), 3110–3121. doi:10.1016/j.jenvman.2009.05.007 PMID:19482410

Lülfs, R., & Hahn, R. (2015). *Sustainable Behavior in the Business Sphere: A Comprehensive Overview of the Explanatory Power of Psychological Models*. https://doi.org/10.1177/1086026614522631

Malaysia, I. (2012). *Tourism & Hospitality Report*. Retrieved from http://etp.pemandu.gov.my/upload/Inside Investor - Tourism.pdf

Mandip, G. (2012). Green HRM: People Management Commitment to Environmental Sustainability. *Research Journal of Recent Sciences*, *1*(2277–2502), 244–252.

Marcus, A., & Fremeth, A. R. (2009). Green Management Matters Regardless. *The Academy of Management Perspectives*, *23*(3), 17–26. doi:10.5465/AMP.2009.43479261

McGuire, D., & Garavan, T. N. (2010). Closing Comments: A Call to Action. *Advances in Developing Human Resources, 12*(5), 614–616. doi:10.1177/1523422310394435

Mehta, K., & Chugan, P. K. (2015). Green HRM in Pursuit of Environmentally Sustainable Business. *Universal Journal of Industrial and Business Management, 3*(3), 74–81. https://doi.org/10.13189/ujibm.2015.030302

Mensah, I. (2006). Environmental management practices among hotels in the greater Accra region. *International Journal of Hospitality Management, 25*(3), 414–431. doi:10.1016/j.ijhm.2005.02.003

Miles, M. P., & Covin, J. G. (2000). Environmental marketing: A source of reputational competitive and financial advantage. *Journal of Business Ethics, 23*(3), 299–311. doi:10.1023/A:1006214509281

Molina-Azorín, J. F., Claver-Cortés, E., López-Gamero, M. D., & Tarí, J. J. (2009). Green management and financial performance: A literature review. *Management Decision, 47*(7), 1080–1100. doi:10.1108/00251740910978313

Moorthy, M. K., Yacob, P., Chelliah, M. K., & Arokiasamy, L. (2012). Drivers for Malaysian SMEs to Go Green. *International Journal of Academic Research in Business and Social Science, 2*(9), 74–86.

Mostafa, M. M. (2006). Antecedents of Egyptian Consumers' Green Purchase Intentions. *Journal of International Consumer Marketing*. https://doi.org/10.1300/J046v19n02_06

Nabiha, A. k. S., R.a, G., Wahid, N. A., Amran, A., Abustan, I., & Mahadi, R. (2011). A field survey of environmental initiatives at selected resorts in Malaysia. *World Applied Science Journal, 12*, 56–63.

Opatha, H. H. D. N. P., & Arulrajah, A. (2014). Green Human Resource Management: Simplified General Reflections. *International Business Research, 7*(8), 101–112. https://doi.org/10.5539/ibr.v7n8p101

Paillé, P., Chen, Y., Boiral, O., & Jin, J. (2013). The Impact of Human Resource Management on Environmental Performance: An Employee-Level Study. *Journal of Business Ethics, 121*(3), 451–466. doi:10.1007/s10551-013-1732-0

Pierce, J. C., Lovrich, N. P., & Dalton, R. J. (2000). Contextual influences on environmental knowledge: Public familiarity with technical terms in nuclear weapons production in Russia and the United States. *Environment and Behavior, 32*(2), 188–208. doi:10.1177/00139160021972496

Pooley, J., & OConnor, M. (2000). Environmental Education and Attitudes: Emotions and Beliefs are What is Needed. *Environment and Behavior, 32*(5), 711–723. doi:10.1177/0013916500325007

Quazi, H. (1999). Implementation of an environmental management system: The experience of companies operating in Singapore. *Industrial Management & Data Systems, 99*(7), 302–311. doi:10.1108/02635579910262526

Rani, S., & Mishra, D. K. (2014). Green HRM : Practices and Strategic Implementation in the Organizations. *International Journal on Recent and Innovation Trends in Computing and Communication, 2*(11), 3633–3639.

Renwick, D. W. S., Redman, T., & Maguire, S. (2013a). Green Human Resource Management: A Review and Research Agenda*. *International Journal of Management Reviews*, *15*(1), 1–14. doi:10.1111/j.1468-2370.2011.00328.x

Renwick, D. W. S., Redman, T., & Maguire, S. (2013b). Green Human Resource Management: A Review and Research Agenda* Green Human Resource Management: A Review and Research Agenda. *International Journal of Management Reviews*, *15*(1), 1–14. doi:10.1111/j.1468-2370.2011.00328.x

Rodríguez-Antón, J. M., del Mar Alonso-Almeida, M., Celemín, M. S., & Rubio, L. (2012). Use of different sustainability management systems in the hospitality industry. The case of Spanish hotels. *Journal of Cleaner Production*, *22*(1), 76–84. doi:10.1016/j.jclepro.2011.09.024

Roxas, B., & Coetzer, A. (2012). Institutional Environment, Managerial Attitudes and Environmental Sustainability Orientation of Small Firms. *Journal of Business Ethics*, *111*(4), 461–476. doi:10.1007/s10551-012-1211-z

Russo, M. V., & Fouts, P. A. (1997). A Resource-Based Perspective on Corporate Environmental Performance and Profitability. *Academy of Management Journal*, *40*(3), 534–559. doi:10.2307/257052

Scott, W. R. (2004). Institutional Theory: Contributing to a Theoretical Research Program. *Great Minds in Management The Process of Theory Development, 37*(3–4), 460–484. https://doi.org/10.1042/BJ20100043.Electrostatic

Scott, W. R. (2008). *Institutions and organizations: Ideas and interests.* Sage Publications. https://doi.org/10.1016/S0263-2373(97)89895-7

Shah, K. U. (2011). Strategic organizational drivers of corporate environmental responsibility in the Caribbean hotel industry. *Policy Sciences*, *44*(4), 321–344. doi:10.1007/s11077-011-9130-x

Sharma, S. (2000). Managerial interpretations and organizational context as predictors of corporate choice of environmental strategy. *Academy of Management Journal*, *43*(4), 681–697. doi:10.2307/1556361

Sharma, S., & Aragòn-Correa, J. A. (2007). The contingent influence of organizational capabilities on proactive environmental strategy in the service sector: An analysis of North American and European ski. *Canadian Journal of*, *283*, 268–283. https://doi.org/10.1002/CJAS.35

Shwom, R. (2009). Strengthening Sociological Perspectives on Organizations and the Environment. *Organization & Environment*, *22*(3), 271–292. doi:10.1177/1086026609345216

Stern, P., Dietz, T., & Kalof, L. (1993). Value Orientations, Gender and Environmental Concern. *Environment and Beahvior,* *25*(3), 322–348. https://doi.org/0803973233

Tang, F. E. (2012). A study of Water Consumption in Two Malaysian Resorts. *International Journal of Environment, Chemical, Ecological. Geological and Geophysical Engineering*, *6*(8), 506–511.

Taylor, S. R. (1992). Green management: The next competitive weapon. *Futures*, *24*(7), 669–680. doi:10.1016/0016-3287(92)90075-Q

Teixeira, A. A., Jabbour, C. J. C., & Jabbour, A. B. L. D. S. (2012). Relationship between green management and environmental training in companies located in Brazil: A theoretical framework and case studies. *International Journal of Production Economics*, *140*(1), 318–329. doi:10.1016/j.ijpe.2012.01.009

Wagner, M. (2013). Green Human Resource Benefits: Do they Matter as Determinants of Environmental Management System Implementation? *Journal of Business Ethics*, *114*(3), 443–456. doi:10.1007/s10551-012-1356-9

Wagner, M. (2014). A European perspective on country moderation effects: Environmental management systems and sustainability-related human resource benefits. *Journal of World Business*, *50*(2), 379–388. doi:10.1016/j.jwb.2014.08.005

Williamson, D., Lynch-Wood, G., & Ramsay, J. (2006). Drivers of environmental behaviour in manufacturing SMEs and the implications for CSR. *Journal of Business Ethics*, *67*(3), 317–330. doi:10.1007/s10551-006-9187-1

Williamson, O. E. (1998). Transaction cost economics and organization theory. In Technology, organization, and competitiveness: Perspectives on industrial and corporate change (pp. 17–66). Academic Press.

Yadav, P. L., Han, S. H., & Rho, J. J. (2015). Impact of Environmental Performance on Firm Value for Sustainable Investment: Evidence from Large US Firms. *Business Strategy and the Environment*. https://doi.org/10.1002/bse.1883

Zein, K., Wazner Semlali, M., & Meylan, G. (2008). *Best Environmental Practices for the Hotel Industry*. Academic Press.

Compilation of References

Aagerup, U., & Nilsson, J. (2016). Green consumer behavior: Being good or seeming good? *Journal of Product and Brand Management*, *25*(3), 274–284. doi:10.1108/JPBM-06-2015-0903

Aaker, D. A., & Equity, M. B. (1991). Capitalizing on the Value of a Brand Name. New York: Academic Press.

Aaker, D. A., & Joachimsthaler, E. (2000). The brand relationship spectrum: The key to the brand architecture challenge. *California Management Review*, *42*(4), 8–23. doi:10.2307/41166051

Aaker, D. A., & Joachimsthaler, E. (2012). *Brand Leadership*. New York: Free Press.

Aaker, J. L. (1997). Dimensions of brand personality. *JMR, Journal of Marketing Research*, *34*(3), 347–356. doi:10.2307/3151897

Aaker, J., Fournier, S., & Brasel, S. A. (2004). When good brands do bad. *The Journal of Consumer Research*, *31*(1), 1–16. doi:10.1086/383419

Aarset, B., Beckmann, S., Bigne, E., Beveridge, M., Bjorndal, T., Bunting, J., & Young, J. et al. (2004). The European consumers understanding and perceptions of the organic food regime: The case of aquaculture. *British Food Journal*, *106*(2), 93–105. doi:10.1108/00070700410516784

Abdul Samad, M. H., Abdul Rahman, A., & Ibrahim, F. (2008). Green Performance Ratings for Malaysian Buildings With Particular Reference to Hotels. *International Conference on Environment Research and Technology (ICERT 08)*.

Abdul Wahid, N., Abustan, I., Khalid, S.-N., & Amran, A. (2008). Green indicators in hospitality industry: Identification of common attributes applied by hotels in American and Latin American continents. *Proceedings of National Symposium on Tourism Research*, 79–90.

Accenture, UN Global Compact. (2013). *UN global compact—accenture CEO study on sustainability 2013. Architects of a better world.* Retrieved June 5, 2016, from https://www.unglobalcompact.org/docs/news_events/8.1/UNGC_Accenture_CEO_Study_2013.pdf

Acharya, A., & Gupta, M. (2016). An Application of Brand Personality to Green Consumers: A Thematic Analysis. *Qualitative Report*, *21*(8), 1531–1545.

Agrawal, A. D., & Das, M. (2013). Green marketing: Sustainable marketing strategy. *Indira Management Review*, *7*(1), 17–31.

Aguilera-Caracuel, J., & Ortiz-de-Mandojana, N. (2013). Green Innovation and Financial Performance: An Institutional Approach. *Organization & Environment*, *26*(4), 365–385. https://doi.org/10.1177/1086026613507931 doi:10.1177/1086026613507931

Ajzen, I. (1991). The Theory of Planned Behavior. *Organizational Behavior and Human Decision Processes, 50*, 179–211. 10.1016/0749-5978(91)90020-T

Ajzen, I., & Fishbein, M. (1980). *Understanding attitudes and predicting social behavior.* Englewood Cliffs, NJ: Prentice Hall.

Ajzen, I., & Sexton, J. (1999). Depth of processing, belief congruence, and attitude-behavior correspondence. *Dual-process theories in social psychology*, 117-138.

Ajzen, I. (1985). From intentions to actions: A theory of planned behavior. In J. Kuhl & J. Beckman (Eds.), *Action control: From cognition to behavior*. Heidelberg, Germany: Springer. doi:10.1007/978-3-642-69746-3_2

Ajzen, I. (1991). The theory of planned behavior. *Organizational Behavior and Human Decision Processes, 50*(2), 179–211. doi:10.1016/0749-5978(91)90020-T

Ajzen, I., & Fishbein, M. (1980). *Understanding attitudes and predicting social behavior*. Englewood Cliffs, NJ: Prentice-Hall.

Akaichi, F., Nayga, R. M. Jr, & Gil, J. M. (2012). Assessing consumer's willingness to pay for different units of organic milk: Evidence from multiunit auctions. *Canadian Journal of Agricultural Economics, 60*(4), 469–494. doi:10.1111/j.1744-7976.2012.01254.x

Akbar, M. M., & Parvez, N. (2009). Impact of service quality, trust, and customer satisfaction on customers loyalty. *ABAC Journal, 29*(1), 24–38.

Akenji, L. (2014). Consumer scapegoatism and limits to green consumerism. *Journal of Cleaner Production, 63*, 13–23. doi:10.1016/j.jclepro.2013.05.022

Al Khattab, S. A., & Asad, H. (2015). The Impact of the Green Supply Chain Management on Environmental-Based Marketing Performance. *Journal of Service Science and Management, 8*(4), 588–597. doi:10.4236/jssm.2015.84059

Ali, A., & Ahmad, I. (2012). Environment Friendly Products: Factors that influence the green purchase intentions of Pakistani consumers. *Pak. J. Eng. Technol. Sci., 2*(1), 84–117.

Ali, M. H., & Suleiman, N. (2016). Sustainable food production: Insights of Malaysian halal small and medium sized enterprises. *International Journal of Production Economics*, 1–12.

Allcott, H. (2011). Social norms and energy conservation. *Journal of Public Economics, 95*(9-10), 1082–1095. doi:10.1016/j.jpubeco.2011.03.003

Allen, D. E., & Olson, J. (1995). Conceptualizing and creating brand personality: A narrative theory approach. *Advances in Consumer Research. Association for Consumer Research (U. S.), 22*(1), 392–393.

Almli, V. L., Næsa, T., Enderli, G., Sulmont-Rossé, C., Issanchou, S., & Hersleth, M. (2011). Consumers acceptance of innovations in traditional cheese. A comparative study in France and Norway. *Appetite, 57*(1), 110–120. doi:10.1016/j.appet.2011.04.009 PMID:21550369

Al-Shourah, A. A. (2007). *The Relationship Between Environmental Management Practices (Emp) And Hotel Performance : Emp Drivers And The Moderating Role Of Perceived Benefits*. Academic Press.

Alsmadi, S. (2007). Green marketing and the concern over the environment: Measuring environmental consciousness of Jordanian consumers. *Journal of Promotion Management, 13*(3-4), 339–361. doi:10.1080/10496490802306905

Altschiller, D. (2000). Do Dot-Coms' Ads Reveal a More Basic Flaw? *Brandweek, 41*(12), 32.

Ambler, T., Kokkinaki, F., & Puntoni, S. (2004). Assessing marketing performance: Reasons for metrics selection. *Journal of Marketing Management*, *20*(3-4), 475–498. doi:10.1362/026725704323080506

American Association for the Advancement of Science. (2007). *AAAS Board Statement on Climate Change.* Retrieved August 15, 2015, from http://www.aaas.org/sites/default/files/migrate/uploads/aaas_climate_statement.pdf

Amirnejad, H., & Tonakbar, P. (2015). The willingness to pay for organic milk by consumers in Tehran. *Journal of Agricultural Science and Technology*, *17*, 1685–1694.

Ancarani, F., & Gisco, A. (2014). *Wellness Marketing: New strategies for new trends.* EGEA spa.

Angulo, A. M., Gil, J. M., & Tamburo, L. (2008). Food safety and consumers willingness to pay for labelled beef in Spain. *Journal of Food Products Marketing*, *11*(3), 89–105. doi:10.1300/J038v11n03_06

Annunziata, A., & Vecchio, R. (2016). Organic farming and sustainability in food choices: An analysis of consumer preference in Southern Italy. *Agriculture and Agricultural Science Procedia*, *8*, 193–200. doi:10.1016/j.aaspro.2016.02.093

Antony, T. K., & Pakutharıvu, D. N. (2016). Go green and save green (Issues faced by green marketing). *Indian Journal of Applied Research*, *6*(5), 191–193.

Aragon-Correa, J. A., Martin-Tapia, I., & de la Torre-Ruiz, J. (2015). Sustainability issues and hospitality and tourism firms strategies. *International Journal of Contemporary Hospitality Management*, *27*(3), 498–522. doi:10.1108/IJCHM-11-2014-0564

Arokiasamy, A. R. a. (2013). *A Study on Employee Satisfaction Perspectives in the Hotel.* Academic Press.

Arulrajah, A. A., Opatha, H. H. D. N., & Nawaratne, N. N. (2015). *Green Human Resource Management Practices: A Review Literature Review on Green HRM Practices.* Academic Press.

Aschemann-Witzel, J., & Hamm, U. (2010). Do consumers prefer foods with nutrition and health claims? Results of a purchase simulation. *Journal of Marketing Communications*, *16*(1-2), 47–58. doi:10.1080/13527260903342746

Asgharian, R., Salehi, M., Saleki, Z. S., Hojabri, R., & Nikkheslat, M. (2012). Green product quality, green customer satisfaction, and green customer loyalty. *International Journal of Research in Management & Technology*, *2*(5), 499–503.

Assadourian, E. (2010). Transforming cultures: From consumerism to sustainability. *Journal of Macromarketing*, *30*(2), 186–191. doi:10.1177/0276146710361932

Atkinson, L., & Kim, Y. (2014, June). "I Drink It Anyway and I Know I Shouldn't": Understanding Green Consumers' Positive Evaluations of Norm-violating Non-green Products and Misleading Green Advertising. *Environmental Communication: A Journal of Nature and Culture*, 1–21. 10.1080/17524032.2014.932817

Atuahene-Gima, K. (2005). Resolving the capability—rigidity paradox in new product innovation. *Journal of Marketing*, *69*(4), 61–83. doi:10.1509/jmkg.2005.69.4.61

Atuahene-Gima, K., Slater, S. F., & Olson, E. M. (2005). The contingent value of responsive and proactive market orientations for new product program performance. *Journal of Product Innovation Management*, *22*(6), 464–482. doi:10.1111/j.1540-5885.2005.00144.x

Awang, K. W., Ishak, N. O. R. K., Radzi, S. M., & Taha, A. Z. (2008). Environmental Variables and Performance : Evidence from the Hotel Industry in Malaysia. *International Journal of Economics and Management*, *2*, 59–79.

Aydoğan, R., Sharpanskykh, A., & Lo, J. (2014). *A Trust-Based Situation Awareness Model.* Paper presented at the European Conference on Multi-Agent Systems.

Ayers, N. (2008). *Consumption of Organic Foods from a Life History Perspective: An Exploratory Study among British Consumers*. Aberystwyth: University of Wales, School of Business and Management.

Ayuk, E., Oku, E., Asubonteng, K., & Nutakor, P. (2017). *Promoting Green Economy: Implications for Natural Resources Development, Food Security and Poverty Reduction in Africa*. United Nations University Institute for Natural Resources in Africa.

Azzone, G., & Noci, G. (1996). Measuring the environmental performance of new products: an integrated approach. *International Journal of Production Research, 34*(11), 3055–3078. https://doi.org/10.1080/00207549608905077

Bagozzi, R. P., Yi, Y., & Baumgartner, J. (1990). The level of effort required for behaviour as a moderator of the attitude-behaviour relation. *European Journal of Social Psychology*, *20*(1), 45–59. doi:10.1002/ejsp.2420200105

Baines, T., Brown, S., Benedettini, O., & Ball, P. (2012). Examining green production and its role within the competitive strategy of manufacturers. *Journal of Industrial Engineering and Management*, *5*(1), 53. doi:10.3926/jiem.405

Baker, M. A., Davis, E. A., & Weaver, P. A. (2013). Eco-friendly attitudes, barriers to participation, and differences in behavior at green hotels. *Cornell Hospitality Quarterly*.

Banerjee, S. B. (2002). Corporate environmentalism: The construct and its measurement. *Journal of Business Research*, *55*(3), 177–191. doi:10.1016/S0148-2963(00)00135-1

Banerjee, S. B., Iyer, E. S., & Kashyap, R. K. (2003). Corporate environmentalism: Antecedents and influence of industry type. *Journal of Marketing*, *67*(2), 106–122. doi:10.1509/jmkg.67.2.106.18604

Bansal, P., & Roth, K. (2000). Why Companies Go Green: A model of Ecological Responsiveness. *Academy of Management, 43*(4), 717–736. https://doi.org/10.2307/1556363

Bansal, P. (2005). Evolving sustainably: A longitudinal study of corporate sustainable development. *Strategic Management Journal*, *26*(3), 197–218. doi:10.1002/smj.441

Bansal, P., & Gao, J. (2006). Building the Future by Looking to the Past: Examining Research Published on Organizations and Environment. *Organization & Environment*, *19*(4), 458–478. doi:10.1177/1086026606294957

Banytė, J., Brazionienė, L., & Gadeikienė, A. (2010). investigation of green consumer profile: A case of lithuanian market of eco-friendly food products. *Economics & Management*, *15*, 374–383.

Barbarossa, C., & Pastore, A. (2015). Why environmentally conscious consumers do not purchase green products: A cognitive mapping approach. *Qualitative Market Research: An International Journal*, *18*(2), 188–209. doi:10.1108/QMR-06-2012-0030

Barney, J. (1991). Firm Resources and Sustained Competitive Advantage. *Journal of Management*, *17*(1), 99–120. doi:10.1177/014920639101700108

Baron, R., & Kenny, D. (1986). The moderator-mediator variable distinction in social psychological research. *Journal of Personality and Social Psychology*, *51*(6), 1173–1182. doi:10.1037/0022-3514.51.6.1173 PMID:3806354

Barr, S., Gilg, A. W., & Ford, N. J. (2001). Differences between household waste reduction, reuse and recycling behaviour: A study of reported behaviours, intentions and explanatory variables. *Environmental & Waste Management*, *4*(2), 69–82.

Barr, S., Shaw, G., & Gilg, A. W. (2011). The policy and practice of sustainable lifestyles. *Journal of Environmental Planning and Management*, *54*(10), 1331–1350. doi:10.1080/09640568.2011.574996

Basili, V. R., Caldiera, G., & Rombach, H. D. (2002). Experience Factory. In J. J. Marciniak (Ed.), *Encyclopaedia of Software Engineering*. Hoboken, NJ: John Wiley & Sons, Inc. doi:10.1002/0471028959.sof110

Bati, U. (2016). Green marketing activities to support corporate reputation on a sample from Turkey. *International Journal of Marketing Studies*, *8*(3), 189–201. doi:10.5539/ijms.v8n3p189

Bauer, M., Blattman, C., Chytilová, J., Henrich, J., Miguel, E., & Mitts, T. (2016). Can war foster cooperation? *The Journal of Economic Perspectives*, *30*(3), 249–274. doi:10.1257/jep.30.3.249

Baum, A., Singer, J. E., & Baum, C. S. (1981). Stress and the Environment. *The Journal of Social Issues*, *37*(1), 4–35. doi:10.1111/j.1540-4560.1981.tb01056.x

Baumgartner, H., & Homburg, C. (1996). Applications of structural equation modeling in marketing and consumer research: A review. *International Journal of Research in Marketing*, *13*(2), 139–161. doi:10.1016/0167-8116(95)00038-0

Bekkers, R., & Wiepking, P. (2011). A literature review of empirical studies of philanthropy: Eight mechanisms that drive charitable giving. *Nonprofit and Voluntary Sector Quarterly*, *40*(5), 924–973. doi:10.1177/0899764010380927

Bellows, A. C., Onyango, B., Diamond, A., & Hallman, W. K. (2008). Understanding Consumer Interest in Organics: Production Values vs. Purchasing Behavior. *Journal of Agricultural & Food Industrial Organization*, *6*(2), 1–28.

Bellows, J., & Miguel, E. (2009). War and local collective action in Sierra Leone. *Journal of Public Economics*, *93*(11), 1144–1157. doi:10.1016/j.jpubeco.2009.07.012

Bem, D. J. (1967). Self-Perception: An Alternative Interpretation of Cognitive Dissonance Phenomena. *Psychological Review*, *74*(3), 183–200. doi:10.1037/h0024835 PMID:5342882

Bercea, M. D. (2013). *Quantitative versus qualitative in neuromarketing research.* Retrieved from https://mpra.ub.uni-muenchen.de/44134/

Berezan, O., Millar, M., & Raab, C. (2014). Sustainable hotel practices and guest satisfaction levels. *International Journal of Hospitality & Tourism Administration*, *15*(1), 1–18. doi:10.1080/15256480.2014.872884

Berezan, O., Raab, C., Yoo, M., & Love, C. (2013). Sustainable hotel practices and nationality: The impact on guest satisfaction and guest intention to return. *International Journal of Hospitality Management*, *34*(1), 227–233. doi:10.1016/j.ijhm.2013.03.010

Berger, I. E., & Corbin, R. M. (1992). Perceived Consumer Effectiveness and Faith in Others as Moderators of Environmentally Responsible Behavior. *Journal of Public Policy & Marketing*, *11*(2), 79–89.

Berlin, L., Lockeretz, W., & Bell, R. (2009). Purchasing foods produced on organic, small and local farms: A mixed method analysis of New England consumers. *Renewable Agriculture and Food Systems*, *24*(04), 267–275. doi:10.1017/S1742170509990111

Bernués, A., Olaizola, A., & Corcoran, K. (2003a). Extrinsic attributes of red meat as indicators of quality in Europe: An application for market segmentation. *Food Quality and Preference*, *14*(4), 265–276. doi:10.1016/S0950-3293(02)00085-X

Bernués, A., Olaizola, A., & Corcoran, K. (2003b). Labelling information demanded by European consumers and relationships with purchasing motives, quality and safety of meat. *Meat Science*, *65*(3), 1095–1106. doi:10.1016/S0309-1740(02)00327-3 PMID:22063692

Beukes, C., & Van Wyk, G. (2016). An investigation of the marketing performance measurement practices in Hatfield Volkswagen group. *African Journal of Business Management*, *10*(6), 131–139. doi:10.5897/AJBM2015.7772

Bhaskaran, S., Polonsky, M., Cary, J., & Fernandez, S. (2006). Environmentally sustainable food production and marketing: Opportunity or hype? *British Food Journal*, *108*(8), 677–690. doi:10.1108/00070700610682355

Bhate, S. (2001). One world, one environment, one vision: Are we close to achieving this? An exploratory study of consumer environmental behaviour across three countries. *Journal of Consumer Behaviour*, *2*(2), 169–184. doi:10.1002/cb.98

Bhate, S., & Lawler, K. (1997). Environmentally friendly products: Factors that influence their adoption. *Technovation*, *17*(8), 457–465. doi:10.1016/S0166-4972(97)00006-0

Bhattacharya, C. B. (2016). Responsible Marketing: Doing Well by Doing Good. *GfK Marketing Intelligence Review*, *8*(1), 8–17. doi:10.1515/gfkmir-2016-0002

Black, I. (2010). Editorial: Sustainability through anti-consumption. *Journal of Consumer Behaviour*, *9*(6), 403–411. doi:10.1002/cb.340

Blackston, M. (1993). Beyond brand personality: Building brand relationships. In D. Aaker & A. Biel (Eds.), *Brand equity and advertising: Advertising's role in building strong brands* (pp. 113–124). Hillsdale, NJ: Erlbaum.

Blattman, C. (2009). From violence to voting: War and political participation in Uganda. *The American Political Science Review*, *103*(02), 231–247. doi:10.1017/S0003055409090212

Bodenhausen, G. V., & Gawronski, B. (2013). Attitude Change. In D. Reisberg (Ed.), *The Oxford Handbook of Cognitive Psychology* (pp. 957–969). Oxford University Press.

Bodlaj, M. (2010). The impact of a responsive and proactive market orientation on innovation and business performance. *Economic and Business Review for Central and South-Eastern Europe*, *12*(4), 241–261.

Bodlaj, M., Coenders, G., & Zabkar, V. (2012). Responsive and proactive market orientation and innovation success under market and technological turbulence. *Journal of Business Economics and Management*, *13*(4), 666–687. doi:10.3846/16111699.2011.620143

Bohdanowicz, P. (2005). European hoteliers environmental attitudes: Greening the Business. *The Cornell Hotel and Restaurant Administration Quarterly*, *46*(2), 188–204. doi:10.1177/0010880404273891

Bohdanowicz, P., Simanic, B., & Martinac, I. (2005). Article. *Sustainable Hotels*, *2005*(September), 1–8.

Bolin, G. (2011). *Value and the Media: Cultural Production and Consumption in Digital Markets*. Ashgate Publishing, Ltd.

Bond, C. A., Thilmany, D. D., & Bond, J. K. (2008). What to choose? The value of label claims to fresh produce consumers. *Journal of Agricultural and Resource Economics*, *33*(3), 402–427.

Bonsi, R., Hammett, A. L., & Smith, B. (2008). Eco–labels and International Trade: Problems and Solutions. *Journal of World Trade*, *42*(3), 407–432.

Borkfelt, S., Kondrup, S., Röcklinsberg, H., Bjørkdahl, K., & Gjerris, M. (2015). Closer to nature? A critical discussion of the marketing of ethical animal products. *Journal of Agricultural & Environmental Ethics*, *28*(6), 1053–1073. doi:10.1007/s10806-015-9577-4

Bose, A., Vira, B., & Garcia, C. (2016). Does environmental certification in coffee promote business as usual? A case study from the Western Ghats, India. *Ambio*, *45*(8), 946–955. doi:10.1007/s13280-016-0796-3 PMID:27329139

Boselie, P., Paauwe, J., & Jansen, P. (2001). Human resource management and performance: Lessons from the Netherlands. *International Journal of Human Resource Management*, *12*(7), 1107–1125. doi:10.1080/09585190110068331

Boyer, P. (1996). What makes anthropomorphism natural: Intuitive ontology and cultural representations. *Journal of the Royal Anthropological Institute*, *2*(1), 83–98. doi:10.2307/3034634

Brakus, J. J., Schmitt, B. H., & Zarantonello, L. (2009). Brand experience: What is it? How is it measured? Does it affect loyalty? *Journal of Marketing*, *73*(3), 52–68. doi:10.1509/jmkg.73.3.52

Brécard, D. (2014). Consumer confusion over the profusion of eco-labels: Lessons from a double differentiation model. *Resource and Energy Economics*, *37*, 64–84. doi:10.1016/j.reseneeco.2013.10.002

Bridges, C. M., & Wilhelm, W. B. (2008). Going beyond green: The why and how of integrating sustainability into the marketing curriculum. *Journal of Marketing Education*, *30*(1), 33–46. doi:10.1177/0273475307312196

Brockhoff, K., Chakrabarti, A. K., & Kirchgeorg, M. (1999, July). *Corporate Strategies in Environmental Management. Research-Technology Management.*

Brown, E., & Ferris, J. M. (2007). Social capital and philanthropy: An analysis of the impact of social capital on individual giving and volunteering. *Nonprofit and Voluntary Sector Quarterly*, *36*(1), 85–99. doi:10.1177/0899764006293178

Brück, T., Naudé, W., & Verwimp, P. (2011). Small Business, Entrepreneurship and Violent Conflict in Developing Countries. *Journal of Small Business and Entrepreneurship*, *24*(2), 161–178. doi:10.1080/08276331.2011.10593532

Brück, T., Naudé, W., & Verwimp, P. (2012). Business under Fire: Entrepreneurship and Violent Conflict in Developing Countries. *The Journal of Conflict Resolution*, *57*(1), 3–19. doi:10.1177/0022002712464846

Bruns-smith, A., Choy, V., Chong, H., Ph, D., Verma, R., & Ph, D. (2015). Cornell Hospitality Report Cornell Hospitality Report Environmental Sustainability in the Hospitality Industry: Best practices. *Guest Participation, and Customer Satisfaction*, *15*(March), 6–16.

Buergelt, D., Christoph-Schulz, I. B., Salamon, P., & Weible, D. (2013). Impacts of sustainability labels on consumers' purchasing decisions for fish. In H. Röcklinsberg & P. Sandin (Eds.), *The ethics of consumption. The citizen, the market, and the law* (pp. 39–46). Wageningen: Wageningen Academic Publishers. doi:10.3920/978-90-8686-784-4_5

Bullot, N. J., & Reber, R. (2013). The artful mind meets art history: Toward a psycho-historical framework for the science of art appreciation. *Behavioral and Brain Sciences*, *36*(02), 123–137. doi:10.1017/S0140525X12000489 PMID:23507091

Burke, R. J., & Cooper, C. L. (2005). *Reinventing human resources management: Challenges and new directions*. Routledge.

Butler, J. (2008). The Compelling Hard Case for Green Hotel Development. *Cornell Hospitality Quarterly*, *49*(3), 234–244. doi:10.1177/1938965508322174

Carlo, G., & Randall, B. A. (2002). The development of a measure of prosocial behaviors for late adolescents. *Journal of Youth and Adolescence*, *31*(1), 31–44. doi:10.1023/A:1014033032440

Carlson, A. (2010). Contemporary environmental aesthetics and the requirements of environmentalism. *Environmental Values*, *19*(3), 289–314. doi:10.3197/096327110X519844

Carmona-Moreno, E., Céspedes-Lorente, J., & De Burgos-Jiménez, J. (2004). Environmental strategies in spanish hotels: Contextual factors and performance. *Service Industries Journal*, *24*(3), 101–130. doi:10.1080/0264206042000247786

Carpio, C. E., & Isengildina-Massa, O. (2009). Consumers willingness to pay for locally grown products: The case of South Carolina. *Agribusiness*, *25*(3), 412–426. doi:10.1002/agr.20210

Carrete, L., Castaño, R., Felix, R., Centeno, E., & González, E. (2012). Green consumer behavior in an emerging economy: Confusion, credibility, and compatibility. *Journal of Consumer Marketing*, *29*(7), 470–481. doi:10.1108/07363761211274983

Carrington, M. J., Neville, B. A., & Whitwell, G. J. (2014). Lost in translation: Exploring the ethical consumer intention–behavior gap. *Journal of Business Research*, *67*(1), 2759–2767. doi:10.1016/j.jbusres.2012.09.022

Caruana, A., Money, A. H., & Berthon, P. R. (2000). Service quality and satisfaction - the moderating role of value. *European Journal of Marketing*, *34*(11/12), 1338–1352. doi:10.1108/03090560010764432

Cassar, A., Grosjean, P., & Whitt, S. (2013). Legacies of violence: Trust and market development. *Journal of Economic Growth*, *18*(3), 285–318. doi:10.1007/s10887-013-9091-3

Central Intelligence Agency. (2015). *The World Factbook- Environmental- Current issues*. Retrieved August 24, 2015, from https://www.cia.gov/library/publications/the-world-factbook/fields/2032.html

Chamorro, A., & Bañegil, T. M. (2006). Green marketing philosophy: A study of Spanish firms with ecolabels. *Corporate Social Responsibility and Environmental Management*, *13*(1), 11–24. doi:10.1002/csr.83

Chandrasekar, R. S. (2010). *Marketing Management. Text and cases, India*. McGraw Hill.

Chan, E. S. W. (2013). Managing green marketing: Hong Kong hotel managers perspective. *International Journal of Hospitality Management*, *34*(1), 442–461. doi:10.1016/j.ijhm.2012.12.007

Chan, E. S. W., & Hawkins Rebecca, R. (2010). Attitude towards EMSs in an international hotel: An exploratory case study. *International Journal of Hospitality Management*, *29*(4), 641–651. doi:10.1016/j.ijhm.2009.12.002

Chan, E. S. W., Hon, A. H. Y., Chan, W., & Okumus, F. (2014). What drives employees intentions to implement green practices in hotels? The role of knowledge, awareness, concern and ecological behaviour. *International Journal of Hospitality Management*, *40*, 20–28. doi:10.1016/j.ijhm.2014.03.001

Chan, E. S. W., & Wong, S. C. K. (2006). Motivations for ISO 14001 in the hotel industry. *Tourism Management*, *27*(3), 481–492. doi:10.1016/j.tourman.2004.10.007

Chang, C. H., Hooker, N. H., & Sam, A. (2011). Organic and conventional milk purchase behaviors in Central Ohio. *Agribusiness*, *27*(3), 311–326. doi:10.1002/agr.20269

Chan, R. Y. K. (2001). Determinants of Chinese Consumers Green Purchase Behavior. *Psychology and Marketing*, *18*(4), 389–413. doi:10.1002/mar.1013

Chan, T. Y., & Wong, C. W. (2012). The consumption side of sustainable fashion supply chain: Understanding fashion consumer eco-fashion consumption decision. *Journal of Fashion Marketing and Management: An International Journal*, *16*(2), 193–215. doi:10.1108/13612021211222824

Chan, W., Wong, K., & Lo, J. (2009). Hong Kong hotels sewage: Environmental cost and saving technique. *Journal of Hospitality & Tourism Research (Washington, D.C.)*, *33*(2), 329–346. doi:10.1177/1096348009338525

Charter, M. (1992). *Greener marketing: A responsible approach to business*. Greenleaf Publishing.

Chen, T. B., & Chai, L. T. (2010). Attitude towards the Environment and Green Products: Consumers' Perspective. *Management Science and Engineering*, *4*(2), 27–39.

Chen, Y. S. (2013). Towards green loyalty: Driving from green perceived value, green satisfaction, and green trust. *Sustainable Development*, *21*(5), 294–308. doi:10.1002/sd.500

Chen, Y. S., & Chang, C. H. (2013). Greenwash and green trust: The mediation effects of green consumer confusion and green perceived risk. *Journal of Business Ethics*, *114*(3), 489–500. doi:10.1007/s10551-012-1360-0

Chen, Y. S., Lai, S. B., & Wen, C. T. (2006). The influence of green innovation performance on corporate advantage in Taiwan. *Journal of Business Ethics*, *67*(4), 331–339. doi:10.1007/s10551-006-9025-5

Chen, Y.-S. (2007). The Driver of Green Innovation and Green Image – Green Core Competence. *Journal of Business Ethics*, *81*(3), 531–543. doi:10.1007/s10551-007-9522-1

Chen, Y.-S. (2009). The Drivers of Green Brand Equity: Green Brand Image, Green Satisfaction, and Green Trust. *Journal of Business Ethics*, *93*(2), 307–319. doi:10.1007/s10551-009-0223-9

Chen, Y.-S., & Chang, C.-H. (2012a). Enhance green purchase intentions: The roles of green perceived value, green perceived risk, and green trust. *Management Decision*, *50*(3), 502–520. doi:10.1108/00251741211216250

Chen, Y.-S., & Chang, C.-H. (2013). Towards green trust: The influences of green perceived quality, green perceived risk, and green satisfaction. *Management Decision*, *51*(1), 63–82. doi:10.1108/00251741311291319

Cherian, J., & Jacob, J. (2012). Green marketing: A study of consumers attitude towards environment friendly products. *Asian Social Science*, *8*(12), 117. doi:10.5539/ass.v8n12p117

Chong, H. G., & Verma, R. (2013). Hotel sustainability : Financial analysis shines a cautious green light. *Cornell Hospitality Report*, *13*(10), 1–15.

Christensen, C. M. (2011). *The innovators' dilemma: The revolutionary book that will change the way you do business*. New York, NY: Harper Collins Publisher Inc. doi:10.15358/9783800642816

Christmann, P. (1999). Forthcoming in the Academy of Management Journal Effects Of "Best Practices" Of Environmental Management On Cost Advantage: The Role Of Complementary Assets. Academy of Management Journal.

Clark, B. H., Abela, A. V., & Ambler, T. (2006). An information processing model of marketing performance measurement. *Journal of Marketing Theory and Practice*, *14*(3), 191–208. doi:10.2753/MTP1069-6679140302

Clark, B., Stewart, G. B., Panzone, L. A., Kyriazakis, I., & Frewer, L. J. (2016). A systematic review of public attitudes, perceptions and behaviours towards production diseases associated with farm animal welfare. *Journal of Agricultural & Environmental Ethics*, *29*(3), 455–478. doi:10.1007/s10806-016-9615-x

Claver-Cortes, E., Molina-Azorin, J. F., Pereira-Moliner, J., & Lopez-Gamero, M. D. (2007). Environmental strategies and their impact on hotel performance. *Environmental Strategies and Their Impact on Hotel Performance.*, *15*(6), 663–679.

Cohen, S. (2014). *The Growing Level of Environmental Awareness*. Retrieved December 11, 2015, from http://www.huffingtonpost.com/steven-cohen/the-growing-level-of-envi_b_6390054.html

Cohen, N. (2011). *Green business: and A-to-Z guide*. Sage Pub. doi:10.4135/9781412973793

Conner, M., & Armitage, C. J. (1998). Extending the Theory of Planned Behavior: A Review and Avenues for Further Research. *Journal of Applied Social Psychology*, *28*(15), 1429–1464. doi:10.1111/j.1559-1816.1998.tb01685.x

Connolly, J., & Prothero, A. (2008). Green consumption: Life-politics, risk and contradictions. *Journal of Consumer Culture*, *8*(1), 117–145. doi:10.1177/1469540507086422

Conradi, R., & Wang, A. I. (Eds.). (2003). Empirical Methods and Studies in Software Engineering. Berlin, Germany: Academic Press.

Conway, G. R. (1987). The properties of egroecosystem. *Agricultural Systems*, *24*(2), 95–117. doi:10.1016/0308-521X(87)90056-4

Cook, D. T., & Ryan, J. M. (2015). *The Wiley Blackwell encyclopedia of consumption and consumer*. John Wiley & Sons. doi:10.1002/9781118989463

Corsi, A., & Novelli, S. (2003). Measuring quantity-constrained and maximum prices consumers are willing to pay for quality improvements: the case of organic beef meat. In *Proceedings of the 25th International Conference of Agricultural Economists (IAAC)*. Durban, South Africa: Document Transformation Technologies.

Costanigro, M., McFadden, D. T., Kroll, S., & Nurse, G. (2011). An in-store valuation of local and organic apples: The role of social desirability. *Agribusiness*, *27*(4), 465–477. doi:10.1002/agr.20281

Costa, Pinto, D., Nique, W. M., Herter M., M., & Borges, A. (2016). Green consumers and their identities: How identities change the motivation for green consumption. *International Journal of Consumer Studies*, 1–12.

Cowan, K., & Kinley, T. (2014). Green spirit: Consumer empathies for green apparel. *International Journal of Consumer Studies*, *38*(5), 493–499. doi:10.1111/ijcs.12125

Cox, R. (2010). *Environmental communication and the public sphere*. Sage.

Cramer, J. (1998). Environmental management: From fit to stretch.. *Business Strategy and the Environment*, *7*(3), 162–172. doi:10.1002/(SICI)1099-0836(199807)7:3<162::AID-BSE149>3.0.CO;2-Q

Crane, A. (2000). Facing the backlash: Green marketing and strategic reorientation in the 1990s. *Journal of Strategic Marketing*, *8*(3), 277–296. doi:10.1080/09652540050110011

Crane, A., Matten, D., & Moon, J. (2008). Ecological Citizenship and the Corporation: Politicizing the New Corporate Environmentalism. *Organization & Environment*, *21*(4), 371–389. doi:10.1177/1086026608326075

Creswell, J. W. (1994). *Research Design, Qualitative and Quantitative Approaches*. Sage Publications.

Cronin, J. J. Jr, Smith, J. S., Gleim, M. R., Ramirez, E., & Martinez, J. D. (2011). Green marketing strategies: An examination of stakeholders and the opportunities they present. *Journal of the Academy of Marketing Science*, *39*(1), 158–174. doi:10.1007/s11747-010-0227-0

Dacin, M. T., Kostova, T., & Roth, K. (2008). Institutional Theory in the Study of Multinational Corporations : A Critique and New Directions. *Academy of Management Review*, *33*(4), 994–1006. doi:10.5465/AMR.2008.34422026

Daily, B. F., Bishop, J. W., & Massoud, J. (2012). The role of training and empowerment in environmental performance: A study of the Mexican *maquiladora* industry. *International Journal of Operations & Production Management*, *32*(5), 631–647. doi:10.1108/01443571211226524

Danaher, K., Biggs, S., & Mark, J. (2016). *Building the Green Economy: Success Stories from the Grassroots*. Routledge.

Daştan, İ., & Gürler, C. (2016). Yeşil bilgi teknolojileri ürün tercihinde tüketici satın alma niyetlerini etkileyen faktörlerin tespiti. *Atatürk University Journal of Economics & Administrative Sciences*, *30*(1), 173–186.

Davenport, C., Gillis, J., Chan, S., & Eddy, M. (2015). Inside the Paris Climate Deal. *The New York Times*. Retrieved from http://www.nytimes.com/interactive/2015/12/12/world/paris-climate-change-deal-explainer.html?action=click&contentCollection=earth&region=rank&module=package&version=highlights&contentPlacement=1&pgtype=collection&_r=0

Davidson, M. C. G., Mcphail, R., & Barry, S. (2011). *Hospitality HRM: past, present and the future*. Retrieved from https://doi.org/10.1108/09596111111130001

Davidsson, P., Klofsten, M., & Hunter, E. (2006). Institutional Forces: The Invisible Hand that Shapes Venture Ideas? *International Small Business Journal*, *24*(2), 115–131. doi:10.1177/0266242606061834

Davies, S., & Alperson, P. (2015). *The philosophy of art*. John Wiley & Sons.

Dawes, R. M. (1980). Social Dilemmas. *Annual Review of Psychology, 31*(1), 169–193. doi:10.1146/annurev.ps.31.020180.001125

Day, J., & Cai, L. (2012). Environmental and energy-related challenges to sustainable tourism in the United States and China. *International Journal of Sustainable Development and World Ecology, 19*(5), 379–388. doi:10.1080/13504509.2012.675600

De Boer, J. (2003). Sustainability labelling schemes: The logic of their claims and their functions for stakeholders. *Business Strategy and the Environment, 12*(4), 254–264. doi:10.1002/bse.362

De Houwer, J., Teige-Mocigemba, S., Spruyt, A., & Moors, A. (2009). Implicit measures: A normative analysis and review. *Psychological Bulletin, 135*(3), 347–368. doi:10.1037/a0014211 PMID:19379018

Del Brio, J. A., Fernandez, E., & Junquera, B. (2007). *Management and employee involvement in achieving an environmental action-based competitive advantage: an empirical study. The International Journal of Human Resource Management, 18.* https://doi.org/10.1080/09585190601178687

Delafrooz, N., Taleghani, M., & Nouri, B. (2014). Effect of green marketing on consumer purchase behavior. *QScience Connect*, 5.

Delmas, M. A., & Grant, L. E. (2014). Eco-labeling strategies and price-premium: The wine industry puzzle. *Business & Society, 53*(1), 6–44. doi:10.1177/0007650310362254

Denison, E., & Ren, G. Y. (2001). *Packaging prototypes 3: Thinking green* (Vol. 3). Rotovision.

Denver, S., & Jensen, J. D. (2014). Consumer preferences for organically and locally produced apples. *Food Quality and Preference, 31*, 129–134. doi:10.1016/j.foodqual.2013.08.014

Denzin, N. K., & Lincoln, Y. S. (1994). *Handbook of Qualitative Research.* London, UK: Sage Publications.

Desai, S. (2011). A Tale of Entrepreneurship in Two Iraqi Cities. *Journal of Small Business and Entrepreneurship, 24*(2), 283–292. doi:10.1080/08276331.2011.10593539

Desai, S. (2016). Destructive entrepreneurship and the security context: Program design considerations for disarmament, demobilization and reintegration (DDR) and counterinsurgency. *Journal of Entrepreneurship and Public Policy, 5*(2), 240–250. doi:10.1108/JEPP-03-2016-0009

DeSimone, L. D., & Popoff, F. (1997). *Eco-efficiency: The Business Link to Sustainable Development.* London: The MIT Press.

Devi Juwaheer, T., Pudaruth, S., & Monique Emmanuelle Noyaux, M. (2012). Analysing the impact of green marketing strategies on consumer purchasing patterns in Mauritius. *World Journal of Entrepreneurship. Management and Sustainable Development, 8*(1), 36–59.

Diamantopoulos, A., Schlegelmilch, B. B., Sinkovics, R. R., & Bohlen, G. M. (2003). Can socio-demographics still play a role in profiling green consumers? A review of the evidence and an empirical investigation. *Journal of Business Research, 56*(6), 465–448. doi:10.1016/S0148-2963(01)00241-7

Dief, M. E., & Font, X. (2010). The determinants of hotels marketing managers green marketing behaviour. *Journal of Sustainable Tourism, 18*(2), 157–174. doi:10.1080/09669580903464232

Diego-Mas, J. A., Poveda-Bautista, R., & Alcaide-Marzal, J. (2016). Designing the appearance of environmentally sustainable products. *Journal of Cleaner Production, 135*, 784–793. doi:10.1016/j.jclepro.2016.06.173

Dimaggio, P., & Powell, W. (1991). The New Institutionalism in organizational analysis. *The International Encyclopedia of Organization Studies*, 144–145. Retrieved from http://web.stanford.edu/group/song/papers/NewInstitutionalism.pdf

DiMaggio, P. J., & Powell, W. W. (1983). The Iron Cage Revisited: Institutional Isomorphism and Collective Rationality in Organizational Fields. *American Sociological Review*, *48*(2), 147. doi:10.2307/2095101

Djip, V. (2014). Entrepreneurship and SME development in post-conflict societies: The case of Bosnia & Herzegovina. *Journal of Entrepreneurship and Public Policy*, *3*(2), 254–274. doi:10.1108/JEPP-09-2012-0048

Dobni, D., & Zinkhan, G. M. (1990). In search of brand image: A foundation analysis. *Advances in Consumer Research. Association for Consumer Research (U. S.)*, *17*(1), 110–119.

Dobson, A. (2003). *Citizenship and the environment*. Oxford, UK: Oxford University Press. doi:10.1093/0199258449.001.0001

Doherty, L. (2013). *Environmental sustainability practices in the hospitality industry of orange county*. California Polytechnic State University.

Dolnicar, S., & Otter, T. (2003). Which hotel attributes matter? A review of previous and a framework for future research. In *Proceedings of the 9th Annual Conference of the Asia Pacific Tourism Association (APTA)*. University of Technology Sydney. http://doi.org/http://ro.uow.edu.au/commpapers/268

Dolores Lopez-Gamero, M., Claver-Cortes, E., & Francisco Molina-Azorin, J. (2011). Environmental Perception, Management, and Competitive Opportunity in Spanish Hotels. *Cornell Hospitality Quarterly*, *52*(4), 480–500. doi:10.1177/1938965511420694

Dominici, G., & Guzzo, R. (2010). Customer satisfaction in the hotel industry : A case study from Sicily. *International Journal of Marketing Studies*, *2*(2), 3–12. doi:10.5539/ijms.v2n2p3

D'Souza, C., Taghian, M., Lamb, P., & Peretiatkos, R. (2006). Green products and corporate strategy: an empirical investigation. *Society and Business Review*, *1*(2), 144-157.

Dunlap, R. E., & Van Liere, K. D. (1978). The New Environmental Paradigm.. *The Journal of Environmental Education*, *9*(4), 10–19. doi:10.1080/00958964.1978.10801875

Dunlap, R., Liere, K., Mertig, A., & Jones, R. E. (2000). Measuring endorsement of the new ecological paradigm: A revised NEP scale. *The Journal of Social Issues*, *56*(3), 425–442. doi:10.1111/0022-4537.00176

Dureja, H., Kaushik, D., Gupta, M., Kumar, V., & Lather, V. (2005). Cosmeceuticals: An emerging concept. *Indian Journal of Pharmacology*, *37*(3), 155. doi:10.4103/0253-7613.16211

Eagly, A. H., & Chaiken, S. (1993). *The psychology of attitudes*. Fort Worth, TX: Harcourt Brace Jovanovich.

Eckhardt, G. M., Belk, R., & Devinney, T. M. (2010). Why dont consumers consume ethically? *Journal of Consumer Behaviour*, *9*(6), 426–436. doi:10.1002/cb.332

Economic Planning Unit. (2015). *Eleventh Malaysia Plan 2016-2020. Rancangan Malaysia Kesebelas (Eleventh Malaysia Plan): 2016-2020*. Kuala Lumpur: Percetakan Nasional Malaysia Berhad. Retrieved from http://rmk11.epu.gov.my/book/eng/Elevent-Malaysia-Plan/RMKe-11 Book.pdf

Edstrom, A., & Lorange, P. (1984). Matching strategy and HR in multinational corporation. Journal of International Business Studies.

Eggeling, J. (2010). *Sustainable Tourism Practices in the Hospitality Sector : A Case Study of Scandic*. Mid Sweden University Östersund.

Eldesouky, A., Mesías, F. J., Elghannam, A., Gaspar, P., & Escribano, M. (2016). Are packaging and presentation format key attributes for cheese consumers? *International Dairy Journal*, *61*, 245–249. doi:10.1016/j.idairyj.2016.06.011

Eldesouky, A., Pulido, A. F., & Mesías, F. J. (2015). The role of packaging and presentation format in consumers preferences for food: An application of projective techniques. *Journal of Sensory Studies*, *30*(5), 360–369. doi:10.1111/joss.12162

Elkington, J. (2004). Enter the triple bottom line. In The triple bottom line: Does it all add up?. Routledge.

Elkington, J. (1997). *Cannibals with forks. The triple bottom line of 21st century*. Mankato, MN: Capstone.

Elliott, R. (1994). Exploring the symbolic meaning of brands. *British Journal of Management*, *5*(s1), S13–S19. doi:10.1111/j.1467-8551.1994.tb00126.x

Emmet, S., & Sood, V. (2010). *Green supply chains: an action manifesto*. John Wiley & Sons.

Engel, J. F., Blackwell, R. D., & Miniard, P. W. (1990). *Customer Behavior* (6th ed.). Hinsdale: Chicago Dryden Press.

Enneking, U. (2002). Analysis of food preferences using discrete choice modelling – The case of organic sausages. *Agrarwirtschaft*, *52*(5), 254–267.

Epstein, M., & Roy, M.-J. (1998). Managing corporate environmental performance. *European Management Journal*, *16*(3), 284–296. doi:10.1016/S0263-2373(98)00005-X

Erdil, O., & Kitapçı, H. (2007). TKY araçlarının kullanımı ve firma yenilikçiliğinin yeni ürün geliştirme hızı ve işletme performansına etkisi. *Atatürk Üniversitesi İktisadi ve İdari Bilimler Dergisi*, *21*(1), 233–145.

Erdogan, N., & Baris, E. (2007). Environmental protection programs and conservation practices of hotels in Ankara, Turkey. *Tourism Management*, *28*(2), 604–614. doi:10.1016/j.tourman.2006.07.003

Erdogan, N., & Tosun, C. (2009). Environmental performance of tourism accommodations in the protected areas: Case of Goreme Historical National Park. *International Journal of Hospitality Management*, *28*(3), 406–414. doi:10.1016/j.ijhm.2009.01.005

Escribano, A. J. (2016a). Beef cattle farms conversion to the organic system. Recommendations for success in the face of future changes in a global context. *Sustainability*, *8*(6), 572. doi:10.3390/su8060572

Escribano, A. J. (2016b). Organic livestock farming: Challenges, perspectives, and strategies to increase its contribution to the agrifood system's sustainability. In P. Konvalina (Ed.), *Organic Farming—A Promising Way of Food Production* (pp. 229–260). Rijeka, Croatia: InTech; doi:10.5772/61272

Escribano, A. J., Escribano, M., Gaspar, P., Mesías, F. J., & Pulido, F. (2015). Comparative sustainability assessment of extensive beef cattle farms in a high nature value agroforestry system. In V. R. Squires (Ed.), *Rangeland ecology, management and conservation benefits* (pp. 65–85). Lanzhou, China: Nova Publishers.

Essa, S. A. G., Dekker, H., & Groot, T. (2015). Improving outsourcing negotiations. *Amsterdam in Science, Business and Society*, *2015*(2), 28-29.

Esty, D., & Winston, A. (2009). *Green to gold: How smart companies use environmental strategy to innovate, create value, and build competitive advantage*. John Wiley & Sons.

European Commission. (2012). *Technical Report section 061: Policies to encourage sustainable consumption*. Retrieved from http://ec.europa.eu/environment/eussd/pdf/report_22082012.pdf

Falguera, V., Aliguer, N., & Falguera, M. (2012). An integrated approach to current trends in food consumption: Moving toward functional and organic products?. *Food Control*, *26*(2), 274–281. doi:10.1016/j.foodcont.2012.01.051

Faulkner, B., Mascardo, G., & Laws, E. (2000). *Tourism in the 21st century: Lessons from experience*. London: Continuum.

Fayyazi, M., Shahbazmoradi, S., Afshar, Z., & Shahbazmoradi, M. R. (2015). Investigating the barriers of the green human resource management implementation in oil industry. *Management Science Letters, 5*(1), 101–108. https://doi.org/10.5267/j.msl.2014.12.002

Fazio, R. H. (1990). Multiple processes by which attitudes guide behaviour: The MODE model as an integrative framework. In M. P. Zanna (Ed.), *Advances in experimental psychology* (Vol. 23, pp. 75–109). San Diego, CA: Academic Press.

Fazio, R. H., & Olson, M. A. (2003). Implicit measures in social cog- nition research: Their meaning and use. *Annual Review of Psychology, 54*(1), 297–327. doi:10.1146/annurev.psych.54.101601.145225 PMID:12172003

Ferrari, M. D., & Sternberg, R. J. (1998). *Self-awareness: Its nature and development*. Guilford press.

Ferrell, W. P. (2008). *Marketing*. Cengage Learning.

Festinger, L. (1957). *A theory of cognitive dissonance*. Evanston, IL: Row, Peterson.

Finisterra do Paço, A. M., & Raposo, M. L. (2010). Green consumer market segmentation: Empirical findings from Portugal. *International Journal of Consumer Studies, 34*(4), 429–436. doi:10.1111/j.1470-6431.2010.00869.x

Fishbein, M., & Ajzen, I. (1975). *Beliefs, attitude, intention and behavior*. Reading, MA: Addison-Wesley.

Fiske, S. T., & Taylor, S. E. (2013). Social Cognition: From Brains to Culture. *Sage (Atlanta, Ga.)*.

Florea, N.V. (2013). *Auditul resurselor umane*. Bucuresti, Romania: C. H. Beck.

Florea, N.V. (2014). *Planul de marketing*. Bucuresti, Romania: C. H. Beck.

Florea, N. V. (2011). Using branding to attract, recruit and retain talented staff. *Marketing & Management Review, 9*(2), 283–297.

Florea, N. V., & Florea, D. (2009). *Integrating sustainable development in human resources recruitment and employment processes. In Conferinta Dezvoltarea Durabila şi energii regenerabile, Univ* (pp. 260–264). Spiru Haret.

Folashade, O., Omoregie, H., & Ochogu, P. (2012). Standardization of herbal medicines-A review. *International Journal of Biodiversity and Conservation, 4*(3), 101–112.

Font i Furnols, M., Realini, C., Montossi, F., Sañudo, C., Campo, M. M., Oliver, M. A., & Guerrero, L. et al. (2011). Consumers purchasing intention for lamb meat affected by country of origin, feeding system and meat price: A conjoint study in Spain, France and United Kingdom. *Food Quality and Preference, 22*(5), 443–451. doi:10.1016/j.foodqual.2011.02.007

Font i Furnols, M., San Julián, R., Guerrero, L., Sañudo, C., Campo, M. M., Olleta, J. L., & Montossi, F. et al. (2006). Acceptability of lamb meat from different producing systems and ageing time to German, Spanish and British consumers. *Meat Science, 72*(3), 545–554. doi:10.1016/j.meatsci.2005.09.002 PMID:22061739

Food and Agriculture Organization of the United Nations (FAO). (2016). FAO's work on climate change: Livestock and climate change. In *United Nations Climate Change Conference 2016*. Marrakech, Morocco: FAO.

Forte, M., & Lamont, B. T. (1998). The bottom line effects of greening. *The Academy of Management Executive, 12*(1), 89–90.

Foster, S. (2012). *Tyler's honest herbal: a sensible guide to the use of herbs and related remedies*. Routledge.

Fotopoulos, C., & Krystallis, A. (2002b). Purchasing motives and profile of the Greek consumer: A country-wide survey. *British Food Journal, 104*(9), 730–765. doi:10.1108/00070700210443110

Fotopoulus, C., & Krystallis, A. (2002a). Organic product avoidance. Reasons for rejection and potential buyers' identification in a countrywide survey. *British Food Journal, 104*(3/4/5), 233-260. doi:10.1108/00070700210425697

Fraj-Andrés, E., Martínez Salinas, E., & Matute Vallejo, J. (2009b). Factors affecting corporate environmental strategy in Spanish industrial firms. *Business Strategy and the Environment, 18*(8), 500–514. doi:10.1002/bse.611

Fraj-Andrés, E., Martinez-Salinas, E., & Matute-Vallejo, J. (2009a). A multidimensional approach to the influence of environmental marketing and orientation on the firms organizational performance. *Journal of Business Ethics, 88*(2), 263–286. doi:10.1007/s10551-008-9962-2

Fraj, E., Martínez, E., & Matute, J. (2011). Green marketing strategy and the firms performance: The moderating role of environmental culture. *Journal of Strategic Marketing, 19*(4), 339–355. doi:10.1080/0965254X.2011.581382

Friend, G. (2009). *The truth about green business.* Que Publishing.

Fritz, A. J. (2013). A Critique of the Relationship between Scientific Cognitivism and Positive Aesthetics. American Society for Aesthetics Graduate E-Journal, 5(2).

Fujii, S., Gärling, T., & Kitamura, R. (2001). Changes in drivers perceptions and use of public transport during a freeway closure: Effects of temporary structural change on cooperation in a real-life social dilemma. *Environment and Behavior, 33*(6), 796–808. doi:10.1177/00139160121973241

Fuller, D. A. (1999). *Sustainable marketing: Managerial-ecological issues.* Sage Publications.

Furqan, A., Mat Som, A. P., & Hussin, R. (2010). Promoting green tourism for future sustainability. *Theoretical and Empirical Researches in Urban Management, 8*(17), 64–74.

Gadenne, D. L., Kennedy, J., & McKeiver, C. (2009). An empirical study of environmental awareness and practices in SMEs. *Journal of Business Ethics, 84*(1), 45–63. doi:10.1007/s10551-008-9672-9

Gao, Y., & Mattila, A. S. (2014). Improving consumer satisfaction in green hotels: The roles of perceived warmth, perceived competence, and CSR motive. *International Journal of Hospitality Management, 42*, 20–31. doi:10.1016/j.ijhm.2014.06.003

García-Torres, S., López-Gajardo, A., & Mesías, F. J. (2016). Intensive vs. free-range organic beef. A preference study through consumer liking and conjoint analysis. *Meat Science, 114*, 114–120. doi:10.1016/j.meatsci.2015.12.019 PMID:26771143

Garg, A. (2015). Green marketing for sustainable development: An industry perspective. *Sustainable Development, 23*(5), 301–316. doi:10.1002/sd.1592

Garvin, D. A. (1998). Building a Learning Organization. Harvard Business Review on Knowledge Management, 47-80.

Gasparatos, A., & Willis, K. (2015). *Biodiversity in the green economy.* Routledge.

Gassler, B., Meyer-Höfer, M., & Spiller, A. (2016). Exploring Consumers' Expectations of Sustainability in Mature and Emerging Markets. *Journal of Global Marketing*, 1–14.

Gatersleben, B., Steg, L., & Vlek, C. (2002). Measurement and Determinants of Environmentally Significant Consumer Behavior. *Environment and Behavior, 34*(3), 335–362. doi:10.1177/0013916502034003004

Gbadamosi. (2016). *Handbook of Research on Consumerism and Buying Behavior in Developing Nations.* IGI Global.

GBES. (2015). Starbucks: The World's Greenest Retailer. *Green Building Education Services(GBES).* Retrieved from http://www.gbes.com/blog/starbucks-the-worlds-greenest-retailer/

Gerini, F., Alfnes, F., & Schjøll, A. (2016). Organic- and animal welfare-labelled eggs: Competing for the same consumers? *Journal of Agricultural Economics*, *67*(2), 471–490. doi:10.1111/1477-9552.12154

Geuens, M., Weijters, B., & De Wulf, K. (2009). A new measure of brand personality. *International Journal of Research in Marketing*, *26*(2), 97–107. doi:10.1016/j.ijresmar.2008.12.002

Gifford, R. (2011). The dragons of inaction: Pychological barriers that limit climate change mitigation and adaptation. *The American Psychologist*, *66*(4), 290–302. doi:10.1037/a0023566 PMID:21553954

Gill, J. D., Crosby, L. A., & Taylor, J. R. (1986). Ecological concern, attitudes, and social norms in voting behavior. *Public Opinion Quarterly*. https://doi.org/10.1086/269002

Gilligan, M. J., Pasquale, B. J., & Samii, C. (2014). Civil war and social cohesion: Lab-in-the-field evidence from Nepal. *American Journal of Political Science*, *58*(3), 604–619. doi:10.1111/ajps.12067

Ginsberg, J. M., & Bloom, P. N. (2004). Choosing the right green-marketing strategy. *MIT Sloan Management Review*, *46*(1), 79–84.

Gleim, M. R., Smith, J. S., Andrews, D., & Cronin, J. J. Jr. (2013). Against the Green: A Multi-method Examination of the Barriers to Green Consumption. *Journal of Retailing*, *89*(1), 44–61. doi:10.1016/j.jretai.2012.10.001

Global Footprint Network. (n.d.). Retrieved from http://www.footprintnetwork.org/

Global. (2015). Green generation: Millennials say sustainability is a shopping priority. *Nielsen*. Retrieved from http://www.nielsen.com/in/en/insights/news/2015/green-generation-millennials-say-sustainability-is-a-shopping-priority.html

Goh, Y.-N., & Wahid, N. A. (2014). A Review on Green Purchase Behaviour Trend of Malaysian Consumers. *Asian Social Science*, *11*(2), 103. doi:10.5539/ass.v11n2p103

González-Roa, M. C., & Calatrava, J. (2009). *El comportamiento del consumidor español respecto a los alimentos ecológicos: Algunos resultados del proyecto Ecomarket II*. Paper presented at the Congreso Nacional de Economía Agraria, Almería, Spain.

Goodland, R. (2002). *Sustainability: Human, social, economic and environmental*. John Wiley & Sons.

Gössling, S., Peeters, P., Ceron, J. P., Dubois, G., Patterson, T., & Richardson, R. B. (2005). The eco-efficiency of tourism. *Ecological Economics*, *54*(4), 417–434. doi:10.1016/j.ecolecon.2004.10.006

Graci, S., & Kuehnel, J. (2010). How to increase your bottom line by going green. *Green Hotels & Responsible Tourism Initiative*, 1–28.

Gracia, A., & de Magistris, T. (2013). Organic food product purchase behaviour: A pilot study for urban consumers in the South of Italy. *Spanish Journal of Agricultural Research*, *5*(4), 439–451. doi:10.5424/sjar/2007054-5356

Grant, J. (2007). *Green is a principle, not a proposition: a review of the green marketing manifesto*. Academic Press.

Grant, J. (2009). *The green marketing manifesto*. West Sussex, UK: John Wiley & Sons.

Grau, S. L., & Folse, J. A. G. (2008). Cause-Related Marketing (CRM): The Influence of Donation Proximity and Message-Framing Cues on the Less-Involved Consumer. *Journal of Advertising*, *36*(4), 19–33. doi:10.2753/JOA0091-3367360402

Greenwald, A. G., McGhee, D. E., & Schwartz, J. L. (1998). Measuring individual differences in implicit cognition: The implicit association test. *Journal of Personality and Social Psychology*, *74*(6), 1464–1480. doi:10.1037/0022-3514.74.6.1464 PMID:9654756

Greenwood, R., & Hinings, C. R. (1996). Understanding radical organizational change: Bringing together the old and the new institutionalism. *Academy of Management Review*, *21*(4), 1022–1054. https://doi.org/10.5465/AMR.1996.9704071862

Gregory, G. D., & Leo, M. D. (2003). Repeated behavior and environmental psychology: The role of personal involvement and habit formation in explaining water consumption. *Journal of Applied Social Psychology*, *33*(6), 1261–1296. doi:10.1111/j.1559-1816.2003.tb01949.x

Grimmer, M., & Bingham, T. (2013). Company environmental performance and consumer purchase intentions. *Journal of Business Research*, *66*(10), 1945–1953. doi:10.1016/j.jbusres.2013.02.017

Grosjean, P. (2014). Conflict and social and political preferences: Evidence from World War II and civil conflict in 35 European countries. *Comparative Economic Studies*, *56*(3), 424–451. doi:10.1057/ces.2014.2

Grunert, K. G., Bredahl, L., & Brunsø, K. (2004). Consumer perception of meat quality and implications for product development in the meat sector—a review. *Meat Science*, *66*(2), 259–272. doi:10.1016/S0309-1740(03)00130-X PMID:22064127

Gulsrud, N. M., Gooding, S., & van den Bosch, C. C. K. (2013). Green space branding in Denmark in an era of neoliberal governance. *Urban Forestry & Urban Greening*, *12*(3), 330–337. doi:10.1016/j.ufug.2013.03.001

Gupta, S., & Ogden, D. T. (2009). To buy or not to buy? A social dilemma perspective on green buying. *Journal of Consumer Marketing*, *26*(6), 376–391. doi:10.1108/07363760910988201

Hacioglu, G., & Gök, O. (2013). Marketing performance measurement: marketing metrics in Turkish firms. *Journal of Business Economics and Management, 14*(sup1), 413-432.

Hair, J. F., Jr., Black, W. C., Babin, B. J., & Anderson, R. E. (2013). Multi-variate Data Analysis (7th ed.). Delhi: Dolrling Kindersley(India) Pvt. Ltd.

Hambrick, D. C. (2007). Upper Echelons Theory: An Update. *Source: The Academy of Management Review, 32*(2), 334–343. https://doi.org/10.5465/AMR.2007.24345254

Han, H. (2015). Travelers pro-environmental behavior in a green lodging context: Converging value-belief-norm theory and the theory of planned behavior. *Tourism Management*, *47*, 164–177. doi:10.1016/j.tourman.2014.09.014

Han, H., Hsu, L.-T., & Sheu, C. (2010). Application of the Theory of Planned Behavior to green hotel choice: Testing the effect of environmental friendly activities. *Tourism Management*, *31*(3), 325–334. doi:10.1016/j.tourman.2009.03.013

Hansson, S. O. (2014). Agricultural Biotechnology for Health and the Environment. In Biotechnology and Biodiversity (pp. 67-76). Springer International Publishing. doi:10.1007/978-3-319-09381-9_5

Harrow, J. (2010). *Philanthropy. In Third sector research* (pp. 121–137). Springer. doi:10.1007/978-1-4419-5707-8_10

Hartmann, P., & Ibáñez, V. A. (2006). Green value added. *Marketing Intelligence & Planning*, *24*(7), 673–680. doi:10.1108/02634500610711842

Hasler, C. M. (2000). The changing face of functional foods. *Journal of the American College of Nutrition, 19*(sup5), 499S-506S.

Hassan, H., & Nezakati, H. (2014). Green Tourism Practices in Malaysia. In Selected Issues in Hospitality and Tourism (pp. 24–36). Serdang, Selangor: Universiti Putra Malaysia Press.

Ha, T. (2008). *The Australian green consumer guide: choosing products for a healthier home,planet and bank balance*. UNSW.

Haws, K., Winterich, K. P., & Reczek, R. W. (2013). Seeing the world through GREEN-tinted glasses: Green consumption values and responses to environmentally friendly products. *Journal of Consumer Psychology*.

Heasman, M., & Mellentin, J. (2001). *The functional foods revolution: healthy people, healthy profits?* Routledge.

Hemmerling, S., Hamm, U., & Spiller, A. (2015). Consumption behaviour regarding organic food from a marketing perspective—a literature review. *Organic Agriculture*, *5*(4), 277–313. doi:10.1007/s13165-015-0109-3

Herremans, I. M., Herschovis, M. S., & Bertels, S. (2009). Leaders and laggards: The influence of competing logics on corporate environmental action. *Journal of Business Ethics*, *89*(3), 449–472. doi:10.1007/s10551-008-0010-z

Herrera, T. (2010). 10 Green NGOs Businesses Should Know About. *GreenBiz*. Retrieved from https://www.greenbiz.com/blog/2010/06/14/10-green-ngos-businesses-know-about

Heyl, M., Díaz, E. M., & Cifuentes, L. (2013). Environmental attitudes and behaviors of college students: A case study conducted at a chilean university. *Revista Latinoamericana de Psicología*, *45*(3), 487. doi:10.14349/rlp.v45i3.1489

Hines, J. M., Hungerford, H. R., & Tomera, A. N. (1987). Analysis and Synthesis o f Research on Responsible Environmental Behavior: A Meta-Analysis. *The Journal of Environmental Education*, *18*(2), 1–8. doi:10.1080/00958964.1987.9943482

Hobson, K. (2001). Sustainable lifestyles: rethinking barriers and behaviour change. *Exploring sustainable consumption: Environmental policy and the social sciences*, 191-209.

Hoffman, A. J. (1999). Institutional evolution and change: Environmentalism and the U.S. chemical industry. *Academy of Management Journal*, *42*(4), 351–371. doi:10.2307/257008

Holbeche, L. (2012). *Aligning human resources and business strategy*. Butterworth-Heinemann.

Hong, J. W., & Zinkhan, G. M. (1995). Self-concept and advertising effectiveness: The influence of congruency, conspicuousness, and response mode. *Psychology and Marketing*, *12*(1), 53–77. doi:10.1002/mar.4220120105

Houle, B. J., Sagarin, B. J., & Kaplan, M. F. (2005). A Functional Approach to Volunteerism: Do Volunteer Motives Predict Task Preference? *Basic and Applied Social Psychology*, *27*(4), 337–344. doi:10.1207/s15324834basp2704_6

Hoyer, W. D. (1984). An examination of consumer decision making for a common repeat purchase product. *The Journal of Consumer Research*, *11*(3), 822–829. doi:10.1086/209017

Hughner, R. S., McDonagh, P., Prothero, A., Shultz, C. J., & Stanton, J. (2007). Who are organic food consumers? A compilation and review of why people purchase organic food. *Journal of Consumer Behaviour*, *6*(23), 94–110. doi:10.1002/cb.210

Hummel, R. P. (2016). Arendt, Kant and the beauty of politics: a phenomenological view. In *Political Phenomenology* (pp. 93–120). Springer International Publishing. doi:10.1007/978-3-319-27775-2_7

Hunt, L., Rosin, C., Campell, H., & Fairweather, J. (2015). Organic Farmers: Contributing to the Resilience of the Food System?. In Re-Thinking Organic Food and Farming in a Changing World (pp. 187-211). Springer Netherlands.

Husted, B. W., Russo, M. V., Meza, C. E. B., & Tilleman, S. G. (2014). An exploratory study of environmental attitudes and the willingness to pay for environmental certification in Mexico. *Journal of Business Research*, *67*(5), 891–899. doi:10.1016/j.jbusres.2013.07.008

Iacobucci, D. (2010). Structural equations modeling: Fit indices, sample size, and advanced topics. *Journal of Consumer Psychology*, *20*(1), 90–98. doi:10.1016/j.jcps.2009.09.003

Iannuzzi, A. (2016). *Greener products: the making and marketing of sustainable brands.* CRC Press.

Ilinitch, A. Y., Soderstrom, N. S., & Thomas, E. T. (1998). Measuring corporate environmental performance. *Journal of Accounting and Public Policy, 17*(4–5), 383–408. https://doi.org/10.1016/S0278-4254(98)10012-1

Imada, M. (2010). *Civil Society in Japan: Democracy, voluntary action, and philanthropy. In Civic Engagement in Contemporary Japan* (pp. 21–40). Springer. doi:10.1007/978-1-4419-1504-7_2

Iozzi, L. A. (1989a). What research says to the educator. Part one: Environmental education and the affective domain. *The Journal of Environmental Education, 20*(3), 3–9. doi:10.1080/00958964.1989.9942782

Iozzi, L. A. (1989b). What Research Says to the Educator Part Two: Environmental Education and the Affective Domain. *The Journal of Environmental Education, 20*(4), 6–13. doi:10.1080/00958964.1989.9943033

Islam, N. (2008). Public Awareness About Environmental Issues: Perspective Bangladesh. *Asian Affairs, 30*(2), 30–56.

Jabbour, C. J. C., & Santos, F. C. A. (2008). The central role of human resource management in the search for sustainable organizations. *International Journal of Human Resource Management, 19*(12), 2133–2154. doi:10.1080/09585190802479389

Jackson, T. (2004). Consuming Paradise? - Unsustainable consumption in cultural and social-psychological context. *International Workshop on Driving Forces of and Barriers to Sustainable Consumption*, 402.

Jackson, T. (2005). *Motivating sustainable consumption: a review of evidence on consumer behaviour and behavioural change: a report to the Sustainable Development Research Network.* Centre for Environmental Strategy, University of Surrey.

Jain, S. K., & Kaur, G. (2006). Role of socio-demographics in segmenting and profiling green consumers: An exploratory study of consumers in India. *Journal of International Consumer Marketing, 18*(3), 107–146. doi:10.1300/J046v18n03_06

Jamal, A., & Naser, K. (2002). Customer satisfaction and retail banking: An assessment of some of the key antecedents of customer satisfaction in retail banking. *International Journal of Bank Marketing, 20*(4), 146–160. doi:10.1108/02652320210432936

Jamali, D., & Karam, C. (2016). Corporate Social Responsibility in Developing Countries as an Emerging Field of Study. *International Journal of Management Reviews*. doi:10.1111/ijmr.12112

Jennings, P. D., & Zandbergen, P. (1995). Ecologically Sustainable Organizations : An Institutional Approach. *Academy of Management Review, 20*(4), 1015–1052. https://doi.org/10.5465/AMR.1995.9512280034

Jerzyk, E. (2016). Design and communication of ecological content on sustainable packaging in young consumers opinions. *Journal of Food Products Marketing, 22*(6), 707–716. doi:10.1080/10454446.2015.1121435

Jianu, I., Ţurlea, C., & Guşatu, I. (2016). The reporting and sustainable business marketing. *Sustainability, 8*(1), 23. doi:10.3390/su8010023

Johnson, F. K. (2011). *Green marketing concepts. How to cash in with ecological Niche marketing.* PLR Rights Marketing.

Johnstone, M. L., & Tan, L. P. (2015). An exploration of environmentally-conscious consumers and the reasons why they do not buy green products. *Marketing Intelligence & Planning, 33*(5), 804–825. doi:10.1108/MIP-09-2013-0159

Jones, P., Clarke-Hill, C., Comfort, D., & Hillier, D. (2008). Marketing and sustainability. *Marketing Intelligence & Planning, 26*(2), 123–130. doi:10.1108/02634500810860584

Jones, P., Hillier, D., & Comfort, D. (2014). Sustainability in the global hotel industry. *International Journal of Contemporary Hospitality Management, 26*(1), 5–17. doi:10.1108/IJCHM-10-2012-0180

José, C., Jabbour, C., Beatriz, A., & De Sousa, L. (2015). Green human resource management and green supply chain management: Linking two emerging agendas. *Journal of Cleaner Production*, 1–10. https://doi.org/10.1016/j.jclepro.2015.01.052

Jose, C., Jabbour, C., Jugend, D., Beatriz, A., De Sousa, L., Gunasekaran, A., & Latan, H. (2015). Green product development and performance of Brazilian fi rms : Measuring the role of human and technical aspects. *Journal of Cleaner Production*, *87*, 442–451. doi:10.1016/j.jclepro.2014.09.036

Jungbluth, N., Tietje, O., & Scholz, R. W. (2000). Food Purchases: Impacts from the Consumers Point of View Investigated with a Modular LCA. *The International Journal of Life Cycle Assessment*, *5*(3), 134–142. doi:10.1007/BF02978609

Juvan, E., & Dolnicar, S. (2014). The attitude–behaviour gap in sustainable tourism. *Annals of Tourism Research*, *48*, 76–95. doi:10.1016/j.annals.2014.05.012

Kahle, L., & Gurel-Atay, E. (2015). *Communicating sustainabilityfor the green economy*. Routledge.

Kaiser, F. G., Oerke, B., & Bogner, F. X. (2007). Behavior-based environmental attitude: Development of an instrument for adolescents. *Journal of Environmental Psychology*, *27*(3), 242–251. doi:10.1016/j.jenvp.2007.06.004

Kaiser, F. G., Wölfing, S., & Fuhrer, U. (1999). Environmental attitude and ecological behaviour. *Journal of Environmental Psychology*, *19*(1), 1–19. doi:10.1006/jevp.1998.0107

Kalafatis, S. P., Pollard, M., East, R., & Tsogas, M. H. (1999). Green marketing and Ajzens theory of planned behaviour: A cross-market examination. *Journal of Consumer Marketing*, *16*(5), 441–460. doi:10.1108/07363769910289550

Kang, K. H., Lee, S., & Huh, C. (2010). Impacts of positive and negative corporate social responsibility activities on company performance in the hospitality industry. *International Journal of Hospitality Management*, *29*(1), 72–82. doi:10.1016/j.ijhm.2009.05.006

Kang, K. H., Stein, L., Heo, C. Y., & Lee, S. (2012). Consumers willingness to pay for green initiatives of the hotel industry. *International Journal of Hospitality Management*, *31*(2), 564–572. doi:10.1016/j.ijhm.2011.08.001

Kangun, N., Carlson, L., & Grove, S. J. (1991). Environmental advertising claims: A preliminary investigation. *Journal of Public Policy & Marketing*, *10*(2), 47–58.

Kapferer, J. N. (1998). *The role of branding in medical prescription: An empirical investigation*. HEC working paper. Jouy en Josas, France.

Kapferer, J. N. (2012). *The new strategic brand management: Advanced insights and strategic thinking*. Kogan Page Publishers.

Kaplan, S. (2000). New ways to promote proenvironmental behavior: Human nature and environmentally responsible behavior. *The Journal of Social Issues*, *56*(3), 491–508. doi:10.1111/0022-4537.00180

Kapoor, V. P. (2005). Herbal cosmetics for skin and hair care. *Nat Prod Radiance*, *4*(4), 306–314.

Kärnä, J., Hansen, E., & Juslin, H. (2003). Social responsibility in environmental marketing planning. *European Journal of Marketing*, *37*(5/6), 848–871. doi:10.1108/03090560310465170

Kasim, A. (2004). Socio-environmentally responsible hotel business: Do tourists to Penang Island, Malaysia care? *Journal of Hospitality & Leisure Marketing*, *11*(4), 5–28. doi:10.1300/J150v11n04_02

Kasim, A. (2007). Towards a Wider Adoption of Environmental Responsibility in the Hotel Sector. *International Journal of Hospitality & Tourism Administration*, *8*(2), 25–49. doi:10.1300/J149v08n02_02

Kasim, A. (2009). Managerial attitudes towards environmental management among small and medium hotels in Kuala Lumpur. *Journal of Sustainable Tourism*, *17*(6), 709–725. doi:10.1080/09669580902928468

Kasim, A., & Scarlat, C. (2007). Business Environmental Responsibility in the Hospitality Industry. *Management*, *2*(1), 5–23.

Kasimu, A. B., Zaiton, S., & Hassan, H. (2012). Hotels involvement in sustainable tourism practices in Klang Valley, Malaysia. *International Journal of Economics and Management*, *6*(1), 21–34.

Kates, R., Parris, T. M., & Leiserowitz, A. A. (2005). What is Sustainable Development? Goals, Indicators, Values, and Practice. *Environment*, *47*(3), 9–21.

Katz, D. (1960). The Functional Approach to the Study of Attitudes. *Public Opinion Quarterly*, *24*(2), 163–204. doi:10.1086/266945

Kaufmann, H. R. (2014). *Hanbook of reserach an consumerism in business and marketing: concepts and practices*. IGI Global. doi:10.4018/978-1-4666-5880-6

Keller, K. L., Apéria, T., & Georgson, M. (2008). *Strategic brand management: A European perspective*. Pearson Education.

Kelman, H. C. (1958). Compliance, identification and internalization: Three process of attitude change. *Conflict Resolution*, *2*(1), 51–60. doi:10.1177/002200275800200106

Kesidou, E., & Demirel, P. (2012). On the drivers of eco-innovations: Empirical evidence from the UK. *Research Policy*, *41*(5), 862–870. doi:10.1016/j.respol.2012.01.005

Khan, I. A., & Abourashed, E. A. (2011). *Leung's encyclopedia of common natural ingredients: used in food, drugs and cosmetics*. John Wiley & Sons.

Khare, A. (2014). Consumers susceptibility to interpersonal influence as a determining factor of ecologically conscious behaviour. *Marketing Intelligence & Planning*, *32*(1), 2–20. doi:10.1108/MIP-04-2013-0062

Khare, A. (2015). Antecedents to green buying behaviour: A study on consumers in an emerging economy. *Marketing Intelligence & Planning*, *33*(3), 309–329. doi:10.1108/MIP-05-2014-0083

Kibert, C. J. (2016). *Sustainable construction: Green building design and delivery*. John Wiley & Sons.

Kim, H. S. (2000). Examination of brand personality and brand attitude within the apparel product category. *Journal of Fashion Marketing and Management: An International Journal*, *4*(3), 243–252. doi:10.1108/eb022593

Kim, H. S., & Damhorst, M. L. (1998). Environmental concern and apparel consumption. *Clothing & Textiles Research Journal*, *16*(3), 126–133. doi:10.1177/0887302X9801600303

Kim, S. Y., Kim, S. Y., Yoon, J., Yoon, J., Choi, I., & Choi, I. (2016). What matters to promote consumers intention to patronize sustainable business-and-industry (B&I) food services?. *British Food Journal*, *118*(11), 2710–2731. doi:10.1108/BFJ-02-2016-0050

King, S. (1970). *What is a Brand?*. London: Walter Thompson Company Limited.

Kirgiz, A. (2016). *Green marketing: a case study of the sub-industry in Turkey*. Springer.

Kirk, D. (1995). Environmental management in hotels. *International Journal of Contemporary Hospitality Management*, *7*(6), 3–8. doi:10.1108/09596119510095325

Kirkpatrick, D. (1990). *Environmentalism: The new crusade*. Retrieved February 21, 2015, from http://archive.fortune.com/magazines/fortune/fortune_archive/1990/02/12/73069/ index.htm

Kitchenham, B., Pickard, L., & Pfleeger, S. L. (1995, July). Case Studies for Method and Tool Evaluation. *J IEEE Software*, 52-62.

Kleindorfer, P. R., Singhal, K., & Wassenhove, L. N. (2005). Sustainable operations management. *Production and Operations Management, 14*(4), 482–492. doi:10.1111/j.1937-5956.2005.tb00235.x

Klöckner, C. A., & Ohms, S. (2009). The importance of personal norms for purchasing organic milk. *British Food Journal, 111*(11), 1173–1187. doi:10.1108/00070700911001013

Koester, E. (2016). *Green entrepreneur handbook: the guide to building and growing a green and clean business.* CRC Press.

Kormos, C., & Gifford, R. (2014). The validity of self-report measures of proenvironmental behavior : A meta-analytic review. *Journal of Environmental Psychology, 40*, 359–371. doi:10.1016/j.jenvp.2014.09.003

Kostadinova, E. (2016). Sustainable consumer behavior: Literature overview. *Economic Alternatives*, (2), 224-234.

Köster, E. P., & Mojet, J. (2007). Boredom and the reasons why some new products fail. In H. J. H. MacFie (Ed.), Consumer-led food product development (pp. 262-280). Abington, UK: Woodhead Publishing. doi:10.1533/9781845693381.2.262

Kostova, T. (1997). Country institutional profiles: concept and measurement. *Academy of Management Best Papers Proceedings, 8*(1), 180–184. https://doi.org/10.5465/AMBPP.1997.4981338

Kostova, T., & Roth, K. (2002). Adoption of an Organizational Practice By Subsidiaries of Multinational Corporations: Institutional and Relational Effects. ^. *Academy of Management Journal, 45*(1), 215–233. doi:10.2307/3069293

Kotler, P. (2011). Reinventing Marketing to Manage the Environmental Imperative. *Journal of Marketing, 75*(July), 132–135. doi:10.1509/jmkg.75.4.132

Kotler, P., & Keller, K. L. (2012). *Marketing Management* (14th ed.). Boston: Prentice-Hall.

Kremer, P., & DeLiberty, T. L. (2011). Local food practices and growing potential: Mapping the case of Philadelphia. *Applied Geography (Sevenoaks, England), 31*(4), 1252–1261. doi:10.1016/j.apgeog.2011.01.007

Krishna, V. V., & Qaim, M. (2008). Consumer attitudes toward GM food and pesticide residues in India. *Applied Economic Perspectives and Policy, 30*(2), 233–251.

Krosnick, J. A. (1988). Attitude importance and attitude change. *Journal of Experimental Social Psychology, 24*(3), 240–255. doi:10.1016/0022-1031(88)90038-8

Krystallis, A., Arvanitoyannis, I., & Chryssohoidis, G. M. (2006). Is there a real difference between conventional and organic meat? Investigating consumers attitudes towards both meat types as an indicator of organic meats market potential. *Journal of Food Products Marketing, 12*(2), 47–78. doi:10.1300/J038v12n02_04

Krystallis, A., & Chryssohoidis, G. (2005). Consumers willingness to pay for organic food: Factors that affect it and variation per organic product type. *British Food Journal, 107*(5), 320–343. doi:10.1108/00070700510596901

Kumar, P., & Ghodeswar, B. (2015). Green Marketing Mix: A Review of Literature and Direction for Future Research. *International Journal of Asian Business and Information Management, 6*(3), 42–59.

La Via, G., Antonio, & Nucifora, M. D. (2002). The determinants of the price mark-up for organic fruit and vegetable products in the European Union. *British Food Journal, 104*(3/4/5), 319-336.

Lacasse, K. (2016). Dont be satisfied, identify! Strengthening positive spillover by connecting pro-environmental behaviors to an environmentalist label. *Journal of Environmental Psychology, 48*, 149–158. doi:10.1016/j.jenvp.2016.09.006

Lamberti, L., & Noci, G. (2010). Marketing strategy and marketing performance measurement system: Exploring the relationship. *European Management Journal, 28*(2), 139–152. doi:10.1016/j.emj.2009.04.007

Laroche, M., Bergeron, J., & Barbaro-Forleo, G. (2001). Targeting consumers who are willing to pay more for environmentally friendly products. *Journal of Consumer Marketing, 18*(6), 503–520. doi:10.1108/EUM0000000006155

Larsen, R. H., & Tambo, T. (2014). Managing cosmetics technologies in dynamic environments. In *Proceedings of the 4th Nordic Retail and Wholesale Conference*. Nordic Retail and Wholesale Association.

Lau, W. K., Chiu, S. M., & Yau, Y. (2014). Economising subsidies for green housing features: A stated preference approach. *Urbani Izziv, 25*(2).

Lay, J. C., & Hoppmann, C. A. (2015). Altruism and Prosocial Behavior. In N. A. Pachana (Ed.), *Encyclopedia of Geropsychology* (pp. 1–9). Singapore: Springer Singapore. doi:10.1007/978-981-287-080-3_69-1

Leder, H., & Nadal, M. (2014). Ten years of a model of aesthetic appreciation and aesthetic judgments: The aesthetic episode–developments and challenges in empirical aesthetics. *British Journal of Psychology, 105*(4), 443–464. doi:10.1111/bjop.12084 PMID:25280118

Lee, C. H., Wahid, N. A., & Goh, Y. N. (2012). Assessing determinants of green practices adoption : A conceptual framework. *Elixir Marketing Mgmt, 45*, 7760–7766.

Lee, K. (2008). Opportunities for green marketing: Young consumers. *Marketing Intelligence & Planning, 26*(6), 573–586. doi:10.1108/02634500810902839

Lee, K. (2009). Gender differences in Hong Kong adolescent consumers green purchasing behavior. *Journal of Consumer Marketing, 26*(2), 87–96. doi:10.1108/07363760910940456

Leiserowitz, A. A., Kates, R. W., & Parris, T. M. (2006). Sustainability values, attitudes and behaviors: a review of multi-national and global trends. *Annual Review of Environment and Resources, 31*(1), 413–444. doi:10.1146/annurev.energy.31.102505.133552

Leonidou, C. N., Katsikeas, C. S., & Morgan, N. A. (2013). Greening the marketing mix: Do firms do it and does it pay off? *Journal of the Academy of Marketing Science, 41*(2), 151–170. doi:10.1007/s11747-012-0317-2

Leonidou, C. N., & Leonidou, L. C. (2011). Research into environmental marketing/management: A bibliographic analysis. *European Journal of Marketing, 45*(1/2), 68–103. doi:10.1108/03090561111095603

Levy, S. J. (1959). Symbols for sales. *Harvard Business Review, 37*(Summer).

Li, C. R., Lin, C. J., & Chu, C. P. (2008). The nature of market orientation and the ambidexterity of innovations. *Management Decision, 46*(7), 1002–1026. doi:10.1108/00251740810890186

Ligade, V., Sreedhar, D., Manthan, J., & Udupa, N. (2009). Cosmeceuticals: Are they truly worth the cost? *Indian Journal of Dermatology, Venereology and Leprology, 75*(1), 8. doi:10.4103/0378-6323.45213 PMID:19172024

Lillemo, S. C. (2014). Measuring the effect of procrastination and environmental awareness on households energy-saving behaviours: An empirical approach. *Energy Policy, 66*, 249–256. doi:10.1016/j.enpol.2013.10.077

Ling-yee, L. (1997). Effect of Collectivist Orientation and Ecological Attitude on Actual Environmental Commitment. *Journal of International Consumer Marketing, 9*(4), 31–53. doi:10.1300/J046v09n04_03

Lita, R. P., Surya, S., Maruf, M., & Syahrul, L. (2014). Green attitude and behavior of local tourists towards hotels and restaurants in West Sumatra, Indonesia. *Procedia Environmental Sciences, 20*, 261–270. doi:10.1016/j.proenv.2014.03.033

Lober, D. D. J. (1996). Evaluating the environmental performance of corporations. *Journal of Managerial Issues*, *8*, 184–205.

López-Gamero, M. D., Molina-Azorín, J. F., & Claver-Cortés, E. (2009). The whole relationship between environmental variables and firm performance: Competitive advantage and firm resources as mediator variables. *Journal of Environmental Management*, *90*(10), 3110–3121. doi:10.1016/j.jenvman.2009.05.007 PMID:19482410

Luck, E., & Ginanti, A. (2013). Online environmental citizenship: Blogs, green marketing and consumer sentiment in the 21st Century. *Electronic Green Journal*, *1*(35), 1–26.

Lülfs, R., & Hahn, R. (2015). *Sustainable Behavior in the Business Sphere: A Comprehensive Overview of the Explanatory Power of Psychological Models*. https://doi.org/10.1177/1086026614522631

Luszczynska, A., & Schwarzer, R. (2005). Social cognitive theory. *Predicting Health Behaviour, 2*, 127-169.

MacDonald, E., Milfont, T., & Gavin, M. (2015). Applying the Elaboration Likelihood Model to increase recall of conservation messages and elaboration by zoo visitors. *Journal of Sustainable Tourism*, *9582*(November), 1–16. doi:10.1080/09669582.2015.1091464

Mainieri, T., Barnett, E. G., Valdero, T. R., Unipan, J. B., & Oskamp, S. (1997). Green Buying: The Influence of Environmental Concern on Consumer Behavior. *The Journal of Social Psychology*, *137*(2), 189–204. doi:10.1080/00224549709595430

Makower. (2014). *State of Green Business: Collaboration becomes an accelerator*. Retrieved from https://www.greenbiz.com/blog/2014/01/27/state-green-business-collaboration-becomes-accelerator

Malaysia, I. (2012). *Tourism & Hospitality Report*. Retrieved from http://etp.pemandu.gov.my/upload/Inside Investor - Tourism.pdf

Maloney, M. P., & Ward, M. P. (1973). Ecology: Lets Hear from the People An Objective Scale for the Measurement of Ecological Attitudes and Knowledge. *The American Psychologist*, *28*(July), 583–586. doi:10.1037/h0034936

Management Assoc. Info Ress. (2014). Marketing and consumer behavior: Concepts, methodologies, tools, and applications. IGI Global

Manaktola, K., & Jauhari, V. (2007). Exploring consumer attitude and behavior towards green practices in the lodging industry in India. *International Journal of Contemporary Hospitality Management*, *19*(5), 364–377. doi:10.1108/09596110710757534

Mandip, G. (2012). Green HRM: People Management Commitment to Environmental Sustainability. *Research Journal of Recent Sciences, 1*(2277–2502), 244–252.

Mandoki, K. (2016). *Everyday aesthetics: Prosaics, the play of culture and social identities*. Routledge.

Maniatis, P. (2016). Investigating factors influencing consumer decision-making while choosing green products. *Journal of Cleaner Production*, *132*, 215–228. doi:10.1016/j.jclepro.2015.02.067

Manly, B. F. J. (1994). *Multivariate Statistical Methods - A Primer* (2nd ed.). London: Chapman & Hall.

Mansvelt, J. (2010). *Green consumerism: an A-to-Z guide*. London, UK: Sage Pub.

Marcus, A., & Fremeth, A. R. (2009). Green Management Matters Regardless. *The Academy of Management Perspectives*, *23*(3), 17–26. doi:10.5465/AMP.2009.43479261

Marinova, D., Annandale, D., & Phillimore, J. (2008). *The international handbook on environmental technology management*. Edward Elgar Oublishing.

Martineau, P. (1958). The personality of a retail store. *Harvard Business Review*, *36*(Nov–Dec).

Martínez-Cerezo, S., Sañudo, C., Medel, I., & Olleta, J. L. (2005). Breed, slaughter weight and ageing time effects on sensory characteristics of lamb. *Meat Science*, *69*(3), 571–578. doi:10.1016/j.meatsci.2004.10.009 PMID:22062998

Marzano, S. (2003). *The new everyday: Views on ambient intelligence*. 010 Publishers.

Mat Said, A., & Ahmadun, F. l.-R., Hj. Paim, L., & Masud, J. (2003). Environmental concerns, knowledge and practices gap among Malaysian teachers. *International Journal of Sustainability in Higher Education*, *4*(4), 305–313. doi:10.1108/14676370310497534

Mattera, M., & Moreno-melgarejo, A. (2012). Strategic Implications of Corporate Social Responsibility in Hotel Industry : A Comparative Research Between NH Hotels and Meliá Hotels International. *Higher Learning Research Communications*, *2*(4), 37–53. doi:10.18870/hlrc.v2i4.85

Mattis, J. S., Jagers, R. J., Hatcher, C. A., Lawhon, G. D., Murphy, E. J., & Murray, Y. F. (2000). *Religiosity, volunteerism, and community involvement among African American men: An exploratory analysis*. Academic Press.

May, C., Finch, T., Mair, F., Ballini, L., Dowrick, C., Eccles, M., & Rogers, A. et al. (2007). Understanding the implementation of complex interventions in health care: The normalization process model. *BMC Health Services Research*, *7*(1), 148. doi:10.1186/1472-6963-7-148 PMID:17880693

McAlexander, J. H., Schouten, J. W., & Koenig, H. F. (2002). Building brand community. *Journal of Marketing*, *66*(1), 38–54. doi:10.1509/jmkg.66.1.38.18451

McDonagh, P., & Prothero, A. (2014). Sustainability marketing research: Past, present and future. *Journal of Marketing Management*, *30*(11–12), 1186–1219. doi:10.1080/0267257X.2014.943263

McEachern, M. G., & Schröeder, M. J. A. (2002). The role of livestock production ethics in consumer values towards meat. *Journal of Agricultural & Environmental Ethics*, *15*(2), 221–237. doi:10.1023/A:1015052816477

McEachern, M. G., & Willock, J. (2004). Producers and consumers of organic meat: A focus on attitudes and motivations. *British Food Journal*, *106*(7), 534–552. doi:10.1108/00070700410545737

McGuire, D., & Garavan, T. N. (2010). Closing Comments: A Call to Action. *Advances in Developing Human Resources*, *12*(5), 614–616. doi:10.1177/1523422310394435

McIntyre, A., & Milfont, T. L. (2016). Who Cares? Measuring Environmental Attitudes. In Research Methods for Environmental Psychology (pp. 93–114). John Wiley & Sons, Inc. doi:10.1002/9781119162124.ch6

McKechnie, G. E. (1977). The Environmental Response Inventory in Application. *Environment and Behavior*, *9*(2), 255–276. doi:10.1177/001391657792006

McKinnon, A., Browne, M., & Whiteing, A. (2015). *Green logistics: improving the environmental sustainability of logistics*. London, UK: Kogan Page Pub.

McMichael, P. (2016). *Development and social change: A global perspective*. Sage Publications.

Md Salleh, N. Z., Abdul Hamid, A. B., Hashim, N. H., & Omain, S. Z. (2010). *Issues and challenges in Malaysian hotel operations. In 3rd Asia-Euro Tourism, Hospitality and Gastronomy*. Subang: Taylor's College.

Megicks, P., Donnelly, R., & Harrison, G. (2009). *The marketing planning process*. Butterworth-Heinemann.

Mehta, K., & Chugan, P. K. (2015). Green HRM in Pursuit of Environmentally Sustainable Business. *Universal Journal of Industrial and Business Management, 3*(3), 74–81. https://doi.org/10.13189/ujibm.2015.030302

Mei, O. J., Ling, K. C., & Piew, T. H. (2012). The antecedents of green purchase intention among Malaysian consumers. *Asian Social Science*, *8*(13), 246. doi:10.5539/ass.v8n13p246

Mendleson, N., & Polonsky, M. J. (1995). Using strategic alliances to develop credible green marketing. *Journal of Consumer Marketing*, *12*(2), 4–18. doi:10.1108/07363769510084867

Mensah, I. (2006). Environmental management practices among hotels in the Greater Accra Region. *Journal Hospitality Management*, *25*(3), 414–431. doi:10.1016/j.ijhm.2005.02.003

Mesías, F. J., Escribano, M., Gaspar, P., & Pulido, F. (2008). Consumers' attitudes towards organic, PGI and conventional meats in Extremadura (Spain). *Archivos de Zootecnia*, *57*(218), 139–146.

Mesías, F. J., Martínez-Carrasco, F., Martínez, J. M., & Gaspar, P. (2011). Functional and organic eggs as an alternative to conventional production: A conjoint analysis of consumers preferences. *Journal of the Science of Food and Agriculture*, *91*(3), 532–538. doi:10.1002/jsfa.4217 PMID:21218489

Mesías, F. J., Pulido, F., Escribano, M., Gaspar, P., Pulido, A. F., Escribano, A., & Rodríguez Ledesma, A. (2013). Evaluation of new packaging formats for dry-cured meat products using conjoint analysis: An application to cry-cured Iberian ham. *Journal of Sensory Studies*, *28*(3), 238–247. doi:10.1111/joss.12040

Midmore, P., Naspetti, S., Sherwood, A.-M., Vairo, D., Wier, M., & Zanoli, R. (2005). Consumer attitudes to quality and safety of organic and low input foods: a review. Aberystwyth: University of Wales. Retrieved from https://www.researchgate.net/publication/265191937_CONSUMER_ATTITUDES_TO_QUALITY_AND_SAFETY_OF_ORGANIC_AND_LOW_INPUT_FOODS_A_REVIEW

Miles, M. P., & Covin, J. G. (2000). Environmental marketing: A source of reputational competitive and financial advantage. *Journal of Business Ethics*, *23*(3), 299–311. doi:10.1023/A:1006214509281

Milfont, T. L., & Duckitt, J. (2007). *A brief version of the environmental attitudes inventory.* Unpublished manuscript.

Milfont, T. L. (2009). The effects of social desirability on self-reported environmental attitudes and ecological behaviour. *The Environmentalist*, *29*(3), 263–269. doi:10.1007/s10669-008-9192-2

Milfont, T. L., & Duckitt, J. (2010). The environmental attitudes inventory: A valid and reliable measure to assess the structure of environmental attitudes. *Journal of Environmental Psychology*, *30*(1), 80–94. doi:10.1016/j.jenvp.2009.09.001

Milfont, T. L., Sibley, C. G., & Duckitt, J. (2009). Testing the Moderating Role of the Components of Norm Activation on the Relationship Between Values and Environmental Behavior. *Journal of Cross-Cultural Psychology*, *41*(1), 124–131. doi:10.1177/0022022109350506

Millar, M., & Baloglu, S. (2008). Hotel guests' preferences for green hotel attributes. *Proceedings of the European Council for Hotel, Restaurant, and Institutional Education Conference.*

Ministry of Tourism and Sports of Thailand. (2013). *ASEAN Tourism Standards.* Bangkok: ASEAN Tourism Standards.

Mishra, P., & Sharma, P. (2010). Green marketing in India: Emerging opportunities and challenges. *Journal of Engineering. Science and Management Education*, *3*(1), 9–14.

Mitchell, R. W., Wooliscroft, B., & Higham, J. (2010). Sustainable market orientation: A new approach to managing marketing strategy. *Journal of Macromarketing*, *30*(2), 160–170. doi:10.1177/0276146710361928

Mitchell, V.-W., & Papavassiliou, V. (1999). Marketing causes and implications of consumer confusion. *Journal of Product and Brand Management*, *8*(4), 319–342. doi:10.1108/10610429910284300

Mohamad, Z. Z., Tengku Arifin, T. R., Samsuri, A. S., & Mior Badrul Munir, M. F. (2014). Intention to visit green hotel in Malaysia : The impact of personal traits and marketing strategy. *International Journal of Business and Social Science, 5*(7), 167–173.

Mohamed, B. (2008). *Pelancongan lestari.* Kuala Lumpur: Dewan Bahasa dan Pustaka.

Mohd Noor, N. A., & Kumar, D. (2014). Eco friendly "Activities" vs Eco friendly "Attitude": Travelers intention to choose green hotels in Malaysia. *World Applied Sciences Journal, 30*(4), 506–513. doi:10.5829/idosi.wasj.2014.30.04.14062

Moher. (2009). *Preferred Reporting Items for Systematic Reviews and Meta-Analyses: The PRISMA Statement.* Available at: http://journals.plos.org/plosmedicine/article?id=10.1371/journal.pmed.1000097

Molina-Azorín, J. F., Claver-Cortés, E., López-Gamero, M. D., & Tarí, J. J. (2009). Green management and financial performance: A literature review. *Management Decision, 47*(7), 1080–1100. doi:10.1108/00251740910978313

Mondelaers, K., Verbeke, W., & Van Huylenbroeck, G. (2009b). Importance of health and environment as quality traits in the buying decision of organic products. *British Food Journal, 111*(10), 1121–1140. doi:10.1108/00070700910992952

Montgomery, D. C. (1997). *Design and Analysis of Experiments* (4th ed.). New York: John Wiley & Sons.

Moorthy, M. K., Yacob, P., Chelliah, M. K., & Arokiasamy, L. (2012). Drivers for Malaysian SMEs to Go Green. *International Journal of Academic Research in Business and Social Science, 2*(9), 74–86.

Mostafa, M. M. (2006). Antecedents of Egyptian Consumers' Green Purchase Intentions. *Journal of International Consumer Marketing.* https://doi.org/10.1300/J046v19n02_06

Mudrack, P. (2007). Individual personality factors that affect normative beliefs about the rightness of corporate social responsibility. *Business & Society, 46*(1), 33–62. doi:10.1177/0007650306290312

Mukherjee, P. K., Maity, N., Nema, N. K., & Sarkar, B. K. (2011). Bioactive compounds from natural resources against skin aging. *Phytomedicine, 19*(1), 64–73. doi:10.1016/j.phymed.2011.10.003 PMID:22115797

Müller, B., & Chandon, J. L. (2003). The impact of visiting a brand website on brand personality. *Electronic Markets, 13*(3), 210–221. doi:10.1080/1019678032000108301

Muntean, A., & Stremtan, F. (2010). Green marketing: A new challenge for Romanian organisations. *Journal of Environmental Protection and Ecology, 11*(4), 1472–1474.

Muralidharan, S., Rejón-Guardia, F., & Xue, F. (2016). Understanding the green buying behavior of younger Millennials from India and the United States: A structural equation modeling approach. *Journal of International Consumer Marketing, 28*(1), 54–72. doi:10.1080/08961530.2015.1056328

Murphy, P. E. (2005). Sustainable marketing. *Business & Professional Ethics Journal, 24*(1/2), 171–198. doi:10.5840/bpej2005241/210

Nabiha, A. k. S., R.a, G., Wahid, N. A., Amran, A., Abustan, I., & Mahadi, R. (2011). A field survey of environmental initiatives at selected resorts in Malaysia. *World Applied Science Journal, 12*, 56–63.

Nair, S. R., & Menon, C. G. (2008). An environmental marketing system–a proposed model based on Indian experience. *Business Strategy and the Environment, 17*(8), 467–479. doi:10.1002/bse.586

Narver, J. C., Slater, S. F., & MacLachlan, D. L. (2004). Responsive and proactive market orientation and new product success. *Journal of Product Innovation Management, 21*(5), 334–347. doi:10.1111/j.0737-6782.2004.00086.x

NASA. (2015a). *Climate change: How do we know?.* Retrieved August 15, 2015, from http://climate.nasa.gov/evidence/

NASA. (2015b). *Scientific consensus: Earth's climate is warming*. Retrieved August 15, 2015, from http://climate.nasa.gov/scientific-consensus/

Natural Resources Canada. (2016). Funding Programs. *Natural Resources Canada*. Retrieved from http://www.nrcan.gc.ca/energy/funding/programs-funding/12400

Needle, D. (2010). *Business in context: An introduction to business and its environment*. Cengage Learning EMEA.

Neumayer, E. (2003). *Weak Versus Strong Sustainability: Exploring the Limits of Two Opposing Paradigms*. Edward Elgar.

Neves, M. F. (2014). *The future of food business: the facts, the impacts and the acts*. World Scientific. doi:10.1142/8567

Newhouse, N. (1990). Implications of Attitude and Behavior Research for Environmental Conservation. *The Journal of Environmental Education*, *22*(1), 26–32. doi:10.1080/00958964.1990.9943043

Nhamo, G., & Mjimba, V. (2017). *Sustainability, climate change and the green economy*. Africa Institute of South Africa.

Nickel, P. M., & Eikenberry, A. M. (2010). Philanthropy in an Era of Global Governance. In R. Taylor (Ed.), *Third Sector Research* (pp. 269–279). New York, NY: Springer New York. doi:10.1007/978-1-4419-5707-8_19

Nigbur, D., Lyons, E., & Uzzell, D. (2010). Attitudes, norms, identity and environmental behaviour: using an expanded theory of planned behaviour to predict participation in a kerbside recycling programme. *The British Journal of Social Psychology*, *49*(Pt 2), 259–84. http://doi.org/10.1348/014466609X449395

Nittala, R. (2014). Green Consumer Behavior of the Educated Segment in India. *Journal of International Consumer Marketing*, *26*(2), 138–152. doi:10.1080/08961530.2014.878205

Nolan, J. M., Schultz, P. W., Cialdini, R. B., Goldstein, N. J., & Griskevicius, V. (2008). Normative social influence is underdetected. *Personality and Social Psychology Bulletin*, *34*(7), 913–923. doi:10.1177/0146167208316691 PMID:18550863

Nunes, B., Bennett, D., & Júnior, S. M. (2014). Sustainable agricultural production: An investigation in Brazilian semi-arid livestock farms. *Journal of Cleaner Production*, *64*, 414–425. doi:10.1016/j.jclepro.2013.07.023

Nunnally, J. C. (1978). *Psychometric theory*. New York, NY: Mc Graw-Hill.

Nurul Syaqirah, Z., & Putra Faizurrahman, Z. (2014). Managing customer retention of hotel industry in Malaysia. *Procedia: Social and Behavioral Sciences*, *130*, 379–389. doi:10.1016/j.sbspro.2014.04.045

O'Donovan, P., & McCarthy, M. (2002). Irish consumer preference for organic meat. *British Food Journal, 104*(3/4/5), 353-370. doi:10.1108/00070700210425778

Oates, C., Alevizou, P., & McDonald, S. (2016). Challenges for Marketers in Sustainable Production and Consumption. *Sustainability, 8*(1), 75.

Obermiller, C., Spangenberg, E., & MacLachlan, D. L. (2005). Ad skepticism: The consequences of disbelief. *Journal of Advertising*, *34*(3), 7–17. doi:10.1080/00913367.2005.10639199

Öberseder, M., Schlegelmilch, B. B., & Murphy, P. E. (2013). CSR practices and consumer perceptions. *Journal of Business Research*, *66*(10), 1839–1851. doi:10.1016/j.jbusres.2013.02.005

OECD. (2015). *OECD Green Growth Studies Material Resources, Productivity and the Environment*. Paris: OECD Publishing.

Oliver, R. L. (1999). Whence consumer loyalty?. *Journal of Marketing*, *63*(Special Issue), 33–44. doi:10.2307/1252099

Olson, J. M., & Stone, J. (2005). The influence of behavior on attitudes. In D. Albarracín, B. T. Johnson, & M. P. Zanna (Eds.), *Handbook of attitudes and attitude change* (pp. 223–271). Mahwah, NJ: Erlbaum.

One Green Planet. (n.d.). Retrieved from http://www.onegreenplanet.org/environment/village-in-india-plants-plants-trees-every-time-a-little-girl-is-born/

Onozaka, Y., Nurse, G., & McFadden, D. T. (2010). Local food consumers: how motivations and perceptions translate to buying behavior. *Choices: The Magazine of Food, Farm and Resource Issues, 25*(1).

Opatha, H. H. D. N. P., & Arulrajah, A. (2014). Green Human Resource Management: Simplified General Reflections. *International Business Research, 7*(8), 101–112. https://doi.org/10.5539/ibr.v7n8p101

Oppenheim, A. N. (2000). *Questionnaire design, interviewing and attitude measurement.* Bloomsbury Publishing.

Osterhus, T. L. (1997). Pro-social consumer influence strategies: When and how do they work?. *Journal of Marketing, 61*(4), 16–29. doi:10.2307/1252084

Oswald, M., Brettel, M., & Engelen, A. (2012). How departments decision-making influence and interdepartmental dynamics relate to two facets of strategic market orientation. *Journal of Strategic Marketing, 20*(6), 483–507. doi:10.1080/0965254X.2012.711346

Ottman, J., & Books, N. B. (1998). Green marketing: opportunity for innovation. *The Journal of Sustainable Product Design, 60.*

Ottman. (2011). *The New Rules of Green Marketing.* Academic Press.

Ottman, J. (2011). *The new rules of green marketing: Strategies, tools, and inspiration for sustainable branding.* Berrett-Koehler Publishers.

Ottman, J. A. (2011). *The new rules of green marketing. Strategies, tools, and inspiration for sustainable branding.* Berrett-Koehler Pub.Inc.

Ottman, J. A., Stafford, E. R., & Hartman, C. L. (2006). Avoiding green marketing myopia: Ways to improve consumer appeal for environmentally preferable products. *Environment: Science and Policy for Sustainable Development, 48*(5), 22–36.

Paillé, P., Chen, Y., Boiral, O., & Jin, J. (2013). The Impact of Human Resource Management on Environmental Performance: An Employee-Level Study. *Journal of Business Ethics, 121*(3), 451–466. doi:10.1007/s10551-013-1732-0

Pap, A., Ham, M., & Turalija, A. (2015). Product policy management as part of sustainable marketing strategy. *Interdisciplinary Management Research, 11*, 131–140.

Parasuraman, R., Sheridan, T. B., & Wickens, C. D. (2008). Situation awareness, mental workload, and trust in automation: Viable, empirically supported cognitive engineering constructs. *Journal of Cognitive Engineering and Decision Making, 2*(2), 140–160. doi:10.1518/155534308X284417

Parguel, B., Benoît-Moreau, F., & Larceneux, F. (2011). How sustainability ratings might deter greenwashing: A closer look at ethical corporate communication. *Journal of Business Ethics, 102*(1), 15–28. doi:10.1007/s10551-011-0901-2

Parker, H. (2005). Normalization as a barometer: Recreational drug use and the consumption of leisure by younger Britons. *Addiction Research and Theory, 13*(3), 205–215. doi:10.1080/16066350500053703

Park, J. (2009). *The Relationship Between Top Managers' Environmental Attitudes and Environmental Management in Hotel Companies.* Virginia Polytechnic Institute and State University.

Park, J., & Ha, S. (2012). Understanding pro-environmental behavior. *International Journal of Retail & Distribution Management*, *40*(5), 388–403. doi:10.1108/09590551211222367

Patil, D. B., & Bhakkad, D. D. (2014). *Redifining management practices and marketing in modern age*. Atharva Pub.

Pawar, R., & Kambale, R. N. (2016). Green marketing-future challenges and opportunities. *Asian Journal of Multidisciplinary Studies*, *4*(3), 149–155.

Paxton, P., Reith, N. E., & Glanville, J. L. (2014). Volunteering and the dimensions of religiosity: A cross-national analysis. *Review of Religious Research*, *56*(4), 597–625. doi:10.1007/s13644-014-0169-y

Payne, J. W., Bettman, J. R., & Johnson, E. J. (1988). Adaptive strategy selection in decision making. *Journal of Experimental Psychology. Learning, Memory, and Cognition*, *14*(3), 534–552. doi:10.1037/0278-7393.14.3.534

Peattie, K. (1995). *Environmental marketing management: Meeting the green challenge*. Financial Times Management.

Peattie, K. (1999). Trappings versus substance in the greening of marketing planning. *Journal of Strategic Marketing*, *7*(2), 131–148. doi:10.1080/096525499346486

Peiry, K., Ziegler, A., & Baumgartner, J. (2016). *Waste managementand the green economy*. Edward Elgar Pub. doi:10.4337/9781783473816

Penn. (2016). Collaborative Efforts. *Penn*. Retrieved from http://www.facilities.upenn.edu/sustainability/collaborative-efforts

Penner, L. A., Dovidio, J. F., Piliavin, J. A., & Schroeder, D. A. (2005). Prosocial behavior: Multilevel perspectives. *Annual Review of Psychology*, *56*(1), 365–392. doi:10.1146/annurev.psych.56.091103.070141 PMID:15709940

Penzenstadler, B., & Femmer, H. (2013). A generic model for sustainability with process-and product-specific instances. *Proceedings of the 2013 workshop on Green in/by software engineering*, 3–8. doi:10.1145/2451605.2451609

Petticrew, M., & Roberts, H. (2008). *Systematic Reviews in the Social Sciences. In Systematic Reviews in the Social Sciences*. Blackwell Publishing Ltd.

Petty, R. E., & Briñol, P. (2006). Understanding Social Judgment: Multiple Systems and Processes. *Psychological Inquiry*, *17*(3), 217–223.

Petty, R., & Cacioppo, J. (1986). The elaboration likelihood model of persuasion. *Advances in Experimental Social Psychology*, *19*, 123–205. doi:10.1016/S0065-2601(08)60214-2

Phalke, V., & Ranade, A. (2016). Green marketing: Complementing Swachh Bharat mission (SBM). *Asian Journal of Multidisciplinary Studies*, *4*(4), 167–173.

Phelan, H. (2012). 10 Eco-friendly fashion brands we can get behind. *Fashionista*. Retrieved from http://fashionista.com/2012/04/10-eco-friendly-fashion-brands-we-can-get-behind

Philipp, D., Popp, M. P., Rumley, E. R., Savin, M. C., & Coffey, K. P. (2015). Regulatory, production, and consumer based challenges of forage-based cattle production systems in the southeastern United States. *Animal frontiers*, *5*(4), 24–31. doi:10.2527/af.2015-0043

phys.org. (2008, May 7). *First-of-its-kind 14-country study ranks consumers according to environmental behavior.* Retrieved June 8, 2016, from http://phys.org/news/2008-05-first-of-its-kind-country-consumers-environmental-behavior.html

Pierce, J. C., Lovrich, N. P., & Dalton, R. J. (2000). Contextual influences on environmental knowledge: Public familiarity with technical terms in nuclear weapons production in Russia and the United States. *Environment and Behavior*, *32*(2), 188–208. doi:10.1177/00139160021972496

Pirkkalainen, P., & Abdile, M. (2009). *The diaspora-conflict-peace-nexus: A literature review*. University of Jyväskylä.

Pirog, R. (2004). Eco-label value assessment phase II: consumer perceptions of local foods. *Leopold Center Pubs and Papers, 140*. Retrieved from www.leopold.iastate.edu/pubs/staff/ecolabels2/ecolabels2.htm

Pirog, R., & Larson, A. (2007). Consumer perceptions of the safety, health and environmental impact of various scales and geographic origin of food supply chains. *Leopold Center Pubs and Papers, 169*. Retrieved from http://lib.dr.iastate.edu/leopold_pubspapers/169

Poku, K., Zakari, M., & Soali, A. (2013). Impact of service quality on customer loyalty in the hotel industry: An empirical study from Ghana. *International Review of Management and Business Research*, *2*(2), 600–609.

Polonsky, M. J. (1994). Green marketing regulation in the US and Australia: The Australian checklist. *Greener Management International*, *5*(January), 44–52.

Polonsky, M. J. (1999). *Greener marketing: a responsible approach to business*. Greenleaf Pub.

Polonsky, M. J. (2011). Transformative green marketing: Impediments and opportunities. *Journal of Business Research*, *64*(12), 1311–1319. doi:10.1016/j.jbusres.2011.01.016

Polonsky, M. J., & Rosenberger, P. J. III. (2001). Reevaluating green marketing: A strategic approach. *Business Horizons*, *44*(5), 21–30. doi:10.1016/S0007-6813(01)80057-4

Pooley, J., & OConnor, M. (2000). Environmental Education and Attitudes: Emotions and Beliefs are What is Needed. *Environment and Behavior*, *32*(5), 711–723. doi:10.1177/0013916500325007

Poortinga, W., Whitmarsh, L., & Suffolk, C. (2013). The introduction of a single-use carrier bag charge in Wales: Attitude change and behavioural spillover effects. *Journal of Environmental Psychology*, *36*, 240–247. doi:10.1016/j.jenvp.2013.09.001

Prakash, A. (2002). Green marketing, public policy and managerial strategies. *Business Strategy and the Environment*, *11*(5), 285–297. doi:10.1002/bse.338

Pramod, V. (2016). Green marketing -an eco-friendly revolution. *Indian Journal of Applied Research*, *6*(1), 594–596.

Pujari, D. (2006). Eco-innovation and new product development: Understanding the influences on market performance. *Technovation*, *26*(1), 76–85. doi:10.1016/j.technovation.2004.07.006

Quazi, H. (1999). Implementation of an environmental management system: The experience of companies operating in Singapore. *Industrial Management & Data Systems*, *99*(7), 302–311. doi:10.1108/02635579910262526

Rabinovich, A., Morton, T., & Postmes, T. (2010). Time perspective and attitude-behaviour consistency in future-oriented behaviours. *The British Journal of Social Psychology*, *49*(1), 69–89. doi:10.1348/014466608X401875 PMID:19224678

Rajagopal & Castano, R. (2015). Understanding consumer behavior and consumption experience. IGI Global.

Raj, S., Jose, S., Sumod, U. S., & Sabitha, M. (2012). Nanotechnology in cosmetics: Opportunities and challenges. *Journal of Pharmacy and Bioallied Sciences*, *4*(3), 186. doi:10.4103/0975-7406.99016 PMID:22923959

Ramli, N. (2009). *Awareness of Eco-label in Malaysia's Green Marketing Initiative*. Academic Press.

Rani, S., & Mishra, D. K. (2014). Green HRM : Practices and Strategic Implementation in the Organizations. *International Journal on Recent and Innovation Trends in Computing and Communication*, *2*(11), 3633–3639.

Ranjbarian, B., Dabestani, R., Khajeh, E., & Noktehdan, I. (2011). An investigation of influencing factors customers' loyalty in a four star hotel in Iran. *International Journal of Business and Social Science*, *2*(21), 243–246.

Rao, P. K., & Bhargav, V. R. (2016). A Study on Green Packaging-A Case Study Approach With Reference To Dell Inc. *International Educational Scientific Research Journal*, *2*(7), 83–84.

Rastogi, E., & Khan, M. S. (2015). An analytical study of online advertising and its co-relationship with green marketing for facilitating sustainable marketing effectiveness. *International Journal of Applied Research*, *1*(5), 182–184.

Rawwas, M. Y. A., Patzer, G. L., & Vitell, S. J. (1998). A cross-cultural investigation of the ethical values of consumers: The potential effect of war and civil disruption. *Journal of Business Ethics*, *17*(4), 435-448.

Reinhardt, F. (1999). Market failure and the environmental policies of firms: Economic rationales for beyond compliance behavior. *Journal of Industrial Ecology*, *3*(1), 9–21. doi:10.1162/108819899569368

Renwick, D. W. S., Redman, T., & Maguire, S. (2013a). Green Human Resource Management: A Review and Research Agenda*. *International Journal of Management Reviews*, *15*(1), 1–14. doi:10.1111/j.1468-2370.2011.00328.x

Research Institute of Organic Agriculture (FIBL) & International Federation of Organic Agriculture Movements (IFOAM). (2016). *The world of organic agriculture. Statistics & emerging trends*. Rheinbreitbach, Germany: Medienhaus Plump. Retrieved June 16, 2016, from: https://shop.fibl.org/fileadmin/documents/shop/1698-organic-world-2016

Rettberg, A., Leiteritz, R. J., & Nasi, C. (2011). Entrepreneurial Activity in the Context of Violent Conflict: Business and Organized Violence in Colombia1. *Journal of Small Business and Entrepreneurship*, *24*(2), 179–196. doi:10.1080/08276331.2011.10593533

Rettie, R., Burchell, K., & Barnham, C. (2014). Social normalisation: Using marketing to make green normal. *Journal of Consumer Behaviour*, *13*(1), 9–17. doi:10.1002/cb.1439

Rettie, R., Burchell, K., & Riley, D. (2012). Normalising green behaviours: A new approach to sustainability marketing. *Journal of Marketing Management*, *28*(3-4), 420–444. doi:10.1080/0267257X.2012.658840

Richey, R. G. Jr, Musgrove, C. F., Gillison, S. T., & Gabler, C. B. (2014). The effects of environmental focus and program timing on green marketing performance and the moderating role of resource commitment. *Industrial Marketing Management*, *43*(7), 1246–1257. doi:10.1016/j.indmarman.2014.06.014

Richter, T., & Hempfling, G. (2003). Supermarket study 2002: Organic products in European supermarkets. *FiBL*, 1-182.

Rist, S., & Allen, D. (2011). *Tales from the Field: Evaluating a University Residential Living- Learning Community*. Retrieved March 31, 2016, from http://www.performancexpress.org/2011/07/tales-from-the-field-evaluating-a-university-residential-living-learning-community/

Robert, J. A. (1996). Green consumers in the 1990s: Profile and implications for advertising. *Journal of Business Research*, *36*(3), 217–231. doi:10.1016/0148-2963(95)00150-6

Roberts, N. C. (2010). Entrepreneurship in Peace Operations. *Journal of Civil Society*, *6*(1), 1–21. doi:10.1080/17448689.2010.481908

Rödiger, M., & Hamm, U. (2015). How are organic food prices affecting consumer behaviour? A review. *Food Quality and Preference*, *43*, 10–20. doi:10.1016/j.foodqual.2015.02.002

Rodríguez-Antón, J. M., del Mar Alonso-Almeida, M., Celemín, M. S., & Rubio, L. (2012). Use of different sustainability management systems in the hospitality industry. The case of Spanish hotels. *Journal of Cleaner Production, 22*(1), 76–84. doi:10.1016/j.jclepro.2011.09.024

Roettgers, F. (2011). *Going green together: how to align employees with green strategies.* Environmental Pioneers.

Roininen, K., Arvola, A., & Lähteenmäki, L. (2006). Exploring consumers perceptions of local food with two different qualitative techniques: Laddering and word association. *Food Quality and Preference, 17*(1-2), 20–30. doi:10.1016/j.foodqual.2005.04.012

Rousseau, D. M., Sitkin, S. B., Burt, R. S., & Camerer, C. (1998). Not so different after all: A cross-discipline view of trust. *Academy of Management Review, 23*(3), 393–404. doi:10.5465/AMR.1998.926617

Roxas, B., & Coetzer, A. (2012). Institutional Environment, Managerial Attitudes and Environmental Sustainability Orientation of Small Firms. *Journal of Business Ethics, 111*(4), 461–476. doi:10.1007/s10551-012-1211-z

Rucker, D. D., & Petty, R. E. (2006). Increasing the Effectiveness of Communications to Consumers: Recommendations Based on Elaboration Likelihood and Attitude Certainty Perspectives. *Journal of Public Policy & Marketing, 25*(1), 39–52. doi:10.1509/jppm.25.1.39

Russell-Bennett, R., Härtel, C. E. J., & Worthington, S. (2013). Exploring a functional approach to attitudinal brand loyalty. *Australasian Marketing Journal, 21*(1), 43–51. doi:10.1016/j.ausmj.2012.08.001

Russo, M. V., & Fouts, P. A. (1997). A Resource-Based Perspective on Corporate Environmental Performance and Profitability. *Academy of Management Journal, 40*(3), 534–559. doi:10.2307/257052

Saba, A., & Messina, F. (2003). Attitudes towards organic foods and risk/benefit perception associated with pesticides. *Food Quality and Preference, 14*(8), 637–645. doi:10.1016/S0950-3293(02)00188-X

Sabella, A. R., Farraj, W. A., Burbar, M., & Qaimary, D. (2014). Entrepreneurship and economic growth in West Bank, Palestine. *Journal of Developmental Entrepreneurship, 19*(01), 1450003. doi:10.1142/S1084946714500034

Sagalowicz, L., & Leser, M. E. (2010). Delivery systems for liquid food products. *Current Opinion in Colloid & Interface Science, 15*(1), 61–72. doi:10.1016/j.cocis.2009.12.003

Sahay, B. S., Stough, R. R., Sohal, A., & Goyal, S. (2006). *Green business.* Allied Publishers.

Santos, N. (2003). *Financing small, medium and micro enterprises in post-conflict situations Microfinance opportunities in the Democratic Republic of the Congo.* Paper presented at the OECD Development Centre. Discussion Paper Produced for the Seminar "Public Private Partnership for the Development of the Democratic Republic of Congo", Kinshasa.

Sarkar, S., & Pansera, M. (2016). Sustainability-driven innovation at the bottom: Insights from grassroots ecopreneurs. *Technological Forecasting and Social Change.* doi:10.1016/j.techfore.2016.08.029

Saxena, R. (2005). *Marketing management.* New Delhi, India: Tata McGraw-Hill Education.

Saxena, R. P., & Khandelwal, P. K. (2012). Greening of industries for sustainable growth: An exploratory study on durable, non-durable and services industries. *International Journal of Social Economics, 39*(8), 551–586. doi:10.1108/03068291211238437

Saxena, R., & Khandelwal, P. K. (2010). Can green marketing be used as a tool for sustainable growth?: A study performed on consumers in India-An emerging economy. *The International Journal of Environmental, Cultural. Economic and Social Sustainability, 6*(2), 277–291.

Scarpa, R., & Del Giudice, T. D. (2004). Market segmentation via mixed logit: Extra-virgin olive oil in urban Italy. *Journal of Agricultural & Food Industrial Organization*, *2*(1), 141–160. doi:10.2202/1542-0485.1080

Schervish, G. P. (1998). Philanthropy. In R. Wuthnow (Ed.), Encyclopedia of Politics and Religion (Vol. 1, pp. 600-603). Washington, DC: Congressional Quarterly Inc.

Schervish, P., & Havens, J. (1997). Social participation and charitable giving: A multivariate analysis. *VOLUNTAS: International Journal of Voluntary and Nonprofit Organizations*, *8*(3), 235–260. doi:10.1007/BF02354199

Schiffman, L. G., & Kanuk, L. L. (2007). *Consumer Behavior. Its Origins and Strategic Applications. Consumer Behavior* (9th ed.). Upper Saddle River, NJ: Pearson Education Inc.

Schroeder, T., Tonsor, G., Mintert, J., & Pennings, J. M. E. (2007). *Consumer risk perceptions and attitudes about beef food safety: implications for improving supply chain management*. Kansas State University.

Schultz, P. W., Nolan, J., Cialdini, R., Goldstein, N., & Griskevicius, V. (2007). The constructive, destructive, and reconstructive power of social norms. *Psychological Science*, *18*(5), 429–434. doi:10.1111/j.1467-9280.2007.01917.x PMID:17576283

Schultz, P. W., Shriver, C., Tabanico, J. J., & Khazian, A. M. (2004). Implicit connections with nature. *Journal of Environmental Psychology*, *24*(1), 31–42. doi:10.1016/S0272-4944(03)00022-7

Schurr, P. H., & Ozanne, J. L. (1985). Influences on exchange processes: Buyers preconceptions of a sellers trustworthiness and bargaining toughness. *The Journal of Consumer Research*, *11*(4), 939–953. doi:10.1086/209028

Schuyt, T., Bekkers, R., & Smit, J. (2010). The Philanthropy Scale: A sociological perspective in measuring new forms of pro social behaviour. *Social Work & Society*, *8*(1), 121–135.

Schwartz, S. H. (1994). Are there universal aspects in the content and structure of values? *The Journal of Social Issues*, *50*, 19–45. doi:10.1111/j.1540-4560.1994.tb01196.x

Scott, W. R. (2004). Institutional Theory: Contributing to a Theoretical Research Program. *Great Minds in Management The Process of Theory Development, 37*(3–4), 460–484. https://doi.org/10.1042/BJ20100043.Electrostatic

Scott, W. R. (2008). *Institutions and organizations: Ideas and interests*. Sage Publications. https://doi.org/10.1016/S0263-2373(97)89895-7

Scott, M., Ipkin, R., & Wong, A. (2015). Green marketing programs as strategic initiatives in hospitality. *Journal of Services Marketing*, *29*(2).

Self, R. M., Self, D. R., & Bell-Haynes, J. (2010). Marketing tourism in the Galapagos Islands: ecotourism or greenwashing?. *International Business & Economics Research Journal (IBER)*, *9*(6).

Sepúlveda, W. S., Maza, M. T., & Pardos, L. (2011). Aspects of quality related to the consumption and production of lamb meat. Consumers versus producers. *Meat Science*, *87*(4), 366–372. doi:10.1016/j.meatsci.2010.11.013 PMID:21167649

Seretny, M., & Seretny, A. (2012). Sustainable marketing -a new era in the responsible marketing development. *Foundations of Management*, *4*(2), 63–76. doi:10.2478/fman-2013-0011

Seyfang, G. (2006). Ecological Citizenship and Sustainable Consumption: Examining local food networks. *Journal of Rural Studies*, *22*(4), 383–395. doi:10.1016/j.jrurstud.2006.01.003

Shah, K. U. (2011). Strategic organizational drivers of corporate environmental responsibility in the Caribbean hotel industry. *Policy Sciences*, *44*(4), 321–344. doi:10.1007/s11077-011-9130-x

Shamma, H., & Hassan, S. (2013). Customer-driven benchmarking: A strategic approach toward a sustainable marketing performance. *Benchmarking: An International Journal, 20*(3), 377–395. doi:10.1108/14635771311318144

Shao, J., Taisch, M., & Mier, M. O. (2017). Influencing factors to facilitate sustainable consumption: From the experts viewpoints. *Journal of Cleaner Production, 142*(1), 203–216. doi:10.1016/j.jclepro.2015.12.111

Shapshay, S. (2013). Contemporary environmental aesthetics and the neglect of the sublime. *The British Journal of Aesthetics, 53*(2), 181–198. doi:10.1093/aesthj/ays067

Sharma, A., Iyer, G. R., Mehrotra, A., & Krishnan, R. (2010). Sustainability and business-to-business marketing: A framework and implications. *Industrial Marketing Management, 39*(2), 330–341. doi:10.1016/j.indmarman.2008.11.005

Sharma, S. (2000). Managerial interpretations and organizational context as predictors of corporate choice of environmental strategy. *Academy of Management Journal, 43*(4), 681–697. doi:10.2307/1556361

Sharma, S., & Aragòn-Correa, J. A. (2007). The contingent influence of organizational capabilities on proactive environmental strategy in the service sector: An analysis of North American and European ski. *Canadian Journal of, 283*, 268–283. https://doi.org/10.1002/CJAS.35

Shepherd, D. A., Kuskova, V., & Patzelt, H. (2009). Measuring the values that underline sustainable development: The development of a valid scale. *Journal of Economic Psychology, 30*(2), 246–256. doi:10.1016/j.joep.2008.08.003

Shepherd, D. A., & Patzelt, H. (2011). The new field of sustainable entrepreneurship: Studying entrepreneurial action linking what is to be sustained with what is to be developed. *Entrepreneurship Theory and Practice, 35*(1), 137–163. doi:10.1111/j.1540-6520.2010.00426.x

Sheth, J., & Parvatiyar, A. (1995). Ecological imperatives and the role of marketing. *Environmental marketing: Strategies, practice, theory and research*, 3-20.

Shmelev, S. (2016). *Green economy reader*. Springer.

Shove, E., & Warde, A. (2002). Inconspicuous consumption: the sociology of consumption, lifestyles and the environment. *Sociological theory and the environment: classical foundations, contemporary insights, 230*, 51.

Shove, E. (2003). Converging conventions of comfort, cleanliness and convenience. *Journal of Consumer Policy, 26*(4), 395–418. doi:10.1023/A:1026362829781

Shwom, R. (2009). Strengthening Sociological Perspectives on Organizations and the Environment. *Organization & Environment, 22*(3), 271–292. doi:10.1177/1086026609345216

Siguaw, J. A., Mattila, A., & Austin, J. R. (1999). The brand-personality scale. *The Cornell Hotel and Restaurant Administration Quarterly, 40*(3), 48–55.

Singh, J., & Sirdeshmukh, D. (2000). Agency and trust mechanisms in consumer satisfaction and loyalty judgments. *Journal of the Academy of Marketing Science, 28*(1), 150–167. doi:10.1177/0092070300281014

Singh, N., Cranage, D., & Lee, S. (2014). Green strategies for hotels: Estimation of recycling benefits. *International Journal of Hospitality Management, 43*, 13–22. doi:10.1016/j.ijhm.2014.07.006

Singh, P. B., & Pandey, K. K. (2012). Green marketing: Policies and practices for sustainable development. *Integral Review, 5*(1), 22–30.

Sinnappan. (2011). *Antecedents of Green Purchasing Behavior among Malaysian Consumers*. Academic Press.

Sirgy, M. J. (1982). Self-concept in consumer behavior: A critical review. *The Journal of Consumer Research*, *9*(3), 287–300. doi:10.1086/208924

Sirgy, M. J., Grewal, D., Mangleburg, T. F., Park, J. O., Chon, K. S., Claiborne, C. B., & Berkman, H. et al. (1997). Assessing the predictive validity of two methods of measuring self-image congruence. *Journal of the Academy of Marketing Science*, *25*(3), 229–241. doi:10.1177/0092070397253004

Siti-Nabiha, A. K., George, R. A., Abdul Wahid, N., Amran, A., Abustan, I., & Mahadi, R. (2011). A field survey of environmental initiatives at selected resorts in Malaysia. *World Applied Sciences Journal*, *12*, 56–63.

Siti-Nabiha, A. K., Abdul Wahid, N., & Kamalul Ariffin, N. S. (2010). The drivers and the outcomes of environmental management practices in the hotel industry : A proposed framework. *TEAM Journal of Hospitality and Tourism*, *7*(1), 13–26.

Sloan, P., Legrand, W., & Chen, J. S. (2004). Factors influencing German hoteliers attitudes toward environmental management. *Advances in Hospitality and Leisure*, *1*, 179–188. doi:10.1016/S1745-3542(04)01011-2

Small, D. A., & Cryder, C. (2016). Prosocial consumer behavior. *Current Opinion in Psychology*, *10*, 107–111. doi:10.1016/j.copsyc.2016.01.001

Smith, A. C., Graetz, B. R., & Westerbeek, H. M. (2006). Brand personality in a membership--based organisation. *International Journal of Nonprofit and Voluntary Sector Marketing*, *11*(3), 251–266. doi:10.1002/nvsm.51

Snyder, M. (1979). Self-monitoring processes. *Advances in Experimental Social Psychology*, *12*, 85–128. doi:10.1016/S0065-2601(08)60260-9

Sobal, J., Khan, L. K., & Bisogni, C. (1998). A conceptual model of the food and nutrition system. *Social Science & Medicine*, *47*(7), 853–863. doi:10.1016/S0277-9536(98)00104-X PMID:9722106

Soil Association. (2000). *The organic food and farming report*. Bristol: Soil Association.

Sooklal, R., Papadopoulos, T., & Ojiako, U. (2011). Information systems development: A normalisation theory perspective. *Industrial Management & Data Systems*, *111*(8), 1270–1286. doi:10.1108/02635571111170794

Sparks, P., & Guthrie, C. A. (1998). Self--Identity and the theory of planned behavior: A useful addition or an unhelpful artifice? *Journal of Applied Social Psychology*, *28*(15), 1393–1410. doi:10.1111/j.1559-1816.1998.tb01683.x

Sserwanga, A., Kiconco, I., & Rebecca, N. (2014). Social entrepreneurship and post conflict recovery in Uganda. *Journal of Enterprising Communities: People and Places in the Global Economy*, *8*(4), 300–317. doi:10.1108/JEC-02-2014-0001

Stagl, S. (2002). Local organic food markets: Potentials and limitations for contributing to sustainable development. *Empirica*, *29*(2), 145–162. doi:10.1023/A:1015656400998

Stahl, F., Heitmann, M., Lehmann, D. R., & Neslin, S. A. (2012). The impact of brand equity on customer acquisition, retention, and profit margin. *Journal of Marketing*, *76*(4), 44–63. doi:10.1509/jm.10.0522

Staus, A. (2011). Which household attitudes determine the store type choice for meat? *Journal of Retailing and Consumer Services*, *18*(3), 224–234. doi:10.1016/j.jretconser.2010.11.003

Steel, B. S. (1996). Thinking Globally and Acting Locally? Environmental Attitudes, Behaviour and Activism. *Journal of Environmental Management*, *47*(1), 27–36. doi:10.1006/jema.1996.0033

Stegaroiu, I., & Florea, N.V. (2013). *Tehnici si instrumente de recrutare si selectie*. C. H. Beck.

Steg, L., & Vlek, C. (2009). Encouraging pro-environmental behaviour: An integrative review and research agenda. *Journal of Environmental Psychology*, *29*(3), 309–317. doi:10.1016/j.jenvp.2008.10.004

Steiner, R. L., & Barnhart, R. B. (1972). The development of an instrument to assess environmental attitudes utilizing factor analytic techniques. *Science Education*, *56*(3), 427–432. doi:10.1002/sce.3730560320

Stern, P., Dietz, T., & Kalof, L. (1993). Value Orientations, Gender and Environmental Concern. *Environment and Beahvior*, *25*(3), 322–348. https://doi.org/0803973233

Stevens, C. (2010, February). Linking sustainable consumption and production: The government role. [Blackwell Publishing Ltd.]. *Natural Resources Forum*, *34*(1), 16–23. doi:10.1111/j.1477-8947.2010.01273.x

Stolz, H., Bodini, A., Stolze, M., Hamm, U., & Richter, T. (2009). Lebensmittelqualität aus der Verbraucherperspektive - eine Synthese qualitativer Studien zur Wahrnehmung und Beurteilung verschiedener Qualitätskriterien bei Öko-Produkten. *Berichte über Landwirtschaft*, *87*(1), 153–182.

Stolz, H., Stolze, M., Hamm, U., Janssen, M., & Ruto, E. (2010). Consumer attitudes towards organic versus conventional food with specific quality attributes. *NJAS – Wageningen. Journal of Life Science*, *58*(3/4), 67–72. doi:10.1016/j.njas.2010.10.002

Stolz, H., Stolze, M., Janssen, M., & Hamm, U. (2011). Preferences and determinants for organic, conventional and conventional-plus products – The case of occasional organic consumers. *Food Quality and Preference*, *22*(8), 772–779. doi:10.1016/j.foodqual.2011.06.011

Styles, D., Schönberger, H., & Martos, J. L. G. (2013). *Best Environmental Management Practice in the Tourism Sector*. European Union; doi:10.2788/33972

Subedi, D. B. (2013). Pro-Peace Entrepreneur or Conflict Profiteer? Critical Perspective on the Private Sector and Peacebuilding in Nepal. *Peace and Change*, *38*(2), 181–206. doi:10.1111/pech.12011

Suki, N. M., Suki, N. M., & Azman, N. S. (2016). Impacts of corporate social responsibility on the links between green marketing awareness and consumer purchase intentions. *Procedia Economics and Finance*, *37*, 262–268. doi:10.1016/S2212-5671(16)30123-X

Sulek, M. (2010). On the modern meaning of philanthropy. *Nonprofit and Voluntary Sector Quarterly*, *39*(2), 193–212. doi:10.1177/0899764009333052

Sutton, R. K. (2014). *Aesthetics for green roofs and green walls*. Academic Press.

Tahir Albayrak. (2011). *The Influence of Skepticism on Green Purchase Behavior*. Academic Press.

Tan, B., & Lau, T. (2011). Green Purchase Behavior: Examining the Influence of Green Environmental Attitude, Perceived Consumer Effectiveness and Specific Green Purchase Attitude. *Australian Journal of Basic and Applied Sciences*, *5*(8), 559–567.

Tang, F. E. (2012). A study of Water Consumption in Two Malaysian Resorts. *International Journal of Environment, Chemical, Ecological. Geological and Geophysical Engineering*, *6*(8), 506–511.

Tang, M. (2015). Evaluating green hotels in Taiwan from the consumer's perspective. *International Journal of Management Research and Business Strategy*, *4*(1), 1–15.

Tanner, C., Kaiser, F. G., & Wofing Kast, S. (2004). Contextual Conditions of Ecological Consumerism: A Food-Purchasing Survey. *Environment and Behavior*, *36*(1), 94–111. doi:10.1177/0013916503251437

Tarrant, M. A., & Green, G. T. (1999). Outdoor recreation and the predictive validity of environmental attitudes. *Leisure Sciences, 21*(1), 17–30. doi:10.1080/014904099273264

Tarrant, P. V. (1998). Some recent advances and future priorities in research for the meat industry. *Meat Science, 49*, S1–S16. doi:10.1016/S0309-1740(98)90035-3 PMID:22060702

Tayfun, N. Ö., & Öçlü, B. (2016). Çevreci ürünlerin tüketicilerin satın alma kararlarındaki yeri üzerine bir uygulama. *Ömer Halisdemir Üniversitesi İktisadi ve İdari Bilimler Fakültesi Dergisi, 9*(3), 185-198.

Taylor, M. L., Coates, T. L., Anyansi-Archibong, C., & Tanaka, N. (2014). The Twenty-First's Second Decade-Whither the Beauty Industry?. *Business Case Journal, 21*(1).

Taylor, S. R. (1992). Green management: The next competitive weapon. *Futures, 24*(7), 669–680. doi:10.1016/0016-3287(92)90075-Q

Tehrani, N., & Sinha, S. (2011). *Understanding green business*. Bloomington, IN: AuthorHouse.

Teixeira, A. A., Jabbour, C. J. C., & Jabbour, A. B. L. D. S. (2012). Relationship between green management and environmental training in companies located in Brazil: A theoretical framework and case studies. *International Journal of Production Economics, 140*(1), 318–329. doi:10.1016/j.ijpe.2012.01.009

Testa, F., Iraldo, F., Vaccari, A., & Ferrari, E. (2015). Why Eco-labels can be Effective Marketing Tools: Evidence from a Study on Italian Consumers. *Business Strategy and the Environment, 24*(4), 252–265. doi:10.1002/bse.1821

The John Marshal Review of Intellectual Law. (2010). *The intersection of intellectual property law and the green movement: RPL's Green Issue 2010*. Quid Pro Books.

The World Bank. (2013, June 5). *India diagnostic assessment of select environmental challenges: an analysis of physical and monetary losses of environmental health and natural resources.* Retrieved June 6, 2016, from http://www-wds.worldbank.org/external/default/WDSContentServer/WDSP/IB/2013/07/16/000442464_20130716091943/Rendered/PDF/700040v10ESW0P0box0374379B00PUBLIC0.pdf

The World Bank. (2014, March 6). *India: Green Growth - Overcoming Environment Challenges to Promote Development.* Retrieved June 5, 2016, from http://www.worldbank.org/en/news/feature/2014/03/06/green-growth-overcoming-india-environment-challenges-promote-development?cid=SAR_TTWBSAREN_EXT

Thøgersen, J. (2009). The Motivational Roots of Norms for Environmentally Responsible Behavior. *Basic and Applied Social Psychology, 31*(4), 348–362. doi:10.1080/01973530903317144

Thøgersen, J., Haugaard, P., & Olesen, A. (2010). Consumer responses to ecolabels. *European Journal of Marketing, 44*(11), 1787–1810. doi:10.1108/03090561011079882

Thøgersen, J., Jørgensen, A. K., & Sandager, S. (2012). Consumer decision making regarding a green everyday product. *Psychology and Marketing, 29*(4), 187–197. doi:10.1002/mar.20514

Thøgersen, J., & Noblet, C. (2012). Does green consumerism increase the acceptance of wind power? *Energy Policy, 51*, 854–862. doi:10.1016/j.enpol.2012.09.044

Thøgersen, J., & Ölander, F. (2002). Human values and the emergence of a sustainable consumption pattern: A panel study. *Journal of Economic Psychology, 23*(5), 605–632. doi:10.1016/S0167-4870(02)00120-4

Tobias, J. M., & Boudreaux, K. C. (2011). Entrepreneurship and Conflict Reduction in the Post-Genocide Rwandan Coffee Industry. *Journal of Small Business and Entrepreneurship, 24*(2), 217–242. doi:10.1080/08276331.2011.10593535

Tobias, J. M., Mair, J., & Barbosa-Leiker, C. (2013). Toward a theory of transformative entrepreneuring: Poverty reduction and conflict resolution in Rwandas entrepreneurial coffee sector. *Journal of Business Venturing*, *28*(6), 728–742. doi:10.1016/j.jbusvent.2013.03.003

Tobin, D., Thomson, J., & LaBorde, L. (2012). Consumer perceptions of produce safety: A study of Pennsylvania. *Food Control*, *26*(2), 305–312. doi:10.1016/j.foodcont.2012.01.031

Tobin, R., Larkin, T., & Moane, S. (2011). The Irish organic food market: Shortfalls, opportunities and the need for research. *Journal of the Science of Food and Agriculture*, *91*(12), 2126–2131. doi:10.1002/jsfa.4503 PMID:21751220

Tobler, C., Visschers, V. H. M., & Siegrist, M. (2011). Eating green. Consumers willingness to adopt ecological food consumption behaviors. *Appetite*, *57*(3), 674–682. doi:10.1016/j.appet.2011.08.010 PMID:21896294

Todd, A. M. (2004). The aesthetic turn in green marketing: Environmental consumer ethics of natural personal care products. *Ethics and the Environment*, *9*(2), 86–102. doi:10.2979/ETE.2004.9.2.86

Trianna Rosli (2016). *Measuring Environmental Performance Awareness: A Qualitative Approach*. SOSHUM.

Trott, S., & Sople, V. V. (2016). Brand Equity: An Indian Perspective. PHI Learning Pvt. Ltd.

Troy, D. J., & Kerry, J. P. (2010). Consumer perception and the role of science in the meat industry. *Meat Science*, *86*(1), 214–226. doi:10.1016/j.meatsci.2010.05.009 PMID:20579814

Tsai, K. H., Chou, C., & Kuo, J. H. (2008). The curvilinear relationships between responsive and proactive market orientations and new product performance: A contingent link. *Industrial Marketing Management*, *37*(8), 884–894. doi:10.1016/j.indmarman.2007.03.005

Tureac, C. E., Turtureanu, A. G., Bordean, I., Grigore, A., Modiga, G., & Pripoie, R. (2010). Ecological food products-general considerations on green marketing. *10th International Multidisciplinary Scientific GeoConference SGEM2010, 2*, 529-537.

Turnbull, P. W., Leek, S., & Ying, G. (2000). Customer confusion: The mobile phone market. *Journal of Marketing Management*, *16*(1-3), 143–163. doi:10.1362/026725700785100523

Turner, R. K. (Ed.). (1988). *Sustainable Environmental Development. Principles and Practice*. London: Belhaven Press.

Uddin, W., Khan, B., Shaukat, N., Majid, M., Mujtaba, G., Mehmood, A., & Almeshal, A. M. et al. (2016). Biogas potential for electric power generation in Pakistan: A survey. *Renewable & Sustainable Energy Reviews*, *54*, 25–33. doi:10.1016/j.rser.2015.09.083

Umberger, W. J., Boxall, P. C., & Lacy, R. C. (2009). Role of credence and health information in determining US consumers willingness-to-pay for grass-finished beef. *The Australian Journal of Agricultural and Resource Economics*, *53*(4), 603–623. doi:10.1111/j.1467-8489.2009.00466.x

Umberger, W. J., Feuz, D. M., Calkins, C. R., & Killinger, K. (2002). U.S. consumer preference and willingness-to-pay for domestic corn-fed beef versus international grass-fed beef measured through an experimental auction. *Agribusiness*, *18*(4), 491–504. doi:10.1002/agr.10034

UN. (2000). *The United Nations Millennium Declaration*. New York: United Nations.

Unhelkar, B. (2016). *Green IT strategies and applications: using environmental intelligence*. CRC Press.

United Nations General Assembly. (2012). *A/RES/66/288 - The Future We Want*. Available at: http://www.un.org/ga/search/view_doc.asp?symbol=A/RES/66/288&Lang=E

United States Department of Agriculture. Economic Research Service (USDA-ERS). (2009). *Organic prices. Data Sets.* Retrieved from https://www.ers.usda.gov/data-products/organic-prices/

Universal-Publishers. (2011). *International Journal of Economic and Political Integration, 1*(1).

Van den Bulte, C., & Joshi, Y. V. (2007). New product diffusion with influentials and imitators. *Marketing Science, 26*(3), 400–421. doi:10.1287/mksc.1060.0224

Van Der Wiele, T., Boselie, P., & Hesselink, M. (2002). Empirical evidence for the relationship between customer satisfaction and business performance. *Managing Service Quality, 12*(3), 184–193. doi:10.1108/09604520210429259

Van Herpen, E., Van Nierop, E., & Sloot, L. (2012). The relationship between in-store marketing and observed sales for organic versus fair trade products. *Marketing Letters, 23*(1), 293–308. doi:10.1007/s11002-011-9154-1

Van Liere, K. D., & Dunlap, R. E. (1978). Moral Norms and Environmental Behavior: An Application of Schwartzs Norm-Activation Model to Yard Burning. *Journal of Applied Social Psychology, 8*(2), 174–188. doi:10.1111/j.1559-1816.1978.tb00775.x

Varman, R., & Costa, J. A. (2008). Embedded markets, communities, and the invisible hand of social norms. *Journal of Macromarketing, 28*(2), 141–156. doi:10.1177/0276146708314594

Vasile, A., & Nicolo, D. (2017). *Sustainable entrepreneurship and investments in the green economy.* IGI Global. doi:10.4018/978-1-5225-2075-7

Vergragt, P., Akenji, L., & Dewick, P. (2014). Sustainable production, consumption, and livelihoods: Global and regional research perspectives. *Journal of Cleaner Production, 63*, 1–12. doi:10.1016/j.jclepro.2013.09.028

Verhoef, P. C. (2005). Explaining purchases of organic meat by Dutch consumers. *European Review of Agriculture Economics, 32*(2), 245–267. doi:10.1093/eurrag/jbi008

Vernekar, S. S., & Wadhwa, P. (2011). Green consumption: An empirical study of consumers attitudes and perception regarding eco-friendly FMCG products, with special reference to Delhi and NCR Region. *Opinion, 1*(1), 64–74.

Villanueva, J. L. J., López, S. V., & De Dios Guerrero Rodríguez, J. (2015). Behavior of consumers and willingness to pay for quality attributes of organic meat rabbit. *Revista Mexicana de Ciencias Pecuarias, 6*(2), 221–232.

Villarino, J., & Font, X. (2015). Sustainability marketing myopia: The lack of persuasiveness in sustainability communication. *Journal of Vacation Marketing, 21*(4), 326–335. doi:10.1177/1356766715589428

Violeta, S., & Gheorghe, I. G. (2009). The green strategy mix–a new marketing approach. *Knowledge Management and Innovation in Advancing Economics–Analysis and Solutions, 1*, 1344–1347.

Wägeli, S., Janssen, M., & Hamm, U. (2015). Organic consumers preferences and willingness-to-pay for locally produced animal products. *International Journal of Consumer Studies, 40*(3), 357–367. doi:10.1111/ijcs.12262

Wagner, S. A. (2003). *Understanding Green Consumer Behaviour: A Qualitative Cognitive Approach.* Academic Press.

Wagner, M. (2013). Green Human Resource Benefits: Do they Matter as Determinants of Environmental Management System Implementation? *Journal of Business Ethics, 114*(3), 443–456. doi:10.1007/s10551-012-1356-9

Wagner, M. (2014). A European perspective on country moderation effects: Environmental management systems and sustainability-related human resource benefits. *Journal of World Business, 50*(2), 379–388. doi:10.1016/j.jwb.2014.08.005

Walker, L. (2013). 71% of Consumers Think Green When Purchasing. *Environmental Leader.* Retrieved from http://www.environmentalleader.com/2013/04/03/71-of-consumers-think-green-when-purchasing/

Wallace, B. (2005). Exploring the meaning (s) of sustainability for community-based social entrepreneurs. *Social Enterprise Journal, 1*(1), 78–89. doi:10.1108/17508610580000708

Walsh, G., & Mitchell, V.-W. (2010). The effect of consumer confusion proneness on word of mouth, trust, and customer satisfaction. *European Journal of Marketing*, *44*(6), 838–859. doi:10.1108/03090561011032739

Wang, Z., Zhang, B., Yin, J., & Zhang, Y. (2011). Determinants and policy implications for household electricity-saving behaviour: Evidence from Beijing, China. *Energy Policy*, *39*(6), 3550–3557. doi:10.1016/j.enpol.2011.03.055

Warner, L. G., & Defleur, M. L. (1969). Attitude as an Interactional Concept: Social Constraint and Social Distance as Intervening Variables Between Attitudes and Action. *American Sociological Review*, *34*(2), 153–169. doi:10.2307/2092174 PMID:5778086

Wasik, J. F. (1996). *Green marketing and management: A global perspective*. Wiley.

Weigel, R., & Weigel, J. (1978). Environmental Concern: The Development of a Measure. *Environment and Behavior*, *10*(1), 3–15. doi:10.1177/0013916578101001

Weston, R., & Gore, P. A. Jr. (2006). A brief guide to structural equation modeling. *The Counseling Psychologist*, *34*(5), 719–751. doi:10.1177/0011000006286345

White, K., MacDonnell, R., & Ellard, J. H. (2012). Belief in a just world: Consumer intentions and behaviors toward ethical products. *Journal of Marketing*, *76*(1), 103–118. doi:10.1509/jm.09.0581

White, R. R., & Brady, M. (2014). Can consumers willingness to pay incentivize adoption of environmental impact reducing technologies in meat animal production? *Food Policy*, *49*, 41–49. doi:10.1016/j.foodpol.2014.06.007

Wicker, A. W. (1969). Attitudes versus Actions: The Relationship of Verbal and Overt Behavioral Responses to Attitude Objects. *The Journal of Social Issues*, *25*(4), 41–78. doi:10.1111/j.1540-4560.1969.tb00619.x

Wicker, A. W. (1971). An Examination of The Other Variables Explanation of Attitude-Behavior Inconsistency. *Journal of Personality and Social Psychology*, *19*(1), 18–30. doi:10.1037/h0031090

Williamson, O. E. (1998). Transaction cost economics and organization theory. In Technology, organization, and competitiveness: Perspectives on industrial and corporate change (pp. 17–66). Academic Press.

Williamson, D., Lynch-Wood, G., & Ramsay, J. (2006). Drivers of environmental behaviour in manufacturing SMEs and the implications for CSR. *Journal of Business Ethics*, *67*(3), 317–330. doi:10.1007/s10551-006-9187-1

Wilson, M. P., & Schwarzman, M. R. (2016). Toward a new US chemicals policy: rebuilding the foundation to advance new science, green chemistry, and environmental health. *Industrial Chemistry: New Applications, Processes and Systems*, 176.

Wilson, R., & Olson, S. (2004). *Utility green pricing programs: a statistical analysis of program effectiveness*. Diane Pub. Retrieved from http://www.wall-street.ro/articol/Economie/69736/Scadere-de-15-pentru-productia-de-produse-ecologice-in-2009.html

Wittenbrink, B., & Schwarz, N. (2007). *Implicit Measures of Attitudes*. New York: Guilford.

Wolch, J. R., Byrne, J., & Newell, J. P. (2014). Urban green space, public health, and environmental justice: The challenge of making cities just green enough. *Landscape and Urban Planning*, *125*, 234–244. doi:10.1016/j.landurbplan.2014.01.017

Wolff, C. (2008). Second Nature. *Lodging Hospitality*, *64*(2), 24–26.

Wolsko, C., Ariceaga, H., & Seiden, J. (2016). Red, White, and Blue Enough to be Green: Effects of Moral Framing on Climate Change Attitudes and Conservation Behaviors. *Journal of Experimental Social Psychology*. 10.1016/j.jesp.2016.02.005

Wood, E. J. (2003). *Insurgent collective action and civil war in El Salvador*. Cambridge University Press. doi:10.1017/CBO9780511808685

World Bank. (2011). *World development report 2011: Conflict, security, and development*. Retrieved from World Economic Forum: http://wef.ch/risks2016(11th Edition)

World Commission on Environment and Development. (1987). *Our Common Future*. New York: Oxford University Press.

Wright, R. W., Brand, R. A., Dunn, W., & Spindler, K. P. (2007). How to write a systematic review. *Clinical Orthopaedics and Related Research*, *455*, 23–29. doi:10.1097/BLO.0b013e31802c9098 PMID:17279036

Wu, L. (2012). Exploring the New Ecological Paradigm Scale for Gauging Childrens Environmental Attitudes in China. *The Journal of Environmental Education*, *43*(2), 107–120. doi:10.1080/00958964.2011.616554

Wu, S. I., & Lin, S. R. (2016). The effect of green marketing strategy on business performance: A study of organic farms in Taiwan. *Total Quality Management & Business Excellence*, *27*(1-2), 141–156. doi:10.1080/14783363.2014.959256

Xue, J., Zartarian, V., Wang, S. W., Liu, S. V., & Georgopoulos, P. (2010). Probabilistic modeling of dietary arsenic exposure and dose and evaluation with 2003–2004 NHANES data. *Environmental Health Perspectives*, *118*(3), 345–350. doi:10.1289/ehp.0901205 PMID:20194069

Yadav, P. L., Han, S. H., & Rho, J. J. (2015). Impact of Environmental Performance on Firm Value for Sustainable Investment: Evidence from Large US Firms. *Business Strategy and the Environment*. https://doi.org/10.1002/bse.1883

Yang, J., & Liu, C. Y. (2006). New product development: An innovation diffusion perspective. *The Journal of High Technology Management Research*, *17*(1), 17–26. doi:10.1016/j.hitech.2006.05.002

Yannopoulos, P., Auh, S., & Menguc, B. (2012). Achieving fit between learning and market orientation: Implications for new product performance. *Journal of Product Innovation Management*, *29*(4), 531–545. doi:10.1111/j.1540-5885.2012.00923.x

Yiridoe, E. K., Bonti-Ankomah, S., & Martin, R. C. (2005). Comparison of consumer perceptions and preferences toward organic versus conventionally produced foods: A review and update of the literature. *Renewable Agriculture and Food Systems*, *20*(4), 193–205. doi:10.1079/RAF2005113

Yue, C., & Tong, C. (2009). Organic or local? Investigating consumer preference for fresh produce using a choice experiment with real economic incentives. *Horticultural Science*, *44*(2), 366–371.

Zander, K., Bürgelt, D., Christoph-Schulz, I., Salamon, P., & Weible, D. (2015). Consumers' response to sustainability labeling in wild caught fish. In *EAFE 2015 XXII Conference of the European Association of Fisheries Economists*. Salerno, Italy: EAFE.

Zein, K., Wazner Semlali, M., & Meylan, G. (2008). *Best Environmental Practices for the Hotel Industry*. Academic Press.

Zelkowitz, M. V., & Wallace, D. R. (1998). Experimental Models for Validating Technology. *J IEEE Computer*, *31*(5), 23–31. doi:10.1109/2.675630

Zhang, J., & Duan, Y. (2010). The impact of different types of market orientation on product innovation performance: Evidence from Chinese manufacturers. *Management Decision*, *48*(6), 849–867. doi:10.1108/00251741011053433

Zhang, J., & Duan, Y. (2010a). Empirical study on the impact of market orientation and innovation orientation on new product performance of Chinese manufacturers. *Nankai Business Review International*, *1*(2), 214–231. doi:10.1108/20408741011052609

Zhao, C. (2011). *An Analysis of Hotels' Green Activities and Its Influence on Hotels' Projected Image Using a Mixed Methodology*. Purdue University.

Zhao, W., & Schroeder, P. (2010). Sustainable consumption and production: Trends, challenges and options for the Asia-Pacific region. *Natural Resources Forum*, *34*(1), 4–15. doi:10.1111/j.1477-8947.2010.01275.x

Zhu, Q., Li, Y., Geng, Y., & Qi, Y. (2013). Green food consumption intention, behaviors and influencing factors among Chinese consumers. *Food Quality and Preference*, *28*(1), 279–286. doi:10.1016/j.foodqual.2012.10.005

Zhu, Q., & Sarkis, J. (2016). Green marketing and consumerism as social change in china: Analyzing the literature. *International Journal of Production Economics*, *181*, 289–302. doi:10.1016/j.ijpe.2016.06.006

About the Contributors

Farzana Quoquab is a senior lecturer at International Business School, UTM. She has received her Doctorate degree from Universiti Kebangsaan Malaysia. She has presented papers at various international and national conferences and published articles in peer-reviewed international journals such as Asian Case Research Journal, Asia Pacific Journal of Marketing and Logistics, International Journal of Economics and Management, International Review of Management and Marketing, Pertanika Journal of Social Sciences & Humanities, International Journal of Business Governance and Ethics, Emerald Emerging Markets Case Studies, Asian Academy of Management Journal and Journal of Islamic Marketing. Since 2008, she has produced several international conference proceedings and book chapters. She is one of the editorial board members of 'Case Studies in Business and Management' and 'Journal of Economic and Administrative Science'. Her current research interest includes Consumer Behavior, Services Marketing, Green & Sustainability Marketing, Social Marketing, Macro Marketing, and Work Ethics & Values.

Ramayah Thurasamy has an MBA from Universiti Sains Malaysia (USM). Currently he is a Professor at the School of Management in USM. He teaches mainly courses in Research Methodology and Business Statistics. Apart from teaching, he is an avid researcher, especially in the areas of technology management and adoption in business and education. His publications have appeared in Computers in Human Behavior, Resources Conservation and Recycling, Journal of Educational Technology & Society, Direct Marketing: An International Journal, Information Development, Journal of Project Management (JoPM), Management Research News (MRN), International Journal of Information Management, International Journal of Services and Operations Management (IJSOM), Engineering, Construction and Architectural Management (ECAM) and North American Journal of Psychology. He is constantly invited to serve on the editorial boards and program committees of many international journals and conferences of repute. His profile can be accessed from http://www.ramayah.com.

Jihad Mohammad is a senior lecturer at International Business School, UTM, Malaysia. He has received his DBA degree from Universiti Kebangsaan Malaysia. He has taught research methodology course in several years. He has published articles in peer-reviewed international journals such as Cross Cultural & Strategic Management, Asia Pacific Journal of Marketing and Logistics, International Journal of Business Governance and Ethics, Asian Academy of Management Journal, Gadjah Mada International Journal of Business, International Journal of Innovation and Learning and Journal of Islamic Marketing. He has versatile career exposure. He has conducted several workshops for postgraduate students regarding research methodology and PLS-SEM. His area of research interest includes organisational citizenship behaviour, psychological ownership, psychological capital, leadership, innovation, pro-environmental behaviour, consumer citizenship behaviour, and Islamic work ethics.

* * *

Anitha Acharya is an Assistant Professor in the Department of Marketing and Business Strategy at IBS Hyderabad. Prior to her academic career, Anitha worked in banking and insurance sector. Anitha's work has been published in leading international journals such as International Journal of Energy Economics and Policy, The Qualitative Report, and International Food Research Journal. Her research focuses primarily on marketing of services, brand personality, branding, and green products. Her expertise lies in the application of Structural Equation Modeling and Multivariate Techniques in addressing marketing research problems. She has 10 years of industry experience and her areas of interest are branding, services marketing, and strategy.

Fauziah Binti Sh. Ahmad is an Associate Professor of Strategic Marketing and Branding, Marketing of Technology Innovations, Entrepreneurship and few others management subjects at UTM International Business School (IBS) since October 2004. She holds numerous portfolios in IBS including Executive Development Manager from 2011-2014 and also the Deputy Dean (Academic) in 2015. Since March 2016 she is being seconded as a Professor and Vice President at KPJ Healthcare University College (KPJUC).

Shaza Aldairany is currently a PhD candidate at International Business School, Universiti Teknologi Malaysia, Kuala Lumpur. Her recent research interest is philanthropy and pro-social behaviour in conflict areas.

Zainudin Awang is a Professor in the Faculty of Economic and Management Sciences Universiti Sultan Zainal Abidin. He has more than 25 years' experience lecturing in various statistical courses such as Regression Analysis and Structural Equation Modeling (SEM), Research Methodology and Statistical Methods.

Deepak Chawla is a distinguished professor at the International Management Institute, New Delhi, India. He has about three and a half decades of teaching and research experience. He holds a master's degree in statistics from Indian Statistical Institute and has done Fellow program in management from Indian Institute of Management, Ahmedabad. His areas of interest are quantitative methods, marketing research and econometrics. He has publications in both national and international journals of repute.

Ayşen Coşkun, PhD, is an assistant professor of marketing at Akdeniz University, Turkey. Her research primarily focuses on the consumer behaviour along with consumers' attitudes towards environment.

Alfredo J. Escribano has received his PhD in Animal Production from University of Extremadura, Spain. His specialization is in Agro-food Marketing and Sustainability. Dr Alfredo has completed his Master on Science and Technology of Meat-products from University of Extremadura, Spain. He also obtained a Veterinary Science degree. He has been researching for the last 8 years on ruminants production systems, with a particular focus on their sustainability under extensive (low-input, pasture-based) conditions, including organic farming. Apart from that, he has also carried out research on marketing and consumer's behavior toward high quality ("premium") products, such as Iberian dry-cured ham and sausages, and organic food. Moreover, he has been participating with different start-ups: as a consultant for an organic baby food company and as a professor of courses for professionals related to ruminants production. In 2014, he joined the feed industry, where he has been Product & Technical Manager for different products and Ruminants. In March 2017, he joined NUTRION International SLU, where his main responsibility is Business Development globally.

Manish Gupta is Assistant Professor in the Department of Human Resources at IBS Hyderabad, IFHE University. His PhD thesis is in the area of 'work engagement'. Manish is a recipient of Junior Research Fellowship and National Eligibility Test certificate awarded by University Grants Commission, Government of India. He is Editorial Team Member of Australasian Journal of Information Systems. He is a member of ISDS, AIMA, DSI, and IBSAF. Currently, he is authoring books for publication with Sage. He is editing three books- one with IGI Global, USA, and other two with Apple Academic Press Inc., a member of the T&F Group, USA. He is also editing five Special Issues for AJIS (UoQ), ADHR (Sage), JGOSS (Emerald), IJKM (IGI) and ICT (Emerald). His teaching areas include Human Resource Management and Organizational Behavior, among others. His scholastic work is available at https://scholar.google.co.in/citations?user=yJtwSkwAAAAJ&hl=en.

Yahaya Ibrahim is a professor at Universiti Sultan Zainal Abidin. He has also served as a professor in the field of development at the National University of Malaysia and was invited as a visiting Professor at Ritsumeikan University, Kyoto, Japan. His current research interest focuses on developmental studies.

Rossilah Jamil is a Senior Lecturer at the International Business School, Universiti Teknologi Malaysia. She has a Masters in Training and Human Resource Development from the University of Warwick and a PhD in Development Policy and Management from the University of Manchester, United Kingdom. She has been with the academia for 15 years and has taught courses in Leading Talent in Organizations, Human Resource Management, Organizational Behavior, Human Resource Development, Training Needs Analysis, and Training Evaluation at undergraduate and postgraduate levels. Dr. Rossilah is active in numerous PhD and MBA supervisions in the fields of Human Resource Management / Organizational Behaviour and Management Education/ Development. She has conducted studies under various research and consultancy grants in the same field.

Serkan Kılıç, born in 1981, graduated in Business Administration in Bursa, Turkey. He received the Master degree and the PhD degree from the Uludağ University. He is currently working as an Assistant Prof. in the Department of Business Administration at Uludağ University in Turkey. He teaches marketing and innovation related courses at Uludağ University. His research interests are marketing, retailing, branding, consumer behavior and innovation. Dr. Kılıç has written three books named as Private labels in Retailing, Innovation Management and New Product Innovation. He has many published articles in different journals. He has also worked on internationalization and generation related projects as an academician and project manager.

Mehran Nejati is a Senior Lecturer in the School of Business and Law. Prior to joining Edith Cowan University, Mehran was the Programme Manager for Research and Consultancy and a Senior Lecturer at Graduate School of Business, University of Science Malaysia (USM). Mehran has also held visiting appointments at the University of Adelaide Business School and Flinders Business School. Mehran serves as the editorial board member of several international academic journals. Mehran has demonstrated research excellence in his field and has been recognized for his research contributions on various occasions including Outstanding Publication Award 2016, Certified Sentinels of Science Award 2016, and ANZMAC 2015 Best Reviewer Award. Mehran has taught various courses across business and management discipline on Business Sustainability, Corporate Social Responsibility, Business Statistics, Research Method, Strategic Management, and Marketing. He has taught in face-to-face, distance and electronic modes, and has received excellent student and peer evaluation for his teaching. Apart from his research and teaching activities, Mehran is often invited as a trainer for quantitative research methodology and data analysis workshops on structural equation modelling, partial least squares, and software such as AMOS and SmartPLS.

Rosmini Omar is an Associate Professor at IBS, UTM. She has been teaching courses of Human Resource Management, Management Principles & Practices, International Business, International Human Resource Management, Organization Development, Business Ethics & Human Values, Organizational Behavior for both the undergraduate and post graduate level in multiple locations since 1999. She is an adjunct faculty member at College of Business, Minot State University, North Dakota, USA and Helsinki School of Business, Finland. Performing online teaching & face to face for graduate and undergraduate courses in Management. She had led/participated in/audit research & consultancy for governments, non-governmental bodies/foundations and industry at national and international level.

Erkan Özdemir received the Master degree and the PhD degree from the Uludağ University in Turkey. He is currently working as an Assoc. Prof. in the Department of Business Administration at Uludağ University in Turkey. He teaches marketing management, sales management, marketing strategies courses at Uludağ University. His research interests are marketing, consumer behavior, high-tech marketing and innovation. Dr. Özdemir has written three books named as Marketing Strategies to Women Consumers, Marketing Ethics, Marketing of High-Tech Products and Services. He has many published articles in different journals. He also served as an assistant researcher at Uludağ University Technology Transfer Office Project supported by The Scientific and Technological Research Council of Turkey (TÜBİTAK) between 2014 and 2015 and has been in charge of business development and entrepreneurship department at Uludağ University Technology Transfer Office.

Shweta Pandey is a Fellow of the International Management Institute, New Delhi with 11 years of experience in the financial services industry. She holds a master's degree in marketing as well as a bachelor's degree in statistics. She is also a certified six sigma black belt from GE. Her areas of interest include Quantitative Techniques, Internet Marketing and Consumer Behaviour. She has publications in both national and international journals.

Trianna Rosli completed her first degree in Industrial Management in (Hons) in 2008 and she possess her Masters in Supply Chain and Logistics in 2011. Currently, she is a doctoral candidate at Universiti Teknologi Malaysia on Green Marketing topic (Environmental Quality Awareness). She also works as a research assistant. Her research focus is Market Research, Consumer Behavior, and Green Marketing.

Shah Saquib is a Computer Scientist, born in October 1987. He is originated from Bangladesh, worked professionally as an IT expert over the globe including his own start-up company right after availing the Bachelor's degree. He loves IT dilemmas and has chosen web engineering as his area of specialization during his master's study at Technical University Munich. He worked as a Database analyst at KDG, later as a researcher at Fraunhofer Institute and now serving the position of IT Director at Basel Institute of commons and Economics.

Ruzanna Shahrin is a PhD candidate at International Business School, UTM. She has received her master and bachelor degree from International Islamic University Malaysia (IIUM). She has working experience in aviation and banking industry before pursuing her postgraduate studies. She is actively joining academic conferences and works closely with her supervisor Dr Farzana Quoquab from UTM. Her PhD research area is in consumer pro-environmental behaviour in nutricosmetic industry.

Fong Teng serves as an IT support personnel in a private institution. She has obtained her MBA from Universiti Teknologi Malaysia and a Bachelor degree in computer science from Universiti Malaya.

Florea Nicoleta Valentina is a Lecturer at Management-Marketing Department, Valahia University of Targoviste, Romania, from 2012 and with an experience over 14 years as economist at Valahia University of Targoviste. She studied Marketing, between 1993-1997, she obtained her Master degree in Marketing in 2004, and her PhD thesis in Management, in 2011. She published over 60 articles in HRM field, Knowledge Management, Business simulation, Marketing and Communication, and 7 books in Communication, PR, HRM, Business simulation and modeling and Marketing, and two book chapters in Communication and Knowledge Management. Her main course and seminar activities are: Human Resources Management, Marketing, Management, Simulation in marketing, Leadership and management communication, Communication and PR in business, PR and Protocol, Services Management, International Marketing. She was a member of the CEDIMES Institute, Paris, between 2009-2010, and she is a member of AVES and the Centre for Research in Management and Marketing of Valahia University of Targoviste. She received a doctoral scholarship at Paris Est, Creteil, Val-de-Marne, France, during April-July, 2010 and an academic scholarship at ASE Bucharest, between Jan-Feb., 2011. In 2015 she received a diploma for "professorial debut" at national level for the important results in teaching and research career.

Yusnita Yusof is currently PhD Candidate in Tourism Management Field at Universiti Sultan Zainal Abidin. Her research covers on environmental management practices, green image, customer satisfaction and loyalty in Malaysian hotel industry.

Yusmani Mohd Yusoff is an Analyst at Thomson Reuters Malaysia. Prior to joining Thomson Reuters, Yusmani was the lecturer at Island College of Technology, Penang. She has more than 3 years teaching experience; tutor in Universiti Sains Malaysia and lecturer in the Island College of Technology. Furthermore, her teaching experience ranges from diploma to degree programs as well as various focus areas across the management discipline, such as Business Research Method, Human Resource Management, Career Development, Strategic Management, Operation Management, Psychology Management, Performance Appraisal, Human Resource Information System, Public Relations, Entrepreneurship, Information Technology in Business, Principle of Finance, Corporate Finance, International Financial, Islamic Finance, and Financial Statement Analysis. In addition, she was successfully assisted in the obtaining the MQA certification for two programs in Island College of Technology and she also managed to conduct five Corporate Social Responsibility programs in conjunction with the subjects taught in Island College of Technology.

Index

A

B

C

D

E

F

G

H

I

L

M

N

O

P

R

S

T

W

www.ingramcontent.com/pod-product-compliance
Lightning Source LLC
LaVergne TN
LVHW062145300926
849161LV00010B/2628